WALT WHITMAN
The Measure of His Song

"I know I have the best of time and space, and was never measured and never will be measured."

—Song of Myself

"Recorders ages hence,
Come, I will take you down underneath this impassive exterior, I will tell you what to say of me,
Publish my name and hang up my picture as that of the tenderest lover,
. . .
Who was not proud of his songs, but of the measureless ocean of love within him, and freely pour'd it forth . . . ."

—"Recorders Ages Hence"

"Now while the great thoughts of space and eternity fill me I will measure myself by them . . . .
O I see now that life cannot exhibit all to me, as the day cannot,
I see that I am to wait for what will be exhibited by death."

—"Night on the Prairies"

WALT WHITMAN

THE MEASURE OF HIS SONG

Edited by JIM PERLMAN ED FOLSOM & DAN CAMPION

INTRODUCTION BY ED FOLSOM

HOLY COW! PRESS / *Minneapolis* / *1981*

Library of Congress Cataloging in Publication Data
Main entry under title:

Walt Whitman—the measure of his song.

1. Whitman, Walt, 1819-1892—Addresses, essays, lectures.
2. Whitman, Walt, 1819-1892, in fiction, drama, poetry, etc. I. Perlman,
Jim, 1951-   . II. Folsom, Ed, 1947-   . III. Campion, Dan,
1949-   .
PS3238.W37   811'.3   80-85268
ISBN 0-930100-09-3   AACR2
ISBN 0-930100-08-5 (pbk.)

"The Mayflower Moment: Reading Whitman During the Vietnam War" —
Copyright © 1981 by Patricia Hampl

Published by Holy Cow! Press
Post Office Box 618, Minneapolis, Minnesota 55440
Manufactured in the United States of America

Photographs of Walt Whitman are from the Bayley Collection, Beeghly
Library, Ohio Wesleyan University.

Back cover portrait of Walt Whitman by Randall W. Scholes.
Calligraphy by Sandy Gourlay.

Printing by The Colwell Press, Inc. (Minneapolis, Minnesota)
Typesetting by Jim Perlman at the University of Iowa's Weeg Computer
Center and processing by Compositors (Cedar Rapids, Ia.)

First Printing—Fall, 1981

Principal Distributors: Bookslinger (Saint Paul, Minnesota), Bookpeople
(Berkeley, California), and Small Press Distribution (Berkeley, California).

This project is supported by a grant from the National Endowment for the
Arts in Washington, D.C., a federal agency.

CONTENTS

1955–1980

1980s

Acknowledgments

We gratefully acknowledge permission to reprint materials from the following sources:

"Ode to Walt Whitman" by Stephen Vincent Benét. From *Selected Works of Stephen Vincent Benét* (Holt, Rinehart & Winston) copyright © 1935 by Stephen Vincent Benét and renewed 1963 by Thomas C. Benét, Stephanie B. Mahin, and Rachel Benét Lewis. Reprinted by permission of Brandt & Brandt Literary Agents, Inc.

"Song of Myself: Intention and Substance" (an excerpt) by John Berryman. From *The Freedom of the Poet* copyright © 1976 by Kate Berryman and reprinted by permission of Farrar, Straus & Giroux, Inc.

"Despair" by John Berryman. From *Love & Fame* copright © 1970 by John Berryman and reprinted by permission of Farrar, Straus & Giroux, Inc.

"A Note on Whitman" by Jorge Luis Borges. From *Other Inquisitions 1937-1952*, trans. Ruth Sims, copyright © 1964 by the University of Texas Press.

"Camden, 1892" by Jorge Luis Borges, trans. Richard Howard and Cesar Rennert. From *Selected Poems 1923-1967*, ed. Norman DiGiovanni, copyright © 1972 by Delacorte Press.

"Whitman" by Witter Bynner. From *A Canticle of Pan*, copyright 1920 by Alfred A. Knopf, Inc. Copyright renewed 1948 by Witter Bynner. Reprinted with permission of the Witter Bynner Foundation for Poetry, Inc.

"Walt Whitman" by Emanuel Carnevali. From *Poetry* 14, no. 2 (May 1919), copyright 1919 by The Modern Poetry Association. Reprinted by permission of John F. Nims, Editor of *Poetry*.

"Cape Hatteras" by Hart Crane. From *The Bridge*, copyright 1933, © 1958, 1970 by Liveright Publishing Corporation. Reprinted by permission of Liveright Publishing Corporation.

"Introduction to *Whitman Selected by Robert Creeley*" by Robert Creeley. From *Was That A Real Poem & Other Essays*, by Robert Creeley. Copyright © 1979 by Robert Creeley and reprinted by permission of Four Seasons Foundation.

"Hopkins to Whitman: from The Lost Correspondence" by Philip Dacey first appeared in *Poetry Northwest*.

"Walt Whitman" by Edward Dahlberg. From *Cipango's Hinder Door*, copyright © 1965 by the Humanities Research Center, University of Texas. Reprinted by permission of the Humanities Research Center, University of Texas, and the Estate of Edward Dahlberg.

"Walt Whitman" by Rubén Darío. From *Homage to Walt Whitman*, copyright © 1969 by the University of Alabama Press. Reprinted by permission of the translator, Didier Tisdel Jaén.

"Centennial for Whitman" by Richard Eberhart. From *Collected Poems 1930-1976*, copyright © 1976 by Richard Eberhart. Reprinted by permission of Oxford University Press, Inc.

"Comments" by Richard Eberhart first appeared in *West Hills Review*, 1, no. 1 (Fall 1979), copyright © 1979 by the Walt Whitman Birthplace Association. Reprinted by permission of the author.

"Whitman and Tennyson" by T. S. Eliot. From *The Nation & Athenaeum* (18 December 1926), copyright © 1926 by The Nation Limited. Reprinted by permission of The Statesman & Nation Publishing Company Ltd.

"Walt Whitman" by Ezequiel Martínez Estrada. From *Homage to Walt Whitman*, copyright © 1969 by the University of Alabama Press. Reprinted by permission of the translator, Didier Tisdel Jaén.

"Populist Manifesto" by Lawrence Ferlinghetti. From *Who Are We Now?*, copyright © 1975, 1976 by Lawrence Ferlinghetti. Reprinted by permission of New Directions.

"Whitman's Song" by Robert Flanagan first appeared in *Poetry Northwest*.

"Allen Ginsberg on Walt Whitman: Composed on the Tongue" by Allen Ginsberg. Allen Ginsberg read and discoursed on consecutive pages of the Modern Library Edition of *Leaves of Grass* in a sound studio in Boulder, Colorado (1980) for use by Centre Films as a spontaneous sketch of Whitman's works as a sound track for a film.

"Supermarket in California" by Allen Ginsberg. From *Howl and Other Poems*, copyright © 1956, 1959 by Allen Ginsberg. Reprinted by permission of City Lights Books.

"For Walt Whitman" by Patricia Goedicke first appeared in *Big Moon* magazine. From *Crossing the Same River*, copyright © 1980 by The University of Massachusetts Press. Reprinted by permission of the author.

"Essay Beginning and Ending with Poems for Whitman" by William Heyen is expanded from its first appearance in *West Hills Review: A Walt Whitman Journal*, 1, no. 1 (Fall 1979), edited by Vince Clemente.

"The Traffic" and "Witness" by William Heyen. From *Long Island Light: Poems and a Memoir* (New York: Vanguard Press, 1979), © 1979 by William Heyen and used with the permission of Vanguard Press.

"Walt Whitman" by Edwin Honig appeared in *The Moral Circus* (Contemporary Poetry, 1955). From *Selected Poems 1955-1976* (Dallas: Texas Center for Writers), copyright © 1979 by Edwin Honig. Reprinted by permission of the author.

"Introduction" by Langston Hughes. From *I Hear the People Singing*, ed. Langston Hughes, copyright © 1946 by International Publishers.

"Old Walt" by Langston Hughes. From *Selected Poems of Langston Hughes*, by Langston Hughes. Reprinted by permission of Alfred A. Knopf, Inc.

"Communion" by David Ignatow. From *Poems 1934-1969*, copyright © 1970 by David Ignatow. Reprinted by permission of the author and Wesleyan University Press.

"Son to Father" by David Ignatow first appeared in *West Hills Review*, 1, no. 1 (Fall 1979), copyright © 1979 by the Walt Whitman Birthplace Association. Reprinted by permission of the author.

"Letters to Walt Whitman," nos. V and IX, by Ronald Johnson. From *Valley of the Many-Colored Grasses*, copyright © 1969 by Ronald Johnson. Reprinted by permission of the W. W. Norton & Company, Inc.

"For the Sake of a People's Poetry: Walt Whitman and the Rest of Us" by June Jordan. From *Passion* copyright © 1980 by June Jordan. Reprinted by permission of Beacon Press.

"168th Chorus" by Jack Kerouac. From *Mexico City Blues* copright © 1959 by Jack Kerouac and reprinted by permission of Grove Press, Inc.

"Whitman's Indicative Words" by Galway Kinnell. First appeared in an earlier version in *The American Poetry Review* (March/April 1973).

"Retort to Whitman" by D. H. Lawrence. From *The Complete Poems of D. H. Lawrence*, copyright © 1964 by Angelo Ravagli and C. M. Weekley, Executors of the Estate of Frieda Lawrence Ravagli. Reprinted by permission of Viking Penguin, Inc.

"Whitman" by D. H. Lawrence. From *The Nation & Athenaeum* (23 July 1921), copyright © 1921 by The Nation Limited. Reprinted by permission of The Statesman & Nation Publishing Company Ltd.

"A Common Ground," Part iii, by Denise Levertov. From *The Jacob's Ladder*, copyright © 1961 by Denise Levertov Goodman. Reprinted by permission of New Directions.

"To W. W." by George Cabot Lodge. From *George Cabot Lodge: Selected Fiction and Verse*, ed. John W. Crowley, copyright © 1976 by The John Colet Press.

"Ode to Whitman" by Federico García Lorca. From *Lorca's Poet in New York*, trans. Betty Jean Craige, copyright 1977 by the University Press of Kentucky. Reprinted by permission of the publishers.

"Revolutionary Frescoes—the Ascension" by Thomas McGrath first appeared in *Praxis*, in a shorter version.

"Walt Whitman" by Edwin Markham. From *New Poems: Eighty Songs at Eighty*, copyright 1932 by Edwin Markham. Reprinted by permission of Doubleday & Company, Inc.

"Petit the Poet" by Edgar Lee Masters. From *Spoon River Anthology*, copyright 1914, 1915 by William Marion Reedy, copyright 1915 by the Macmillan Company. Reprinted by permission of Mrs. Ellen C. Masters.

"Walt Whitman" by Henry Miller. From *Stand Still Like the Hummingbird*, copyright © 1962 by Henry Miller. Reprinted by permission of New Directions.

"Countersong to Walt Whitman: Song of Ourselves" by Pedro Mir. From *Homage to Walt Whitman*, copyright © 1969 by the University of Alabama Press. Reprinted by permission of the translator, Didier Tisdel Jaén.

"Reaching Around" by Judith Moffett. From *The Kenyon Review*, 2, no. 4 (Fall 1980) and reprinted by permission of Judith Moffett.

"A Modern Poet" by Howard Nemerov. From *The Blue Swallows* by Howard Nemerov. Copyright 1967 by Howard Nemerov and published by the University of Chicago Press. Reprinted by permission of the author.

"I Begin by Invoking Walt Whitman." by Pablo Neruda. From *A Call for the Destruction of*

Nixon . . ." trans. Teresa Anderson. Copyright 1980 by the Estate of Pablo Neruda. Published in 1980 by West End Press. Reprinted by permission of West End Press.

"Ode to Walt Whitman" by Pablo Neruda. From *Homage to Walt Whitman,* copyright © 1969 by the University of Alabama Press. Reprinted by permission of the translator, Didier Tisdel Jaén.

"We Live in a Whitmanesque Age," by Pablo Neruda. Copyright © 1972 by The New York Times Company. Reprinted by permission.

"I, Mencius" by Charles Olson. From *The Distances* by Charles Olson. Copyright © 1960 by Charles Olson, published by Grove Press. Reprinted with the permission of the Estate of Charles Olson.

"The Orange Bears" by Kenneth Patchen. From *The Collected Poems of Kenneth Patchen,* copyright © 1968 by Kenneth Patchen. Reprinted by permission of New Directions.

"Salutation to Walt Whitman" by Fernando Pessoa. From *Selected Poems,* Fernando Pessoa, translated by Edwin Honig, © 1971 by Swallow Press. Reprinted with the permission of The Ohio University Press, Athens, Ohio.

"To a Dame Who Sneered When She Saw My Sox" by Paul Potts. From *Instead of a Sonnet,* by Paul Potts. Published by Editions Poetry London (1944).

"A Pact" by Ezra Pound. From *Personae.* Copyright © 1926 by Ezra Pound. Reprinted by permission of New Directions.

"What I Feel About Walt Whitman" by Ezra Pound. From *Selected Prose 1909-1965.* Copyright © 1955 by Ezra Pound. Reprinted by permission of New Directions.

"The Abyss," Part 2 by Theodore Roethke. From *The Collected Poems of Theodore Roethke.* Copyright © 1963 by Beatrice Roethke, Administrix of the Estate of Theodore Roethke. Reprinted by permission of Doubleday & Company, Inc.

"Face on the Daguerreotype" by Norman Rosten first appeared in *West Hills Review,* 1, no. 1 (Fall 1979). From *Selected Poems* (Braziller), copyright © 1979 by Norman Rosten. Reprinted by permission of the author.

"Whitman and the Problem of Good" by Muriel Rukeyser. From *The Life of Poetry,* copyright (1949) by Muriel Rukeyser and reprinted by permission of Current Books, Inc., A. A. Wyn Publisher.

"Walt Whitman at Bear Mountain" and "Pacific Ideas—A Letter to Walt Whitman" by Louis Simpson. From *At the End of the Open Road,* copyright © 1960 and 1962 by Louis Simpson. Reprinted by permission of Wesleyan University Press.

"With Walt Whitman at Fredericksburg" by Dave Smith. Copyright © 1976 by Dave Smith and reprinted by permission of the University of Illinois Press and the author.

"For You, Walt Whitman" by William Stafford first appeared in *West Hills Review* 1, no. 1 (Fall 1979), copyright © 1979 by the Walt Whitman Birthplace Association. Reprinted by permission of the author.

"Like Decorations in a Nigger Cemetary" Part I by Wallace Stevens. Reprinted from *The Collected Poems of Wallace Stevens,* by Wallace Stevens, by permission of Alfred A. Knopf, Inc. Copyright © 1936 by Wallace Stevens and renewed 1964 by Holly Stevens.

"For Whitman" by Diane Wakoski. From *Dancing on the Grave of a Son of a Bitch* copyright © 1974 and reprinted by permission of Black Sparrow Press.

"Over Colorado" by Derek Walcott. From *Sea Grapes* copyright 1971, 1973, 1974, 1975, 1976 by Derek Walcott. Reprinted by permission of Farrar, Straus & Giroux.

"The Good Grey Poet" by Theodore Weiss. From *Fireweeds* copyright © 1972, 1973, 1974, 1975, 1976 by Theodore Weiss and reprinted by permission of Macmillan Publishing Company, Inc.

"Fastball" and "Autopsy" by Jonathan Williams. From *The Empire Finals at Verona: Poems* by Jonathan Williams. Copyright © 1959 and reprinted by permission of the Jargon Society, Inc. and the author.

"The American Idiom" by William Carlos Williams. From *Interviews with William Carlos Williams: "Speaking Straight Ahead,"* edited by Linda Wagner. Copyright © 1976 by the Estate of William Carlos Williams. Reprinted by permission of New Directions.

"The Delicacy of Walt Whitman" by James Wright. From *The Presence of Walt Whitman,* edited by R. W. B. Lewis. Copyright 1962 by Columbia University Press and The English Institute. Reprinted with the permission of Columbia University Press and Mrs. James Wright.

Illustrations

Cover—A photograph of Walt Whitman taken in 1861, the year the Civil War began.

1. An 1868 photograph of Walt Whitman.

2. A daguerreotype image of Whitman from the early 1840s. During this time, Whitman taught school on Long Island, worked as a printer in New York City, and edited *The Aurora*—a New York City daily newspaper. This image may have been made in one of Mathew Brady's galleries.

3. Dr. R. M. Bucke called this image the "Christ Likeness" of Whitman. This daguerreotype was made at the same time (July, 1854) as the frontispiece for the 1855 edition of *Leaves of Grass*. It is probable that this image was made by Gabriel Harrison—Brady's best cameraman.

4. A photograph circa 1863, probably taken by Alexander Gardner in Gardner's Washington, D.C. gallery.

5. & 6. Photographs taken on April 15, 1887 by George C. Cox—one of Whitman's favorite photographers. Over twenty photographs of Whitman were taken that morning in Cox's studio at Broadway and 12th, including illustrations 16 and 17.

7. Photograph of Whitman from the early 1870s.

8. Photograph of Whitman by Napoleon Sarony in 1879, taken while Whitman was in New York to deliver his Lincoln lecture. Sarony's opulent studio was on 5th Avenue.

9. An 1891 photograph of Whitman by the painter Thomas Eakins. One of many photographs Eakins took in Whitman's Camden, N.J. home.

10. An 1881 photograph of Whitman taken in Boston by Bartlett F. Kenny. Whitman called it "The Pompous Photo."

11. Photograph dated 1871.

12. Photograph circa 1880.

13. (See 9. above.) An 1890 Eakins photograph of Whitman sitting in a buffalo-skin covered chair.

14. Photograph dated 1880 and labeled the "Lear" photo.

15. Photograph of Whitman taken by Alexander Gardner in 1864, Washington, D.C.

16. & 17. (See 5. & 6. above.) The children are Nigel and Catherine Jeannette Cholmeley-Jones, the nephew and niece of Jeannette L. Gilder (1849-1916; founding editor of *The Critic* and sister of Richard Watson Gilder, an editor of *Scribner's Monthly*), who accompanied Whitman to Cox's studio. Cox perceived these children as "soul extensions" of Whitman.

Preface

WHEN R. W. B. LEWIS went in quest of the fundamental American myth, he found its introduction into American letters in words of Walt Whitman: "The Adamic hero is discovered . . . 'surrounded, detached in *measureless oceans* of space.' " Whitman thus introduced "the fundamental theme of American literature . . . : the theme of loneliness." The phenomenon traced in the following pages is the surrounding of the lonely hero of *Leaves of Grass* by almost measureless oceans of messages concerning him, many addressed directly to Walt Whitman in efforts to dispute, maintain a dialogue, and achieve communion with him, by a vast and growing community of writers throughout the world.

Our project began in the spring of 1980, when Professor Ed Folsom chaired a seminar devoted to Whitman at the University of Iowa. Scholarly attention to Walt has always been wide-ranging in its focuses, frequently contentious, and not seldom lively. His presence has also been strongly felt and responded to by visual artists and composers. But we were mainly struck by the vitality with which Whitman's specific rallying cry to "Poets to Come" has been taken up, in divers ways and by diverse voices, not only in the United States but wherever his voice has been heard.

Of course, as Ed Folsom points out in his introduction, it is virtually impossible for any American poet to *ignore* Whitman; and, indeed, Whitman's indirect presence is felt in a very great many succeeding American poets and poems. But the *direct* presence is remarkable in itself, and rare in world literature. Jim Perlman decided that a collection of poems and essays written to and about Whitman by contemporary poets might make a timely and illuminating anthology testifying to this vigorous poetic strain.

As preliminary editing proceeded, our ambitions grew. New articles and poems were requested and commissioned. It became evident from our review of the Whitman literature that a volume of wider historic range would be useful in consolidating within one set of covers representative statements, many of which have been long out of print, from poets and writers from Whitman's day to our own. Such a collection would also provide a background for the new statements and afford the reader a

xvi

well-informed perspective on their place in the continuing dialogue surrounding Whitman. A portfolio of little-known photos of Whitman became
available to us. And finally, we decided that inclusion of a selected bibliography of the many available materials would be helpful in charting those
"measureless oceans" beyond the selections we could offer here.

Confronted at last with a diversity of materials akin to *Leaves of Grass,*
we too were faced with Whitmanian problems of organization. Whitman
liked to date events from the publication of the Declaration of Independence. We decided finally to organize our collection by reference to America's poetic Declaration of Independence. Thus, the first section contains
materials from the fifty years following the first edition of *Leaves of Grass;*
the second section the ensuing fifty years; the third section the twenty-five
years following the centennial of the *Leaves,* and the fourth section, very
recent works (most of them written especially for this volume) surrounding
the centennial of the final arrangement of the *Leaves* by Whitman in 1881.
We believe the resulting collection can be read straight through with pleasure and is also sufficiently formal in organization to facilitate its use for
reference, but we also encourage the reader to upset the chronology, to read
selections out of order, to create new juxtapositions. These essays and
poems all talk to and about Walt Whitman, but they also clearly talk to and
about each other; the more familiar pieces take on a new vitality when read
in the context of the long tradition of writers talking back to Whitman.

"Men execute nothing so faithfully as the wills of the dead, to the last
codicil and letter. *They* rule this world, and the living are but their executors," wrote Thoreau one blue Monday. It was, of course, specifically to
elude the dead, to front life, that Thoreau, and Whitman, wrote, giving rise
to the "American Adam." Naturally, this provided their successors with
nicely convoluted problems in the "anxiety of influence." What is refreshing
in the following pages is the degree, not so much of anxiety, but rather of
tolerance, empathy, family feeling both affectionate and irascible, deadeyed
analysis, and freedom, that informs the words of poets who have read Walt
Whitman and who have taken the measure of his song.

Finally, we would like to acknowledge the generous spirit of cooperation
that prevailed throughout this project. We were continually pleased by the
friendliness of our contributors and their willingness to support our efforts.
Perhaps this eagerness and openness are a reaction, in part, to the current
wave of conservatism in the United States—and reaffirm that the Whitmanic
democratic tradition is essential to the survival of our most important
cultural values. There are several people who deserve our special thanks:
Randall Waldron, John Reed (Archivist, Ohio Wesleyan University Library),

Norman Sage, Jim Dochniak (*Sez* magazine), William Kupersmith, Jeff Bart-lett, and Ron Prieve.

Iowa City, Iowa, 1981   D. C., J. P., E. F.

Poets to Come

Poets to come! orators, singers, musicians to come!
Not to-day is to justify me and answer what I am for,
But you, a new brood, native, athletic, continental, greater than
      before known,
Arouse! for you must justify me.

I myself but write one or two indicative words for the future,
I but advance a moment only to wheel and hurry back in the
      darkness.

I am a man who, sauntering along without fully stopping, turns a
      casual look upon you and then averts his face,
Leaving it to you to prove and define it,
Expecting the main things from you.

        —Walt Whitman

1.

Talking Back to Walt Whitman: An Introduction

ED FOLSOM

ONE HUNDRED YEARS AGO Walt Whitman finished *Leaves of Grass*. The 1881 edition, his sixth arrangement of the poems of his life, became the definitive edition. It was, as he called it, "the completed book at last," and he never altered the order of his poems again. All poems after 1881 he added—housebuilder that he was—in "annexes," poetic attachments to the main structure, additions that did not alter the careful organic unity of the main body of *Leaves*, a unity he had nourished and watched evolve during the quarter-century after the first edition appeared in 1855. And since Whitman's life-work was this book—the book that literally *became* Whitman (until he could "spring from the pages into your arms")—the centennial of the final edition of *Leaves of Grass* is as significant an event as the more publicized centenary celebration of the first edition. Our book, then, celebrates *his*, and traces out the success of Whitman's experiment, demonstrates the power of a book to be a man, records Whitman's enduring presence: here, a hundred years later, our poets still talk about, talk to, talk back to Walt Whitman.

So palpable is Whitman's presence that it's difficult for an American poet to define himself or herself without direct reference to him. At some point in the lives of most twentieth-century American poets, some encounter with Whitman takes place. Again and again poets come to grips with his definition of what the American poet should (and should not) be, respond to his development of the poetic line, his concepts of poetic subject and object. And, at some point, most American poets after Whitman have directly taken him on—to argue with him, agree with him, revise, question, reject and accept him—in an essay or a poem. It's this intersection and interaction of a twentieth-century poet's life with the continuing presence of Whitman that is the focusing point of this volume: that recorded moment in a poet's life

xxi

when Whitman's presence is most vividly felt. And that moment is often
a highly charged encounter that forces the poet to define his or her role as
a writer in America.

The encounter is different for each poet: some take on Whitman's voice,
imagine themselves to be Whitman talking; others view him from an ironic
distance, or imagine scenes in which he is the major character; some deal
with him more analytically, carefully examining their attitudes toward him
in prose. But most talk directly *to* him; this remarkable and unique dialogue,
now more than a hundred years old, is the most surprising aspect of his
continuing influence. The fact that today's poets continue to talk with
Whitman confirms his boast that time and space can be conquered:

> What is it then between us?
> What is the count of the scores or hundreds of years between us?
> Whatever it is, it avails not. . . .

Roy Harvey Pearce, in *The Continuity of American Poetry*, suggests that
"All American poetry [since *Leaves of Grass*] is, in essence if not in substance,
a series of arguments with Whitman." But what is remarkable is how much
American poetry has been in *substance* a record of that argument. Whitman
is not only an *influence*, he is a *presence*, and this distinction defines the unique
relationship poets have had with him over the past century.

I

> Listener up there! What have you to confide to me?
> Look in my face while I snuff the sidle of evening,
> (Talk honestly, no one else hears you, and I stay only a minute longer.)
> . . .
> Will you speak before I am gone? will you prove already too late?

The temptation to talk back to Walt Whitman has always been great, and
poets over the years have made something of a tradition of it. There's
nothing quite like it anywhere else in English or American poetry—a sustained tradition, a century old, of directly invoking or addressing another
poet. It has become a litany running through our poetry, this call to Whitman, a rough muse, to enter our poems, our time, and pass on his secrets
about how to deal with experience in this country. American poets cannot
rid themselves of his presence; he always seems to stop somewhere, as he
said he would, waiting for them, and sooner or later they must come to
terms with him.

British poets have no ongoing tradition of addressing their past masters:

Keats wrote with Shakespeare's portrait above his desk, but he never actually beckons the bard in his poetry; Blake feels Milton's spirit filter into his body in "Milton," but the muses addressed there are the sexually-charged "Daughters of Beulah," not Milton himself. Wordsworth is the most conspicuous example of a major poet who talks to a poetic predecessor; in "London, 1802," he futilely beckons Milton's spirit, an absent muse: "Milton! thou shoulds't be living at this hour:/ England hath need of thee: she is a fen/ Of stagnant waters . . ./ Oh! raise us up, return to us again. . . ." For American poets, though, the call to Walt Whitman is no isolated case, but more like a common necessity, an important step in discovering the poet's own calling.

The tradition began early, while Whitman was still alive, and continues to the present day. Poetic direct addresses to Whitman proliferated, of course, around his death and around the centennial of his birth, but these expected occasional pieces are not what make the tradition vital and significant. Most of the poets who address Whitman don't do so to celebrate an occasion, but rather to satisfy a gnawing urge to talk things out with him, to relieve the itching of his words at their ears. So poets as diverse as Joaquin Miller, Hamlin Garland, and George Cabot Lodge; Edwin Markham, Ezra Pound, and Hart Crane; Charles Olson, Allen Ginsberg, and Robert Duncan; Louis Simpson, Theodore Roethke, and Richard Eberhart, have all entered into the dialogue with Whitman. Notable young contemporary poets like Dave Smith, Judith Moffett, and Patricia Goedicke continue to enter the conversation. And British poets like Algernon Charles Swinburne, Robert Buchanan, and D. H. Lawrence, as well as Hispanic poets like Fernando Pessoa, Federico García Lorca, and Pablo Neruda have joined the dialogue too.

Whitman, of course, invited the response; to address Walt Whitman, after all, is in a very real sense to complete his poetic act, to create the other half of the dialogue he initiated:

> Poets to come! orators, singers, musicians to come!
> Not to-day is to justify me and answer what I am for,
> But you, a new brood, native, athletic, continental, greater than
>   before known,
> Arouse! for you must justify me.
> . . .
> Leaving it to you to prove and define it,
> Expecting the main things from you.

No poet has ever made his reader more of an intimate than Whitman has; his poems demand *your* presence—"My left hand hooking you around the

waist"—and *your* response—"Will you speak before I am gone?" He hears
his reader talking and often speaks his words for him: "It is you talking just
as much as myself, I act as the tongue of you. . . ." The reader, like it or not,
is Whitman's comrade, and the book the reader holds is Whitman himself:

> Camerado, this is no book,
> Who touches this touches a man,
> (Is it night? are we here together alone?)
> It is I you hold and who holds you. . . .

Whitman even ends *Leaves of Grass* with a suggestion of ongoing conversation: "Remember my words, I may return again. . ."

Many poets, then, have simply taken Whitman at his word. He is, as he
said he was, someone who can be talked to, confided in, someone who can
be persistently recalled. William Carlos Williams, reflecting on his own
fascination with Whitman, once said: "I don't know why I had that instinctive drive to get in touch with Whitman, but he was a passionate man. . . ."
Whitman would certainly have approved of the poetic drive to get in touch
with him, and he did, in fact, welcome the poems addressed to him during
his lifetime in the same fleshly spirit with which he offered up his own
poetry. Rennell Rodd—British diplomat, classicist, and poet once champi-
oned by Oscar Wilde—sent Whitman a poem in 1887 that castigated Swinburne for recanting his earlier praise of Whitman: "He has turned on you
too, Camerado, has passed from the few to the throng,/ Content you and
smile and remember he called to you once for a song." While Rodd's poem
certainly doesn't amount to much, Whitman pronounces it "mighty good"
even though "It's scholarly and all that: sort of schoolish." What Whitman
likes about it is that "it seems intended seriously—as a real handshake. . . ."
He likes the sense of completion it suggests, the confirmation of a hand out
there that has grasped his own through the medium of his poetry. Whitman's
"listener up there" has ceased to be a spectre and has manifested himself
in a song of answering.

So Robert Buchanan—English poet, novelist, reformer, and like Rennell
Rodd a detractor of Swinburne—actually employed the handshake metaphor in one of his poems addressed to Whitman, this one written at the
poet's death:

> One handshake, Walt! while we, thy little band
> Of lovers, take our last long look at thee—
> One handshake, and one kiss upon the hand
> Thou didst outreach to touch Humanity!

Buchanan here sets the tone for much of the poetry to be addressed to Whitman after his death; there is a continual sense that Whitman's soul could never really be separated from his body, a sense that we would always be able to embrace him, to feel the firm grip of his hand. Manifesting himself so effectively in his poems, Whitman would always seem corporeal, would always radiate *physical* presence. This, then, is one reason he has continued to be addressed—because poets continue to have the remarkable feeling that he is *there*, able to be spoken to. So even as Buchanan bids his final farewell to Whitman, Whitman's own words echo back in the very farewell, and he seems very much alive even at his funeral, his words resounding:

> *So long!*—We seem to hear thy voice again,
> Tender and low, and yet so deep and strong!

Just as his physical being could not "abase itself" to his soul in life, so it seems that in death his physical attributes demand the same immortality as his soul.

But it was while Whitman was still living that Swinburne—the villain for Buchanan and Rodd—addressed Whitman in one of the most rousing (and one of the earliest) calls to the poet. In 1871 he published "To Walt Whitman in America," entreating Whitman to allow his chants, with their air of freedom and youthful democracy, to flow freely to England and Europe to help re-energize a decayed and cruel culture: "Chains are here, and a prison,/ Kings and subjects, and shame;/ If the God upon you be arisen,/ How should our songs be the same?" For Swinburne, Whitman becomes the singer of Freedom, whose poems are capable of initiating a revolution—"A song to put fire in our ears. . . ." Whitman is addressed as "O strong-winged soul with prophetic/ Lips hot with the bloodbeats of song. . . ." His words have actual substance "That pierce men's souls as with swords. . . ." Swinburne's address to Whitman, then, also completes the embrace; he feels through Whitman's poems "A blast of the breath of the West." Swinburne never saw Whitman in the flesh; their camaraderie (such as it was) was entirely through words, and so, like all the poets who would talk to Whitman after his death, Swinburne gave and sought response from a presence he never actually saw. The charged encounter exists solely between poems, words taking on body.

Robert Buchanan, who made a career out of satirizing and condemning Swinburne, admired Whitman as much as he despised Swinburne; he may have been, in fact, one reason for Swinburne's later loss of enthusiasm for Whitman. In the first of several poems addressed to "Friend Whitman," he did his best to distance Walt from the decadent Swinburne: "Ne'er have thy hands for jaded triflers twined/ Sick flowers of rhetoric and weeds of rhyme." Buchanan goes on to discern in Whitman a divine soul that makes him "Christ-like . . . in mien," and then envisions Walt as a reincarnation of not only Christ, but Socrates too: "God bless thee, Walt! . . ./ The wisdom and the charm of Socrates,/ Touch'd with some gentle glory of the Christ!" Buchanan was not the first or only person to see Christ incarnated in Whitman. The perception of Whitman as son of God or divine prophet, in fact, led to several early poems that, while they are addressed to Whitman, really are only disguised prayers. Swinburne's and Buchanan's poems, to be sure, have some of the reverent and beseeching overtones of prayer, but other more minor figures simply replace God with Walt, as does a well-wisher named Leonard Wheeler:

> O pure heart singer of the human frame
> Divine, whose poesy disdains control
> Of slavish bonds! each poem is a soul,
> Incarnate born of thee, and given a name.

There are many more poems like this one, some by well-known literary figures in Whitman's day, like Edmund Clarence Stedman and Francis Howard Williams.

Once we recognize that these early poems initiated the tradition of carrying on a dialogue in poetry with Whitman, we should probably let them retreat to their well-earned obscurity. One interesting aspect, though, should be noted: almost without exception, these early replies to Whitman were written in rhyme, and most in very regular, traditional meters. At least ten of the early responses were traditional sonnets. Some were written by British poets, which may partially explain the insistence on formal qualities; Ernest Rhys, for example, a founding member of the Rhymers' Club (and author of the Rhymers' Club toast) toasted Whitman in gently pointed rhyme, emphasizing the difference between his own nationality and Walt's: "Here health we pledge you in one draft of song,/ Caught in this rhymster's cup from earth's delight,/ Where English fields are green the whole year long. . . ." Rhys, in fact, travelled to America to encourage Whitman to consider "the possible use of rhyme and what may be called pattern-verse in the new poetry he had inaugurated. . . . But, no, he would not budge." Rennell Rodd spoke for many of the early British supporters when he proclaimed that Whitman "often probed to the substance, [but] he missed the form. . . ."

We can imagine Whitman's dismay at this "sort of schoolish" response that his "barbaric yawp" seemed to provoke. The poet, after all, who was

proud to have "found the law of my own poems" in the "elemental abandon" and "entire absence of art" of "primitive nature," and who hoped he
was initiating a distinctly American form of writing, must have been dis-
traught to see all his disciples' answers to him deriving their structures from
inherited European poetic forms. Some of the early rhyming attempts, in
fact, used their formal qualities as a quiet corrective to Whitman's apparent
wildness, and tried to yank him gently back in line. The recurrent rhymes
and meters try to function as a rote reminder that the way to talk of beauty
is in strict and controlled form. And many of the actual parodies of Whitman, which began soon after he published *Leaves of Grass,* were direct
addresses to the poet ridiculing his lack of form; this one is from 1877:

> Multitudinous, Titanic,
> As of many mighty waters in a large-sized panic . . .

> Forgive, O Whitman, large and big and huge,
> These accidental droppings into rhyme,
> Which thou rightly disdainest. . . .

Even when poets wanted to praise his new form, though, they tended to
do so in old forms. Albert Edmund Lancaster's tribute, for example, approaches self-parody as it loudly praises a rough muse who obviously never
visited Lancaster himself:

> Your lonely muse, unraimented with rhyme,
> Her hair unfilleted, her feet unshod,
> Naked and not ashamed demands of God
> No covering for her beauty's youth or prime.

And Joaquin Miller, the flamboyant frontier poet, praises Whitman's rough
form in rhymed iambic pentameter:

> What though thy sounding song be roughly set?
> Parnassus' self is rough! Give thou the thought,
> The golden ore, the gems that few forget;
> In time the tinsel jewel will be wrought.

This is ironic praise from the poet whom Whitman admired because he "has
broken loose some—been more or less free in technique," unlike those who
are still writing "in the old ways, hugging the traditions." Miller's address
to Walt as "Titan soul" somberly portrays Whitman ascending into the skies,
a "lone, sad soul," doomed to be "to the end alone." Such lofty isolation
was something Whitman, of course, feared rather than desired, and the poet

of democracy would have found, at best, an odd comfort in the isolated Olympian image Miller offered him.

There *were* poets, however, who began carrying on the dialogue with Whitman in forms modeled on his own. Sadikichi Hartmann—a Japanese-German immigrant dramatist, art critic, poet, and devoted follower of Whitman—wrote a poem to him in 1887 composed of lines that in length exceed even Whitman's: "Poet of America! The language of thy songs is rough, but its natural sternness penetrates the soul, and is the harbinger of a new poetry, and a higher school of art than even that of Greece." Hartmann's lines get increasingly longer and remain just as prosaic; he calls these early poems "*prose* poems in imitation" of Whitman. Though he tried not to become a slavish imitator of Whitman, Hartmann could never over-state his worship: "Walt Whitman, I do not call thee master, but I am bound to thee for ever, thy works were to me, except Love and Nature, the grandest lessons of my life."

But for the most part the nineteenth-century poets who responded to Whitman struggled with the tensions between traditional forms and the new line Whitman had created. George Cabot Lodge made painstaking analyses of Whitman's rhythms and tried to model his lines and rhythms accurately on those in *Leaves of Grass*. He dedicated his second volume of poetry, *Poems (1899-1902)*, to Whitman, and opened the volume with an address to him:

> Upon Thy grave,—the vital sod how thrilled as from
>   Thy limbs and breast transpired,
> Rises the spring's sweet utterance of flowers,—
> I toss this sheaf of song, these scattered leaves of love!

But Lodge was his whole life a sonneteer, and even this dedicatory address to Whitman turns out to be an unrhymed sonnet; we can feel the Whitman-spirit in Lodge struggling with the formalist-spirit for control of the poem.

Hamlin Garland's *Prairie Songs* of 1893 are called "chants rhymed and unrhymed of the level lands of the Great West," but Garland unaccountably chooses to cast in rhyme the one imitative song he addresses to Whitman. His words to Whitman contain the familiar elements we have seen in most of the early responses. But in bringing the elements together, Garland transcends them and creates one of the most effective and interesting of the pre-twentieth-century poems to Whitman. After the unpromising beginning, where Whitman is immortalized, made godlike, lofty, and bloodless (as he is in so many of the early poems to him), Garland abruptly shifts his tone; the god descends and manifests himself again in friendly flesh; Garland uses the same handshake image that Whitman himself had used to refer to early poetic responses to him: "Thy grasp of hand, thy hearty breath/ Of welcome thrills me yet/ As when I faced thee there." Whitman still exists in body for Garland, a hearty comrade; as in Buchanan's poem, Whitman's breath, even after his death, can be felt through his words. Garland then goes on to argue gently with Walt, to delineate clearly their differences in stance and in geographical affection. Garland thus initiates the tone of much of the twentieth-century response—a tone of love and admiration for, but also an affirmation of separation from, Whitman. While Garland had great respect for Whitman, calling him the "genius of the present," he was no blind disciple. Garland's poems were varied in form, and he believed that "the subject should have its own dress, a garment which would take its shape from the inner urge." Given such an organic view of poetic form, his use of rhyme in the poem to Whitman stands as one more quiet affirmation of an identity separate from Walt's.

Garland's poem is called "A Tribute of Grasses" and, like Lodge's, is based upon "When Lilacs Last in the Dooryard Bloom'd." But instead of Whitman's sprig of lilac or Lodge's "sheaf of song," Garland brings to his idol a distinctively midwestern offering:

> Loving my plain as thou thy sea,
> Facing the east as thou the west,
> I bring a handful of grasses to thee,
> The prairie grasses I know the best—

The shifting rhythm and informal tone pay homage to Whitman; the rhyme, though, and the emphasis on a place Whitman had only once visited (he recorded of that visit in *Specimen Days* that the prairies were "what most impress'd me, and will longest remain with me") suggest the independence of one who is most honoring the style of his teacher by carving out a separate identity.

II

Ezra Pound, twenty years later, picks up on Garland's gentle quarrel and sets the tone the twentieth century would often use to address Whitman. The earlier responses, as we have seen, were either taunting chants of ridicule (early parodies of Whitman would themselves fill a large volume) or, more commonly, comforting words of support for a beleaguered poet. Most were cheering replies of confidence, responding to the poet by assuring him that he had friends who believed in him and who believed in—and would help bring about—the persistence of his poetry. By early in the twentieth century, though, the battle for lasting recognition was won. As the nineteenth century closed, Edwin Arlington Robinson had proclaimed about Whitman: "Last night it was the song that was the man,/ But now it is the man that is the song." Whitman had finally and fully become his words, and it would now be his *words*—and their persistent influence—that poets would address. He had become a poet to be reckoned with; American poets, like it or not, would now inevitably be compared with him. They couldn't ignore him even if they wanted to, and so the nature of their responses changed.

Six years before the centennial of Whitman's birth, Pound published "A Pact" in *Poetry*. When *Poetry* first appeared the year before (1912), its back cover featured a quotation from Whitman, a sign of his pervasive influence. Pound disliked this gesture, and his address to Whitman may be seen in part as a response to the cover of the journal:

> I make a pact with you, Walt Whitman—
> I have detested you long enough.
> I come to you as a grown child
> Who has had a pig-headed father;
> I am old enough now to make friends.
> It was you that broke the new wood,
> Now is the time for carving.
> We have one sap and one root—
> Let there be commerce between us.

Pound here plays the role of a lost son returning to a father he has gradually learned to tolerate. He plays upon one of Whitman's favorite images, that of the pioneer chopping the wilderness up into American forms; Walt had always liked to imagine himself on the cutting edge of the frontier ("Come my tan-faced children,/ ... have you your sharp-edged axes?/ ... We primeval forests felling,/ ... we the virgin soil upheaving,/ Pioneers! O Pioneers!"). Whitman—the poet as pioneer—had flung himself into formlessness to extract new native forms; with great abandon he had sought to make his poetry resonate with the energy and crude muscularity of the American frontier. But now Pound refines this work; he trades Whitman's indiscriminate axe for a more delicate knife: "Mentally I am a Walt Whitman who has learned to wear a collar and a dress shirt (although at times inimical to both)," he said. Originally the first line of Pound's address to Whitman had been, "I make a *truce* with you, Walt Whitman" [italics mine], but this war imagery, with its suggestion of only a temporary cessation of hostility, gave way to a *pact*, a civilized agreement with the force or necessity of law behind it. The thrust of the poem, then, is the increasing civility of America and of its poetry since Whitman; there can now be *commerce*, exchange between two separate entities, but there will be no absorptive identity. With commerce, too, comes a less intense emphasis on nationalism, and more of an interplay between cultures, an internationalism; Pound, after all, would carry on his commerce with Whitman from outside Whitman's America.

Pound's poem captures his lifelong ambivalence toward Whitman: "He *is* America. His crudity is an exceeding great stench, but it *is* America. . . . He is disgusting. He is an exceedingly nauseating pill, but he accomplishes his mission." Pound both hated and admired his "spiritual father," despising his poetry while feeling compelled to read it: "The *Leaves of Grass* is the book. It is impossible to read it without swearing at the author almost continuously." Yet he felt Whitman was the best poet America had produced, and acknowledged that the "vital part of my message, taken from the sap and fibre of America, is the same as his." Their blood and their origins—sap and root—are the same, but they still remain separate—like Garland's prairie grass from Whitman's lilacs—far enough apart so that commerce instead of comradeship best defines their relationship. Pound will take his knife and begin to do the necessary intricate work with the cantos that Whitman had so energetically chopped out of the wilderness. Whitman, Pound said, "came before the nation was self-conscious or introspective or subjective"; he went "bail for the nation." Pound, arriving in his own time, picks up the knife of self-consciousness and introspection and carves out a vastly different song of the self. And this, after all, is what Whitman set himself up for, Pound claimed: "He knew himself, and proclaimed himself 'a start in the right direction.' He never said 'American poetry is to stay where I left it'; he said it was to go on from where he started it." (And the process *does* go on: forty years later Charles Olson, a "pupil" of Pound's, would define his troublesome relationship with *his* mentor in terms—commerce, trade—reminiscent of Pound's words to Whitman. In so doing, Olson finds himself rejecting what Pound has become and instead going back to Whitman, whom he addresses:

> that the great 'ear
> can no longer 'hear!

>> o Whitman,
>> let us keep our trade with you when
>> the Distributor
>> who couldn't go beyond wood,
>> apparently,
>> has gone out of business . . .)

After Pound's pact, poets in the 1920s continued to keep the conversation with Whitman alive, often without much distinction. Witter Bynner, for example, addresses him but affirms little more than that Whitman's "many voices" can still be heard: "And out of your great frame and windy beard,/ As out of earth,/ They are shaken free again. . . ." But it was during this time that Carl Sandburg labelled *Leaves of Grass* "a book to be owned, kept, loaned, fought over, and read till it is dog-eared and dirty all over." It was at this time, too, that James Oppenheim, editor of *The Seven Arts*, so thoroughly absorbed Whitman into his work, especially in his long autobiographical poem, *The Mystic Warrior*, where he recalls a youthful vision of Whitman:

> And one day I was in Central Park with my mother . . .
> (Do I dream this or is it so?)
> Over the walk came swinging an old giant of pink and white,
> His collar open, his flowing luminous beard blowing in the wind . . .

and goes on to recall his first look at *Leaves of Grass:*

> I looked in, shocked, repelled, attracted: a burst of health
>   seemed to envelope me:
> A sea-breeze blew from that book scattering vapours of death:
> I had found my opposite—it would be years before I loved him . . . .

And it was during the 1920s that Hart Crane struggled intensely to get in touch with Whitman, to learn from him, to catch his spirit, to regain his vision of America. His dialogue with Whitman is certainly the most remarkable of them all, for, unlike Pound, Crane begins with the assumption that he *can* carry on Whitman's mission, can recapture Walt's optimism about America and the future, and can apply it to contemporary reality. Crane intially refused to admit that there were any major essential differences between Whitman's times and his own; Whitman thus became a model for Crane, an instructive muse rather than a pigheaded father. Refusing to surrender to the sterility of a technological wasteland, Crane saw the problem of modern poetry as one of simply uncovering the persistent spirit lurking beneath the gaudy machine surface of America: "unless poetry can absorb the machine, i.e., *acclimatize* it as naturally and casually as trees, cattle, galleons, castles and all other human associations of the past, then poetry has failed of its full contemporary function." And the master-singer of the machine, of course, was Whitman, who (Crane said) "better than any other, was able to coordinate those forces in America which seem most intractable, fusing them into a universal vision which takes on additional significance as time goes on." Whitman, then, would guide Crane to a way of finding the spirit behind the technological facade. It is fitting that Crane's great address to Whitman—the "Cape Hatteras" section of *The Bridge,* which he called "a kind of ode to Whitman"—begins with an epigraph from "Passage to India," Whitman's giant affirmation of the spiritual charge of man's technological achievement. The transatlantic cable, the Suez Canal, and the transcontinental railroad, Whitman suggests in this poem, are really all emblems of the human spirit, reaching to affirm the rondure of the world and the oneness of men. So Crane sought to make the great engineering feat of the Brooklyn Bridge symbolize the same things: a redeeming union of past, present, and future, a new spiritual unity. And so (in ringing rhyme) he beckons Whitman, the technological spirit: "Our Meistersinger, thou set breath in steel:/ And it was thou who on the boldest heel/ Stood up and flung the span on even wing/ Of that great Bridge, our Myth, whereof I sing!"

As he began to map out *The Bridge* in 1923, Crane felt the spirit of Whitman coming alive in him: "I begin to feel myself directly connected with Whitman. I feel myself in currents that are positively awesome in their extent and possibilities." But only three years later his emerging poem seemed a ruins: "intellectually judged the whole theme and project seems more and more absurd. . . . If only America were half as worthy today to be spoken of as Whitman spoke of it fifty years ago there might be something for me to say. . . ." Crane was at this point coming to share Pound's belief that Whitman's attitude was no longer viable, was instead a product of a distinctly different time: "time has shown how increasingly lonely and ineffectual his confidence stands." But a couple of months later Crane was again enthusiastic about the way in which he could "realize suddenly . . . how much of the past is living under only slightly altered forms, even in machinery and such-like. . . ." So his rhapsodic address to Whitman embodies his ambivalence, his wavering attitude toward Whitman's relevance for the twentieth century.

Picturing himself on the shores of Cape Hatteras on the verge of the age of the airplane, Crane wants Whitman to explain infinity to him: "Walt, tell me, Walt Whitman, if infinity/ Be still the same as when you walked the beach near Paumanok. . . ." Crane senses Whitman's presence everywhere, and he needs his guidance to write the new "gleaming cantos of unvanquished space," the new songs that the airborne dynamo will make possible. So, echoing Whitman (" 'Recorders ages hence'—ah, syllables of faith!") in line after line, Crane sets out to sing the spiritual glory of the airplane—"The soul, by naphtha fledged into new reaches/ Already knows the closer clasp of Mars." But his song, like the plane, plunges from its lofty heights and disintegrates into wrecked fragments; no sooner do the Wright brothers get their machine aloft than the plane—emblem of man's soul soaring, off to explore infinity—embraces Mars and turns into a massive force of destruction in the First World War. Crane imagines a war plane, shot down, plunging to the ground: "By Hatteras bunched the beached heap of high bravery!"

The next lines of "Cape Hatteras" are startling in their abrupt shift from the foregoing raucous energy and mechanistic noise, to utter calm and quiet, to nature, to a restful drifting into the past: "The stars have grooved our eyes with old persuasions. . . ." Crane begins to feel Whitman's presence again, but now recalls how easily Walt had soared without the contrivance of an airplane: "But who has held the heights more sure than thou,/ O Walt!—Ascensions of thee hover in me now. . . ." The Whitman that Crane turns to here is a different Whitman, not the prophet of machinery; he is the loafer at his ease "observing a spear of summer grass": "The competent loam, the probable grass . . . fail/ Not . . ./ To answer deepest soundings!" And then the Whitman of *Drum-Taps* suddenly manifests himself, the unifying, comforting wound-dresser: "Thou bringest tally, and a pact, new bound/ Of living brotherhood!/ . . . Thou, pallid there as chalk,/ Hast kept of wounds, O mourner. . . ." This shift from the Whitman of "Passage to India" forward to the twentieth-century airplane and then back to the Whitman of the 1855 *Leaves* and the Whitman of *Drum-Taps* has led, understandably, to a good deal of critical confusion over "Cape Hatteras." One critic, for example, sees Crane's tributes to Whitman "ill-placed in an exploration of mechanics and air-travel." But such a comment ignores the fact that after the crash of the plane—the demise of hope for twentieth-century America and its jungle of machines—there is *need* for a wound-dresser, for someone to soothe, heal, unify; the poet, his poem, and his country (not to mention the pilot and his plane) need patching, need new direction. Whitman in the Civil War, after all, experienced the shattering of his vision of the "transcendental Union" of America; Crane seeks him out, then, to find a way out of his despair over the equivalent wreckage in the present. And so Crane willingly plunges into the past—beyond the Whitman of the later years back to the early Whitman (exploring all the multitudes that Walt contains)—to find that comfort. It is a plunge for security: "no, never to let go/ My hand/ in yours,/ Walt Whitman—/ so—" It is a fleeing from a mechanical world out of control, back to a less complex, slower time, when, instead of bowing to a whirl of mechanical force, the poet could "to the greensward" kneel and contemplate leaves of grass. It is a retreat to the

Whitman whose poetry was an endless plunge into the wilderness: "thy lines, rife as the loam/ Of prairies. . . ."

Although it was Whitman who "set breath in steel," gave spirit to the machine, Crane now praises him more for his ability to go "Beyond all sesames of science" and to offer awareness of "something green," a wilderness, an organic life, a promise that existed in the past and that can be reclaimed only by an imaginative merger with that past. And so, leaving Whitman's poetry of technology behind, Crane embraces an earlier Whitman: "O Walt, . . . this, thine other hand, upon my heart. . . ." Indeed, Whitman as wound-dresser is the most "recent" comfort Crane can find; after the Civil War and the incipience of industrialization, American history seems for Crane somehow diminished and empty. In *The Bridge,* he finds sustenance further back in time than the Civil War, but nowhere does he find it after that event.

Crane's imaginative merger with the early Whitman is a success—"thy vision is reclaimed!"—and it is Whitman's guiding spirit who "Stood up and flung the span on even wing/ Of that great Bridge, our Myth, whereof I sing!" It is not the Brooklyn Bridge itself—steel feat of engineering—that Whitman inspires, but the myth of America, the span the bridge represents, spanning in its horizontality east and west, and, in its verticality, past and present; Whitman is pictured as a continental giant heaving the bridge like a javelin, assimilating America into one vast unified expanse; a meaningful myth. For it is while reading Whitman that the poet becomes aware of the original "She," the virgin land, that once existed under the mechanized creation of modern America: ". . . to read you, Walt,—knowing us in thrall/ To that deep wonderment, our native clay/ Whose depth of red, eternal flesh of Pocahontus—/ Those continental folded aeons, surcharged/ With sweetness below derricks, chimneys, tunnels—." The operative word here is "below," for that is where Crane must descend to find his Pocahontus: a descent in time below the "derricks, chimneys, tunnels" of the present, back to the sensual She, the virgin continent of potentiality. His healing merger with the pre-industrialized Whitman opens the way for Crane to drift further and further back, all the way to the pre-Americanized continent: "I must ask slain Iroquois to guide/ Me further than scalped Yankees knew to go. . . ."

It is Crane, then, who begins the serious, probing conversations with Whitman, who comes to him asking for advice about how to endure in the modern world, asking for ways of recapturing his vision. He is the first poet to discuss with Whitman the distance America had come since Walt, seemingly so easily, could sing its spiritual unity and its expansive democracy. And he is the first to ask Whitman, in effect, what *Walt* would do of *he* were alive and forced to write in an America that seemed so diminished in spirit and hope, a country overrun by an accelerating technology that Whitman could not have anticipated. Could Whitman's vision transform the new sensual emptiness into a spiritual ideal again, as Crane hoped, or would Whitman's vision, too, collapse and surrender if forced to confront the twentieth century, as Crane feared? Poets kept probing these questions, and Whitman's buoyant vision of America was quickly put to its sternest test; *The Bridge* was published in 1930 just as America entered the Great Depression, and the subsequent addresses to Whitman turned increasingly somber as the distance between the nineteenth- and twentieth-century versions of the country grew, painfully and rapidly.

Edwin Markham, over thirty years after his initial success with "The Man with the Hoe," read a poem to Whitman at the unveiling of the Whitman bust at the New York University Hall of Fame in 1931. Markham was never an unqualified supporter of Whitman, and in his address to him he assumes the querulous tone of Ezra Pound—"I mix some discords in the chant"—but his argument with Walt, unlike Pound's, has very little to do with poetics. In the 1930s, poets became much more concerned with Whitman's social and political stances than with his forms. And so Markham takes Whitman to task for his philosophical naiveté and his inability to deal with real hardship in the world:

> You laud 'the average man,' and yet his feet
> Are mired in clay, his soul beholds no star,
> Hears only a far faint music from the skies.
> You dare annouce your optimistic news
> That good is good and evil is also good.
> Yet, Whitman, there is something wild in the world. . . .

Speaking for the thirties, Markham finds that Whitman's comforting words grate against the harsh reality evident everywhere in America. Markham especially dislikes Whitman's all-embracing democracy and emphasis on the Ego, for these things take away "the Ideal" from man, and, especially in depression times, leave the men with their dusty hoes nothing to do but to stare at their own impotence, their own want:

> You find all equal: no one is above:
> You leave bewildered souls no place to kneel,
> Leave them no Altar where their eyes may turn
> To something higher than themselves. . . .

By offering only comfort, then, Whitman doesn't prepare man for the necessary struggle for existence: "Whitman, there is no battle in your song;/ Yet true life is a battle and a march,/ And in this we are kindred to the gods." Markham's Whitman, in fact, lacks an overriding vision: "Where is your peak, your all-commanding peak?" But, after he vents his frustration, Markham ends his poem with moderate praise: "Sometimes we hear in your chant/ The belch of chaos, the babble of Caliban;/ And then sometimes we hear sweet homely sounds. . . ." In fact, Whitman's very emphasis on the commonplace, which has taken away the altar of the Ideal, has also brought a compensating virtue, a new way of seeing, of being awake to the reality around us: "Your conjuring touch has opened our eyes to see/ A strange, sweet gladness in all common things." When all else has been taken from man, he may still comfort himself with an intensified appreciation of the simple things around him. The poem nearly cancels itself out as Markham ends by praising Whitman for the very things he had just condemned him for: "And you have left great words to cheer our hearts—/ Democracy and the dear comrade-love." Whitman teaches joy and a promise of immortality, Markham claims, and such lessons are particularly needed in the bleak world of 1931.

By 1935, in the heart of the depression, Stephen Vincent Benét's "Ode to Walt Whitman" carried a more deferential tone. After evoking the scene of Whitman's death and contemplating the distance of forty years that separates him from the present, the poet goes out to look for Walt in the dirt, where he said he would be. He needs to talk with him: "Let us go to the hillside and ask; he will like to hear us. . . ." But, in a surprising reversal of the standard formula, it is *Whitman* who ends up asking the embarrassing questions about what has become of his America: "Is it well with these States?" Whitman keeps asking the poet, who continually evades the question with half-truths: "The old wound of your war is healed and we are one nation./ We have linked the whole land with the steel and the hard highways./ We have fought new wars and won them." But when Whitman persists with his simple question, the poet is finally forced to admit the truth:

'We have many, fine new toys.
We—
There is a rust on the land.
A rust and a creeping blight and a scaled evil,
For six years eating, yet deeper than those six years,
Men labor to master it but it is not mastered.'

Whitman asks about his "tan-faced children," and the poet's response is even bleaker: "These are your tan-faced children./ These skilled men, idle, with the holes in their shoes./ . . . The women with dry breasts and phantom eyes./ The walkers upon nothing, the four million." Whitman asks about the land, and receives a darker answer yet: "Over the great plains of the buffalo-land,/ The dust-storm blows, the choking, sifting, small dust." Whitman's once-ecstatic process of "beating the wilderness up into fertile farms" has turned into a nightmare of sterility: "We tore the buffalo's pasture with the steel blade./ We made the waste land blossom and it has blossomed./ That was our fate; now that land takes its own revenge,/ And the giant dust-flower blooms above five States." Benét plays upon the words "waste land"; the wilderness waste beyond Whitman's frontier has blossomed into fertile farms only to become, through man's greed, a new, more forbidding sterile land, Eliot's waste land, dry, filled with the hollow-eyed. Whitman, of course, is deeply saddened by the scene, and begins to question the relevance of his life-work and the validity of the war that was fought to preserve the country: "Was the blood spilt for nothing, then?"

The poem ends with Benét dismissing all the Markham-like quarrels with Whitman: "They say, they say, they say and let them say/ . . . And who cares?/ You're still the giant lode we quarry/ For gold .../ Still the trail-breaker, still the rolling river." And, despite the vast blight on the land, Benét affirms that the years of America "are not ended yet." As Crane does in *The Bridge,* Benét turns to the Mississippi River for the emblem of America's strong, turbulent energy, its persistence; in Benét's poem, it is a symbol too of Whitman, "the rolling river," absorbing all elements of America, melding them into an "eternal motion": "Always, forever, Mississippi, the god." The specifics of Benét's affirmation are not clear; the poem works more as a Whitman-inspired answer to *The Waste Land,* with rolling water replacing sterile dust, essential nature enduring the greedy, empty men who prey upon it. But the crucial part of the poem is the conversation with Whitman, the poet's attempt to avert his face from Walt's dismayed gaze, the admission of national failure, and the persistent urge to get back in touch with Whitman's muscular faith in America, predicated on a return to the land and the land's values.

III

Benét's poem appeared in his book entitled *Burning City;* in his conversation with Whitman, Benét tells of America's "great, portentous" cities, both a marvel (with their "bridges arched like the necks of beautiful horses") and a nightmare. Many of the poems in *Burning City* are in fact evocations of the nightmare of modern New York; they form a catastrophic vision of what Whitman's Mannahatta had come to be. In 1929 and 1930, Federico García

Lorca also was in New York, where he began to study Whitman's poetry in Spanish translation. Here he wrote the poems of *Poeta en Nueva York* (*The Poet in New York*) in which the city is depicted with a nightmarish intensity similar to Benét's. As it was for Benét, New York for Lorca becomes a destructive and inhuman nexus—"New York of mud,/ New York of wires and death"—and, again like Benét, he looks to Whitman for a reaffirmation of man's spirit, a reclamation of the American values buried beneath the rubble of the present. Lorca's "Ode to Walt Whitman" is a conversation with Whitman about what has become of his Mannahatta; in the poems of *Poet in New York* the ode stands penultimate to the section entitled "Flight from New York," and it records, as the poet leaves the city, his horror of modern America mixed with a lingering affection for the lost America of Whitman:

> And you, handsome Walt Whitman, sleep on the rivers of the Hudson,
> with your beard towards the pole and your hands open.
> Soft clay or snow, your tongue is calling
> comrades to watch your disembodied gazelle.
> Sleep, nothing remains.
> A dance of walls shakes the meadows
> and America is flooded in machines and sobs.

The tone finally is much like that of Benét's ode—a deep despair over the degraded present, but an even deeper affirmation of hope, only vaguely realized. For Benét, Whitman ultimately becomes associated with the Mississippi River and its persistent fertility ("A growing, a swelling torrent"), and for Lorca, too, Whitman is like a river, in harmony with natural flow beneath the waste land present: "virile beauty,/ who of mountains of carbon, advertisements and railroads,/ dreamed of being a river and sleeping as a river. . . ." So Lorca concludes his poem with a plea for the "reign of wheat," a depression-call for the poor and downtrodden to rise up and share in the bread, precipitate a renewal of spiritual and physical fertility.

Lorca is part of a corresponding tradition in Spanish and Portuguese—as vital and compelling as the one in English—of addressing Whitman; the continuing dialogue with Walt crosses the bounds of language, and has been especially active in Hispanic tongues. It was in 1887 that José Martí, a Cuban writer and revolutionary living in exile in New York, wrote "El Poeta Walt Whitman," an influential essay that introduced Whitman to the Spanish-speaking world. There were few translations of Whitman's poetry into Spanish until well into the twentieth century, so Martí's and other early prose accounts of Whitman's form and ideas were often more familiar to Spanish readers than was Walt's actual poetry. Martí opens his essay with a newspaper account of the aged Whitman in Camden: "Last night he seemed a god, sitting in his red velvet chair, his hair completely white, his beard upon his breast, his brows like a thicket, his hand upon a cane." Martí embellishes the portrait, always emphasizing Whitman's venerable age—"this elderly poet . . . Walt Whitman the father-man, muscular and angelic. . . ." It is this portrait of an ancient bearded prophet that Spanish poets tend to address; Whitman enters Spanish poetry as an old man, not as the brash, youthful comrade of 1855 but as a wizened prophet, and as such he falls naturally into the Hispanic tradition of the prophet/bard. His beard—emblem of his role as wise prophet and frame for all the words he would embouchure—is continually emphasized by the Hispanic poets who address him. Lorca, for instance, sees it as symbolic of his divinity: "Not for one moment, beautiful aged Walt Whitman,/ have I failed to see your beard full of butterflies,/ nor your shoulders of corduroy worn out by the moon,/ nor your thighs of virginal Apollo. . . ." But in this poem the beard also becomes the focal point of a surrealistic homosexual rape; Lorca laments the fact that empty, frustrated, effeminate homosexuals claim Whitman for their own and thus diminish his more revolutionary homosexuality of a universal camaraderie. He portrays these "maricas" attacking Whitman: ". . . And they fling them-selves/ on your luminous and chaste beard,/ blonds from the north, blacks from the sand,/ . . . the perverts, Walt Whitman, the perverts, turbid with tears, flesh for the whiplash,/ . . . Stained fingers/ point to the bank of your dream. . . ." Lorca once explained that, while "I have known only men," still "the homosexual, the fairy makes me laugh, amuses me with his womanish itch to wash, iron and sew, to paint himself, to wear skirts, to speak with effeminate faces and gestures. But I don't like it." Instead, Lorca envisioned a new kind of relationship, one free of all sexual stereotypes:

There is no one who gives orders; there is no one who dominates; there is no submission. There is no assigning of roles. There is no substitution or imitation. There is only abandon and joyous mutual possession. But it would take a real revolution. A new morality, a morality of complete freedom. That is what Walt Whitman was asking for.

So, in Lorca's ode, Whitman and his beard, and his ideal of manly love, rise pure above the degradation around him.

Fifteen years before Lorca's poem, Fernando Pessoa, the Portuguese poet who wrote under three heteronyms (created personalities whom he claimed were distinct from himself), wrote a long and passionate "Saudação a Walt Whitman" ("Salutation to Walt Whitman"); his heteronym for this poem was his Whitman-like poetic self, Alvaro de Campos. The salutation clamors for openness and "pressing forward," and celebrates the "abandon and joyous mutual possession" and the "morality of complete freedom" that Lorca too came to see embodied in Whitman. Pessoa claims that de Campos is far more than a follower of Whitman, is rather an actual *incarnation* carrying on Walt's sensual release:

> Walt, my beloved old man, my great Comrade, I evoke you!
> I belong to your Bacchic orgy of free sensations,
> I am yours, from the tingling of my toes to the nausea of my dreams,
> I am yours, look at me—up there where you are near God, you see
>   me contrariwise,
> From inside out . . . My body is what you divine but you see my soul—
> You see it properly, and through its eyes you glimpse my body—
> Look at me: you know that I, Alvaro de Campos, engineer,
> Sensationist poet,
> Am not your disciple, am not your friend, am not your singer,
> You know that I am You, and you are happy about it!

In 1929, the Argentinian essayist and poet Ezequiel Martinez Estrada also addressed Whitman; although there is no transubstantiation here, Estrada does reassure Walt that he will continue to follow him and affirms that even the poetic act of imagining oneself in a dialogue with the dead poet gives the impression of a renewed physical embrace with him. As he does for Pessoa, Whitman lives on, intensely, even in physical death, for Estrada:

> I will follow your trail with the zeal of the hound,
> among the rhythmic stars or the earth-molded human,
> wherever you are now repeating, Walt Whitman,
> the autochthonous canticles of your iron land.
> . . .
> receive this salutation cast to the wind and the sky
> with the certain impression of embracing you briefly
> and the agonizing fear of losing you again.

Estrada, who would go to Cuba near the end of his life in support of Castro's revolution, talks to Whitman in this early poem as a fellow revolutionary, finding him "at the iron gate where the serfs are rebelling. . . ." And Pedro Mir, poet from the Dominican Republic, also discusses such matters with Whitman, addressing him in his "Contracanto a Walt Whitman: Canto a Nosotros Mismos" ("Countersong to Walt Whitman: Song of Ourselves"). His countersong, published in 1952, also focuses on Whitman's beard, seen here in a striking metaphor: "OH WALT WHITMAN, your sensitive beard/ was a net in the wind!" The beard as wind-net, allowing Whitman to capture and move with all the various currents of America, is for Mir the perfect image of Walt's open, expanding nineteenth-century America: "Oh Walt

Whitman with candid beard,/ I reach through the years your red blaze of fire!" Whitman could capture all the diverse elements of society in his beard-net and unite them in his massive democratic "I," sign of a rugged and proud individualism that could still utter the word "En-Masse":

> and all the people listened to themselves in your song
> when they listened to the word
>> I, Walt Whitman, a cosmos
>> of Manhattan the son.
> Because you were the people, you were I,
> and I was Democracy, the people's last name,
> and I was also Walt Whitman, a cosmos
> of Manhattan the son . . . !

But now, Mir tells Whitman, the world has changed and America's rugged individualism has perversely spawned the greed of capitalism. So now a new song must be sung, the song of the collective We: "AND NOW/ it is no longer the word/ I/ the accomplished word,/ the touch-word to begin the world./ And now, now it is the word/ we." The countersong is then sung as Mir, in Whitman-like catalogues, reunites the dispossessed, the common men who have lost the proud stance Whitman taught them. Mir, like Whitman leading the pioneers into the wilderness, now leads the workers with his song into a new hope for a socialist world. In this way, Mir tells Whitman, the poets of today can justify Whitman's faith anew; Whitman's beard becomes aroused again as the gathering masses from around the world join to follow his rhythmic song once more: "No, Walt Whitman, here are the poets of today,/ workers of today, pioneers of today, peasants/ of today,/ firm and aroused to justify you!/ Oh Walt Whitman with aroused beard!"

Mir's exhortation to Whitman, coercing him into the role of socialist revolutionary, is far removed from Pablo Neruda's quiet intimate conversation with Walt, "Oda a Walt Whitman," written in the 1950s (though Neruda later certainly did come to invoke Whitman for social action, too: "Because I love my country/ I claim you, essential brother,/ old Walt Whitman with your gray hands,/ so that, with your special help/ line by line, we will tear out by the roots/ and destroy this bloodthirsty President Nixon"). Neruda's 1950s ode recurs to the familiar metaphor of the handshake, or to Crane's image of holding Whitman's hand for security: "During/ my entire/ youth/ I had the company of that hand. . . ." Whitman permeated Neruda's childhood and his native Chile just as he had permeated New York:

> To every corner of your town

> a verse
> of yours arrived for a visit,
> and it was like a piece
> of clean body,
> the verse that arrived,
> like
> your own fisherman beard
> or the solemn tread of your acacia legs.

Here is Whitman's beard again, but unlike the prophetic butterfly-filled beard in Lorca's poem or the aroused angry beard in Mir's, this is the beard of a friendly old fisherman bringing gifts of health and clarity. Like Lorca and Mir, Neruda does tell Whitman of the dark days of the contemporary world, of the loss of a healthy democratic America, but—as it did for Lorca, Mir, and Benét—Whitman's song still flows through the waste land, an eternal source of fresh inspiration, unassailable by the death-dealing society it seems so removed from: "New/ and cruel years in your Fatherland:/ persecutions,/ tears,/ prisons,/ poisoned weapons/ and wrathful wars/ have not crushed/ the grass of your book;/ the vital fountainhead/ of its freshness." And just as Benét was forced to suggest that the war to preserve the union seems now to have been fought in vain since the union no longer seems a thing worthy of preservation, so Neruda tells Whitman of the ironic reversal of American values in a passage that anticipates his later passionate invocation to Whitman to "destroy this bloodthirsty President Nixon . . . who practices genocide from the White House": "And, alas!/ those/ who murdered/ Lincoln/ now/ lie in his bed." But Neruda concludes by comforting Whitman with the affirmation that the people do not forget him— "Your people,/ white/ and black,/ poor/ people/ do not forget/ your bell"—and they move, if not with the fervor Mir suggests, still slowly toward his ideals: "They walk among the peoples with your love/ caressing/ the pure development/ of brotherhood on earth."

Jorge Luis Borges, like Neruda, has had a long and fascinating relationship with Whitman in his work; he continues to write of him and to him with passion. At the end of a 1968 lecture on Whitman at The University of Chicago, Borges stood up and directly addressed the shade of Whitman:

And if Walt Whitman's ghost be around, and for all we know it may be, I would like to tell him, "You can forget men of ill will, you may forget the miseries you have undergone, you may forget your loneliness, your sickness, all the wrongs that have been piled on you. Now you are no longer those things. Now you are Walt Whitman, Walt Whitman of the Leaves of Grass. Now you are as one disembodied, triumphant, dead."

Whitman's influence on Hispanic peoples has been great, of course, and, as these few examples can only suggest, Spanish-speaking and Portuguese-speaking poets have felt, like their English-speaking counterparts, the urge to get in touch with Whitman, to engage him in a continuing conversation to help guide them through their times, to re-call them to ideals. And, as in the English poems, the reader is always cast in the role of eavesdropper, listening in on an intimate and probing ongoing discussion—sometimes heated and political, sometimes affectionate and personal—between our modern poets and Walt Whitman, whom time and space seem unable to remove as a continual contemporary. For poets, he seems to be perpetually within reach.

IV

"Whitman's beard unrolled like the Pacific": so begins Derek Walcott's poem "Over Colorado." The massive whiteness of Walt's beard, emphasized in the familiar photographs of Whitman in his final years, continues to fascinate contemporary poets. His beard suggests to some the growing and aging of America, the mass of flowing white surrounding the mouth that "embouchered" the country, giving voice to its rivers, prairies, towns. And it suggests, too, a comforting intimacy, as Whitman himself used the image in his poetry: "Passing stranger! . . ./ You give me the pleasure of your eyes, face, flesh, as we pass, you take of my beard, breast, hands, in return,/ . . . I do not doubt I am to meet you again. . . ." His beard—emblem of wisdom and grandfatherly comfort, prophetic pointer and sensitive wind-net, field of butterflies—has been grasped as often as his hands have as poets seek his presence and counsel, seek to meet him again. So it is not surprising to encounter his beard again in Allen Ginsberg's mid-1950s address to Whitman: "Where are we going, Walt Whitman? The doors close in an hour. Which way does your beard point tonight?"

Ginsberg's poem to Whitman, "A Supermarket in California," echoes Lorca's ode in a number of ways: besides the striking beard images, it shares the same surrealistic quality, again raises the issue of Whitman's homosexuality, and even addresses Lorca directly. Ginsberg, wandering alone through the sidestreets of America, thinks of Whitman and heads into a supermarket (where he finds Lorca in a suggestive pose) to begin a Whitmanesque catalogue of the things in contemporary America:

> What thoughts I have of you tonight, Walt Whitman, . . .
> In my hungry fatigue, and shopping for images, I went into the neon
>   fruit supermarket, dreaming of your enumerations!
> What peaches and what penumbras! Whole families shopping at night!

Aisles full of husbands! Wives in the avocados, babies in the tomatoes!—and
you, Garcia Lorca, what were you doing down by the watermelons?

Ginsberg's absorptive lines, imitating Whitman's, seem to accumulate empty
or absurd images rather than the rugged, ennobling catalogues Whitman
could so easily collect as he wandered the roads of America. The country
has changed, and Ginsberg charts the change by simply opening up Whitman's flowing line to sterile contemporary reality. Unlike Pound, Ginsberg
does not repudiate Whitman's expansive form: "Pound complains that
Whitman was not interested enough in developing his line, I have tried to
rescue long line for further use. . . ."

As Ginsberg wanders the grocery aisles, then, Whitman suddenly appears:
"I saw you, Walt Whitman, childless, lonely old grubber, poking among the
meats in the refrigerator and eyeing the grocery boys." The Open Road has
given way to "open corridors" of the grocery store where Whitman now,
instead of freely absorbing the vast variety of an expanding America, is
reduced to consuming what's left, "tasting artichokes, possessing every
frozen delicacy, and never passing the cashier." But the nightmarish hilarity
of the poem gives way to a somber realization of what has truly been lost
since Whitman's death: "I touch your book and dream of our odyssey in
the supermarket and feel absurd." And the poem ends with Ginsberg
picturing himself walking quietly with Whitman—"we'll both be lonely"—
through the "solitary streets" of what's left of Whitman's grand Union:
"Will we stroll dreaming of the lost America of love past blue automobiles
in driveways . . . ?" And in a final intimate address, Ginsberg asks Whitman
for help, for a description of the ideal America he foresaw, a conception
that seems to have faded in the twentieth century as the waters of Lethe
separate us further and further from the time Whitman inhabited: "Ah, dear
father, graybeard, lonely old courage-teacher, what America did you have
when Charon quit poling his ferry and you got out on a smoking bank and
stood watching the boat disappear on the black waters of Lethe?"

Ginsberg here sets the tone of the contemporary American dialogue with
Whitman, a dialogue that involves a deep concern with the loss of the Open
Road, a loss of American direction, openness, and purpose, and a concomitant loss of love. The concern of many of these recent poets is that Whitman's ideal democracy of love and camaraderie has yielded to a fierce
capitalistic enterprise based on greed and lack of trust. And so in his journal
in 1960, Ginsberg records a vast catalogue of this perverted and paranoid
America: ". . . eek! I just saw FBI/ hiding behind my mother's skull./ . . .
Big eyes on the editorial pages searching my soul for secret affiliation
afflictions/ . . . Democracy! Bah!" And in the midst of this harangue Gins-

berg again addresses Whitman, echoing and updating Wordsworth's appeal to Milton to draw England back to its ideals: "Walt Whitman thou shdst be living at this Hour!" In an attempt to incarnate that living Whitman, to become the bard of love, Ginsberg appropriates Whitman's all-embracing form and imagines himself heading out with it into America as the heir of Whitman, anxious to infuse his country again with an ideal: "America what's wrong? . . ./ America when will you stop destroying human souls? Your soul and my soul?/ America when will you send me a lover?/ I Allen Ginsberg Bard out of New Jersey take up the laurel tree cudgel from Whitman." *The Fall of America: Poems of These States,* the book by Ginsberg that is most clearly a Whitman-like attempt to span the entire continent, is dedicated to Whitman and his "Intense and loving comradeship." This desire to talk with Walt, to get in touch with his vision, is the essence of the beat generation's feelings toward him; Ginsberg's friend Gregory Corso, in *Elegiac Feelings American,* expresses it succinctly: "How a Whitman we were always wanting, a hoping, an America, that America ever an America to be, never an America to sing about or to, but ever an America to sing hopefully for. . . ."

Although he was an early supporter of Ginsberg, Richard Eberhart is a poet hardly identified with the beat generation. But in the mid-1950s he, too, entered the dialogue with Whitman and ended up asking (in a different tone and form, to be sure) the same essential questions Ginsberg did:

> What shall I say to Walt Whitman tonight?
> Give us a share of your love, your simplicity,
> The large scope, the strong health of the soul,
> Love be our guide, and love be our redemption,
> Love make miracles, animate us now.

Whitman's love and simple faith (his ability, as Eberhart says in his prose piece, "to love the whole of life") are much needed today, Eberhart believes, for contemporary man with his "New bombs, new wars, new hatreds, new insecurities" is now "ready to destroy himself." It has become a dark world, Eberhart tells Walt, but he disagrees with Ginsberg about the current status of America in this destructive world, seeing himself rather an "Inheritor of [Whitman's] America maybe at its great height. . . ." Throughout his conversation with Whitman, though, Eberhart keeps his distance; he does not desire to walk as intimately as Ginsberg does with Walt. He will not follow Whitman in cataloguing the reality around him, but rather will turn his attention to a deeper look into the human soul, for Whitman's "words were a mask of the true soul";

> What shall I say to Walt Whitman tonight?
> I look not upon the world of facts and figures
> But in the heart of man. Ineradicable evil
> Sits enthroned there. . . .

Eberhart, with his Cambridge background, his precise diction and controlled form, is certainly not in the Whitman tradition: "I always admired Whitman from my earliest reading of poetry but he was not one of several poets who influenced my life." So, like Pound, he rejects the lessons of Whitman's techniques: "I praise him not in a loose form, not in outpouring,/ . . . It is not the forms you evoked, these are changed,/ But the force you spoke with, the heart's holy rapture. . . ." Eberhart's poem is a carefully controlled dialogue which clearly delineates the limits of allowable influence: Whitman's forceful rapture, his cosmic love, though threatened by the dark complexity of the contemporary world, can still be a source of inspiration to the contemporary poet, even if his formal contributions to poetry are negligible and out of fashion.

Similar attitudes were expressed by others addressing Whitman on the hundredth anniversary of the first edition of *Leaves of Grass*. Russell Atkins writes an ironic poem to Whitman, telling him of the diminishment of the muse in America: "Ah Whitman, she's the alack/ Of Muses. Tried to be/ English even./ . . . Listen, she is quoting!/ 'Let us go you and I—'/ She does but little else./ . . . She has professor's ears./ Not so loud Walt, will you?" And Norman Friedman, echoing many of the very earliest poetic responses to Whitman, addresses Walt in mildly taunting rhyme: "You would bellow through your beard at this puny rhyme,/ and hoot at the rust of these indoor feet;/ roar for my trouble, how I try to be neat. . . ." Friedman goes on to say that he has "yawped in my time too," but now has settled down into a more formal pattern; he echoes Pound's querulous tone and calls up the same frontier imagery as he engages in another battle of the son with his poetic paternity: "You taught me how to chop . . ./ But grace is wild, and sweet also. You, you never bothered/ to watch your swing. Your rhyming dad you felled;/ here is my axe: behold your rhyming child." Ernest Kroll, in more casual rhyme, offers Whitman a bleak centennial picture; unlike the Hispanic poets who affirm that Whitman still is heard by the people, Kroll tells him that his message has now lost its audience: "Not looking for you under their bootsoles,/ The people do not find you now, a century gone. . . ." Only the poet, in intimate dialogue with Walt, heeds his message anymore. Like Ginsberg, Kroll sees Whitman's Open Road a hopelessly outmoded ideal, unadaptable to the modern world; Kroll's poem ends in utter despair:

> The open road leads only into space,
> By rocket poised against the void.
> Riders to the stars might take your leaves along
> For guidance elsewhere. This is the wrong
> Planet. The love of comrades is a hopeless case.

In 1963 Louis Simpson expanded on this theme in his book of poems called *At the End of the Open Road*. The whole book, as the title implies, is essentially an extended conversation with Whitman about what has happened to his America, a country in which love now seems absent—"And can it be that love is an illusion?" Simpson calls out for help:

> 'Where are you, Walt?
> The Open Road goes to the used-car lot.
>
> Where is the nation you promised?
> These houses built of wood sustain
> Colossal snows,
> And the light above the street is sick to death.'

Wherever we go on the continent now, someone has been there before us; the used-car lot is there to prove it. It suggests used-up dreams, discarded journeys, perhaps a desire to trade-in and try again. At any rate, the country seems to be over, its manifest destiny complete: "Every night at the end of America/ We taste our wine, looking at the Pacific./ How sad it is, the end of America!" Not only is the youth and energy of the frontier push westward gone, but so is the dream of a great country fulfilling its democratic ideals; the finished product has turned out to be an ecological nightmare: "While we were waiting for the land/ They'd finished it—with gas drums/ On the hilltops, cheap housing in the valleys/ Where lives are mean and wretched./ But the banks thrive and realtors/ Rejoice. . . ." (David Ignatow, in his 1950s "Communion" with Whitman, sees the same twentieth century diminished and money-hungry America springing directly out of Whitman's possessive desire for the land and for a consuming camaraderie: "Let us be friends, said Walt,/ and buildings sprang up/ quick as corn and people/ were born into them, stock/ brokers, admen, lawyers and doctors. . . ." And Dave Smith, addressing Whitman, also is troubled by the America that has sprung up out of Whitman's time: "I want/ to tell you how progress has not changed us much," Smith says as he lies down on the grass of the battlefield at Fredericksburg, but the traffic booming by on the nearby highway chants the lie of such a desire: "*wrong, wrong, wrong, wrong.*")

Simpson, as did Whitman, considers America while facing west from

California's shores. When Whitman imagined himself at the edge of the Pacific, he was forced into asking despondent questions about what the whole American creation had come to mean now that it was nearing completion: "But where is what I started for so long ago?/ And why is it yet unfound?" Simpson, in "In California," finds himself similarly troubled, "Bearing among the realtors/ And tennis-players my dark preoccupation." He advises Whitman to remain back in the more open spaces of the nineteenth century where he could, like Huck Finn, still (at least in his imagination) light out for the territory ahead of the rest: "Lie back, Walt Whitman,/ There, on the fabulous raft with the King and the Duke!/ Turn round the wagons here./ . . . Lie back! We cannot bear/ The stars any more, those infinite spaces." And, like Kroll, Simpson finds himself forced to tell Whitman that he has been forgotten by the people he hoped to reach and is now only heard by the occasional poet who renews the persistent conversation: "As for the people—see how they neglect you!/ Only a poet pauses. . . ." (This lament is heard again and again in the poetry of our time; James Wright, for one, adds his voice: "The old man Walt Whitman our countryman/ Is now in America our country/ Dead.") Whitman, for his part, is happy to be "found out" by Simpson, but he can offer no solutions and little comfort about the contry's bleak present: ". . . did I not warn you that it was Myself/ I advertised? . . ./ I gave no prescriptions,/ And those who have taken my moods for prophecies/ Mistake the matter."

In "Song of the Exposition" Whitman had begged the muse to come to youthful, fresh America and leave behind the decayed cultures of Greece, Rome and Europe where she had long favored generations of poets with "immensely overpaid accounts"; Simpson, though, now sees *America* on the verge of becoming a future ruins—"All that grave weight of America/ Cancelled! Like Greece and Rome./ The future in ruins!"—and reveals to Walt that America has ended up another failure of civilization: "Those 'immensely overpaid accounts,'/ Walt, it seems that we must pay them again." And so he takes Whitman's advice and turns inward, away from America, its obsessions and failures: "Whitman was wrong about the People,/ But right about himself. The land is within./ At the end of the open road we come to ourselves." Simpson, then, turns from the depressing meaning of present America to investigate instead the meaning of himself and of death; it is the Whitman of "Out of the Cradle Endlessly Rocking" that finally is of the most help to Simpson, certainly not the Whitman of "Pioneers! O Pioneers!" (Whitman's "whooping it up over the chest-expansion of the United States didn't do a thing for me," he says in the essay he writes for this volume.) Forced to turn our attention from continual escape across the frontier and perpetual future-orientation, Americans increasingly will be forced to look within their own minds; we must come face to face with ourselves.

While the style of the poems in Simpson's book is not as Whitmanesque as, say, Ginsberg's, his poems are, for the most part, written in a much more open form than his earlier work; it's as if Simpson's direct encounter with Whitman somehow shakes his line free of traditional meters. Up to the publication of this book, in fact, Simpson had been identified with the formalist or academic poets in battle against the beats, but he now went so far as to define his *End of the Open Road* form as something approximating projective verse: "Now I just simply got away from the old fixed patterns because I couldn't speak in them freely, and I couldn't move around in them freely enough. . . . I write poems that depend very much on a rhythmic line, which is determined somewhat by the rhythm of my body, the motions." Unlike Friedman and Eberhart, then, who refused to praise Whitman in "a loose form" and who rejected the influence of his style, Simpson in his conversations with Walt picks up some of the free rhythms of Walt's own speech: "I never made a formal study of Whitman's line, but I probably know as much about it as anyone does. . . . I think he's an extremely good teacher. . . ." In the essay he writes for this volume, Simpson recalls the effect Whitman had on him: "On the whole I found Whitman exhilarating. His freedom of line and style, and his interest in pots and pans, bringing them over into poetry, were what I needed at the time."

The "freedom of line and style" is exactly what attracts contemporary poets of "open form" to Whitman. He is the progenitor of organic style, of the physiological line—inhaling, exhaling, a rhythm like breath itself. So Robert Creeley, in his essay in this volume, celebrates "the seeming large-nesses of act which Whitman grants to the poet" through the development of his new measure, and Robert Duncan talks of "the adventure of Whit-man's line": "the line itself as a going forth, instituting itself as a new event and presence in the world—a *sortie* Whitman named it. . . ." Duncan sees Whitman's line as symbol and emblem—enactment—of his vision of life:

The new line advances in an acknowledgment that there is no line to be drawn but only to follow through the line of going out there, declaring one's self, problematic. It was, for Whitman—it is his great insight—the informing principle at work in ideas of democracy, of faring forth where no lines are to be drawn between classes or occupations, between kinds of intelligence, between private and public, but daring the multitude of lives to be lived and seeking in each life its own individual potentialities. . . . Whitman's lines are journeymen's lines, working lines.

And so, in addressing Whitman, Duncan feels those lines "present in the verdict of my own lines," as he mingles his voice with Walt's:

Let me join you again this morning, Walt Whitman, emulous press forward,
    the sea is here again then—
for the Spirit is a Sea "the tones of unseen mystery," "the liquid-flowing
    syllables," "the boundless vista and horizon far and dim are all here,"
as particularly mine because of this great spirit in which we are
    enduring fellows, you and I,
once I swing out into your stride, stepping out. . . .
    . . .
even now my line just now walking with yours, then with yours striding the
    rounds of an identity with the sun in whose energy fields my life
    energies charged, anticipating,
hears, in your line from whose generations—many other poets' forces
    conjoining—my line inherits a design. . . .

Duncan acknowledges that Whitman's phrase "the field of the world" lies
behind his own title, *The Opening of the Field;* in his address to Whitman,
his own titles and phrases merge with Walt's: "in the opening of the field
of grass you made for me facing the nation we inhabit together. . . ." And
in "A Poem Beginning with a Line from Pindar," Duncan tells how he, like
Crane, seeks a bridge from the scarred present back to the creative vistas
of Whitman: "It is across great scars of wrong/ I reach toward the song of
kindred men/ and strike again the naked string/ Old Whitman sang from."
Whitman is a continual source for Duncan—from Whitman's avowal of
tender strength in a man's love to Whitman's adventurous form.

The sustaining power of Whitman's lines—strong, open, absorptive, awake
to the impulses of the world—is a quality sought by many poets of this
century, a century of accelerating forces that requires, as Henry Adams
foresaw, a new mind capable of dealing with "supersensuous chaos": "In
the earlier stages of progress, the forces to be assimilated were simple and
easy to absorb, but, as the mind of man enlarged its range, it enlarged the
field of complexity, and must continue to do so, even into chaos. . . ."
Whitman's poems reveal the form of this new mind, the urban, democratic,
expansive sensibility. So, like Crane before him, Theodore Roethke calls to
Whitman (and his absorptive line) when the sensual inflow ("Too much
reality can be a dazzle, a surfeit") threatens to break the floodgate and plunge
him into the "abyss": "Be with me, Whitman, maker of catalogues/ For the
world invades me again,/ And once more the tongues begin babbling./ And
the terrible hunger for objects quails me. . . ."

*

The real testament to Whitman's largeness, his multitudes, is that he has
been and continues to be called on so often by so many poets for such a

variety of reasons. It's true that most of the poets who have called on
Whitman over the years have been white males, but until recently, of course,
most recognized American poets have *been* white males. Fortunately that
recognition has changed, and with the change have come illuminating new
calls to Whitman: his message continues to grow as his poetry is read in new
lights. More than ever before his radical democratic poetics is being called
on for all it is worth. Black American poets have begun to find origins in
him: Langston Hughes talks of Whitman's "sympathy for the Negro people"
and affirms that "his poems contain us all," and June Jordan states: "I too
am a descendant of Walt Whitman." Joseph Bruchac, with his American
Indian heritage, finds "much in Whitman which reminds me of the American Indian way of looking at the world" and senses "Whitman's spirit" in
his own writing and in the work of some of "the finest of the new generation
of Native American writers." Feminist poets are returning to him in recognition of his insistence on "the perfect equality of the female with the male."
Muriel Rukeyser believes Whitman's poems "speak for a struggle between
elements in one man, and give us a resolution of components that are
conventionally considered to be male and female—a resolution that expresses very much indeed." In rereading *Leaves of Grass*, Patricia Hampl comes
to "see how much Whitman has mattered to me in ways I hadn't been aware
of." Judith Moffett, in her poem "for Walt Whitman," learns a kind of
"reaching around" from him, a possibility of touch through words ("This
long hug made of words"): "how stirring it can be/ to touch a book and
seem to touch a man." Patricia Goedicke, in her address to Whitman, quiets
his democratic yawp but affirms his democratic connectedness, the roots of
his leaves of grass: ". . . to my mind it is more a matter/ Of quiet roots, of
connections,/ Of speaking out, loud/ Or just soft enough/ For a few friends
to hear. . . ." His feminism, his homoeroticism, his universal love, his democratic affection; his revolutionary fervor; his open forms, his new line, his
catalogues and images of the commonplace: Whitman's legacy is manifold
and often unpredictable. And that is as it should be. His *words* are the man
now, and his words reach out in new ways to each new reader, initiating
"unexpected things," as Theodore Weiss says in his poem to Whitman:

> But then you surely realize
> how lucky you are, not only to have them,
> these words, striking out on their own,
> bearded with faces you scarcely recognize,
> refusing to bend to your wishes or regrets,
> refusing to acknowledge you in any way,
> but to be able to use them—most because
> they refuse—to measure that essential music

as it, and at its own sweet pace, moves on
to find the latest version of the truth
in the changes it is making.
    Beyond that,
your words work, and work for you, but what
they do to others, bringing you—this
from far-off continents—reports of pleasure,
love, the tender night your poems go on
gathering as they inspire it.

This volume is one measure of that "essential music," recording several versions of the truth of Whitman's song, tracing out the effect his words have had on others. Here, a hundred years after he completed *Leaves of Grass*, we record the current state of the gathering and the inspiring.

Bibliographic Note

Most of the quotations in the introduction are from essays and poems that appear in this volume or that are listed in the bibliography. Roy Harvey Pearce's remark on Whitman is from his book *The Continuity of American Poetry* (Princeton: Princeton University Press, 1961), p. 57. W. C. Williams's comment is from Walter Sutton's "A Visit with William Carlos Williams," in Linda Wagner, ed., *Interviews with William Carlos Williams* (New York: New Directions, 1976), p. 42. Ernest Rhys's comments are from his *Everyman Remembers* (New York: Cosmopolitan Book Corporation, 1931), p. 124. Rennell Rodd's remarks are from the essay, "The Essence of Poetry," in Theodore Koch, *Reading: A Vice or a Virtue?* (Dayton: University of Dayton, 1929), p. 82. For Henry Adams's analysis of George Cabot Lodge, see his *The Life of George Cabot Lodge* (Delmar, New York: Scholars' Facsimiles, 1978; orig. pub., 1911). Garland's comment on Whitman is quoted in Donald Pizer's *Hamlin Garland's Early Work and Career* (Berkeley: University of California, 1960), p. 148. Pound's comments are from D. D. Paige, ed., *The Letters of Ezra Pound* (New York: Harcourt, Brace and World, 1950); Pound's *Selected Prose: 1909-1965*, ed. William Cookson (New York: New Directions, 1973); and T. S. Eliot, ed., *Literary Essays of Ezra Pound* (New York: New Directions, 1968). Crane's comments are from his essay "Modern Poetry," in Brom Weber, ed., *The Complete Poems and Selected Letters and Prose of Hart Crane* (Garden City: Anchor, 1966), and Brom Weber, ed., *The Letters of Hart Crane: 1916-1932* (Berkeley: University of California, 1965). The critic referred to in the section on Crane is Vincent Quinn, *Hart Crane* (New York: Twayne, 1963). José Martí's essay, "The Poet Walt Whitman," is translated by Arnold Chapman in Gay Wilson Allen, ed., *Walt Whitman Abroad* (Syracuse: Syracuse University Press, 1955). Lorca's comment is quoted in Richard L. Predmore, *Lorca's New York Poetry* (Durham: Duke University Press, 1980), pp. 82-83. Borges's lecture on Whitman was printed in *Critical Inquiry*, I (1975), 707-18. Ginsberg's comments are from Jane Kramer's *Allen Ginsberg in America* (New York: Vintage, 1970), p. 171, and Ginsberg's *Journals: Early Fifties, Early Sixties* (New York: Grove Press, 1977), pp. 91, 155-6. Some of Simpson's comments are in Lawrence R. Smith's "A Conversation with Louis Simpson," *Chicago Review*, 27 (Summer 1975). Robert Duncan's essay and poetic address to Whitman, "The Adventure of Whitman's Line," was delivered to a conference on Whitman at the Rutgers University campus in Camden, New Jersey, in November, 1978. All quotations from Whitman's poetry are from Sculley Bradley and Harold W. Blodgett, eds., *Leaves of Grass: Comprehensive Reader's Edition* (New York: New York University Press, 1965).

2.

1855-1905

Walt Whitman at thirty five

3.

A Letter

RALPH WALDO EMERSON

DEAR SIR—I am not blind to the worth of the wonderful gift of "LEAVES OF GRASS." I find it the most extraordinary piece of wit and wisdom that America has yet contributed. I am very happy in reading it, as great power makes us happy. It meets the demand I am always making of what seemed the sterile and stingy nature, as if too much handiwork, or too much lymph in the temperament, were making our western wits fat and mean.

I give you joy of your free and brave thought. I have great joy in it. I find incomparable things said incomparably well, as they must be. I find the courage of treatment which so delights us, and which large perception only can inspire.

I greet you at the beginning of a great career, which yet must have had a long foreground somewhere, for such a start. I rubbed my eyes a little, to see if this sunbeam were no illusion; but the solid sense of the book is a sober certainty. It has the best merits, namely, of fortifying and encouraging.

I did not know until I last night saw the book advertised in a newspaper that I could trust the name as real and available for a post-office. I wish to see my benefactor, and have felt much like striking my tasks, and visiting New York to pay you my respects.

Concord, Massachusetts, 21 July, 1855.   R. W. EMERSON

A Letter to Harrison Blake

HENRY DAVID THOREAU

THAT WALT WHITMAN, of whom I wrote to you, is the most interesting fact to me at present. I have just read his second edition (which he gave me), and it has done me more good than any reading for a long time. Perhaps I remember best the poem of Walt Whitman, an American, and the Sun-Down Poem. There are two or three pieces in the book which are disagreeable, to say the least; simply sensual. He does not celebrate love at all. It is as if the beasts spoke. I think that men have not been ashamed of themselves without reason. No doubt there have always been dens where such deeds were unblushingly recited, and it is no merit to compete with their inhabitants. But even on this side he has spoken more truth than any American or modern that I know. I have found his poem exhilarating, encouraging. As for its sensuality,—and it may turn out to be less sensual than it appears,—I do not so much wish that those parts were not written, as that men and women were so pure that they could read them without harm, that is, without understanding them. One woman told me that no woman could read it,—as if a man could read what a woman could not. Of course Walt Whitman can communicate to us no experience, and if we are shocked, whose experience is it that we are reminded of?

On the whole, it sounds to me very brave and American, after whatever deductions. I do not believe that all the sermons, so called, that have been preached in this land put together are equal to it for preaching.

We ought to rejoice greatly in him. He occasionally suggests something a little more than human. You can't confound him with the other inhabitants of Brooklyn or New York. How they must shudder when they read him! He is awfully good.

To be sure I sometimes feel a little imposed on. By his heartiness and broad generalities he puts me into a liberal frame of mind prepared to see

2

wonders,—as it were, sets me upon a hill or in the midst of a plain,—stirs me well up, and then—throws in a thousand of brick. Though rude, and sometimes ineffectual, it is a great primitive poem,—an alarum or trumpet-note ringing through the American camp. Wonderfully like the Orientals, too, considering that when I asked him if he had read them, he answered, "No: tell me about them."

I did not get far in conversation with him,—two more being present,—and among the few things which I chanced to say, I remember that one was, in answer to him as representing America, that I did not think much of America or of politics, and so on, which may have been somewhat of a damper to him.

Since I have seen him, I find that I am not disturbed by any brag or egoism in his book. He may turn out the least of a braggart of all, having a better right to be confident.

He is a great fellow.

December 7th, 1856

from **A Letter to W. D. O'Connor**

MATTHEW ARNOLD

AS TO THE GENERAL QUESTION of Mr Walt Whitman's poetical achievement, you will think that it savours of our decrepit old Europe when I add that while you think it is his highest merit that he is so unlike anyone else, to me this seems to be his demerit; no one can afford in literature to trade merely on his own bottom and to take no account of what the other ages and nations have acquired: a great original literature America will never get in this way, and her intellect must inevitably consent to come, in a considerable measure, into the European movement. That she may do this and yet be an independent intellectual power, not merely as you say an intellectual colony of Europe, I cannot doubt; and it is on her doing this, and not on her displaying an eccentric and violent originality that wise Americans should in my opinion set their desires.

16 September 1866

To Walt Whitman in America •
Algernon Charles Swinburne

Send but a song oversea for us,
  Heart of their hearts who are free,
Heart of their singer, to be for us
  More than our singing can be;
Ours, in the tempest at error,
With no light but the twilight of terror;
  Send us a song oversea!

Sweet-smelling of pine-leaves and grasses,
  And blown as a tree through and through
With the winds of the keen mountain-passes,
  And tender as sun-smitten dew;
Sharp-tongued as the winter that shakes
The wastes of your limitless lakes,
  Wide-eyed as the sea-line's blue.

O strong-winged soul with prophetic
  Lips hot with the bloodbeats of song,
With tremor of heartstrings magnetic,
  With thoughts as thunders in throng,
With consonant ardours of chords
That pierce men's souls as with swords
  And hale them hearing along,

Make us too music, to be with us
  As a word from a world's heart warm,
To sail the dark as a sea with us,
  Full-sailed, outsinging the storm,
A song to put fire in our ears
Whose burning shall burn up tears,
  Whose sign bid battle reform;

A note in the ranks of a clarion,
  A word in the wind of cheer,
To consume as with lightning the carrion
  That makes time foul for us here;
In the air that our dead things infest
A blast of the breath of the west,
  Till east way as west way is clear.

Out of the sun beyond sunset,
  From the evening whence morning shall be,
With the rollers in measureless onset,
  With the van of the storming sea,
With the world-wide wind, with the breath
That breaks ships driven upon death,
  With the passion of all things free,

With the sea-steeds footless and frantic,
  White myriads for death to bestride
In the charge of the ruining Atlantic
  Where deaths by regiments ride,
With clouds and clamours of waters,
With a long note shriller than slaughter's
  On the furrowless fields world-wide,

With terror, with ardour and wonder,
  With the soul of the season that wakes
When the weight of a whole year's thunder
  In the tidestream of autumn breaks,
Let the flight of the wide-winged word
Come over, come in and be heard,
  Take form and fire for our sakes.

For a continent bloodless with travail
  Here toils and brawls as it can,
And the web of it who shall unravel
  Of all that peer on the plan;
Would fain grow men, but they grow not,
And fain be free, but they know not
  One name for freedom and man?

One name, not twain for division;
  One thing, not twain, from the birth;
Spirit and substance and vision,
  Worth more than worship is worth;
Unbeheld, unadored, undivined,
The cause, the centre, the mind,
  The secret and sense of the earth.

Here as a weakling in irons,
  Here as a weanling in bands,
As a prey that the stake-net environs,
  Our life that we looked for stands;
And the man-child naked and dear,
Democracy, turns on us here
  Eyes trembling with tremulous hands.

It sees not what season shall bring to it
  Sweet fruit of its bitter desire;
Few voices it hears yet sing to it,
  Few pulses of hearts reaspire;
Foresees not time, nor forehears
The noises of imminent years,
  Earthquake, and thunder, and fire:

When crowned and weaponed and curbless
It shall walk without helm or shield
The bare burnt furrows and herbless
Of war's last flame-stricken field,
Till godlike, equal with time,
It stands in the sun sublime,
In the godhead of man revealed.

Round your people and over them
Light like raiment is drawn,
Close as a garment to cover them
Wrought not of mail nor of lawn;
Here, with hope hardly to wear,
Naked nations and bare
Swim, sink, strike out for the dawn.

Chains are here, and a prison,
Kings, and subjects, and shame;
If the God upon you be arisen,
How should our songs be the same?
How, in confusion of change,
How shall we sing, in a strange
Land, songs praising his name?

God is buried and dead to us,
Even the spirit of earth,
Freedom; so have they said to us,
Some with mocking and mirth,
Some with heartbreak and tears;
And a God without eyes, without ears,
Who shall sing of him, dead in the birth?

The earth-god Freedom, the lonely
  Face lightening, the footprint unshod,
Not as one man crucified only
  Nor scourged with but one life's rod;
The soul that is substance of nations,
Reincarnate with fresh generations;
  The great god Man, which is God.

But in weariest of years and obscurest
  Doth it live not at heart of all things,
The one God and one spirit, a purest
  Life, fed from unstanchable springs?
Within love, within hatred it is,
And its seed in the stripe as the kiss,
  And in slaves is the germ, and in kings.

Freedom we call it, for holier
  Name of the soul's there is none;
Surelier it labours, if slowlier,
  Than the metres of star or of sun;
Slowlier than life into breath,
Surelier than time into death,
  It moves till its labour be done.

Till the motion be done and the measure
  Circling through season and clime,
Slumber and sorrow and pleasure,
  Vision of virtue and crime;
Till consummate with conquering eyes,
A soul disembodied, it rise
  From the body transfigured of time.

Till it rise and remain and take station
  With the stars of the worlds that rejoice;
Till the voice of its heart's exultation
  Be as theirs an invariable voice;
By no discord of evil estranged,
By no pause, by no breach in it changed,
  By no clash in the chord of its choice.

It is one with the world's generations,
  With the spirit, the star, and the sod;
With the kingless and king-stricken nations,
  With the cross, and the chain, and the rod;
The most high, the most secret, most lonely,
The earth-soul Freedom, that only
  Lives, and that only is God.

To Walt Whitman • *Joaquin Miller*

O Titan soul, ascend your starry steep,
　On golden stair, to gods and storied men!
Ascend! nor care where thy traducers creep.
　For what may well be said of prophets, when
A world that's wicked comes to call them good?
Ascend and sing! As kings of thought who stood
　On stormy heights, and held far lights to men,
Stand thou, and shout above the tumbled roar,
Lest brave ships drive and break against the shore.

What though thy sounding song be roughly set?
　Parnassus' self is rough! Give thou the thought,
The golden ore, the gems that few forget;
　In time the tinsel jewel will be wrought.
Stand thou alone, and fixed as destiny,
　An imaged god that lifts above all hate;
　Stand thou serene and satisfied with fate;
Stand thou as stands the lightning-riven tree,
That lords the cloven clouds of gray Yosemite.

Yea, lone, sad soul, thy heights must be thy home;
　Thou sweetest lover! love shall climb to thee
Like incense curling some cathedral dome,
　From many distant vales. Yet thou shalt be,
O grand, sweet singer, to the end alone.
　But murmur not. The moon, the mighty spheres,
　Spin on alone through all the soundless years;
Alone man comes on earth; he lives alone;
Alone he turns to front the dark unknown.

To Walt Whitman, from Some Younger English Friends • *Ernest Rhys*

Here health we pledge you in one draught of song,
Caught in this rhymster's cup from earth's delight,
Where English fields are green the whole year long—
The wine of might,
That the new-come spring distills, most sweet and
strong,
In the viewless air's alembic, that's wrought too fine for
sight.
Good health! we pledge, that care may lightly sleep,
And pain of age be gone for this one day,
As of this loving cup you take, and, drinking deep,
Are glad at heart straightway
To feel once more the friendly heat of the sun
Creative in you (as when in youth it shone),
And pulsing brainward with the rhythmic wealth
Of all the summer whose high minstrelsy
Shall soon crown field and tree,
To call back age to youth again, and pain to perfect
health.

A Letter to Robert Bridges

GERARD MANLEY HOPKINS

Dearest Bridges,

... FIRST I MAY as well say what I should not otherwise have said, that I always knew in my heart Walt Whitman's mind to be more like my own than any other man's living. As he is a very great scoundrel this is not a pleasant confession. And this also makes me the more desirous to read him and the more determined that I will not.

. . . . .

Now prose rhythm in English is always one of two things (allowing my convention about scanning upwards or from slack to stress and not from stress to slack)—either iambic or anapaestic. You may make a third measure (let us call it) by intermixing them. One of these three simple measures then, all iambic or all anapaestic or mingled iambic and anapaestic, is what [Whitman] in every case means to write. He dreams of no other and he *means* a rugged or, as he calls it in that very piece 'Spirit that formed this scene' (which is very instructive and should be read on this very subject), a 'savage' art and rhythm.

Extremes meet, and (I must for truth's sake say what sounds pride) this savagery of his art, this rhythm in its last ruggedness and decomposition into common prose, comes near the last elaboration of mine.

. . . . .

The above remarks are not meant to run down Whitman. His 'savage' style has advantages, and he has chosen it; he says so. But you cannot eat your cake and keep it: he eats his offhand, I keep mine. It makes a very great difference. Neither do I deny all resemblance. In particular I noticed in *Spirit that Formed this Scene* a preference for the alexandrine. I have the same preference: I came to it by degrees, I did not take it from him. . . .

18 October 1882

Walt Whitman • *Edwin Arlington Robinson*

The master-songs are ended, and the man
That sang them is a name. And so is God
A name; and so is love, and life, and death,
And everything. But we, who are too blind
To read what we have written, or what faith
Has written for us, do not understand:
We only blink and wonder.

Last night it was the song that was the man,
But now it is the man that is the song.
We do not hear him very much to-day:
His piercing and eternal cadence rings
Too pure for us—too powerfully pure,
Too lovingly triumphant, and too large;
But there are some that hear him, and they know
That he shall sing to-morrow for all men,
And that all time shall listen.

The master-songs are ended? Rather say
No songs are ended that are ever sung,
And that no names are dead names. When we write
Men's letters on proud marble or on sand,
We write them there forever.

A Letter

LOUIS H. SULLIVAN

My dear and honored Walt Whitman: It is less than a year ago that I made your acquaintance so to speak, quite by accident, searching among the shelves of a book store. I was attracted by the curious title: Leaves of Grass, opened the book at random, and my eyes met the lines of Elemental Drifts. You then and there entered my soul, have not departed, and never will depart.

Be assured that there is at least one (and I hope there are many others) who understands you as you wish to be understood; one, moreover, who has weighed you in the balance of his intuition and finds you the greatest of poets.

To a man who can resolve himself into subtle unison with Nature and Humanity as you have done, who can blend the soul harmoniously with materials, who sees good in all and overflows in sympathy toward all things, enfolding them with his spirit: to such a man I joyfully give the name of Poet—the most precious of all names.

At the time I first met your work, I was engaged upon the essay which I herewith send you. I had just finished Decadence. In the Spring Song and the Song of the Depths my orbit responded to the new attracting sun. I send you this essay because it is your opinion above all other opinions that I should most highly value. What you may say in praise or encouragement will please me, but sympathetic surgery will better please. I know that I am not presuming, for have you not said: "I concentrate toward them that are nigh"—"will you speak before I am gone? Will you prove already too late?"

After all, words fail me in writing to you. Imagine that I have expressed to you my sincere conviction of what I owe you.

The essay is my first effort at the age of thirty. I, too, "have sweated through fog with linguists and contenders." I, too, "have pried through the strata, analyzed to a hair," reaching for the basis of a virile and indigenous art. Holding on in silence to this day, for fear of foolish utterances, I hope at least that my words may carry the weight of conviction.

Trusting that it may not be in vain that I hope to hear from you, believe me, noble man, affectionately your distant friend,

Chicago, Feb. 3rd, 1887.

LOUIS H. SULLIVAN

Walt Whitman • *Rubén Darío*

In his land of iron lives the great elder,
Beautiful patriarch, serene and holy;
His furrowed brow, of Olympic splendor,
Commands and conquers with noble glory.

His soul, like a mirror, the cosmos evokes,
And his tired shoulders merit the mantle;
With a lyre chiseled from an ancient oak,
As a new prophet he sings his canticles.

A high priest inspired with divine avail
Heralds, in the future, a better spring,
He tells the eagle: "Fly!"; the sailor: "Sail!";

And the robust worker to keep on working.
Thus, the poet passes along his trail,
with the splendid countenance of a king.

(translated by Didier Tisdel Jaén)

18

A Tribute of Grasses • *Hamlin Garland*

To W. W.

Serene, vast head, with silver cloud of hair
Lined on the purple dusk of death,
A stern medallion, velvet set—
Old Norseman, throned, not chained upon thy chair,
Thy grasp of hand, thy hearty breath
  Of welcome thrills me yet
  As when I faced thee there!

Loving my plain as thou thy sea,
Facing the East as thou the West,
I bring a handful of grass to thee—
The prairie grasses I know the best;
Type of the wealth and width of the plain,
Strong of the strength of the wind and sleet,
Fragrant with sunlight and cool with rain,
I bring it and lay it low at thy feet,
  Here by the eastern sea.

from Walt Whitman

EDMUND GOSSE

FATIMA WAS PERMITTED, nay encouraged, to make use of all the rooms, so elegantly and commodiously furnished, in Bluebeard Castle, with one exception. It was in vain that the housemaid and the cook pointed out to her that each of the ladies who had preceded her as a tenant had smuggled herself into that one forbidden chamber and had never come out again. Their sad experience was thrown away upon Fatima, who penetrated the fatal apartment and became an object of melancholy derision. The little room called "Walt Whitman," in the castle of literature, reminds one of that in which the relics of Bluebeard's levity were stored. We all know that discomfort and perplexity await us there, that nobody ever came back from it with an intelligible message, that it is piled with the bones of critics; yet such is the perversity of the analytic mind, that each one of us, sooner or later, finds himself peeping through the keyhole and fumbling at the lock.

As the latest of these imprudent explorers, I stand a moment with the handle in my hand and essay a defence of those whose skeletons will presently be discovered. Was it their fault? Was their failure not rather due to a sort of magic that hangs over the place? To drop metaphor, I am sadly conscious that, after reading what a great many people of authority and of assumption have written about Whitman—reading it, too, in a humble spirit—though I have been stimulated and entertained, I have not been at all instructed. Pleasant light, of course, has been thrown on the critics themselves and on their various peculiarities. But upon Whitman, upon the place he holds in literature and life, upon the questions, what he was and why he was, surely very little. To me, at least, after all the oceans of talk, after all the extravagant eulogy, all the mad vituperation, he remains perfectly cryptic and opaque. I find no reason given by these authorities why he should have made his appearance, or what his appearance signifies. I am told

20

that he is abysmal, putrid, glorious, universal and contemptible. I like these excellent adjectives, but I cannot see how to apply them to Whitman. Yet, like a boy at a shooting-gallery, I cannot go home till I, too, have had my six shots at this running-deer.

On the main divisions of literature it seems that a critic should have not merely a firm opinion, but sound argument to back that opinion. It is a pilgarlicky mind that is satisfied with saying, "I like you, Dr. Fell, the reason why I cannot tell." Analysis is the art of telling the reason why. But still more feeble and slovenly is the criticism that has to say, "I liked Dr. Fell yesterday and I don't like him to-day, but I can give no reason." The shrine of Walt Whitman, however, is strewn around with remarks of this kind. Poor Mr. Swinburne has been cruelly laughed at for calling him a "strong-winged soul, with prophetic lips hot with the blood-beats of song," and yet a drunken apple-woman reeling in a gutter. But he is not alone in this inconsistency. Almost every competent writer who has attempted to give an estimate of Whitman has tumbled about in the same extraordinary way. Something mephitic breathes from this strange personality, something that maddens the judgment until the wisest lose their self-control.

Therefore, I propound a theory. It is this, that there is no real Walt Whitman, that is to say, that he cannot be taken as any other figure in literature is taken, as an entity of positive value and defined characteristics, as, for instance, we take the life and writings of Racine, or of Keats, or of Jeremy Taylor, including the style with the substance, the teaching with the idiosyncrasy. In these ordinary cases the worth and specific weight of the man are not greatly affected by our attitude towards him. An atheist or a quaker may contemplate the writings of the Bishop of Dromore without sympathy; that does not prevent the *Holy Dying* from presenting, even to the mind of such an opponent, certain defined features which are un-modified by like or dislike. This is true of any fresh or vivid talent which may have appeared among us yesterday. But I contend that it is not true of Whitman. Whitman is mere *bathybius;* he is literature in the condition of protoplasm—an intellectual organism so simple that it takes the instant impression of whatever mood approaches it. Hence the critic who touches Whitman is immediately confronted with his own image stamped upon that viscid and tenacious surface. He finds, not what Whitman has to give, but what he himself has brought. And when, in quite another mood, he comes again to Whitman, he finds that other self of his own stamped upon the provoking protoplasm.

If this theory is allowed a moment's consideration, it cannot, I think, but tend to be accepted. It accounts for all the difficulties in the criticism of

Whitman. It shows us why Robert Louis Stevenson has found a Stevenson in *Leaves of Grass,* and John Addington Symonds a Symonds. It explains why Emerson considered the book "the most extraordinary piece of wit and wisdom that America has yet [in 1855] produced;" why Thoreau thought all the sermons ever preached not equal to it for divinity; why Italian *dilettanti* and Scandinavian gymnasts, anarchists and parsons and champions of women's rights, the most opposite and incongruous types, have the habit of taking Whitman to their hearts for a little while and then flinging him away from them in abhorrence, and, perhaps, of drawing him to them again with passion. This last, however, I think occurs more rarely. Almost every sensitive and natural person has gone through a period of fierce Whitmanomania; but it is a disease which rarely afflicts the same patient more than once. It is, in fact, a sort of highly-irritated egotism come to a head, and people are almost always better after it.

Unless we adopt some such theory as this, it is difficult to account in any way for the persistent influence of Walt Whitman's writings. They have now lasted about forty years, and show no sign whatever of losing their vitality. Nobody is able to analyse their charm, yet the charm is undeniable. They present no salient features, such as have been observed in all other literature, from Homer and David down to the latest generation. They offer a sort of Plymouth Brethrenism of form, a negation of all the laws and ritual of literature. As a book, to be a living book, must contain a vigorous and appropriate arrangement of words, this one solitary feature occurs in *Leaves of Grass.* I think it is not to be denied by any candid critic, however inimical, that passages of extreme verbal felicity are to be found frequently scattered over the pages of Whitman's rhapsodies. But, this one concession made to form, there is no other. Not merely are rhythm and metre conspicuously absent, but composition, evolution, vertebration of style, even syntax and the limits of the English tongue, are disregarded. Every reader who comes to Whitman starts upon an expedition to the virgin forest. He must take his conveniences with him. He will make of the excursion what his own spirit dictates. There are solitudes, fresh air, rough landscape, and a well of water, but if he wishes to enjoy the latter he must bring his own cup with him. When people are still young and like roughing it, they appreciate a picnic into Whitman-land, but it is not meant for those who choose to see their intellectual comforts round them.

. . . . .

. . . I am inclined to admit that in Walt Whitman we have just missed receiving from the New World one of the greatest of modern poets, but that we have missed it must at the same time be acknowledged. To be a poet it is not necessary to be a consistent and original thinker, with an elaborately-balanced system of ethics. The absence of intellectual quality, the superabundance of the emotional, the objective, the pictorial, are no reasons for undervaluing Whitman's imagination. But there is one condition which distinguishes art from mere amorphous expression; that condition is the result of a process through which the vague and engaging observations of Whitman never passed. He felt acutely and accurately, his imagination was purged of external impurities, he lay spread abroad in a condition of literary solution. But there he remained, an expanse of crystallisable substances, waiting for the structural change that never came; rich above almost all his coevals in the properties of poetry, and yet, for want of a definite shape and fixity, doomed to sit for ever apart from the company of the Poets.

1893

Walt Whitman • *Robert Buchanan*

One handshake, Walt! while we, thy little band
  Of lovers, take our last long look at thee—
One handshake, and one kiss upon the hand
  Thou didst outreach to bless Humanity!

The dear, kind hand is cold, the grave sweet eyes
  Are closed in slumber, as thou liest there.
We shed no tears, but watch in sad surmise
  The face still smiling thro' the good grey hair!

No tears for *thee!* Tears rather, tears of shame,
  For those who saw that face yet turn'd away;
Yet even *these,* too, didst thou love and claim
  As brethren, tho' they frown'd and would not stay.

And so, dear Walt, thine Elder Brother passed,
  Unknown, unblest, with open hand like thine—
Till lo! the open Sepulchre at last,
  The watching angels, and the Voice Divine!

God bless thee, Walt! Even Death may never seize
  Thy gifts of goodness in no market priced—
The wisdom and the charm of Socrates,
  Touch'd with some gentle glory of the Christ!

So long!—We seem to hear thy voice again,
  Tender and low, and yet so deep and strong!
Yes, we will wait, in gladness not in pain,
  The coming of thy Prophecy. (*'So long!'*)

To W. W. • *George Cabot Lodge*

I toss upon Thy grave,
(After Thy life resumed, after the pause, the backward
  glance of Death;
Hence, hence the vistas on, the march continued,
In larger spheres, new lives in paths untrodden,
On! till the circle rounded, ever the journey on!)
Upon Thy grave,—the vital sod how thrilled as from Thy limbs
  and breast transpired,
Rises the spring's sweet utterance of flowers,—
I toss this sheaf of song, these scattered leaves of love!
For thee, Thy Soul and Body spent for me,
—And now still living, now in love, transmitting still Thy
  Soul, Thy Flesh to me, to all!—
These variant phrases of the long-immortal chant
I toss upon Thy grave!

4.

1905-1955

5.

A Pact • *Ezra Pound*

I make a pact with you, Walt Whitman—
I have detested you long enough.
I come to you as a grown child
Who has had a pig-headed father;
I am old enough now to make friends.
It was you that broke the new wood,
Now is a time for carving.
We have one sap and one root—
Let there be commerce between us.

What I Feel About Walt Whitman

EZRA POUND

FROM THIS SIDE of the Atlantic I am for the first time able to read Whitman, and from the vantage of my education and—if it be permitted a man of my scant years—my world citizenship: I see him America's poet. The only Poet before the artists of the Carmen-Hovey period, or better, the only one of the conventionally recognised 'American Poets' who is worth reading.

He *is* America. His crudity is an exceeding great stench, but it *is* America. He is the hollow place in the rock that echoes with his time. He *does* 'chant the crucial stage' and he is the 'voice triumphant.' He is disgusting. He is an exceedingly nauseating pill, but he accomplishes his mission.

Entirely free from the renaissance humanist ideal of the complete man or from the Greek idealism, he is content to be what he is, and he is his time and his people. He is a genius because he has vision of what he is and of his function. He knows that he is a beginning and not a classically finished work.

I honour him for he prophesied me while I can only recognise him as a forebear of whom I ought to be proud.

In America there is much for the healing of the nations, but woe unto him of the cultured palate who attempts the dose.

As for Whitman, I read him (in many parts) with acute pain, but when I write of certain things I find myself using his rhythms. The expression of certain things related to cosmic consciousness seems tainted with this maramis.

I am (in common with every educated man) an heir of the ages and I demand my birth-right. Yet if Whitman represented his time in language acceptable to one accustomed to my standard of intellectual-artistic living he would belie his time and nation. And yet I am but one of his 'ages and ages' encrustations' or to be exact an encrustation of the next age. The vital part of my message, taken from the sap and fibre of America, is the same as his.

Mentally I am a Walt Whitman who has learned to wear a collar and a dress shirt (although at times inimical to both). Personally I might be very glad to conceal my relationship to my spiritual father and brag about my more congenial ancestry—Dante, Skakespeare, Theocritus, Villon, but the descent is a bit difficult to establish. And, to be frank, Whitman is to my fatherland (*Patriam quam odi et amo* for no uncertain reasons) what Dante is to Italy and I at my best can only be a strife for a renaissance in America of all the lost or temporarily mislaid beauty, truth, valour, glory of Greece, Italy, England and all the rest of it.

And yet if a man has written lines like Whitman's to the *Sunset Breeze* one has to love him. I think we have not yet paid enough attention to the deliberate artistry of the man, not in details but in the large.

I am immortal even as he is, yet with a lesser vitality as I am the more in love with beauty (If I really do love it more than he did). Like Dante he wrote in the 'vulgar tongue,' in a new metric. The first great man to write in the language of his people.

Et ego Petrarca in lingua vetera scribo, and in a tongue my people understood not.

It seems to me I should like to drive Whitman into the old world. I sledge, he drill—and to scourge America with all the old beauty. (For Beauty *is* an accusation) and with a thousand thongs from Homer to Yeats, from Theocritus to Marcel Schwob. This desire is because I am young and impatient, were I old and wise I should content myself in seeing and saying that these things will come. But now, since I am by no means sure it would be true prophecy, I am fain set my own hand to the labour.

It is a great thing, reading a man to know, not 'His Tricks are not as yet my Tricks, but I can easily make them mine' but 'His message is my message. We will see that men hear it.'

Salutation to Walt Whitman • *Fernando Pessoa*

Infinite Portugal, June eleventh, nineteen hundred and fifteen . . .
A-hoy-hoy-hoy-hoy!

From here in Portugal, with all the ages in my brain,
I salute you, Walt, I salute you, my brother in the Universe,
I, with my monocle and tightly buttoned frock coat,
I am not unworthy of you, Walt, as you well know,
I am not unworthy of you, as my greeting you shows . . .
I, so like you in indolence, so easily bored,
I am with you, as you well know, and understand you and love you,
And though I never met you, born the same year you died,
I know you loved me too, you knew me and I am happy.

I know that you knew me, that you considered me and explained me,
I know that this is what I am, whether on Brooklyn Ferry ten
    years before I was born
Or strolling up *Rua do Ouro* thinking about everything that is
    not *Rua do Ouro*,
And just as you felt everything, so I feel everything, and so
    here we are clasping hands,
Clasping hands, Walt, clasping hands, with the universe doing
    a dance in our soul.

O singer of concrete absolutes, always modern and eternal,
Fiery concubine of the scattered world,
Great pederast brushing up against the diversity of things,
Sexualized by rocks, by trees, by people, by their trades,
Rutting on the move, with casual encounters, with mere
    observations,
My enthusiast for the contents of everything,
My great hero going to meet death by leaps and bounds,
Roaring, screaming, bellowing greetings to God!

Singer of cruel and tender brotherhood with everything,
Great epidermic democrat, close to all in body and soul,
Carnival of all deeds, bacchanalia of all intentions,
Twin brother of all impulses,

Jean-Jacques Rousseau of the world destined to produce machines,
Homer of all ungraspable and wavering carnality,
Shakespeare of the sensation that begins to be steam-propelled,
Milton-Shelley of the dawn of Electricity!
Incubus of all gestures,
Inner spasm of all force in objects,
Pimp of the whole Universe,
Whore of all solar systems . . .

How many times have I kissed your picture!
Wherever you are now (I don't know where it is but it is God),
You feel this, I know you feel it, and my kisses are warmer
    (among us)
And you like it that way, dear old man, and you thank me
    for them—
I know this well, something tells me, like a feeling of pleasant
    warmth in my spirit,

An abstract, oblique erection at the bottom of my soul.

There was nothing of the *engageant* in you—rather the muscular,
    the cyclopic,
Though in facing the Universe yours was the attitude of a woman,
For every blade of grass, every stone, every man was a Universe
    for you.

Walt, my beloved old man, my great Comrade, I evoke you!
I belong to your Bacchic orgy of free sensations,
I am yours, from the tingling of my toes to the nausea of my
    dreams,
I am yours, look at me—up there where you are near God,
    you see me contrariwise,
From inside out . . . My body is what you divine but you see
    my soul—
You see it properly, and through its eyes you glimpse my body—
Look at me: you know that I, Alvaro de Campos, engineer,
Sensationist poet,
Am not your disciple, am not your friend, am not your singer,
You know that I am You, and you are happy about it!

I could never read all your verses through . . . There's too much
feeling in them . . .
I go through your lines as through a teeming crowd brushing
past me,
And I smell the sweat, the grease, the human and mechanical
activity.
At a given moment, reading your poems, I can't tell if I'm reading
or living them,
I don't know if my actual place is in the world or in your verse,

I don't know if I'm standing here, with both feet on the ground,
Or hanging upside down in some sort of institution,
From the natural ceiling of your tumultuous inspiration,
From the middle of the ceiling of your inaccessible intensity.

Open all the doors for me!
Because I have to go in!
My password? Walt Whitman!
But I don't give any password . . .
I go in without explaining . . .
If I must, I'll knock the doors down . . .
Yes, slight and civilized though I am, I'll knock the doors down,
Because at this moment I'm not slight or civilized at all,
I'm ME, a thinking universe of flesh and bone, wanting to get in
And having to get in by force, because when I want to go in
        I am God!

Take this garbage out of my way!
Put those emotions away in drawers!
Get out of here, you politicians, literati,
You peaceful businessmen, policemen, whores, pimps,
All your kind is the letter that kills, not the spirit giving life.
The spirit giving life at this moment is ME!

Let no son of a bitch get in my way!
My path goes through Infinity before reaching its end!
It's not up to you whether I reach this end or not,
It's up to me, up to God—up to what I mean by the word *Infinite* . . .

Go on!
Press onward!
I feel the spurs, I am the very horse I mount
Because I, since I want to be consubstantial with God,
Can be everything, or I can be nothing, or anything,
Just as I please ... It's nobody's business ...
Raging madness! Wanting to yelp, jump,
Scream, bray, do handsprings and somersaults, my body yelling,
Wanting to grab hold of car wheels and go under them,
Get inside the whirling whip that's about to strike,
Be the bitch to all dogs and they not enough for me,
Be the steering wheel of all machines and their limitless speed,
Be the one who's crushed, abandoned, dislocated, or done for,
Come dance this fury with me, Walt, you there in that other world,
Let's swing into this rock dance, knocking at the stars,
Fall exhausted to the ground with me,
Beat the walls with me like mad,
Break down, tear yourself apart with me,
Through everything, in everything, around everything, in nothing,
In an abstract body rage that stirs up maelstroms in the soul ...

Damn it! Get going, I said!
Even if God himself stops us, let's get going ... it makes no
    difference ...
Let's go on and get nowhere ...
Infinity! Universe! End without end! What's the difference?

(Let me take off my tie, unbutton my collar.
You can't let off steam with civilization looped around your
    neck ...)
All right now, we're off to a flying start!

In a great torchlight parade of all the cities of Europe,
In a great military parade of industry, trade and leisure,
In a great race, a great incline, a great decline,
Thundering and leaping, and everything with me,
I jump up to salute you,
I yell out to salute you,
I burst loose to salute you, bounding, handstanding, yawping!

This is how I send you
My leaping verses, my bounding verses, my spasmodic verses,
My attacks-of-hysteria verses,
Verses that pull the cart of my nerves.

My crazy tumbling inspires me,
Barely able to breathe, I get to my feet exalted,
For the verses stem from my being unable to burst with life.

Open all the windows for me!
Throw open all the doors!
Pull the whole house up over me!
I want to live freely, out in the open,
I want to make gestures outside my body,
To run like the rain streaming down over walls,
To be stepped on like stones down the broad streets,
To sink like heavy weights to the bottom of the sea,
And all this voluptuously, a feeling remote from me now!

I don't want the doors bolted!
I don't want the safes locked!
I want to horn in there, put my nose in, be dragged off,
I want to be somebody else's wounded member,
I want to be spilled from crates,
I want to be thrown in the ocean,
I want them to come looking for me at home with lewd intentions—
Just so I'm not always sitting here quietly,
Just so I'm not simply writing these verses!

I'm against spaces-between in the world!
I'm for the compenetrated, material contiguity of objects!
I'm for physical bodies commingling like souls,
Not just dynamically but statically too!

I want to fly and fall from way up high!
To be thrown like a hand grenade!
To be brought to a sudden stop ... To be lifted to ...
The highest, abstract point of me and it all!

Climax of iron and motors!
Accelerated escalator without any stairs!
Hydraulic pump tearing out my smashed up guts!

Put me in chains, just so I can break them,
Just so I can break them with my teeth bleeding,
Bleeding away in spurts, with the masochistic joy of life!

The sailors took me prisoner,
Their hands gripped me in the dark,
For the moment I died of the pain,
My soul went on licking the floors of my private cell
While the whirling of impossibilities circled my spite.

Jump, leap, take the bit between your teeth,
Red-hot iron Pegasus of my twitching anxieties,
Wavering parking place of my motorized destiny!

He's called Walt:
Entryway to everything!
Bridge to everything!
Highway to everything!
Your omnivorous soul,
Your soul that's bird, fish, beast, man, woman,
Your soul that's two where two exist,
Your soul that's one becoming two when two are one,
Your soul that's arrow, lightning, space,
Amplex, nexus, sex and Texas, Carolina and New York,
Brooklyn Ferry in the twilight,
Brooklyn Ferry going back and forth,
Libertad! Democracy! the Twentieth Century about to dawn!
Boom! Boom! Boom! Boom! Boom!
BOOM!

You who lived it, you who saw it, you who heard it,
Subject and object, active and passive,
Here, there, everywhere you,
Circle closing off all possibilities of feeling,
Quintessence of all things that might still happen,
God-Terminus of all imaginable objects, and it is you!
You are the Hour,
You the Minute,
You the Second!
You interpolated, liberated, unfurled, and sent,
Interpolating, liberating, unfurling, sending,
You, the interpolator, liberator, unfurler, sender,
The seal on all letters,
The name on all addressed envelopes,
Goods delivered, returned, and to follow . . .
Trainful of feelings at so many soul-miles per hour,
Per hour, per minute, per second, BOOM!

Now that I'm almost dead and see everything so clearly,
I bow to you, Great Liberator.

Surely my personality has had some purpose.
Surely it meant something, since it expressed itself,
Yet looking back today, only one thing troubles me—
Not to have had your self-transcending calm,
Your star-clustered liberation from Infinite Night.

Maybe I had no mission at all on earth.

That's why I'm calling out,
For the ear-splitting privilege of greeting you,
All the ant-swarming humanity in the Universe,
All the ways of expressing all emotions,
All the consequences of all thoughts,
All the wheels, all the gears, all the pistons of the soul.

That's why I'm crying out
And why, in this homage to you from Me, they all begin to buzz
In their real and metaphysical gibberish,
In the uproar of things going on inside without nexus.

Goodbye, bless you, live forever, O Great Bastard of Apollo,
Impotent and ardent lover of the nine muses and of the graces,
Cable-car from Olympus to us and from us to Olympus.

(*translated by Edwin Honig*)

Petit, the Poet • *Edgar Lee Masters*

Seeds in a dry pod, tick, tick, tick,
Tick, tick, tick, like mites in a quarrel—
Faint iambics that the full breeze wakens—
But the pine tree makes a symphony thereof.
Triolets, villanelles, rondels, rondeaus,
Ballades by the score with the same old thought:
The snows and the roses of yesterday are vanished;
And what is love but a rose that fades?
Life all around me here in the village:
Tragedy, comedy, valor and truth,
Courage, constancy, heroism, failure—
All in the loom, and oh what patterns!
Woodlands, meadows, streams and rivers—
Blind to all of it all my life long.
Triolets, villanelles, rondels, rondeaus,
Seeds in a dry pod, tick, tick, tick,
Tick, tick, tick, what little iambics,
While Homer and Whitman roared in the pines?

Walt Whitman • *Emanuel Carnevali*

Noon on the mountain!—
And all the crags are husky faces powerful with love for
　the sun;
All the shadows
Whisper of the sun.

Whitman • *Witter Bynner*

As voices enter earth,
Into your great frame and windy beard
Have entered many voices,
And out of your great frame and windy beard,
As out of earth,
They are shaken free again . . .

With the thunder and the butterfly,
With the sea crossing like runners the tape of the
    beach,
With machinery and tools and the sweat of men,
With all lovers and comrades combining,
With the odor of redwoods and the whisper of
    death,
Comes your prophetic presence,
Never to be downed, never to be dissuaded from
    singing
The comfortable counsel of the earth
And from moving, athletic, intimate, sure, non-
    chalant,
Friending whoever is friends with himself,
Accusing only avoiders, tamperers, fabricators,
And yet touching with your finger-tips
All men,
As Michael Angelo imagined God
Touching with sap the finger-tips of Adam.

Whitman

D. H. LAWRENCE

WHITMAN IS THE GREATEST of the Americans. One of the greatest poets of the world, in him an element of falsity troubles us still. Something is wrong; we cannnot be quite at ease in his greatness.

This may be our own fault. But we sincerely feel that something is overdone in Whitman; there is something that is too much. Let us get over our quarrel with him first.

All the Americans, when they have trodden new ground, seem to have been conscious of making a breach in the established order. They have been self-conscious about it. They have felt that they were trespassing, transgressing, or going very far, and this has given a certain stridency, or portentousness, or luridness to their manner. Perhaps that is because the steps were taken so rapidly. From Franklin to Whitman is a hundred years. It might be a thousand.

The Americans have finished in haste, with a certain violence and violation, that which Europe began two thousand years ago or more. Rapidly they have returned to lay open the secrets which the Christian epoch has taken two thousand years to close up.

With the Greeks started the great passion for the ideal, the passion for translating all consciousness into terms of spirit and ideal or idea. They did this in reaction from the vast old world which was dying in Egypt. But the Greeks, though they set out to conquer the animal or sensual being in man, did not set out to annihilate it. This was left for the Christians.

The Christians, phase by phase, set out actually to *annihilate* the sensual being in man. They insisted that man was in his reality *pure spirit*, and that he was perfectible as such. And this was their business, to achieve such a perfection.

They worked from a profound inward impulse, the Christian religious impulse. But their proceeding was the same, in living extension, as that of the Greek esoterics, such as John the Evangel or Socrates. They proceeded, by will and by exaltation, to overcome *all* the passions and all the appetites and prides.

Now, so far, in Europe, the conquest of the lower self has been objective. That is, man has moved from a great impulse within himself, unconscious. But once the conquest has been effected, there is a temptation for the conscious mind to return and finger and explore, just as tourists now explore battlefields. This self-conscious *mental* provoking of sensation and reaction in the great affective centres is what we call sentimentalism or sensationalism. The mind returns upon the affective centres, and sets up in them a deliberate reaction.

And this is what all the Americans do, beginning with Crêvecoeur, Hawthorne, Poe, all the transcendentalists, Melville, Prescott, Wendell Holmes, Whitman, they are all guilty of this provoking of mental reactions in the physical self, passions exploited by the mind. In Europe, men like Balzac and Dickens, Tolstoi and Hardy, still act direct from the passional motive, and not inversely, from mental provocation. But the aesthetes and symbolists, from Baudelaire and Maeterlinck and Oscar Wilde onwards, and nearly all later Russian, French, and English novelists set up their reactions in the mind and reflect them by a secondary process down into the body. This makes a vicious living and a spurious art. It is one of the last and most fatal effects of idealism. Everything becomes self-conscious and spurious, to the pitch of madness. It is the madness of the world of to-day. Europe and America are all alike; all the nations self-consciously provoking their own passional reactions from the mind, and *nothing* spontaneous.

And this is our accusation against Whitman, as against the others. Too often he deliberately, self-consciously *affects* himself. It puts us off, it makes us dislike him. But since such self-conscious secondariness is a concomitant of all American art, and yet not sufficiently so to prevent that art from being of rare quality, we must get over it. The excuse is that the Americans have had to perform in a century a curve which it will take Europe much longer to finish, if ever she finishes it.

Whitman has gone further, in actual living expression, than any man, it seems to me. Dostoevsky has burrowed underground into the decomposing psyche. But Whitman has gone forward in life-knowledge. It is he who surmounts the grand climacteric of our civilization.

Whitman enters on the last phase of spiritual triumph. He really arrives at that stage of infinity which the seers sought. By subjecting the *deepest centres* of the lower self, he attains the maximum consciousness in the higher self: a degree of extensive consciousness greater, perhaps, than any man in the modern world.

We have seen Dana and Melville, the two adventurers, setting out to conquer the last vast *element,* with the spirit. We have seen Melville touching at last the far end of the immemorial, prehistoric Pacific civilization, in "Typee." We have seen his terrific cruise into universality.

Now we must remember that the way, even towards a state of infinite comprehension, is through the externals toward the quick. And the vast elements, the cosmos, the big things, the universals, these are always the externals. These are met first and conquered first. That is why science is so much easier than art. The quick is the living being, the quick of quicks is the individual soul. And it is here, at the quick, that Whitman proceeds to find the experience of infinitude, his vast extension, or concentrated intensification into Allness. He carries the conquest to its end.

If we read his paeans, his chants of praise and deliverance and accession, what do we find? All-embracing, indiscriminate, passional acceptance; surges of chaotic vehemence of invitation and embrace, catalogues, lists, enumerations. "Whoever you are, to you endless announcements. . . ." "And of these one and all I weave the song of myself." "Lovers, endless lovers."

Continually the one cry; I am everything and everything is me. I accept everything in my consciousness; nothing is rejected:—

> "I am he that aches with amorous love:
>   Does the earth gravitate? does not all matter, aching, attract
>   all matter?
> So the body of me to all I meet or know."

At last everything is conquered. At last the lower centres are conquered. At last the lowest plane is submitted to the highest. At last there is nothing more to conquer. At last all is one, all is love, even hate is love, even flesh is spirit. The great oneness, the experience of infinity, the triumph of the living spirit, which at last includes everything, is here accomplished.

It is man's accession into wholeness, his knowledge in full. Now he is united with everything. Now he embraces everything into himself in a oneness. Whitman is drunk with the new wine of this new great experience, really drunk with the strange wine of infinitude. So he pours forth his words, his chants of praise and acclamation. It is man's maximum state of consciousness, his highest state of spiritual being. Supreme spiritual consciousness, and the divine drunkenness of supreme consciousness. It is reached through embracing love. "And whoever walks a furlong without sympathy walks to his own funeral dressed in his own shroud." And this supreme state, once reached, shows us the One Identity in everything, Whitman's cryptic *One Identity*.

Thus Whitman becomes in his own person the whole world, the whole universe, the whole eternity of time. Nothing is rejected. Because nothing opposes him. All adds up to one in him. Item by item he identifies himself with the universe, and this accumulative identity he calls Democracy, En Masse, One Identity, and so on.

But this is the last and final truth, the last truth is at the quick. And the quick is the single individual soul, which is never more than itself, though it embrace eternity and infinity, and never *other* than itself, though it include all men. Each vivid soul is unique, and though one soul embrace another, and include it, still it cannot *become* that other soul, or livingly dispossess that other soul. In extending himself, Whitman still remains himself; he does not become the other man, or the other woman, or the tree, or the universe: in spite of Plato.

Which is the maximum truth, though it appears so small in contrast to all these infinites, and En Masses, and Democracies, and Almightynesses. The essential truth is that a man is himself, and only himself, throughout all his greatnesses and extensions and intensifications.

The second truth which we must bring as a charge against Whitman is the one we brought before, namely, that his Allness, his One Identity, his En Masse, his Democracy, is only a half-truth—an enormous half-truth. The other half is Jehovah, and Eygpt, and Sennacherib: the other form of Allness, terrible and grand, even as in the Psalms.

Now Whitman's way to Allness, he tells us, is through endless sympathy, merging. But in merging you must merge away from something, as well as towards something, and in sympathy you must depart from one point to arrive at another. Whitman lays down this law of sympathy as the one law, the direction of merging as the one direction. Which is obviously wrong. Why not a right-about-turn? Why not turn slap back to the point from which you started to merge? Why not *that* direction, the reverse of merging, back to the single and overweening self? Why not, instead of endless dilation of sympathy, the retraction into isolation and pride?

Why not? The heart has its systole diastole, the shuttle comes and goes, even the sun rises and sets. We know, as a matter of fact, that all life lies between two poles. The direction is twofold. Whitman's *one direction* becomes a hideous tyranny once he has attained his goal of Allness. His One Identity is a prison of horror, once realized. For identities are manifold and each jewel-like, different as a sapphire from an opal. And the motion of merging becomes at last a vice, a nasty degeneration, as when tissue breaks down into a mucous slime. There must be the sharp retraction from isolation, following the expansion into unification, otherwise the integral being is overstrained and will break, break down like disintegrating tissue into slime, imbecility, epilepsy, vice, like Dostoevsky.

And one word more. Even if you reach the state of infinity, you can't sit down there. You just physically can't. You either have to strain still further into universality and become vaporish, or slimy: or you have to hold your toes and sit tight and practise Nirvana; or you have to come back to common dimensions, eat your pudding and blow your nose and be just yourself; or die and have done with it. A grand experience is a grand experience. It brings a man to his maximum. But even at his maximum a man is not more than himself. When he is infinite he is still himself. He still has a nose to wipe. The state of infinity is *only* a state, even if it be the supreme one.

But in achieving this state Whitman opened a new field of living. He drives on to the very centre of life and sublimates even this into consciousness. Melville hunts the remote white whale of the deepest passional body, tracks it down. But it is Whitman who captures the whale. The pure sensual body of man, at its deepest remoteness and intensity, this is the White Whale. And this is what Whitman captures.

He seeks his consummation through one continual ecstacy: the ecstacy of *giving himself,* and of being taken. The ecstacy of his own reaping and merging with another, with others; the sword-cut of sensual death. Whitman's motion is always the motion of *giving himself:* This is my body—take, and eat. It is the great sacrament. He knows nothing of the other sacrament, the sacrament in pride, where the communicant envelops the victim and host in a flame of ecstatic consuming, sensual gratification, and triumph.

But he is concerned with others beside himself: with woman, for example. But what is woman to Whitman? Not much? She is a great function—no more. Whitman's "athletic mothers of these States" are depressing. Muscles and wombs: functional creatures—no more.

> "As I see myself reflected in Nature,
> As I see through a mist, One with inexpressible completeness,
> sanity, beauty,
> See the bent head, and arms folded over the breast, the Female
> I see."

That is all. The woman is reduced, really, to a submissive function. She is no longer an individual being with a living soul. She must fold her arms and bend her head and submit to her functioning capacity. Function of sex, function of birth.

> "This, the nucleus—after the child is born of woman, man is
>   born of woman,
> This is the bath of birth, the merge of small and large, and the
>   outlet again—"

Acting from the last and profoundest centres, man acts womanless. It is no longer a question of race continuance. It is a question of sheer, ultimate being, the perfection of life, nearest to death. Acting from these centres, man is an extreme being, the unthinkable warrior, creator, mover, and maker.

And the polarity is between man and man. Whitman alone of all moderns has known this positively. Others have known it negatively, *pour épater les bourgeois*. But Whitman knew it positively, in its tremendous knowledge, knew the extremity, the perfectness, and the fatality.

Even Whitman becomes grave, tremulous, before the last dynamic truth of life. In *Calamus* he does not shout. He hesitates: he is reluctant, wistful. But none the less he goes on. And he tells the mystery of manly love, the love of comrades. Continually he tells us the same truth: the new world will be built upon the love of comrades, the new great dynamic of life will be manly love. Out of this inspiration the creation of the future.

The strange Calamus has its pink-tinged root by the pond, and it sends up its leaves of comradeship, comrades at one root, without the intervention of woman, the female. This comradeship is to be the final cohering principle of the new world, the new Democracy. It is the cohering principle of perfect soldiery, as he tells in "Drum Taps." It is the cohering principle of final *unison* in creative activity. And it is extreme and alone, touching the confines of death. It is something terrible to bear, terrible to be responsible for. It is the soul's last and most vivid responsibility, the responsibility for the circuit of final friendship, comradeship, manly love.

> "Yet, you are beautiful to me, you faint-tinged roots, you make
>   me think of death;
> Death is beautiful from you (what, indeed, is finally beautiful
>   except death and love?).
> I think it is not for life I am chanting here my chant of lovers, I
>   think it must be for death.
> For how calm, how solemn it grows to ascend to the atmosphere
>   of lovers;
> Death or life, I am then indifferent, my soul declines to prefer

> (I am not sure but the high soul of lovers welcomes death
> most),
> Indeed, O death, I think now these leaves mean precisely the
> same as you mean—"

Here we have the deepest, finest Whitman, the Whitman who knows the extremity of life, and of the soul's responsibility. He has come near now to death, in his creative life. But creative life must come near to death, to link up the mystic circuit. The pure warriors must stand on the brink of death. So must the men of a pure creative nation. We shall have no beauty, no dignity, no essential freedom otherwise. And so it is from Sea-Drift, where the male bird sings the lost female: not that she is lost, but lost to him who has had to go beyond her, to sing on the edge of the great sea, in the night. It is the last voice on the shore.

> "Whereto answering, the sea
> Delaying not, hurrying not,
> Whispered me through the night, very plainly before daybreak,
> Lisp'd to me the low and delicious word death,
> And again death, death, death, death,
> Hissing melodious, neither like the bird nor like my aroused
> child's heart,
> But edging near as privately for me rustling at my feet,
> Creeping thence steadily up to my ears and laving me softly all
> over,
> Death, death, death, death, death—"

What a great poet Whitman is: great like a great Greek. For him the last enclosures have fallen, he finds himself on the shore of the last sea. The extreme of life: so near to death. It is a hushed, deep responsibility. And what is the responsibility? It is for the new great era of mankind. And upon what is this new era established? On the perfect circuits of vital flow between human beings. First, the great sexless normal relation between individuals, simple sexless friendships, unison of family, and clan, and nation, and group. Next, the powerful sex relation between man and woman, culminating in the eternal orbit of marriage. And, finally, the sheer friendship, the love between comrades, the manly love which alone can create a new era of life.

The one state, however, does not annul the other: it fulfils the other. Marriage is the great step beyond friendship, and family, and nationality, but it does not supersede these. Marriage should only give repose and perfection to the great previous bonds and relationships. A wife or husband who sets about to annul the old, pre-marriage affections and connections ruins the foundations of marriage. And so with the last, extremest love, the love of comrades. The ultimate comradeship which sets about to destroy marriage destroys its own *raison d'être*. The ultimate comradeship is the final progression from marriage; it is the last seedless flower of pure beauty, beyond purpose. But if it destroys marriage it makes itself purely deathly. In its beauty, the ultimate comradeship flowers on the brink of death. But it flowers from the root of all life upon the blossoming tree of life.

The life-circuit now depends entirely upon the sex-unison of marriage. This circuit must never be broken. But it must still be surpassed. We cannot help the laws of life.

If marriage is sacred, the ultimate comradeship is utterly sacred, since it has no ulterior motive whatever, like procreation. If marriage is eternal, the great bond of life, how much more is this bond eternal, being the great life-circuit which borders on death in all its round. The new, extreme, the sacred relationship of comrades awaits us, and the future of mankind depends on the way in which this relation is entered upon by us. It is a relation between fearless, honorable, self-responsible men, a balance in perfect polarity.

The last phase is entered upon, shakily, by Whitman. It will take us an epoch to establish the new, perfect circuit of our being. It will take an epoch to establish the love of comrades, as marriage is really established now. For fear of going on, forwards, we turn round and destroy, or try to destroy, what lies behind. We are trying to destroy marriage, because we have not the courage to go forward from marriage to the new issue. Marriage must never be wantonly attacked. *True* marriage is eternal; in it we have our consummation and being. But the final consummation lies in that which is beyond marriage.

And when the bond, or circuit of perfect comrades is established, what then, when we are on the brink of death, fulfilled in the vastness of life? Then, at last, we shall know a starry maturity.

Whitman put us on the track years ago. Why has no one gone on from him? The great poet, why does no one accept his greatest word? The Americans are not worthy of their Whitman. They take him like a cocktail, for fun. Miracle that they have not annihilated every word of him. But these miracles happen.

The greatest modern poet! Whitman, at his best, is purely himself. His verse springs sheer from the spontaneous sources of his being. Hence its lovely, lovely form and rhythm: at the best. It is sheer, perfect, *human* spontaneity, spontaneous as a nightingale throbbing, but still controlled, the highest loveliness of human spontaneity, undecorated, unclothed. The whole being is there, sensually throbbing, spiritually quivering, mentally, ideally speaking. It is not, like Swinburne, an exaggeration of the one part of being. It is perfect and whole. The whole soul speaks at once, and is too pure for mechanical assistance of rhyme and measure. The perfect utterance of a concentrated, spontaneous soul. The unforgettable loveliness of Whitman's lines!

"Out of the cradle endlessly rocking."

Ave America!

Retort to Whitman • *D. H. Lawrence*

And whoever walks a mile full of false sympathy
walks to the funeral of the whole human race.

[Bouquets and Brickbats] *from* Introduction to 1921 Modern Library Edition of *Leaves of Grass*

IN CERTAIN PARTICULARS Walt Whitman's book, "Leaves of Grass,"
stands by itself and is the most peculiar and noteworthy monument amid
the work of American literature.

First, as to style. In a large and growing circle of readers and critics, it
is regarded as the most original book, the most decisively individual, the
most sublimely personal creation in American literary art.

Second, as to handling by critics and commentators. It is the most highly
praised and the most deeply damned book that ever came from an American
printing press as the work of an American writer; no other book can
compete with it in the number of bouquets handed it by distinguished
bystanders on one side of the street and in the number of hostile and nasty
brickbats flung by equally distinguished bystanders on the other side of the
street.

Third, as to personality. It is the most intensely personal book in American literature, living grandly to its promissory line, "who touches this
touches a man," spilling its multitude of confessions with the bravery of a
first-rate autobiography.

Fourth, as to scope of life work. It packs within its covers, does "Leaves
of Grass," the life and thought and feeling of one man; it was first published
when the author was 36 years of age and he actually never wrote another
book even though he lived to be 73 years of age; what he did all the rest
of his life after publishing the first edition of "Leaves of Grass," was to
rewrite and extend the first book.

Fifth, as to literary rank abroad. No other American poet, except Poe,
has the name, the persistent audiences across decades of time, and the
pervasive influence, credited to Walt Whitman as an American writer, an

53

American force in Europe, Asia, Africa, Australia, and the archipelagoes of the sea.

Sixth, as to influence in America. No other American book has so persistent a crowd of friends, advocates and sponsors as that which from decade to decade carries on the ballyhoo for "Leaves of Grass"; in Chicago, as an instance, Walt Whitman is the only dead or living American author whose memory is kept by an informal organization that memorializes its hero with an annual dinner.

Seventh, as to Americanism. "Leaves of Grass" is the most wildly keyed solemn oath that America means something and is going somewhere that has ever been written; it is America's most classic advertisement of itself as having purpose, destiny, banners and beacon-fires.

Therefore—because of the foregoing seven itemized points—and because there are further points into which the annals might be lengthened—and because still furthermore there are great and mystic points of contact that cannot be captured in itemized information—therefore "Leaves of Grass" is a book to be owned, kept, loaned, fought over, and read till it is dog-eared and dirty all over.

It was in 1855 that Whitman offered the American public its first chance at his poetry. Because no publisher of that day cared to undertake publication of the book, "Leaves of Grass," the poet was his own publisher. That is, he invited himself to take a header into literature, accepted the invitation, and went to the party unabashed, in his shirtsleeves and in a slouch hat.

There has been mention on occasion of American "shirtsleeve diplomacy." Whitman is the commanding instance in shirtsleeve literature. A second edition of "Leaves of Grass" came out in 1856. And the poet published as a frontispiece a picture of himself in shirtsleeves, knockabout clothes, the left hand in the pants pocket, the right hand on the hip akimbo, the hat tossed at a slant, and the head and general disposition of the cosmos indicating a statement and an inquiry, "Well, here we are; it looks good to us; and while it isn't important, how do you like us?"

On the cover of the book were the words gilded on a green background: "I greet you at the beginning of a great career—R. W. Emerson." The generally accredited foremost reputable figure of American letters and philosophy had written those words to Whitman the year before.

And in order to let everybody in and give free speech full play, there was printed as the last thing in the book, a criticism by a reviewer in the Boston *Intelligencer* of May 3, 1856, closing with this paragraph: "This book should find no place where humanity urges any claim to respect, and the author should be kicked from all decent society as below the level of the brute.

There is neither wit nor method in his disjointed babbling, and it seems to us he must be some escaped lunatic, raving in pitiable delirium."

That was a beginning. It isn't over yet. The controversy yet rises and subsides.

The best loved figure in American literature—by those who loved him—he is counted also the most heartily damned figure—by those who damned him.

The most highly praised and the most roundly excoriated book America has produced—that is Walt Whitman's "Leaves of Grass."

"He is the poet who brought the slop-pail into the parlor," wrote one critic. "He is one of the sublime figures of all human annals, one to be set for companionship with Confucius, Socrates, and the teachers of high and sacred living," wrote another critic.

"The man was mad, mad beyond the cavil of a doubt," wrote Max Nordau. Another European critic, Gabriel Sarrazin, wrote: "He is the apostle of the idea that man is an indivisible fragment of the universal Divinity."

Walt Whitman is the only established epic poet of America. He is the single American figure that both American and European artists and critics most often put in a class or throw into a category with Shakespeare, Dante, Homer. He is the one American writer that Emerson, Burroughs, John Muir, Edward Carpenter, and similar observers enter in their lists as having a size in history and an importance of utterance that places him with Socrates, Confucius, Lao Tse, and the silver-grey men of the half-worlds who left the Bhagavad Gita and writings known most often as sacred.

In stature, pride, stride, and scope of personality, he is a challenger. He warns us to come with good teeth if we are to join in his menu—to bring along our rough weather clothes. He is likely any time to tip us out of the boat to see whether we swim or sink. And there are blanks to be filled in among his writings where he seems to have whispered, "I am going away now and I leave you alone to work it out for yourself—you came alone and you will have to go away alone."

Walt Whitman wrote his vital passages at the height of America's most stormily human period of history. "We live in the midst of alarms; anxiety beclouds the future; we expect some new disaster with each newspaper we read," said Abraham Lincoln in the famous "Lost Speech" delivered the same year Walt Whitman's "Leaves of Grass" was first published.

"Blood will flow . . . and brother's hand will be raised against brother!" was the passionate outcry of that same speech, which because of its tenor of violence was withheld from publication and distribution by its orator.

In the same decade, Charles A. Dana, managing editor of the *New York*

Tribune, was writing: "It may be that the day of revolutions is past, but, if so, why are they there in such abundance? ... Let others give aid and comfort to despots. Be it ours to stand for Liberty and Justice, nor fear to lock arms with those who are called hotheads and demagogues." The luminous fringes of romance attaching to those abstractions, "Liberty and Justice," as a result of the American and French revolutions, were still in the air. Dana wrote friendly explanations of just what the Frenchman, Proudhon, meant by his thesis, "Property is Robbery." Thoreau was writing an essay, "On the Duty of Civil Disobedience." John Brown was stealing horses, running slaves by the underground railroad from slave to free soil, stocking arsenals, praying over strange, new projects. These all have their significance in showing the tint of the time spirit. Brook Farm, and its Utopian socialist outlooks, Fourier and his phalanxes of workmen, the 1848 revolutions, these were hot topics of the time. The far-reaching tides and backwashes of thought and emotion resulting from the French and American revolutions, and all that weave of circumstance touching the secession rights of states of the Union with its ramifications into chattel slavery, besides the swirl of events riding into that epic upheaval, the sectional war—these things, tangibles and intangibles, were in the air and the breath of men in the years when Walt Whitman was bringing his book to focus, getting ready to launch "Leaves of Grass."

The poem of Whitman's most often published in public school readers is "Captain, My Captain." His best single characteristic and authentic poem is "The Song of the Open Road," earlier published under the title, "The Public Road," and still earlier as the "Poem of the Road."

Probably the most majestic threnody to death in the English language is the long piece, written just after the assassination of President Lincoln, entitled, "When Lilacs Last in the Dooryard Bloom'd." Some readers consider "Passage to India" the poem of profoundest meanings and vision.

Among lovers of Whitman the one line that probably haunts most often is "Out of the Cradle Endlessly Rocking." The epithet most frequently quoted in political controversy is "the never-ending audacity of elected persons." Of hostile criticism the most vivid line is, "He brought the slop-pail into the parlor," a commentary antedating modern plumbing. The most poignantly human note struck in any one line is that in the poem "To a Common Prostitute," where he declares, "Not till the sun excludes you do I exclude you." As "intriguing" as any title is "A Woman Waits for Me."

. . . . .

"Song of Myself," which in the earliest editions was titled, "Poem of Walt Whitman, An American," is a specimen of the massive masterpiece. "I do not ask who you are, that is not important to me," he declares in one line, and, "I wear my hat as I please indoors and out," in another line. Such lines are easily understood even by those who question whether it should classify as poetry. "What is a man anyhow? What am I? What are you?" or "I do not call one greater and one smaller," or "These are really the thoughts of all men in all ages, they are not original with me," or "I launch all men and women forward with me into the Unknown," these are further instances of the understandable.

It is among the inarticulates of the primitive, the abysmal, on the borders where time, mystic dimensions, and the sphinxes of Nowhere ask their riddles, it is in this territory that Walt Whitman gives some people a grand everlasting thrill, while still other people get only a headache and a revulsion. "Rise after rise bow the phantoms behind me, Afar down I see the huge first Nothing, I know I was even there," he murmurs in "Song of Myself," "Long I was hugg'd close—long and long."

. . . . .

Throughout "Leaves of Grass" there recurs often a wild soft laughter carrying the hint that it is impossible for a poet to tell you anything worth knowing unless you already know it and no song can be sung to you that will seem a song deeply worth hearing unless you have already in some strange, far-off fashion heard that song. An instance of this wild soft laughter is in the closing lines of "Song of Myself," where it is written:

> The spotted hawk swoops by and accuses me, he complains
> of my gab and my loitering.
>
> I too am not a bit tamed, I too am untranslatable.
> I sound my barbaric yawp over the roofs of the world.
>
> The last scud of day holds back for me,
> It flings my likeness after the rest and true as any on
> the shadow'd wilds,
> It coaxes me to the vapor and the dusk.
>
> I depart as air, I shake my white locks at the runaway
> sun,
> I effuse my flesh in eddies, and drift it in lacy jags.

I bequeath myself to the dirt to grow from the grass
I love,
If you want me again look for me under your boot-
soles.

You will hardly know who I am or what I mean.
But I shall be good health to you nevertheless,
And filter and fibre your blood.

Failing to fetch me at first keep encouraged,
Missing me one place search another,
I stop somewhere waiting for you.

What he is trying to sing is a theme fluid, flowing, elusive, and so he goes out of his way to flip in the face those who are too sure they are flying the same wild sea-winds with him. "Even while you should think you had unquestionably caught me, already, behold! you see I have escaped you," he writes.

He is at a funeral looking into a coffin. A girl stands on her toes and joins him looking in on the white face in the black box. "You don't understand this, do you, my child?" he asks. "No," she answers. "Neither do I," is his muttered and kindly rejoinder.

The anecdote fits Whitman as feathers a duck. From such a poet might be expected the line, "I charge you forever reject those who would expound me."

Cape Hatteras • *Hart Crane*

> The seas all crossed,
> weathered the capes, the voyage done . . .—Walt Whitman

Imponderable the dinosaur
          sinks slow,
                  the mammoth saurian
                        ghoul, the eastern
                              Cape. . .
While rises in the west the coastwise range,
    slowly the hushed land—
Combustion at the astral core—the dorsal change
Of energy—convulsive shift of sand. . .
But we, who round the capes, the promontories
Where strange tongues vary messages of surf
Below grey citadels, repeating to the stars
The ancient names—return home to our own
Hearths, there to eat an apple and recall
The songs that gypsies dealt us at Marseille
Or how the priests walked—slowly through Bombay—
Or to read you, Walt,—knowing us in thrall

To that deep wonderment, our native clay
Whose depth of red, eternal flesh of Pocahontus—
Those continental folded aeons, surcharged
With sweetness below derricks, chimneys, tunnels—
Is veined by all that time has really pledged us. . .
And from above, thin squeaks of radio static,
The captured fume of space foams in our ears—
What whisperings of far watches on the main
Relapsing into silence, while time clears
Our lenses, lifts a focus, resurrects
A periscope to glimpse what joys or pain
Our eyes can share or answer—then deflects
Us, shunting to a labyrinth submersed
Where each sees only his dim past reversed. . .

59

But that star-glistered salver of infinity,
The circle, blind crucible of endless space,
Is sluiced by motion,—subjugated never.
Adam and Adam's answer in the forest
Left Hesperus mirrored in the lucid pool.
Now the eagle dominates our days, is jurist
Of the ambiguous cloud. We know the strident rule
Of wings imperious... Space, instantaneous,
Flickers a moment, consumes us in its smile:
A flash over the horizon—shifting gears—
And we have laughter, or more sudden tears.
Dream cancels dream in this new realm of fact
From which we wake into the dream of act;
Seeing himself an atom in a shroud—
Man hears himself an engine in a cloud!

"—Recorders ages hence"—ah, syllables of faith!
Walt, tell me, Walt Whitman, if infinity
Be still the same as when you walked the beach
Near Paumanok—your lone patrol—and heard the wraith
Through surf, its bird note there a long time falling...
For you, the panoramas and this breed of towers,
Of you—the theme that's statured in the cliff.
O Saunterer on free ways still ahead!
Not this our empire yet, but labyrinth
Wherein your eyes, like the Great Navigator's without ship,
Gleam from the great stones of each prison crypt
Of canyoned traffic ... Confronting the Exchange,
Surviving in a world of stocks,—they also range
Across the hills where second timber strays
Back over Connecticut farms, abandoned pastures,—
Sea eyes and tidal, undenying, bright with myth!

The nasal whine of power whips a new universe...
Where spouting pillars spoor the evening sky,
Under the looming stacks of the gigantic power house
Stars prick the eyes with sharp ammoniac proverbs,
New verities, new inklings in the velvet hummed
Of dynamos, where hearing's leash is strummed...
Power's script,—wound, bobbin-bound, refined—

Is stropped to the slap of belts on booming spools, spurred
Into the bulging bouillon, harnessed jelly of the stars.
Towards what? The forked crash of split thunder parts
Our hearing momentwise; but fast in whirling armatures,
As bright as frogs' eyes, giggling in the girth
Of steely gizzards—axle-bound, confined
In coiled precision, bunched in mutual glee
The bearings glint,—O murmurless and shined
In oilrinsed circles of blind ecstasy!

Stars scribble on our eyes the frosty sagas,
The gleaming cantos of unvanquished space. . .
O sinewy silver biplane, nudging the wind's withers!
There, from Kill Devils Hill at Kitty Hawk
Two brothers in their twinship left the dune;
Warping the gale, the Wright windwrestlers veered
Capeward, then blading the wind's flank, banked and spun
What ciphers risen from prophetic script,
What marathons new-set between the stars!
The soul, by naphtha fledged into new reaches
Already knows the closer clasp of Mars,—
New latitudes, unknotting, soon give place
To what fierce schedules, rife of doom apace!

Behold the dragon's covey—amphibian, ubiquitous
To hedge the seaboard, wrap the headland, ride
The blue's cloud-templed districts unto ether. . .
While Iliads glimmer through eyes raised in pride
Hell's belt springs wider into heaven's plumed side.
O bright circumferences, heights employed to fly
War's fiery kennel masked in downy offings,—
This tournament of space, the threshed and chiselled height,
Is baited by marauding circles, bludgeon flail
Of rancorous grenades whose screaming petals carve us
Wounds that we wrap with theorems sharp as hail!

Wheeled swiftly, wings emerge from larval-silver hangars.
Taut motors surge, space-gnawing, into flight;
Through sparkling visibility, outspread, unsleeping,
Wings clip the last peripheries of light. . .
Tellurian wind-sleuths on dawn patrol,
Each plane a hurtling javelin of winged ordnance,
Bristle the heights above a screeching gale to hover;
Surely no eye that Sunward Escadrille can cover!
There, meaningful, fledged as the Pleiades
With razor sheen they zoom each rapid helix!
Up-chartered choristers of their own speeding
They, cavalcade on escapade, shear Cumulus—
Lay siege and hurdle Cirrus down the skies!
While Cetus-like, O thou Dirigible, enormous Lounger
Of pendulous auroral beaches,—satellited wide
By convoy planes, moonferrets that rejoin thee
On fleeing balconies as thou dost glide,
—Hast splintered space!

           Low, shadowed of the Cape,
Regard the moving turrets! From grey decks
See scouting griffons rise through gaseous crepe
Hung low ... until a conch of thunder answers
Cloud-belfries, banging, while searchlights, like fencers,
Slit the sky's pancreas of foaming anthracite
Toward thee, O Corsair of the typhoon,—pilot, hear!
Thine eyes bicarbonated white by speed, O Skygak, see
How from thy path above the levin's lance
Thou sowest doom thou hast nor time nor chance
To reckon—as thy stilly eyes partake
What alcohol of space .. ! Remember, Falcon-Ace,
Thou hast there in thy wrist a Sanskrit charge
To conjugate infinity's dim marge—
Anew .. !

           But first, here at this height receive
The benediction of the shell's deep, sure reprieve!
Lead-perforated fuselage, escutcheoned wings
Lift agonized quittance, tilting from the invisible brink

Now eagle-bright, now
                    quarry-hid, twist-
                                        -ing, sink with
Enormous repercussive list-
                        -ings down
Giddily spiralled
                    gauntlets, upturned, unlooping
In guerrilla sleights, trapped in combustion gyr-
Ing, dance the curdled depth
                        down whizzing
Zodiacs, dashed
                (now nearing fast the Cape!)
                        down gravitation's
                            vortex into crashed
. . . . dispersion . . . into mashed and shapeless debris. . . .
By Hatteras bunched the beached heap of high bravery!

                .   .   .   .   .   .

The stars have grooved our eyes with old persuasions
Of love and hatred, birth,—surcease of nations. . .
But who has held the heights more sure than thou,
O Walt!—Ascensions of thee hover in me now
As thou at junctions elegiac, there, of speed
With vast eternity, dost wield the rebound seed!
The competent loam, the probable grass,—travail
Of tides awash the pedestal of Everest, fail
Not less than thou in pure impulse inbred
To answer deepest soundings! O, upward from the dead
Thou bringest tally, and a pact, new bound
Of living brotherhood!

            Thou, there beyond—
Glacial sierras and the flight of ravens,
Hermetically past condor zones, through zenith havens
Past where the albatross has offered up
His last wing-pulse, and downcast as a cup
That's drained, is shivered back to earth—thy wand
Has beat a song, O Walt,—there and beyond!

And this, thine other hand, upon my heart
Is plummet ushered of those tears that start
What memories of vigils, bloody, by that Cape,—
Ghoul-mound of man's perversity at balk
And fraternal massacre! Thou, pallid there as chalk
Hast kept of wounds, O Mourner, all that sum
That then from Appomattox stretched to Somme!

Cowslip and shad-blow, flaked like tethered foam
Around bared teeth of stallions, bloomed that spring
When first I read thy lines, rife as the loam
Of prairies, yet like breakers cliffward leaping!
O, early following thee, I searched the hill
Blue-writ and odor-firm with violets, 'til
With June the mountain laurel broke through green
And filled the forest with what clustrous sheen!
Potomac lilies,—then the Pontiac rose,
And Klondike edelweiss of occult snows!
White banks of moonlight came descending valleys—
How speechful on oak-vizored palisades,
As vibrantly I following down Sequoia alleys
Heard thunder's eloquence through green arcades
Set trumpets breathing in each clump and grass tuft—'til
Gold autumn, captured, crowned the trembling hill!

Panis Angelicus! Eyes tranquil with the blaze
Of love's own diametric gaze, of love's amaze!
Not greatest, thou,—not first, nor last,—but near
And onward yielding past my utmost year.
Familiar, thou, as mendicants in public places;
Evasive—too—as dayspring's spreading arc to trace is:—
Our Meistersinger, thou set breath in steel;
And it was thou who on the boldest heel
Stood up and flung the span on even wing
Of that great Bridge, our Myth, whereof I sing!

Years of the Modern! Propulsions toward what capes?
But thou, *Panis Angelicus,* hast thou not seen
And passed that Barrier that none escapes—
But knows it leastwise as death-strife?—O, something green,
Beyond all sesames of science was thy choice
Wherewith to bind us throbbing with one voice,
New integers of Roman, Viking, Celt—
Thou, Vedic Caesar, to the greensward knelt!

And now, as launched in abysmal cupolas of space,
Toward endless terminals, Easters of speeding light—
Vast engines outward veering with seraphic grace
On clarion cylinders pass out of sight
To course that span of consciousness thou'st named
The Open Road—thy vision is reclaimed!
What heritage thou'st signalled to our hands!

And see! the rainbow's arch—how shimmeringly stands
Above the Cape's ghoul-mound, O joyous seer!
Recorders ages hence, yes, they shall hear
In their own veins uncancelled thy sure tread
And read thee by the aureole 'round thy head
Of pasture-shine, *Panis Angelicus!*

                              yes, Walt,
Afoot again, and onward without halt,—
Not soon, nor suddenly,—no, never to let go
     My hand
               in yours,
                    Walt Whitman—
                         so—

from "Whitman and Tennyson"

T. S. ELIOT

... THE TIME, OF COURSE, is the epoch of American history known to readers of "Martin Chuzzlewit." To most Europeans, I imagine, this is a time which hardly exists; its difference, that is, from the Colonial Period (which we may say ended in 1829 with the defeat of Adams by Jackson) on the one hand, and the Age of Jazz on the other. But with relation to Whitman, it must be recognized that his was a time with a character of its own, and one in which it was possible to hold certain notions, and many illusions, which are now untenable. Now Whitman was ... a "man with a message," even if that message was sometimes badly mutilated in transmission; he was interested in what he had to say; he did not think of himself primarily as the inventor of a new technique of versification. His "message" must be reckoned with, and it is a very different message from that of Mr. Carl Sandburg.

The world of the American voyage in "Martin Chuzzlewit" is the same. Dickens knew best what it looked like, but Whitman knew what it felt like. There is another interesting parallel: "Leaves of Grass" appeared in 1856, "Les Fleurs du mal" in 1857: could any age have produced more heterogeneous leaves and flowers? The contrasts should be noted. But perhaps more important than these contrasts is the similarity of Whitman to another master, one whose greatness he always recognized and whose eminence he always acknowledged generously—to Tennyson. Between the ideas of the two men, or, rather, between the relations of the ideas of each to his place and time, between the ways in which each held his ideas, there is a fundamental resemblance. Both were born laureates. Whitman, of course, fought hard against corruption, against Press servility, against slavery, against alcohol (and I dare say Tennyson would have done so under the same conditions); but essentially he was satisfied—too satisfied—with things as they are.

His labourers and pioneers (at that date all Anglo-Saxon, or at least North European, labourers and pioneers) are the counterpart to Tennyson's great broad-shouldered Englishman at whom Arnold pokes fun; Whitman's horror at the monarchical tyranny of Europe is the counterpart to Tennyson's comment on the revolutions of French politics, no "graver than a schoolboy's barring out." Baudelaire, on the other hand, was a disagreeable person who was rarely satisfied with anything: *je m'ennuie en France*, he wrote, *ou tout le monde ressemble à Voltaire*.

I do not mean to suggest that all discontent is divine, or that all self-righteousness is loathesome. On the contrary, both Tennyson and Whitman made satisfaction almost magnificent. It is not the best aspect of their verse; if neither of them had more, neither of them would be still a great poet. But Whitman succeeds in making America as it was, just as Tennyson made England as it was, into something grand and significant. You cannot quite say that either was deceived, and you cannot at all say that either was insincere, or the victim of popular cant. They had the faculty—Whitman perhaps more prodigiously than Tennyson—of transmuting the real into an ideal. Whitman had the ordinary desires of the flesh; for him there was no chasm between the real and the ideal, such as opened before the horrified eyes of Baudelaire. But this, and the "frankness" about sex for which he is either extolled or mildly reproved, did not spring from any particular honesty or clearness of vision: it sprang from what may be called either "idealization" or a faculty for make-believe, according as we are disposed. There is, fundamentally, no difference between the Whitman frankness and the Tennyson delicacy, except in its relation to public opinion of the time. And Tennyson liked monarchs, and Whitman liked presidents. Both were conservative, rather than reactionary or revolutionary; that is to say, they believed explicitly in progress, and believed implicitly that progress consists in things remaining much as they are.

If this were all there is to Whitman, it would still be a great deal; he would remain a great representative of America, but emphatically of an America which no longer exists. It is not the America of Mr. Scott Fitzgerald, or Mr. Dos Passos, or Mr. Hemingway—to name some of the more interesting of contemporary American writers. If I may draw still one more comparison, it is with Hugo. Beneath all the declamations there is another tone, and behind all the illusions there is another vision. When Whitman speaks of the lilacs or of the mocking-bird, his theories and beliefs drop away like a needless pretext.

Walt Whitman

SHERWOOD ANDERSON

> Come close to me warm little thing. It is night—
> I am cold. When I was a boy in my village here in the
> West, I always knew all the old men. How sweet
> they were—quite Biblical too—makers of harness and
> wagons and plows—soldiers and sailors and pioneers.
> We got Walt and Abraham out of that lot.
>
> *(Mid-American Chants)*

WHITMAN IS IN THE BONES of America as Ralph Waldo Emerson is in the American mentality, but what is wanted and needed here now is a return to the bones and blood of life—to Whitman. We Americans need again to have and to be conscious of land hunger, river hunger, sea and sky hunger. For one, two or three generations now the drift of our young American men and women has been away from the land and toward the towns. Industrialism must go on and the machine must be made subservient to man, but there must be also a rebirth of feeling for the fact of America. Now we work too much with our heads. When I was myself a young man and had got into the advertising business, as a writer of advertisements, I had an experience more common to young Americans than is generally believed. I kept getting into a blue funk. It seemed to me that I couldn't go on, day after day, using words to praise and sell someone's soap, toothpaste, or what-not. Other men about me were in the same case. We were often desperate. Why, as to that, we were making money enough, doing very well. We were in the current of our times, swimming with the current. We continually turned to Emerson and he bucked us up. How many days of stupid advertising writing have I myself got through on the strength of Emerson's "Self Reliance." Alas...!

This self reliance, where is it, where does it take us?

68

There is something beyond this success we Americans have been so intent upon. Where is it? What is it?

It is in the land, waving cornfields of Illinois, Kentucky, Tennessee and Virginia hills, piny woods of Georgia, hot red lands of Georgia, Alabama, Mississippi, gigantic flow of the Mississippi River, forests that surround Wisconsin lakes, deserts, skies, men plowing. . . .

Push hard against horse-collars, broad-breasted horses. . . .

There are men of the farms going into the towns and belly-aching. "There is no money in farming any more," they say. Well, what of it? What has money being in a thing or not being in it got to do with anything?

Don't laugh. This isn't sentimentality. It's a matter of getting back national health. Once, I swear, we had men here. . . . Walt Whitman, lone Abe Lincoln, John Brown, others I could name, men with a sense of soil in them, men with guts, patience, stand-up men, men not intent upon success. If I, an American man, cannot learn to love one strip of countryside, turn of a flowing river, white farm house on a slope in an apple orchard, if I cannot love some one spot . . . (if I am a strong man perhaps a dozen such spots) how can I love America . . . ?

. . . or a woman or a brother man?

Whitman is the singer of the strong lustful ones of the men who could love a woman or a field or the sky above prairies, forest or seas. He walked far and wide, bare-throated, brown-armed, and singing . . . not up in the mind only but with his whole body. He was thought too crude, too lustful. They turned away from him. As a boy and young man I myself went into respectable middle-class homes and found there volumes of Whitman's "Leaves of Grass" with the so-called ugly lustful passages cut out with scissors.

How shameful! How can there be real delicacy without strength? I proclaim Whitman the most delicate and tender of all American singers. . . . Read again "When Lilacs Last in the Dooryard Bloomed." . . . "Out of the Cradle Endlessly Rocking." Read the rocking long and short American verses. Who was it who said only the negroes had brought real song into America? Hail, all hail, negro workmen, river hands, plantation hands, makers of songs, but hail also, always Whitman, white American, lustful one. . . .

Singer of the great land, the broad land . . . singer of growing cities, horses plowing, men sowing seed, soft waves breaking on sea shores, forest singer, town and dusty country road singer.

The great sweet land that Walt Whitman sang so lustily is still here. People now forget what America is . . . why forget how huge, varied, strong and flowing it is? We gather too much and stay too long in holes in cities. We forget land-love, river and sky-love. To these we must return before we begin again to get brother to brother love of which Whitman sang and dreamed.

Whitman is in the bones and blood of America. He is the real American singer. What is wanted among us now is a return to Whitman, to his songs, his dreams, his consciousness of the possibilities of the land that was his land and is our land.

Walt Whitman • *Ezequiel Martínez Estrada*

Wandering among abstruse and upper circles,
or else, simply alive and paradoxical
(all wisdom or all contradiction)
you pass, although you have returned to the "eternal uses
of the earth," this time even more categorical,
as in Barbarossa's final incarnation.

I will follow your trail with the zeal of the hound,
among the rhythmic stars or the earth-molded human,
wherever you are now repeating, Walt Whitman,
the autochthonous canticles of your iron land.

Whether you are in the banner of the stars and stripes,
or at the iron gate where the serfs are rebelling,
or at the post that watches upstanding in defiance,
or at the nuptial exchange which the morning revives,
or with the sailors' crew taking arms and uprising,
or in the trampling of bisons crossing the darkness,
or in the endless void where silence and death reign,
receive this salutation cast to the wind and the sky
with the certain impression of embracing you briefly
and the agonizing fear of losing you again.

(translated by Didier Tisdel Jaén)

Ode to Walt Whitman • *Federico García Lorca*

Along the East River and the Bronx,
the young men were singing showing their waists,
with the wheel, the oil, the leather and the hammer.
Ninety thousand miners were taking silver out of the rocks
and the boys were drawing ladders and perspectives.

But nobody was sleeping,
nobody wanted to be the river,
nobody loved the large leaves,
nobody loved the blue tongue of the beach.

Along the East River and Queensborough
the young men were fighting with industry,
and the jews were selling to the faun of the river
the rose of the circumcision
and the sky emptied over the bridges and the roofs
herds of bison pushed by the wind.

But nobody was stopping,
nobody wanted to be a cloud,
nobody was seeking the ferns
or the yellow wheel of the drum

When the moon comes out
the pulleys will turn to disturb the sky;
a border of needles will enclose the memory
and the coffins will carry off those who do not work.

New York of mud,
New York of wire and death.
What angel do you carry hidden in your cheek?
What perfect voice will speak the truths of the wheat?
Who will speak the terrible dream of the stained anemones?

Not a single moment, old beautiful Walt Whitman,
have I stopped seeing your beard full of butterflies,
or your shoulders of corduroy wasted by the moon,

or your muscles of a virginal Apollo,
or your voice like a column of ash;
old man beautiful as the cloud
who cried like a bird
with his sex pierced by a needle,
enemy of the satyr,
enemy of the vine
and lover of bodies under the heavy cloth.
Not a single moment, virile beauty
who on mountains of carbon, advertisements and railroads,
dreamed of being a river and sleeping as a river
with that comrade who would put in your breast
a small pain of an unknowing leopard.

Not a single moment, Adam of blood, male,
lone man in the sea, old beautiful Walt Whitman,
for on the rooftops,
clustered in the bars,
leaving in bunches from the sewers
trembling between the legs of the chauffeurs
or turning around on platforms of wormwood,
the perverts, Walt Whitman, dreamed of you.

Also that! As well! And they fling themselves
upon your luminous and chaste beard,
blonds from the north, blacks from the sand,
crowds of shouts and gestures,
like cats and like serpents,
the perverts, Walt Whitman, the perverts
turbid with tears, flesh for the whiplash,
boot or bite of the animal trainers.

Also that! As well! Stained fingers
point to the bank of your dream
when the friend eats your apple
with a light taste of gasoline
and the sun sings through the navels
of the young men who play beneath the bridges.

But you were not seeking scratched eyes,
or the dark bog where they submerge the boys,
or the frozen saliva,
or the curves wounded like a toad's belly
that the perverts carry in cars and on terraces
while the moon lashes them on the corners of terror.

You were seeking a nude who might be like a river,
bull and dream that might unite the wheel and the seaweed,
father of your agony, camelia of your death,
who would cry in the flames of your hidden equator.

For it is just that man not seek his pleasure
in the jungle of blood of the following morning.
The sky has beaches for the evasion of life
and there are bodies that should not be repeated at dawn.

Agony, agony, dream, ferment and dream.
This is the world, friend, agony, agony.
The dead decompose beneath the clock of the cities,
the war passes crying with a million gray rats,
the rich give to their mistresses
small lighted dying ones,
and life is not noble, or good, or sacred.

Man can, if he wants, conduct his desire
through the coral vein or celestial nude.
Tomorrow the loves will be rocks and Time
a breeze that comes sleeping through the branches.

Therefore I do not raise my voice, old Walt Whitman,
against the boy who writes
the name of a girl on his pillow,
nor against the youth who dresses as a bride
in the darkness of the closet,
nor against the lonely men of the casinos
who drink with nausea the water of prostitution,
nor against the men with the green gaze
who love men and burn their lips in silence.

But I do raise my voice against you, perverts of the cities,
of swelling flesh and filthy thought,
mothers of mud, harpies, sleepless enemies
of the Love that distributes wreaths of joy.

Against you always, who give to the young men
drops of filthy death with bitter venom.
Against you always,
Faeries of North America,
Pájaros of Havana,
Jotos of Mexico,
Sarasas of Cadiz,
Apios of Seville,
Cancos of Madrid,
Floras of Alicante,
Adelaidas of Portugal.

Perverts everywhere, assassins of doves!
Slaves of the woman, bitches of their boudoirs,
open in the plazas with fan fever
or ambushed in motionless landscapes of hemlock.

May there be no district! Death
flows from your eyes
and groups gray flowers on the bank of the mud.
May there be no district! Watch out!
That the confused, the pure,
the classic, the distinguished, the entreating ones
may shut the doors of the bacchanal.

And you, handsome Walt Whitman, sleep on the rivers of
    the Hudson
with your beard towards the pole and your hands open.
Soft clay or snow, your tongue is calling
comrades to watch your disembodied gazelle.
Sleep, nothing remains.

A dance of walls shakes the meadows
and America is flooded in machines and sobs.
I want the strong air of the deepest night
to take away flowers and letters from the arch where you
      sleep
and a black child to announce to the whites of the gold
the coming of the reign of the wheat.

  (*translated by Betty Jean Craige*)

Walt Whitman • *Edwin Markham*

I

O shaggy god of the ground, barbaric Pan!
I mix some discords in the chant, and yet
I mix triumphant praises in it, too.

You laud "the average man," and yet his feet
Are mired in clay, his soul beholds no star,
Hears only a far faint music from the skies.
You dare announce your optimistic news
That good is good and evil is also good.
Yet, Whitman, there is something wild in the world:
Even Christ found here no place to lay his head.

In woman, too, you miss the morning star:
You sing the brood-mare woman, not the one
Who leads us onward, upward to the skies,
The woman of old romance, the woman of song,
The woman that sings into the poet's dream.

You shout the Ego also: this draws down
Toward dust and ashes: never the upward look
Which sees afar the pure Ideal gleam.
You find all equal: no one is above:
You leave bewildered souls no place to kneel,
Leave them no Altar where their eyes may turn
To Something higher than themselves—perhaps
To Someone veiled in the Wonder above Time.

"Cast out humility!" you cry: "cast out
Obedience, reverence, adoration, awe."
Yet only when the Ideal gleams on high
Can we behold our imperfections, rise
And struggle on to nobler heights ahead.

Whitman, there is no battle in your song;
Yet true life is a battle and a march,
And in this we are kindred to the gods.

O thunder-throat, you search the world; and yet
You bring no answer to our mortal cry
To know the meaning of the Mystery,
The meaning of the riddle of the world.
Where is your peak, your all-commanding peak?
Dante stood on a height even when in Hell;
But you, O comrade, have no lighted cliff
From which you look on life and see it whole.

II

Yet after all discountings, mighty bard,
There is a lordly credit to your name.
You have broken chains, have given gifts of joy,
Have drawn our eyes from things polite and pale—
Things measured, labeled, run into a mold.

  Sometimes we hear in your chant
The belch of chaos, the babble of Caliban;
And then sometimes we hear sweet homely sounds,
The lowing of cows, the bustle of heading wheat.
Your conjuring touch has opened our eyes to see
A strange, sweet gladness in all common things.
All scenes, all sounds, all fragrances of earth
Are hailed as with the glad, free cry of youth:
They seem blown down from Eden's far-off fields:
They seem strange things we never knew before.

Two lyrics, torn from Sorrow, lift our hearts—
Your song of the mock-bird wild with widowed grief,
Your song of love in tears; and that other song,
Your chant in lilac-time, when Lincoln lay
Resting at last in the tender arms of death.

And you have left great words to cheer our hearts—
Democracy and the dear comrade-love.
Joy also is your word: it warms the world.
We feel the joy in your triumphant faith
That life outsoars the darkness of the grave,
That the dead are never captives of the tomb,
But are the pilgrims of Eternity.
Your voice cries clear above the world's dark doubt:
'If death ends all, then alarum, for we are betrayed!'

Now in this hour, this high remembering hour,
I see the eternal Lord of Song bend down
With fragrant, fadeless laurels for your brow,
Lay them with reverence on your honored head,
And leave you in your immortality.

Ode to Walt Whitman • *Stephen Vincent Benét*

(May 31, 1819—March 26, 1892)

Now comes Fourth Month and the early buds on the trees.
By the roads of Long Island, the forsythia has flowered,
In the North, the cold will be breaking; even in Maine
The cold will be breaking soon; the young, bull-voiced
    freshets
Roar from green mountains, gorging the chilly brooks
With the brown, trout-feeding waters, the unlocked springs;
Now Mississippi stretches with the Spring rains. . . .

It is forty years and more,
The time of the ripeness and withering of a man,
Since you lay in the house in Camden and heard, at last,
The great, slow footstep, splashing the Third Month snow
In the little, commonplace street
—Town snow, already trampled and growing old,
Soot-flecked and dingy, patterned with passing feet,
The bullet-pocks of rain, the strong urine of horses,
The slashing, bright steel runners of small boys' sleds
Hitching on behind the fast cutters.
They dragged their sleds to the tops of the hills and yelled
The Indian yell of all boyhood, for pure joy
Of the cold and the last gold light and the swift rush down
Belly-flopping into darkness, into bedtime.
You saw them come home, late, hungry and burning-cheeked,
The boys and girls, the strong children,
Dusty with snow, their mittens wet with the silver drops of
    thawed snow.

All winter long, you had heard their sharp footsteps passing,
The skating crunch of their runners,
An old man, tied to a house, after many years,
An old man with his rivery, clean white hair,
His bright eyes, his majestic poverty,
His fresh pink skin like the first strawberry-bloom,

80

His innocent, large, easy old man's clothes
—Brown splotches on the hands of clean old men
At County Farms or sitting on warm park-benches
Like patient flies, talking of their good sons,
"Yes, my son's good to me"—
An old man, poor, without sons, waiting achingly
For spring to warm his lameness,
For spring to flourish,
And yet, when the eyes glowed, neither old nor tied.

All winter long there had been footsteps passing,
Steps of postmen and neighbors, quick steps of friends,
All winter long you had waited that great, snow-treading
    step,
The enemy, the vast comrade,
The step behind, in the wards, when the low lamp flickered
And the sick boy gasped for breath,
*"Lean on me! Lean upon my shoulder! By God, you shall
    not die!"*
The step ahead, on the long, wave-thundering beaches of
    Paumanok,
Invisible, printless, weighty,
The shape half-seen through the wet, sweet sea-fog of youth,
Night's angel and the dark Sea's,
The grand, remorseless treader,
Magnificent Death.

"Let me taste all, my flesh and my fat are sweet,
My body hardy as lilac, the strong flower.
I have tasted the calamus; I can taste the nightbane."

Always the water about you since you were born,
The endless lapping of water, the strong motion,
The gulls by the ferries knew you, and the wild sea-birds,
The sandpiper, printing the beach with delicate prints.
At last, old, wheeled to the wharf, you still watched the
    water,
The tanned boys, flat-bodied, diving, the passage of ships,
The proud port, distant, the people, the work of harbors. . . .

"I have picked out a bit of hill with a southern exposure.
I like to be near the trees. I like to be near
The water-sound of the trees."

Now, all was the same in the cluttered, three-windowed
    room,
Low-ceiled, getting the sun like a schooner's cabin,
The crowding photos hiding the ugly wall-paper.
The floor-litter, the strong chair, timbered like a ship,
The hairy black-and-silver of the old wolfskin;
In the back-yard, neither lilac nor pear yet bloomed
But the branch of the lilac swelling with first sap;
And there, in the house, the figures, the nurse, the woman,
The passing doctor, the friends, the little clan,
The disciple with the notebook who's always there.

All these and the pain and the water-bed to ease you
And you said it rustled of oceans and were glad
And the pain shut and relaxed and shut once more.

"Old body, counsellor, why do you thus torment me?
Have we not been friends from our youth?"

But now it came,
Slow, perceived by no others,
The splashing step through the grey, soft, Saturday rain,
Inexorable footstep of the huge friend.
"Are you there at last, fine enemy?
Ah, haste, friend, hasten, come closer!
Breathe upon me with your grave, your releasing lips!
I have heard and spoken; watched the bodies of boys
Flash in the copper sun and dive to green waters,
Seen the fine ships and the strong matrons and the tall
    axemen,
The young girls, free, athletic; the drunkard, retching
In his poor dream; the thief taken by officers;
The President, calm, grave, advising the nation;
The infant, with milk-wet lips in his bee-like slumber.
They are mine; all, all are mine; must I leave them, truly?

I have cherished them in my veins like milk and fruit.
I have warmed them at my bare breast like the eggs of
    pigeons.
The great plains of the buffalo are mine, the towns, the hills,
    the ship-bearing waters.
These States are my wandering sons.
I had them in my youth; I cannot desert them.
The green leaf of America is printed on my heart forever."

Now it entered the house, it marched upon the stair.
By the bedside the faces dimmed, the huge shoulder blotting
    them,
—It is so they die on the plains, the great, old buffalo,
The herd-leaders, the beasts with the kingly eyes,
Innocent, curly-browed,
They sink to the earth like mountains, hairy and silent,
And their tongues are cut by the hunter.
        Oh, singing tongue!
Great tongue of bronze and salt and the free grasses,
Tongue of America, speaking for the first time,
Must the hunter have you at last?

Now, face to face, you saw him
And lifted the right arm once, as a pilot lifts it,
Signalling with the bell,
In the passage at night, on the river known yet unknown,
—Perhaps to touch his shoulder, perhaps in pain—
Then the rain fell on the roof and the twilight darkened
And they said that in death you looked like a marvelous old,
    wise child.

2

It is Fourth Month now and spring in another century,
Let us go to the hillside and ask; he will like to hear us;
"Is it good, the sleep?"

"It is good, the sleep and the waking.
I have picked out a bit of hill where the south sun warms me.
I like to be near the trees."

Nay, let him ask, rather.
"Is it well with you, comrades?
The cities great, portentous, humming with action?
The bridges mightily spanning wide-breasted rivers?
The great plains growing the wheat, the old lilac hardy,
    well-budded?
Is it well with these States?"

"The cities are great, portentous, a world-marvel,
The bridges arched like the necks of beautiful horses.
We had made the dry land bloom and the dead land
    blossom."

"Is it well with these States?"

"The old wound of your war is healed and we are one nation.
We have linked the whole land with the steel and the hard
    highways.
We have fought new wars and won them. In the French field
There are bones of Texarkana and Little Falls,
Aliens, our own; in the low-lying Belgian ground;
In the cold sea of the English; in dark-faced islands.
Men speak of them well or ill; they themselves are silent."

"Is it well with these States?"

"We have made many, fine new toys.
We—
There is a rust on the land.
A rust and a creeping blight and a scaled evil,
For six years eating, yet deeper than those six years,
Men labor to master it but it is not mastered.
There is the soft, grey, foul tent of the hatching worm
Shrouding the elm, the chestnut, the Southern cypress.
There is shadow in the bright sun, there is shadow upon the
    streets.

They burn the grain in the furnace while men go hungry.
They pile the cloth of the looms while men go ragged.
We walk naked in our plenty."

"My tan-faced children?"

"These are your tan-faced children.
These skilled men, idle, with the holes in their shoes.
These drifters from State to State, these wolvish, bewildered
    boys
Who ride the blinds and the box-cars from jail to jail,
Burnt in their youth like cinders of hot smokestacks,
Learning the thief's crouch and the cadger's whine,
Dishonored, abandoned, disinherited.
These, dying in the bright sunlight they cannot eat,
Or the strong men, sitting at home, their hands clasping
    nothing,
Looking at their lost hands.
These are your tan-faced children, the parched young,
The old man rooting in waste-heaps, the family rotting
In the flat, before eviction,
With the toys of plenty about them,
The shiny toys making ice and music and light,
But no price for the shiny toys and the last can empty.
The sleepers in blind corners of the night.
The women with dry breasts and phantom eyes.
The walkers upon nothing, the four million.
These are your tan-faced children."

"But the land?"

"Over the great plains of the buffalo-land,
The dust-storm blows, the choking, sifting, small dust.
The skin of that land is ploughed by the dry, fierce wind
And blown away, like a torrent;
It drifts foot-high above the young sprouts of grain
And the water fouls, the horses stumble and sicken,
The wash-board cattle stagger and die of drought.
We tore the buffalo's pasture with the steel blade.
We made the waste land blossom and it has blossomed.

That was our fate; now that land takes its own revenge,
And the giant dust-flower blooms above five States."

"But the gains of the years, who got them?"

        "Many, great gains.
Many, yet few; they robbed us in the broad daylight,
Saying, 'Give us this and that; we are kings and titans;
We know the ropes; we are solid; we are hard-headed;
We will build you cities and railroads.'—as if *they* built
    them!
They, the preying men, the men whose hearts were like
    engines,
Gouging the hills for gold, laying waste the timber,
The men like band-saws, moving over the land.
And, after them, the others,
Soft-bodied, lacking even the pirate's candor,
Men of paper, robbing by paper, with paper faces,
Rustling like frightened paper when the storm broke.
The men with the jaws of moth and aphis and beetle,
Boring the dusty, secret hole in the corn,
Fixed, sucking the land, with neither wish nor pride
But the wish to suck and continue.
They have been sprayed, a little.
But they say they will have the land back again, these men."

"There were many such in my time.
I have seen the rich arrogant and the poor oppressed.
I have seen democracy, also. I have seen
The good man slain, the knave and the fool in power,
The democratic vista botched by the people,
Yet not despaired, loving the giant land,
Though I prophesied to these States."

"Now they say we must have one tyranny or another
And a dark bell rings in our hearts."

"Was the blood spilt for nothing, then?"

3

Under dry winter
Arbutus grows.
It is careless of man.
It is careless of man.

Man can tear it,
Crush it, destroy it;
Uproot the trailers,
The thumb-shaped leafings.

A man in gray clothes
May come there also,
Lie all day there
In weak spring sunlight.

White, firm-muscled,
The flesh of his body;
Wind, sun, earth
In him, possessing him.

In his heart
A flock of birds crying.
In his belly
The new grass growing.

In his skull
Sunlight and silence,
Like a vast room
Full of sunlight and silence.

In the lines of his palms
The roads of America,
In the knots of his hands
The anger of America.

In the sweat of his flesh
The sorrows of America,
In the seed of his loins
The glory of America.

The sap of the birch-tree
Is in his pelt,
The maple, the red-bud
Are his nails and parings.

He grows through the earth and is part of it like the roots
   of new grass.

Little arbutus
Delicate, tinted,
Tiny, tender,
Fragile, immortal.

If you can grow,
A man can grow
Not like others
But like a man.

Man is a bull
But he has not slain you
And this man lies
Like a lover beside you.

Beside the arbutus,
The green-leaved Spring,
He lies like a lover
By his young bride,
In the white hour,
The white, first waking.

4

They say, they say, they say and let them say
Call you a revolutionist—you were one—
A nationalist—you were one—a man of peace,
A man describing battles, an old fraud,
A Charlus, an adept self-advertiser,
A "good, gray poet"—oh, God save us all!
God save us from the memoirs and the memories!
And yet, they count. They have to. If they didn't
There'd be no Ph.Ds. And each disciple
Jealously guards his own particular store
Of acorns fallen from the oak's abundance
And spits and scratches at the other gatherers.
"I was there when he died!"

        "He was not there when he died!"
"It was me he trusted, me! X got on his nerves!
He couldn't stand X in the room!"
        "Y's well-intentioned
But a notorious liar—and, as for Z . . ."

So all disciples, always and forever.
—And the dire court at Longwood, those last years,
The skull of Sterne, grinning at the anatomists,
Poe's hospital-bed, the madness of the Dean,
The bright, coughing blood Keats wrote in to the girl,
The terrible corpse of France, shrunk, naked and solitary—
Oh, yes, you were spared some things.
Though why did Mrs. Davis sue the estate
And what did you mean when you said—
        And who cares?

You're still the giant lode we quarry
For gold, fools' gold and all the earthy metals,
The matchless mine.
Still the trail-breaker, still the rolling river.

You and your land, your turbulent, seeking land
Where anything can grow.

And they have wasted the pasture and the fresh valley,
Stunk the river, shot the ten thousand sky-darkening pigeon
To build sham castles for imitation Medici
And the rugged sons of the rugged sons of death.
The slum, the sharecropper's cabin, the senseless tower,
The factory town with the dirty stoops of twilight,
The yelling cheapness, the bitter want among plenty,
But never Monticello, never again.

And there are many years in the dust of America
And they are not ended yet.

Far north, far north are the sources of the great river,
the headwaters, the cold lakes,
By the little sweet-tasting brooks of the blond country,
The country of snow and wheat,
Or west among the black mountains, the glacial springs.
Far north and west they lie and few come to them, few taste
    them,
But, day and night, they flow south,
By the French grave and the Indian, steadily flowing,
By the forgotten camps of the broken heart,
By the countries of black earth, fertile, and yellow earth and
    red earth,
A growing, a swelling torrent:
Rivers meet it, and tiny rivulets,
Meet it, stain it,

Great rivers, rivers of pride, come bowing their watery heads
Like muddy gift-bearers, bringing their secret burdens,
Rivers from the high horse-plains and the deep, green
    Eastern pastures
Sink into it and are lost and rejoice and shout with it, shout
    within it,
They and their secret gifts,

A fleck of gold from Montana, a sliver of steel from
    Pittsburgh,
A wheat-grain from Minnesota, an apple-blossom from
    Tennessee,
Roiled, mixed with the mud and earth of the changing
    bottoms
In the vast, rending floods,
But rolling, rolling from Arkansas, Kansas, Iowa,
Rolling from Ohio, Wisconsin, Illinois,
Rolling and shouting:
Till, at last, it is Mississippi,
The Father of Waters; the matchless; the great flood
Dyed with the earth of States; with the dust and the sun
    and the seed of half the States;
The huge heart-vein, pulsing and pulsing; gigantic; ever
    broader, ever mightier;
It rolls past broken landings and camellia-smelling woods;
    strange birds fly over it;
It rolls through the tropic magic, the almost-jungle, the
    warm darkness breeding the warm, enormous stars;
It rolls to the blue Gulf; ocean; and the painted birds fly.
The grey moss mixes with it, the hawk's feather has fallen
    in it,
The cardinal feather, the feather of the small thrush
Singing spring to New England,
The apple-pip and the pepper-seed and the checkerberry,
And always the water flowing, earthy, majestic,
Fed with snow and heat, dew and moonlight,
Always the wide, sure water,
Over the rotted deer-horn
The gold, Spanish money,

The long-rusted iron of many undertakings,
Over De Soto's bones and Joliet's wonder,
And the long forest-years before them, the brief years after,
The broad flood, the eternal motion, the restless-hearted
Always, forever, Mississippi, the god.

April, 1935

from Like Decorations in a Nigger Cemetery •
Wallace Stevens

[*for Arthur Powell*]

I

In the far South the sun of autumn is passing
Like Walt Whitman walking along a ruddy shore.
He is singing and chanting the things that are part of him,
The worlds that were and will be, death and day.
Nothing is final, he chants. No man shall see the end.
His beard is of fire and his staff is a leaping flame.

To a Dame Who Sneered When She Saw My Sox • *Paul Potts*

What I have here put down in words
Niagara on a piece of paper,
Could have been turned to living action.
Walt Whitman could have been Columbus
And your Bobbie Burns the Young Pretender
With Hopkins at the Vatican
And William Butler Yeats the President of Eire
Then in a world like that
Paul Potts, he would have been a king.

The Ceaseless Rings of Walt Whitman

LANGSTON HUGHES

WALT WHITMAN, greatest of American poets, was born on a farm owned by his father near West Hills, Long Island, New York, on the last day of May, 1819. He died in a tiny old house of his own on Mickle Street in Camden, New Jersey, at the end of March, 1892. The span of his life ran from American slavery through the Civil War to American freedom and the approaching dawn of the twentieth century.

Whitman did not fight in the War Between the States. He hated war and killing, but he devoted much of his time to nursing and caring for the wounded, both Northern and Southern, white or Negro, Yankee or Rebel. At Culpeper, Virginia, a staging area, he saw enough of combat to sicken him against war. But on errands of mercy, he went out to the battlefields and into field hospitals. From his friends he solicited money to buy cookies, candies, ice cream, magazines, and papers for the wounded. He tended them, read to them, wrote letters home for those who could not write, and cheered them with stories. He helped those with leg injuries to learn to walk again.

In 1864, assisting a surgeon in an amputation, Walt Whitman was accidentally cut with a gangrenous scalpel. An infection set in which caused him health complications in later life. While carrying on this voluntary nursing among the wounded in and near Washington, Whitman held a job as a clerk in the Indian Office. The attacks of narrow-minded readers on his poetry caused him to lose this job. But, through the help of friends, he secured a place in the Attorney General's office. In the late night hours, he continued to write his poems of democracy, articles, and letters for the papers.

His position in the Indian Office was not the first that Whitman had lost because of his liberal views. He had been an editor of the Brooklyn *Eagle,* but was fired there in 1848 because he refused to support Governor Cass of Michigan who advocated the continuation of slavery. Whitman called

95

people like Cass "Dough Faces," because of their condonance of Southern
slavery. Whitman abhorred slave catchers and those who gave them aid or
supported their political beliefs. In the New York *Evening Post,* Whitman
wrote:

> We are all docile dough-faces,
> They knead us with the fist,
> They, the dashing Southern Lords,
> We labor as they list.
> For them we speak—or hold our tongue,
> For them we turn and twist.

There had been a half-dozen or so slaves on the ancestral Whitman farm,
and young Walt had played with them as a child. Perhaps that is where he
acquired his sympathy for the Negro people, and his early belief that all men
should be free—a belief that grew to embrace the peoples of the whole
world, expressed over and over throughout his poems, encompassing not
only America but the colonial peoples, the serfs of tsarist Russia, the
suppressed classes everywhere. His spiritual self roamed the earth wherever
the winds of freedom blow however faintly, keeping company with the
foiled revolutionaries of Europe or the suppressed coolies of Asia.

Because the vast sweep of democracy is still incomplete even in America
today, because revolutionaries seeking to break old fetters are still foiled in
Europe and Asia, because the physical life of the Brooklyn ferries and the
Broadway street cars and the Mississippi river banks and the still fresh
battlefields of World War II continue to pulse with the same heartbeats of
humanity as in Whitman's time, his poetry strikes us now with the same
immediacy it must have awakened in its earliest readers in the 1850s.

The good gray poet of democracy is one of literature's great faithholders
in human freedom. Speaking simply for people everywhere and most of all
for the believers in our basic American dream, he is constantly growing in
stature as the twentieth century advances and edition after edition of his
poems appears.

Walt Whitman wrote without the frills, furbelows, and decorations of
conventional poetry, usually without rhyme or measured prettiness. Perhaps
because of his simplicity, timid poetry lovers over the years have been
frightened away from his *Leaves of Grass,* poems as firmly rooted and as
brightly growing as the grass itself. Perhaps, too, because his all-embracing
words lock arms with workers and farmers, Negroes and whites, Asiatics
and Europeans, serfs, and free men, beaming democracy to all, many aca-
demic-minded intellectual isolationists in America have had little use for
Whitman, and so have impeded his handclasp with today by keeping him

imprisoned in silence on library shelves. Still his words leap from their pages and their spirit grows steadily stronger everywhere.

The best indication of the scope of Whitman's poems might be found in his own "Song of the Answerer" where he writes about poetry:

> ... I give the sign of democracy.
> By God! I will accept nothing which all cannot
> have their counterpart of on the same terms ...

So there is no keeping Whitman imprisoned in silence. He proclaims:

> I ordain myself loosed of limits. . . .
> Going where I list. . . .
> Gently, but with undeniable will, divesting myself of the
> holds that would hold me.

One of the greatest "I" poets of all time, Whitman's "I" is not the "I" of the introspective versifiers who write always and only about themselves. Rather it is the cosmic "I" of all peoples who seek freedom, decency, and dignity, friendship and equality between individuals and races all over the world.

> The words of true poems give you more than poems,
> They give you to form for yourself poems, religions, politics,
>   war, peace, behavior, histories, essays, daily life
>   and everything else,
> They balance ranks, colors, races, creeds, and the sexes. . . .
> They bring none to his or her terminus or to be content and full,
> Whom they take they take into space to behold the birth of stars,
>   to learn one of the meanings,
> To launch off with absolute faith, to sweep through the ceaseless
>   rings and never be quiet again.

In this atomic age of ours, when the ceaseless rings are multiplied a millionfold, the Whitman spiral is upward and outward toward a freer, better life for all, not narrowing downward toward death and destruction. Singing the greatness of the individual, Whitman also sings the greatness of unity, cooperation, and understanding.

> ... all the men ever born are also my brothers,
>   and the women my sisters. . . .

As an after-thought he adds:

(I am large, I contain multitudes).

Certainly, his poems contain us all. The reader cannot help but see his own better self therein.

6.

Old Walt • *Langston Hughes*

Old Walt Whitman
Went finding and seeking,
Finding less than sought
Seeking more than found,
Every detail minding
Of the seeking or the finding.

Pleasured equally
In seeking as in finding,
Each detail minding,
Old Walt went seeking
And finding.

The Orange Bears • *Kenneth Patchen*

The orange bears with soft friendly eyes
Who played with me when I was ten,
Christ, before I left home they'd had
Their paws smashed in the rolls, their backs
Seared by hot slag, their soft trusting
Bellies kicked in, their tongues ripped
Out, and I went down through the woods
To the smelly crick with Whitman
In the Haldeman-Julius edition,
And I just sat there worrying my thumbnail
Into the cover—What did he know about
Orange bears with their coats all stunk up with soft coal
And the National Guard coming over
From Wheeling to stand in front of the millgates
With drawn bayonets jeering at the strikers?

I remember you could put daisies
On the windowsill at night and in
The morning they'd be so covered with soot
You couldn't tell what they were anymore.

A hell of a fat chance my orange bears had!

Whitman and the Problem of Good

MURIEL RUKEYSER

IT HAS BEEN SAID, and there are lines in the poems to prove it, that Walt Whitman could not discriminate between good and evil, that indeed with his inclusive benevolence Whitman dismissed the problem of evil altogether. But it is not proved. As the critics add to their quotations, one thing comes through: Whitman from the beginning felt himself to be deeply evil and good. Within that conflict—again like the conflict of his culture—there was a *problem* of good. It was no matter of simple recognition, with direct action to follow. How was it possible to search for the good, find it, and use it? Whitman's answer was "Identify."

But, before Whitman could be, in his own words, likened and restored, he must deal completely with himself; and I think there has been no conflict deeper than the nature of that self ever solved in poetry.

Melville knew the sea, its poising and somnambulism, its levels of revery, the dive to blackness and the corposants, the memories of shore and sleep and love among disaster. Abstract among detail, he finds and finds; in his unresolved Clarel, his Pierre who acts and is doomed, and above all in *Moby-Dick*, everything is essential, and more essential than it seems. But it is what it seems: the myth of tragedy rises up, world-shaped and enormous; Ahab is Ahab, and the Whale the Whale. If there is evil in whalehood; if there is evil in the chase; if darkness leaps from light; even so, there is redemption, and it lies in sympathy with another human being, in the arrival of a touch, and beyond that touch, of "the centre and circumference of all democracy," God our divine equality.

Whitman faced the same period and problem. His critics say that he does not discriminate between good and evil. F. O. Matthiessen in his full and powerful *American Renaissance*, declares of Whitman's "indiscriminate acceptance" that it "becomes real only when it is based on an awareness of the human issues involved, when it rises out of tenderness over man's struggle and suffering, and says: 'I moisten the roots of all that has grown.' "

This awareness of Whitman's is a process, lifelong, and whatever acceptance was finally reached expressed itself in an identification with America as a people, multitudinous and full of contradictions.

But, first, Whitman needed to accept himself. In the testimony of the poems, this most decisive step was the most difficult. Every trap was ready, just here. His idealized image was far from what he knew he was, in the late 1840s. Deeper than the acts of his living or the image-making of himself, his conflicts tore him: truth and reality were both at stake, and unless he could find them both, he would be lost to himself. His struggle was a struggle for identity.

He faced, not only good, but the *problem* of good.

Among his many faces, how was he to reach and insist on the good? How was he to be enough for himself, and take the terrible forms of earth also to be his own? How was he to identify, to talk of the expression of love for men and women, and see flashing that America—with its power, war, Congress, weapons, testimony, and endless gestation? America is what he identified with: not only the "you" in his lifelong singing of love and identification, but "me" also.

It was harder for Whitman to identify with himself than with the "you" of the poems.

To discover his nature as a poet and to make his nature by knowing it is the task before every poet. But to Walt Whitman, crowded with contradictions, the fifteen-year-old large as a man, the conventional verse-maker who learned his own rhythms at the sea-edge, the discovery of his nature was a continual crisis. He speaks of himself as ill-assorted, contradictory. His readers reacted violently from the beginning to his writing about sex—and of course it is not writing *about* sex, it is that physical rhythms are the base of every clear line, and that the avowals and the secrecy are both part of the life of a person who is, himself, a battleground of forces.

In the short conventional meter of *After the Pleasure Party*, Melville's bitter pain at

> The human integral clove asunder

makes its cry. Melville, however, was speaking of a couple—of himself as half, needing to mate with the "co-relative," and crying out for the power to free sex by setting free the sexless essential man, or by remaking himself. Whitman, also, used these terms of need; but the "halves" he fought to bring together were in himself, and he chose, early in his life as a poet, not to allow himself the concept of a central sexless man, but to take the other way: to remake himself.

It is in the remaking of himself that Whitman speaks for the general conflict in our culture. For, in the poems, his discovery of himself is a discovery of America; he is able to give it to anyone who reaches his lines.

Apparent again and again are the relationships with himself, the people, and the "you" of any of the poems. From these relationships, we may derive the fact of his physical split with himself and the heroic quality of his struggle to achieve strength from that conflict. The report on his autopsy—performed necessarily with his consent, but actually at his request—speaks of the virtues as well as the decay of that body of a seventy-three-year-old man, the sound structures of his age, the diseases. The people who have read that report seem struck by nothing beside the statement of tuberculosis. Whitman had not complained of pain, and no diagnosis had been made in his lifetime. But there is another fact that leaps from the lines of the report. Long before any of the critical tests now being projected, little was known of glandular equilibrium. But the poems themselves speak for a struggle between elements in one man, and give us a resolution of components that are conventionally considered to be male and female—a resolution that expresses very much indeed. If you read, as I did, the report on the autopsy after the poems, you will find this deduction borne out by remarks which no writer—medical or lay—seems to have analyzed. The list—and this is a catalogue—includes one's specific expectation as a confirmation of many contradictory gestures, in his poems and his life. The statement is not emphasized, among the list of other tubercular areas and foci of infection, and one wishes simply to bring it to the attention of competent clinicians now. Here is declared, in the baldness of medical writing, that the left suprarenal capsule was tubercular, and contained a cyst the size of a pigeon's egg. The kidney was soft, red, swollen, somewhat granular. The smaller right kidney was in good condition.

Whitman's autopsy is used in Edgar Lee Masters' biography, but neither he nor anyone else has seemed to understand the implications of his finding. In the light of what we know about the suprarenal-pituitary-sex hormone relation, certain conclusions probably may be reached. I venture to suggest that the inclusive personality which Whitman created from his own conflict is heroic proof of a life in which apparent antagonisms have been reconciled and purified into art. If this is true, the definitions of good and evil, in relation to Whitman and his sense of possibility, may be re-explored.

The effort to make a balance must have been intense. When Whitman, in an early poem, speaks of the threat of being

> lost to myself, ill-assorted, contradictory,

he shows us the beginning of a long and conscious work performed according to the challenges before a mythical hero. He wrote of the terrible doubt of appearances, and of himself among the shows of the day and night. He spoke of

> the sense of what is real, the thought if after all it
> should prove unreal . . .

This struggle was not a struggle for conformity in the "normal," but for the most intense reality which the individual can achieve, a struggle of process and hope and possibility which we all make when we desire to include our farthest range and then extend the newly-created self into the new again, when we base our desire in the belief that the most real is the most subtle, in art and in life.

It was Whitman's acceptance of his entire nature that made the work possible. The line of a man full of doubt is

> I never doubt whether that is really me. . . .

Will went into this work on the self, and there are signs of the achievements here as well as the scars. Whitman is accused by many of showing too much will, and we know how unlikely it is for the efforts of will to lead alone to form. The form of Whitman does not arrive as a product of will, line by line. Each poem follows the curves of its own life in passion; it stands or falls, dies or grows, by that. The form is there, but it is a form of details. For the large work is a double work, and we must seek form in its two expressions: the entire collection of *Leaves of Grass,* and the life-image of Whitman as he made himself, able to identify at last with both the people in their contradictions and himself in his. Able to identify—and this is his inner achievement—with his own spirit, of which his body, his life, his poems are the language.

For Whitman grew to be able to say, out of his own fears,

> Be not afraid of my body,

and, out of his own scattering,

> I am a dance.

He remembered his body as other poets of his time remembered English

verse. Out of his own body, and its relation to itself and the sea, he drew
his basic rhythms. They are not the rhythms, as has been asserted, of work
and love-making; but rather of the relation of our breathing to our heartbeat,
and these measured against an ideal of water at the shore, not beginning
nor ending, but endlessly drawing in, making forever its forms of massing
and falling among the breakers, seething in the white recessions of its surf,
never finishing, always making a meeting-place.

Not out of English prosody but the fluids of organism, not so much from
the feet and the footbeat except as they too derive from the rhythms of pulse
and lung, Whitman made his music signify. Rarely, in the sweep of lines,
is the breath harshened and interrupted. The tension of Hopkins is nearer
to activity: it is activity, muscular, violent, and formal. Emily Dickinson's
strictness, sometimes almost a slang of strictness, speaks with an intellectually active, stimulated quick music. But Whitman offers us the rhythms of
resolved physical conflict. When he says, "I have found the law of my own
poems," he celebrates that victory.

Forced by his own time to see the industrial war, the war of the States,
the disavowal of death (one of the deepest sources, in our culture, of the
corruption of consciousness), Whitman's fight for reconciliation was of
profound value as a symbol. The fight was the essential process of democracy: to remake and acknowledge the relationships, to find the truth and
power in diversity, among antagonists; and a poet of that democracy would
have to acknowledge and make that truth emerge from the widest humanity
in himself, among the horizons of his contradicted days and nights. The
reconciliation was not a passive one; the unity was not an identification in
which the range was lost (although "Identify" is a key word in his work);
the peace toward which his poems tended was not simply a lack of war. He
put away the war he had known, in the hospitals, as a pioneer in what is
now called psychiatric nursing. He did that as he put away, in writing a dirge
for Lincoln, the fact of the murder. It was simply that, to Whitman, the life,
the fact of Lincoln's death, and the "debris and debris of all the slain soldiers
of the war" were more immediate in this "victorious song, death's outlet
song." In a minor poem of four lines, he uses one line to call the assassination

> The foulest crime in history known in any land or age—

and we can see that the line is thrown away. It is a "bad line," and with it
Booth is dismissed. So, this poet will say, of slavery,

> On and on to the grapple with it—Assassin! then your
> life or ours be at stake, and respite no more.

These are flat lines, the power of music is lost. On these, and on the "catalogues," charges are made that Whitman is full of "bad lines," and that he is a "bad influence."

Whitman is a "bad influence"; that is, he cannot be imitated. He can, in hilarious or very dull burlesques, be parodied; but anyone who has come under his rhythms to the extent of trying to use them knows how great a folly is there. He cannot be extended; it is as if his own curse on "poems distill'd from poems" were still effective (as it forever is); but what is always possible is to go deeper into one's own sources, the body and the ancient religious poetry, and go on with the work he began.

As for the "cataloguing" lines: it seems to me that they stand in a very clear light, not only among his poems entire, but also in regard to present techniques.

There has been a good deal of regret over the printed poem, since first the press was used; and recently, with the mourning over a supposed breakdown in communication, I have heard simple people and college presidents complain that the function of the poet is past, that the bard is gone. Now it is true that a poem heard does enter very vividly into the consciousness; but, with the habit of reading as widespread as it now is, many prefer to see the poem, at least to see it before hearing it, and this is apart from that number who can imagine better when they read than when they listen. For those who care more for the hearing of poetry, there is the stage and the radio, mediums allowing very little verse to make itself heard, except in such ways as I propose later to show. But, whether a poem is approached through the eyes in a book, or through the ears, the eyes within the eyes, the visual imagination, are reached; and this in itself is a way of reaching the total imagination. This visual summoning may be made often or very seldom, depending on your poet; if the occurrence is well prepared, the impact is unforgettably strong. The visual imagination may be spoken of as including the eyes. The imaginative function includes the senses. It includes, perhaps most easily, a kind of seeing; we are perhaps most used to having sight invoked in the telling of stories and poems.

Whitman draws on this continually, sometimes with a word at a time—

> The birth, the hasting after the physician, the beggar's tramp,
>   the drunkard's stagger, the laughing party of mechanics,
> The escaped youth, the rich person's carriage, the fop,
>   the eloping couple,
> The early market-man, the hearse, the moving of furniture
>   into the town, the return back from the town,
> They pass, I also pass—

sometimes these visual summonings are accomplished in a procession of short phrases:

> Passage to more than India!
> O secret of the earth and sky!
> Of you O waters of the sea! O winding creeks and rivers!
> Of you O woods and fields! of you strong mountains of my land!
> Of you O prairies! of you gray rocks!
> O morning red! O clouds! O rain and snow!
> O day and night, passage to you!

sometimes they follow each other line after line:

> With the fresh sweet herbage under foot, and the pale
>   green leaves of the trees prolific,
> In the distance the flowing glaze, the breast of the
>   river, with a wind-dapple here and there,
> With ranging hills on the banks, with many a line
>   against the sky, and shadows,
> And the city at hand with dwellings so dense, and
>   stacks of chimneys,
> And all the scenes of life and the workshops, and the
>   workmen homeward returning.

These successions are not to be called catalogues. That name has thrown readers off; it is misleading. What we are confronted with here, each time, is not a list, but a sequence with its own direction. It is visual; it is close to another form, and its purpose is the same as the purpose which drives this passage:

> And Sutter, on his way home—
> —passes through the prosperous landscapes of a happy
>   countryside.
> Wealth, fertility, and contentment can be sensed everywhere.
> The rain has ceased ... Myriads of raindrops shimmer in
>   the sunshine.
> Suddenly, he meets a group of working people with picks,
>   and pans for gold-washing.
> Astonished, Sutter follows them with his eyes, then turns
>   his horse and gallops towards the fort.
> The store-keeper from near the fort comes up to Sutter to
>   show him gold dust in the palm of his hand.
> He asks Sutter if this is really gold or not.
> Sutter nods slowly.

That sequence describes a key action; in the next few lines,

> The dams are taut with their heavy loads, the canal locks
> are shattered, and the waters rush through their old courses.

You will recognize the form of that passage, if you imagine it with your eyes. It is typical, and it is very like Whitman. But it is a fragment of the script of a movie called *Sutter's Gold*.

Whitman, writing years before the invention of the moving picture camera, has in his poems given to us sequence after sequence that might be the detailed instructions, not to the director and cameramen only, but to the film editor as well. The rhythm of these sequences is film rhythm, the form is montage; and movies could easily be made of these poems, in which the lines in the longer, more sustained speech rhythms would serve as sound track, while these seemingly broken and choppy descriptive lines would serve well as image track.

But the chief reason for the difficulty that certain critics and imitators have with Whitman is not in his rhythm nor his "lists." These can be translated; we can see in our own time that a powerful poet can take his long, breathing line and transform it to his own uses and his own music. What has to be changed radically is the meaning. In Jeffers' hands, the long line of Whitman—which does, of course, lead us to Biblical and to Greek poetry—has been transformed. The meaning has crossed over, and is with the antagonists in our long conflict, both sides of which we know so well, from both sides of which the various and beautiful strength does arrive. Jeffers in his power has set the alternative of perfection or death. Wanting perfect love, perfect human beings, perfect acts, he sees death as the only other truth. In an organic world, if you set that choice, death is the answer; if you do not see a perfection of its own kind and moment, moving in time through many things, there is no other answer but annihilation. The setting of this alternative is a product of an age of mechanistic science, which could let its people speak of each other in terms of inorganic structure, which saw the universe infinitely large, and dying.

Whitman is the emblem poet, in this conflict, of another relationship. He is the poet of possibility. And he gives the meanings of possibility, produced by his own age, their further meaning and image in poetry.

Melville is the poet of outrage of his century in America, Whitman is the poet of possibility; one cannot be repeated more than the other. But Whitman's significance is based on the possibility realized in this period, as Dante's is based on the system of his religion in his time. As far as their imagination of *possibility* outranges their time, their systems live; for their images are deep in their belief. Melville's outrage lives; he touched perpetual evil, the perpetual hunt, and sea-images, world-images gave these their language. They speak for the backgrounds of our present. In our history, our open history, we know the gifts of many poets: in our buried history are the lost poems and songs; but these two master-poets, in all their work, stand at the doors of conflict, offering both courage and possibility, and choosing, emphasizing one or the other according to the ways in which forces that work in all of us drove them, and were driven, as they lived toward their forms.

from Countersong to Walt Whitman: Song of Ourselves • *Pedro Mir*

9

FOR
    what else is a great, inevitable poet
      but a limpid pool
        where a people discover their perfect image?
What else
    but a submerged garden
      where all men recognize themselves
      in language?
And what else
    but a chord of an endless guitar
      where the people's fingers pluck
        their simple, their own, their
          strong and
      their true, innumerable song?
For that reason, you, numerous Walt Whitman, who
 saw and dreamed
the precise word for singing your people,
who in the midst of night said

I

and the fisherman understood himself in his cape
and the hunter heard himself in the midst of his shot
and the wood-cutter recognized himself in his axe
and the farmer in his field and the gold-
panner in his yellow image on the water
and the maiden in her future city
    that grows and matures
underneath her skirt
and the prostitute in her fountain of joy
and the miner of shadows in his steps below the
      Fatherland ...
When the tall preacher, bowing his head,
between two long hands, said

I

and found himself united to the metal forger and to the
  salesman,
to the obscure wanderer in a soft cloud of dust,
to the dreamer and the climber,
to the earthy bricklayer who resembles a gravestone,
to the farmer and the weaver,
to the sailor in white who resembles a handkerchief . . .
And all the people saw themselves
when they heard the word

I

and all the people listened to themselves in your song
when they listened to the word
    I, Walt Whitman, a cosmos
    of Manhattan the son.
Because you were the people, you were I,
and I was Democracy, the people's last name,
and I was also Walt Whitman, a cosmos
of Manhattan the son . . . !

15

AND NOW
it is no longer the word

I

the accomplished word,
the touch-word to begin the world.
And now,
now it is the word
        w e.
And now,
now has come the hour of the c o u n t e r s o n g .

    We, the railroad workers,
    we, the students,
    we, the miners,
    we, the peasants,
    we, the poor of the earth,
    populators of the world,
    daily-work heroes,
    with our love and our fists,
    enamoured of hope.
    We, the whites,
    the blacks, the yellow,
    the Indians, the bronze,
    Moorish and brunette,
    olive and red,
    platinum and blond,
    united by work,
    by misery, by silence,
    by the shout of a solitary man
    who in the midst of night
    with a perfect whip,
    with a dark salary,
    with a golden knife and an iron face,
    unrestrainedly shouts

I

and feels the crystalline echo
of a shower of blood
which decidedly feeds on
        us
in the midst of wharfs that reach far away
        us
and below the horizon of the factories
        us
in the flower, in the pictures, in the tunnels
        us
in the tall structure on the way to the orbits
        us
on the way to the marbles
        us
on the way to the prisons
        us

(*translated by Didier Tisdel Jaén*)

Walt Whitman

HENRY MILLER

I HAVE NEVER UNDERSTOOD why he should be called "the good gray poet." The color of his language, his temperament, his whole being is electric blue. I hardly think of him as poet. Bard, yes. The bard of the future.

America has never really understood Whitman, or accepted him. America has exalted Lincoln, a lesser figure.

Whitman did not address the masses. He was as far removed from the people as a saint is from the members of a church. He reviled the whole trend of American life, which he characterized as mean and vulgar. Yet only an American could have written what he did. He was not interested in culture, tradition, religion or Democracy. He was what Lawrence called "an aristocrat of the spirit."

I know of no writer whose vision is as inclusive, as all-embracing as Whitman's. It is precisely this cosmic view of things which has prevented Whitman's message from being accepted. He is all affirmation. He is completely outgoing. He recognizes no barriers of any kind, not even evil.

Everyone can quote from Whitman in justification of his own point of view. No one has arisen since Whitman who can include his thought and go beyond it. The "Song of the Open Road" remains an absolute. It transcends the human view, obliges man to include the universe in his own being.

The poet in Whitman interests me far less than the seer. Perhaps the only poet with whom he can be compared is Dante. More than any other single figure, Dante symbolizes the medieval world. Whitman is the incarnation of the modern man, of whom thus far we have only had intimations. Modern life has not yet begun. Here and there men have arisen who have given us glimpses of this world to come. Whitman not only voiced the keynote of this new life in process of creation but behaved as if it already existed. The wonder is that he was not crucified. But here we touch the mystery which shrouds his seemingly open life.

Whoever has studied Whitman's life must be amazed at the skill with which he steered his bark through troubled waters. He never relinquishes his grasp of the oar, never flinches, never wavers, never compromises. From the moment of his awakening—for it was truly an awakening and not a mere development of creative talent—he marches on, calm, steady, sure of himself, certain of ultimate victory. Without effort he enlists the aid of willing disciples who serve as buffers to the blows of fate. He concentrates entirely upon the deliverance of his message. He talks little, reads little, but speculates much. It is not, however, the life of a contemplative which he leads. He is very definitely in and of the world. He is worldly through and through, yet serene, detached, the enemy of no man, the friend of all. He possesses a magic armor against wanton intrusion, against violation of his being. In many ways he reminds one of the "resurrected" Christ.

I stress this aspect of the man deliberately because Whitman himself gave expression to it most eloquently—it is one of his most revelatory utterances—in a prose work. The passage runs as follows: "A fitly born and bred race, growing up in right conditions of outdoor as much as indoor harmony, activity and development, would probably, from and in those conditions, find it enough merely *to live*—and would, in their relations to the sky, air, water, trees, etc., and to the countless common shows, and in the fact of *life* itself, discover and achieve happiness—with Being suffused night and day by wholesome ecstasy, surpassing all the pleasures that wealth, amusement, and even gratified intellect, erudition, or the sense of art, can give." This view, so utterly alien to the so-called modern world, is thoroughly Polynesian. And that is where Whitman belongs, out beyond the last frontiers of the Western world, neither of the West nor of the East but of an intermediary realm, a floating archipelago dedicated to the attainment of peace, happiness and well-being here and now.

I maintain most stoutly that Whitman's outlook is not American, any more than it is Chinese, Hindu or European. It is the unique view of an emancipated individual, expressed in the broadest American idiom, understandable to men of all languages. The flavor of his language, though altogether American, is a rare one. It has never been captured again. It probably never will. Its universality springs from its uniqueness. In this sense it has all tradition behind it. Yet, I repeat, Whitman had no respect for tradition; that he forged a new language is due entirely to the singularity of his vision, to the fact that he felt himself to be a new being. Between the early Whitman and the "awakened" Whitman there is no resemblance whatever. No one, scanning his early writings, could possibly detect the germ of the future genius. Whitman remade himself from head to foot.

I have used the word *message* several times in connection with his writings. Yes, the message is explicit as well as implicit in his work. It is the message which informs all of his work. Remove the message and his poetry falls apart. Like Tolstoy, he may be said to have made of art propaganda. But is this not merely to say that unless used for life, put at the service of life, art is meaningless? Whitman is never a moralist or a religionist. His concern is to open men's vision, to lead them to the center of nowhere in order that they may find their true orientation. He does not preach, he exhorts. He is not content merely to speak his view, he sings it, shouts it triumphantly. If he looks backward it is to show that past and future are one. He sees no evil anywhere. He sees through and beyond, always.

He has been called a pantheist. Many have referred to him as the great democrat. Some have asserted that he possessed a cosmic consciousness. All attempts to label and categorize him eventually break down. Why not accept him as a pure phenomenon? Why not admit that he is without a peer? I am not attempting to divinize him. How could I, since he was so strikingly human? If I insist on the uniqueness of his being, is it not to suggest the clue which will unravel the mysterious claims of democracy?

"Make Room for Man" is the title of a poem by his faithful friend and biographer, Horace Traubel. What is it that has stood in the way of man? *Only man*. Whitman demolishes every flimsy barrier behind which man has sought to take refuge. He expresses utter confidence in man. He is not a democrat, he is an anarchist. He has the faith born of love. He does not know the meaning of hate, fear, envy, jealousy, rivalry. Born on Long Island, moving to Brooklyn at the commencement of his career, serving first as carpenter and builder, later as reporter, typesetter, editor, nursing the wounded during the bloody Civil War, he finally settles in Camden, a most inconspicuous spot. He journeyed over a good part of America and in his poems he has recorded his impressions, hopes and dreams.

It is a grandiose dream indeed. In his prose works he issues warnings to his countrymen, unheeded, of course. What would he say if he could see America today? I think his utterances would be still more impassioned. I believe he would write a still greater *Leaves of Grass*. He would see potentialities "immenser far" than those he had originally visioned. He would see "the cradle endlessly rocking."

Since his departure we have had the "great poems of death" which he spoke of, and they have been *living* poems of death. The poem of life has still to be lived.

Meanwhile the cradle is endlessly rocking. . . .   *[published 1957]*

The American Idiom

WILLIAM CARLOS WILLIAMS

THE AMERICAN IDIOM is the language we speak in the United States. It is characterized by certain differences from the language used among cultured Englishmen, being completely free from all influences which can be summed up as having to do with "the Establishment." This, pared to essentials, is the language which governed Walt Whitman in his choice of words. It constituted a revolution in the language. (In France, only Paul Fort recognized what had happened about him to negate the *Académie*.)

The language had been deracinated in this country, but the English tongue was a tough customer with roots bedded in a tradition of far-reaching cultural power. Every nursery rhyme gave it a firmer grip on the tradition and there were always those interested in keeping their firm hold upon it.

Every high school in America is duty bound to preserve the English language as a point of honor, a requirement of its curriculum. To fail in *English* is unthinkable!

Ignoring the supreme masters of English composition and thinking to go beyond them along the same paths impugns a man's loyalty if not his good sense. In fact, it has been baldly stated in the highest circles and believed that there is no American language at all—so low have we fallen in defense of our speech.

The result is a new and unheralded language which has grown stronger by osmosis, we are asked to believe, but actually by the power of those Whitmans among us who were driven to take a chance by their fellows and the pride of an emerging race, its own. The American idiom had been driven into a secondary place by our scholars, those rats that had abandoned it to seek salvage elsewhere in safer places. No one can blame them, no one can say that we shall survive to plant our genes in another world.

We must go forward—uncertainly it may be, but courageously as we may. Be assured that measure in mathematics as in verse is inescapable; so in reply to the fixed foot of the ancient line, including the Elizabethans, we must have a reply: it is the variable foot which we are beginning to discover after Whitman's advent.

"The Establishment," fixed in its commitments, has arrived at its last stand: the iambic pentameter, blank verse, the verse of Shakespeare and Marlowe which gives it its prestige. A full stop. Until we can go beyond that, "the Establishment" has an edge on us.

Whitman lived in the nineteenth century but he, it must be acknowledged, proceeded instinctively by rule of thumb and a tough head, correctly, in the construction of his verses. He knew nothing of the importance of what he had stumbled on, unconscious of the concept of the variable foot. This new notion of time which we were approaching, leading to the work of Curie and the atom bomb, and other *new* concepts have been pregnant with far-reaching consequences.

We were asleep to the tremendous responsibilities—as poets and as writers generally—that were opening up to us. Our poets especially are asleep from the neck down—only the Russians with their state control of letters are stupider than we. And still we follow the English and teach it to our unsuspecting children.

[published 1961]

7.

1955-1980

8.

A Supermarket in California • *Allen Ginsberg*

What thoughts I have of you tonight, Walt Whitman, for I walked down the sidestreets under the trees with a headache self-conscious looking at the full moon.

In my hungry fatigue, and shopping for images, I went into the neon fruit supermarket, dreaming of your enumerations!

What peaches and what penumbras! Whole families shopping at night! Aisles full of husbands! Wives in the avocados, babies in the tomatoes! — and you, Garcia Lorca, what were you doing down by the watermelons?

I saw you, Walt Whitman, childless, lonely old grubber, poking among the meats in the refrigerator and eyeing the grocery boys.

I heard you asking questions of each: Who killed the pork chops? What price bananas? Are you my Angel?

I wandered in and out of the brilliant stacks of cans following you, and followed in my imagination by the store detective.

We strode down the open corridors together in our solitary fancy tasting artichokes, possessing every frozen delicacy, and never passing the cashier.

Where are we going, Walt Whitman? The doors close in an hour. Which way does your beard point tonight?

(I touch your book and dream of our odyssey in the supermarket and feel absurd.)

Will we walk all night through solitary streets? The trees add shade to shade, lights out in the houses, we'll both be lonely.

Will we stroll dreaming of the lost America of love past blue automobiles in driveways, home to our silent cottage?

Ah, dear father, graybeard, lonely old courage-teacher, what

America did you have when Charon quit poling his ferry and you got out on a smoking bank and stood watching the boat disappear on the black waters of Lethe?

Berkeley 1955

168th Chorus *from* Mexico City Blues
• *Jack Kerouac*

Asking questions and listening
   is sincerity;
Asking questions and listening
   without really listening
Is a kind of sincerity; but
Talking about yourself alla
   time, is not insincere.

It's all the same thing
In the long run, the short run
   the no run

Whitman examined grass
   and concluded
It to be the genesis
   & juice, of pretty girls.

"Hair of Graves," footsteps
Of Lost Children,
Forgotten park meadows,
—Looking over your shoulder
   At the beautiful maidens—

Centennial for Whitman • *Richard Eberhart*

(*Amimetobion, not Synapothanumenon*)

I

What shall I say to Walt Whitman tonight?
Reading him here in the springtime of bursting green,
Foreign from him, held by the same air he breathed of the
    world,
Looking at night to the same stars, white and radiant,
Obsessed with a kindred obsession, at a dark depth,
Inheritor of his America maybe at its great height,

I praise him not in a loose form, not in outpouring,
Not in a positive acclamation of frenetic belief,
Not in the simplicity of a brotherhood, such peace,
And not in the dawn of an original compulsion,
But speak to him in the universe of birth and death.

By a Spring meadow I lay down by a river
And felt the wind play on my cheek. By the sunlight
On the water I felt the strangeness of the world.
Prone in the meadow by the side of the fast brook
I saw the trout shooting his shadow under the willow.

I sank into the mystical nature of memory
And became my beginning. I was one with strong nature,
At the heart of the world, with no need to penetrate her.
In the sheerness and the elegance of this feeling
I destroyed time and dwelled in eternal pleasure.

The vastness of the aim of human nature
Yielded to ease and immediacy of comprehension,
Such is the rarity of the mastery of existence
In the ethereal realm of pure intuition,
Within the subtlety of perfected spiritual balance.

II

What shall I say to Walt Whitman tonight?
Nothing that is not myself. Nothing for himself,
Who spoke the golden chords of a rough soul
Deep below the meeting of the mind
With reality; his words were a mask of the true soul.

I grew up among animal pleasures, hot in sense,
And fought off the lofty reaches of the intellect
As one knowing the soft touches of the night,
Running on the Spring freshets in delight,
Joyful and serene, not to be overcome or quelled.

Then dramatic evil like a blight overcame me,
The dream-like character of eternal knowledge
Was brought in earthly bondage; knowledge of death,
Our old enemy, appeared with his powerful will
And laid waste the garden of my green seeming.

The years began to whirl in a worldly ecstasy
Fulfilling some dark purpose confronting the heart
Of things, and I was loosened to flesh and mind,
Torn asunder from essential unity
And would wander the world in fateful duality.

This was the knowledge of good and evil,
This was the certainty of actual death,
The powerful hold of an ancient, fallen state,
The battering ram of time on the bones and eyes,
The new reality of the unredeemed mankind.

III

What shall I say to Walt Whitman tonight?
I look not upon the world of facts and figures
But in the heart of man. Ineradicable evil
Sits enthroned there, jealously guarding the place,
Only held at arm's length by a comic attitude.

Laughter at the sun and the moon, at the tides,
Laughter at the comedy of the eternal struggle,
And at the institutions and society of mankind
Laughter, I celebrate this tonic attitude,
And go as far as that for the sake of intellect.

And run on bitterness and corrosive pessimism
Standing under the glaring eye of antique satire
And range the fields of powerful condemnation
As one who allows himself such pleasures,
A beast engaged, knowing the gates of escape.

New bombs, new wars, new hatreds, new insecurities!
Man has become the victim of delusions
Thrashing his brains in energies of misaction,
Lost in tribal sin, ready to destroy himself,
Defenceless against all natures of monstrosity.

What shall I say to Walt Whitman tonight?
Give us a share of your love, your simplicity,
The large scope, the strong health of the soul,
Love be our guide, and love be our redemption,
Love make miracle, animate us now.

IV

Love come upon us when the willow bends,
Love come upon us at the child's upturned face,
Love recapture us in the market-place,
In churches, slums, on mountains, in the fog,
Love be with us in the hour of death.

Love be with us in the pang of birth,
And throw out hatred, envy, pride, despair,
Be joyful at the time of the tall daffodil,
Be rampant as the legendary lion,
Be meek and sweet, and sure, so love be here.

Love that is swift creator and saviour
Bless all the infants and the old men,
Bless the middle kingdom of the workers,
Love come in the soft night, in the sensual day,
Let our airs be soft flower-lofts of love.

What would you say to me, Walt Whitman, today?
Is there anything you can give me but your love,
That total devotion to comprehension of the word?
It is not the forms you evoked, these are changed,
But the force you spoke with, the heart's holy rapture,

Your knowledge of the changeless in birth and death,
The merit of man in his eternal suffering,
Your love of the stars, of valour, and of doom
That I would say to you, Walt Whitman, tonight,
That you could say to me, Walt Whitman, today.

Comments

RICHARD EBERHART

I ALWAYS ADMIRED WHITMAN from my earliest reading of poetry but he was not one of several poets who influenced my life. As I have said elsewhere, Wordsworth and Blake changed my life, and later Hopkins. Why Whitman did not do this to me also I will never know. It is not so much that Wordsworth, Blake and Hopkins made me imitate them when young but that they stimulated the inner reaches of my being. They evoked possibility. They were always there in the background. Whitman brought his awareness later. I was always pro-Whitman. I loved Whitman because of his wholeness, the large scope of his mind, the fact that he was international as well as national, metaphysical as well as physical, able to love the whole of life and it is this word that came out as the climax to my Centennial poem. He also had greatness of soul. I do not see how anybody can deny this. He was in Plato's camp rather than Aristotle's, despite the catalogues. Last week a young poet here said the soul was unsuitable for poetry, a word that should not be used. He should read the entire works of Whitman.

Walt Whitman • *Edwin Honig*

Prophet of the body's roving magnitude, he still commands
A hope elusive as the Jewish savior—not dying,
Not yet born, but always imminent: coming in a blaze
One sunny afternoon, defying winter, to everyone's
Distinct advantage, then going on to Eden, half sham,
Half hearsay, like California or Miami, golden.

All his life was squandered in his poverty when he became
The body's prime reunionist, bankrupt exploiter,
From early middle age, of the nation's largest
Unexploited enterprise—baggy, queer, a Johnny
Appleseed freely planting selves the future mashes
Into commonplaces, lops off as flourishes, an unweaned appetite.

Who can shape his mouth's beard-brimming bubble, that violent
Honey sound? Afterwards they just blew hard, Tarzans
Hamming through the swampy lots. His patent, never filed,
Was being man quixotically alive against the hoax
Of sin & dying. Paradise is now. America, whose greatest
War was civil, must be born from Abel's wound

& Cain be welcomed home by Adam—Father Abraham
Opening his blood to continents, all armies, lovers, tramps.
A time for heroes, but the captains, shot or dowdy, died.
(Had old Abe really smiled & tipped his hat or had he
Merely grimaced?) Ulysses, finished, promptly sighed &
    chomped
Cigars & toured the capitals. The people yea'd & shambled

To the greatest fortunes made, while he conveyed the lippy
Cop, the whistling streetcar man, the ferry pilot
Billowing upon the apron of his praise. Nakedly at last
He flailed his own paralysis with mud & flesh-brush. A man,

All men himself alone, a rugged blue-eyed testament,
His looks in Brady's lens are calm with after-rages.

"The real war will never get in the books." Below
The ragged line he signed his chummy name.

Ode to Walt Whitman • *Pablo Neruda*

I do not remember
at what age
nor where:
in the great damp South
or on the fearsome
coast, beneath the brief
cry of the seagulls,
I touched a hand and it was
the hand of Walt Whitman.
I trod the ground
with bare feet,
I walked on the grass,
on the firm dew
of Walt Whitman.

During
my entire
youth
I had the company of that hand,
that dew,
its firmness of patriarchal pine, its prairie-like expanse,
and its mission of circulatory peace.

Not
disdaining
the gifts
of the earth,
nor the copious
curving of the column's capital,
nor the purple
initial
of wisdom,
you taught me
to be an American,
you raised

my eyes
to books,
towards
the treasure
of the grains:
broad,
in the clarity
of the plains,
you made me see
the high
tutelary
mountain. From subterranean
echoes,
you gathered
for me
everything;
everything that came forth
was harvested by you,
galloping in the alfalfa,
picking poppies for me,
visiting
the rivers,
coming into the kitchens
in the afternoon.

But not only
soil
was brought to light
by your spade:
you unearthed
man,
and the
slave
who was humiliated
with you, balancing
the black dignity of his stature,
walked on, conquering
happiness.

To the fireman
below,
in the stoke-hole,
you sent
a little basket
of strawberries.
To every corner of your town
a verse
of yours arrived for a visit,
and it was like a piece
of clean body,
the verse that arrived,
like
your own fisherman beard
or the solemn tread of your acacia legs.

Your silhouette
passed among the soldiers:
the poet, the wound-dresser,
the night attendant
who knows
the sound
of breathing in mortal agony
and awaits with the dawn
the silent
return
of life.

Good baker!
Elder first cousin
of my roots,
araucaria's
cupola,
it is
now
a hundred
years
that over your grass
and its germinations,

the wind
passes
without wearing out your eyes.

New
and cruel years in your Fatherland:
persecutions,
tears,
prisons,
poisoned weapons
and wrathful wars
have not crushed
the grass of your book;
the vital fountainhead
of its freshness.
And, alas!
those
who murdered
Lincoln
now
lie in his bed.
They felled
his seat of honor
made of fragrant wood,
and raised a throne
spattered
with misfortune and blood.

But
your voice
sings
in the suburban
stations,
in
the
vespertine
wharfs,
your word

splashes
like
dark water.
Your people,
white
and black,
poor
people,
simple people
like
all
people
do not forget
your bell:
They congregate singing
beneath
the magnitude
of your spacious life.
They walk among the peoples with your love
caressing
the pure development
of brotherhood on earth.

(translated by Didier Tisdel Jaén)

I Begin by Invoking Walt Whitman •
Pablo Neruda

Because I love my country
I claim you, essential brother,
old Walt Whitman with your gray hands,

so that, with your special help
line by line, we will tear out by the roots
and destroy this bloodthirsty President Nixon.

There can be no happy man on earth,
no one can work well on this planet
while that nose continues to breathe in Washington.

Asking the old bard to confer with me
I assume the duties of a poet
armed with a terrorist's sonnet

because I must carry out with no regrets
this sentence, never before witnessed,
of shooting a criminal under siege,

who in spite of his trips to the moon
has killed so many here on earth
that the paper flies up and the pen is unsheathed

to set down the name of this villain
who practices genocide from the White House.

(translated by Teresa Anderson)

We Live in a Whitmanesque Age
(A Speech to P.E.N.)

PABLO NERUDA

I think I could turn and live with animals, they are so placid
   and self-contain'd,
I stand and look at them long and long.
They do not sweat and whine about their condition,
They do not lie awake in the dark and weep for their sins,
They do not make me sick discussing their duty to God,
Not one is dissatisfied, not one is demented with the mania
   of owning things,
Not one kneels to another, nor to his kind that lived thousands
   of years ago,
Not one is respectable or unhappy over the whole earth.
                    (from Section 32, "Song of Myself")

IN THIS HALF CENTURY, men have reached the moon, complete with penicillin and with television. In the field of warfare, napalm has been invented, to render democratic by means of its purifying fire the ashes of a number of the inhabitants of our planet. In spite of half a century of intellectual understanding, relations between rich and poor—between nations which lend some crumbs of comfort and others which go hungry— continue to be a complex mixture of anguish and pride, injustice and the right to live.

It is important that we should all recognize what it is that we owe to each other. We must continually keep renegotiating the 'internal debt' which weighs upon writers everywhere. Each one of us owes much to his own intellectual heritage and much to that which we have drawn from the cultural treasury of all the world. The writers from the southern half of this continent, like myself, have grown up knowing and admiring—despite the difference of tongues—the vast growth of the world of letters in its northern half. We have been particularly impressed by the amazing awakening of the novel which, from the days of Dreiser to the present time, has displayed a new strength—a convulsive and constructive strength—whose greatness and fierceness has no match in the literatures of the present age, unless it be among your own playwrights.

Your books, often cruel books, have exhibited the singular testimony of great and noble writers, faced with the conflicts involved in the vertiginous growth of your capitalist structure. In those exemplary works, none of the truth was concealed: the souls of multitudes and individuals, of the powerful and the weak, in city or in suburb, were laid bare—the drops of the very lifeblood of your 'body politic,' of your collective and your solitary lives.

For my part, I, who am now nearing seventy, discovered Walt Whitman when I was just fifteen, and I hold him to be my greatest creditor. I stand before you feeling that I bear with me always this great and wonderful debt which has helped me to exist.

I must start by acknowledging myself to be the humble servant of a poet who strode the earth with long, slow paces, pausing everywhere to love, to examine, to learn, to teach and to admire. The fact of the matter is that this great man, this lyric moralist, chose a hard path for himself: he was both a torrential and a didactic singer—qualities which appear opposed, seeming also more appropriate to a leader than to a writer. But what really counts is that Walt Whitman was not afraid to teach—which means to learn at the hands of life and undertake the responsibility of passing on the lesson! To speak frankly: he had no fear of either moralizing or immoralizing, nor did he seek to separate the fields of pure and impure poetry. He was the first totalitarian poet: his intention was not just to sing, but to impose on others his own total and wide-ranging vision of the relationships of men and nations. In this sense, his patent nationalism forms part of a total and organic universal vision: he held himself to be the debtor of happiness and sorrow alike, and also of both the advanced cultures and more primitive societies.

There are many kinds of greatness, but let me say (though I be a poet of the Spanish tongue) that Walt Whitman has taught me more than Spain's Cervantes: in Walt Whitman's work one never finds the ignorant being humbled, nor is the human condition ever found offended.

We continue to live in a Whitmanesque age, seeing how new men and new societies rise and grow, despite their birth-pangs. Walt Whitman was the protagonist of a truly geographical personality: the first man in history to speak with a truly continental American voice, to bear a truly American name. The colonies of the most brilliant countries have left a legacy of centuries of silence: colonialism seems to slay fertility and stultify the power of creation.

In this age, we see how other new nations, other new literatures and new flags, are coming into being with what one hopes is the total extinction of colonialism in Africa and Asia. Almost overnight, the capitals of the world are studded with the banners of people we had never heard of, seeking self-expression with the unpolished and pain-laden voice of birth. Black writers of Africa and America begin to give us the true pulse of the luckless races which had hitherto been silent. Man's liberation may often require bloodshed, but it always requires song—and the song of mankind grows richer day by day, in this age of sufferings and liberation.

Camden 1892 • *Jorge Luis Borges*

The fragrance of coffee and newspapers.
Sunday and its tedium. This morning,
On the uninvestigated page, that vain
Column of allegorical verses
By a happy colleague. The old man lies
Prostrate, pale, even white in his decent
Room, the room of a poor man. Needlessly
He glances at his face in the exhausted
Mirror. He thinks, without surprise now,
That face is me. One fumbling hand touches
The tangled beard, the devastated mouth.
The end is not far off. His voice declares:
I am almost gone. But my verses scan
Life and its splendor. I was Walt Whitman.

(*translated by Richard Howard and César Rennert*)

Note on Walt Whitman

JORGE LUIS BORGES

"The whole of Whitman's work is deliberate."
—Robert Louis Stevenson, 1882

THE PRACTICE OF LITERATURE sometimes fosters the ambition to construct an absolute book, a book of books that includes all the others like a Platonic archetype, an object whose virtue is not lessened by the years. Those who cherished that ambition have chosen lofty subjects: Apollonius of Rhodes, the first ship that braved the dangers of the deep; Lucan, the struggle between Caesar and Pompey, when the eagles waged war against the eagles; Camoëns, the Portuguese armies in the Orient; Donne, the circle of a soul's transmigrations according to Pythagorean dogma; Milton, the most ancient of sins and Paradise; Firdusi, the thrones of the Sassanidae. Góngora, I believe, was the first to say that an important book can exist without an important theme; the vague story told by the *Soledades* is deliberately trite, according to the observation and reproof of Cascales and Gracián (*Cartas filológicas*, VIII; *El Criticón*, II, 4). Trivial themes did not suffice for Mallarmé; he sought negative ones—the absence of a flower or a woman, the whiteness of the piece of paper before the poem. Like Pater, he felt that all the arts gravitate toward music, the art that has form as its substance; his decorous profession of faith *Tout aboutit à un livre* seems to summarize the Homeric axiom that the gods fabricate misfortunes so that future generations will have something to sing about (*Odyssey*, VIII). Around 1900 Yeats searched for the absolute in the manipulation of symbols that would awaken the generic memory, or Great Memory, which pulsates beneath individual minds; those symbols could be compared to the later archetypes of Jung. Barbusse, in *L'Enfer*, a book that has been unjustly neglected, avoided (tried to avoid) the limitations of time by means of the poetical account of man's basic acts. In *Finnegans Wake* Joyce tried to achieve the same objective by the simultaneous presentation of the characteristics of different epochs. The deliberate manipulation of anachronisms to produce an appearance of eternity has also been practiced by Pound and T. S. Eliot.

I have recalled some procedures; none is more curious than the one used by Whitman in 1855. Before considering it, I should like to quote some opinions that more or less prefigure what I am going to say. The first is from the English poet Lascelles Abercrombie, who wrote that Whitman extracted from his noble experience the vivid and personal figure who is one of the few great things in modern literature: the figure of himself. The second is from Sir Edmund Gosse, who said there was no real Walt Whitman, but that Whitman was literature in the protoplasmic state: an intellectual organism that was so simple it only reflected those who approached it. The third one is mine; it is found on page 70 of the book *Discusión* (1932):

Almost everything that has been written about Whitman is falsified by two persistent errors. One is the summary identification of Whitman, the man of letters, with Whitman, the semidivine hero of *Leaves of Grass*, as Don Quixote is the hero of the *Quixote*. The other is the senseless adoption of the style and vocabulary of his poems by those who write about him, that is to say, the adoption of the same surprising phenomenon one wishes to explain.

Imagine that a biography of Ulysses (based on the testimonies of Agamemnon, Laertes, Polyphemus, Calypso, Penelope, Telemachus, the swineherd, Scylla, and Charybdis) indicated that he never left Ithaca. Such a book is fortunately hypothetical, but its particular brand of deception would be the same as the deception in all the biographies of Whitman. To progress from the paradisiacal sphere of his verses to the insipid chronicle of his days is a melancholy transition. Paradoxically, that inevitable melancholy is aggravated when the biographer chooses to overlook the fact that there are two Whitmans: the "friendly and eloquent savage" of *Leaves of Grass* and the poor writer who invented him.[1] The latter was never in California or in Platte Canyon; the former improvises an apostrophe in Platte Canyon ("Spirit that Formed this Scene") and was a miner in California ("Starting from Paumanok," 1). In 1859 the latter was in New York; on December second of that year the former was present at the execution of the old abolitionist, John Brown, in Virginia ("Year of Meteors"). The latter was born on Long Island; so was the former ("Starting from Paumanok," 1), but he was also born in one of the southern states ("Longings for Home"). The latter was chaste, reserved, and somewhat taciturn; the former, effusive and orgiastic. It is easy to multiply such contradictions; but it is more important to understand that the mere happy vagabond proposed by the verses of *Leaves of Grass* would have been incapable of writing them.

Byron and Baudelaire dramatized their unhappiness in famous volumes; Whitman, his joy. (Thirty years later, in Sils-Maria, Nietzsche would discover Zarathustra; that pedagogue is happy or, at any rate, he recommends happiness, but his principal defect is that he does not exist.) Other romantic heroes—Vathek is the first of the series, Edmond Teste is not the last—tediously emphasize their differences; Whitman, with impetuous humility, yearns to be like all men. He says that *Leaves of Grass* "is the song of a great collective, popular individual, man or woman" (*Complete Writings*, V, 192). Or in these immortal words ("Song of Myself," 17):

> These are really the thoughts of all men in all ages and lands,
>   they are not original with me,
> If they are not yours as much as mine they are nothing, or next
>   to nothing,
> If they are not the riddle and the untying of the riddle they are
>   nothing,
> If they are not just as close as they are distant they are nothing.
>
> This is the grass that grows wherever the land is and the water is,
> This is the common air that bathes the globe.

Pantheism has disseminated a variety of phrases which declare that God is several contradictory or (even better) miscellaneous things. The prototype of such phrases is this: "I am the rite, I am the offering, I am the oblation to the parents, I am the grass, I am the prayer, I am the libation of butter, I am the fire" (*Bhagavad-Gita*, IX, 16). Earlier, but ambiguous, is Fragment 67 of Heraclitus: "God is day and night, winter and summer, war and peace, satiety and hunger." Plotinus describes for his pupils an inconceivable sky, in which "everything is everywhere, anything is all things, the sun is all the stars, and each star is all the stars and the sun" (*Enneads*, V, 8, 4). Attar, a twelfth-century Persian, sings of the arduous pilgrimage of the birds in search of their king, the Simurg; many of them perish in the seas, but the survivors discover that they are the Simurg and that the Simurg is each one of them and all of them. Extension of the principle of identity seems to have infinite rhetorical possibilities. Emerson, a reader of the Hindus and of Attar, leaves us the poem "Brahma"; perhaps the most memorable of its sixteen verses is this one: "When me they fly, I am the wings." Similar but more fundamental is "Ich bin der Eine und bin Beide," by Stefan George (*Der Stern des Bundes*). Walt Whitman renovated that procedure. He did not use it, as others had, to define the divinity or to play with the "sympathies and differences" of words; he wanted to identify himself, in a sort of ferocious tenderness, with all men. He said ("Crossing Brooklyn Ferry," 6):

> [I] Was wayward, vain, greedy, shallow, sly, cowardly, malignant,
> The wolf, the snake, the hog, not wanting in me,

And also, ("Song of Myself," 33):

> I am the man, I suffer'd, I was there.

> The disdain and calmness of martyrs,
> The mother of old, condemn'd for a witch, burnt with dry
>   wood, her children gazing on,
> The hounded slave that flags in the race, leans by the fence,
>   blowing, cover'd with sweat,
> The twinges that sting like needles his legs and neck, the
>   murderous buckshot and the bullets,
> All these I feel or am.

Whitman felt and was all of them, but fundamentally he was—not in mere history, in myth—what these two lines denote ("Song of Myself," 24):

> Walt Whitman, a kosmos, of Manhattan the son,
> Turbulent, fleshy, sensual, eating, drinking, and breeding . . .

He was also the one he would be in the future, in our future nostalgia, which is created by these prophecies that announced it ("Full of Life Now"):

> Full of life now, compact, visible,
> I, forty years old the eighty-third year of the States,
> To one a century hence or any number of centuries hence,
> To you yet unborn these, seeking you.

> When you read these I that was visible am become invisible,
> Now it is you, compact, visible, realizing my poems,
>   seeking me,
> Fancying how happy you were if I could be with you and
>   become your comrade;
> Be it as if I were with you. (Be not too certain but I am
>   now with you.)

Or ("Songs of Parting," 4,5):

> Camerado, this is no book,
> Who touches this touches a man,
> (Is it night? are we here together alone?)

> I love you, I depart from materials,
> I am as one disembodied, triumphant, dead.[2]

Walt Whitman, the man, was editor of the *Brooklyn Eagle* and read his basic ideas in the pages of Emerson, Hegel, and Volney; Walt Whitman, the poetic personage, evolved his ideas from contact with America through imaginary experiences in the bedrooms of New Orleans and on the battlefields of Georgia. That does not necessarily imply falsity. A false fact may be essentially true. It is said that Henry I of England never smiled after the death of his son; the fact, perhaps false, can be true as a symbol of the King's grief. In 1914 it was reported that the Germans had tortured and mutilated a number of Belgian hostages; the statement may have been false, but it effectively summarized the infinite and confused horrors of the invasion. Even more pardonable is the case of those who attribute a doctrine to vital experiences and not to a certain library or a certain epitome. In 1874 Nietzsche ridiculed the Pythagorean thesis that history repeats itself cyclically (*Vom Nutzen und Nachtheil der Historie*, 2); in 1881 he suddenly conceived that thesis on a path in the woods of Silvaplana (*Ecce homo*, 9). One could descend to the level of a detective and speak of plagiarism; if he were asked about it, Nietzsche would reply that the important consideration is the change an idea can cause in us, not the mere formulation of it.[3] The abstract proposition of divine unity is one thing; the flash of light that drove some Arab shepherds out of the desert and forced them into a battle that has not ended and which extended from Aquitaine to the Ganges is another. Whitman's plan was to display an ideal democrat, not to devise a theory.

Since Horace predicted his celestial metamorphosis with a Platonic or Pythagorean image, the theme of the poet's immortality has been classic in literature. Those who utilized it did so from motives of vainglory ("Not marble, nor the gilded monuments"), if not from a kind of bribery or even revenge. From his manipulation of the theme, Whitman derives a personal relationship with each future reader. He identifies himself with the reader, and converses with Whitman ("Salut au Monde!," 3):

> What do you hear, Walt Whitman?

And it was thus that he became the eternal Whitman, the friend who is an old American poet of the eighteen hundreds and also his legend and also each one of us and also happiness. Vast and almost inhuman was the task, but no less important was the victory.

NOTES

1   Henry Seidel Canby (*Walt Whitman* [1943]) and Mark Van Doren in the Viking Press Anthology (1945) recognize that difference very well, but, to my knowledge, they are the only ones who do.

2   The mechanism of these apostrophes is intricate. We are touched by the fact that the poet was moved when he foresaw our emotion. Compare these lines by Flecker, addressed to the poet who will read him a thousand years later:

> O friend unseen, unborn, unknown,
> Student of our sweet English tongue,
> Read out my words at night, alone:
> I was a poet, I was young.

3   Reason and conviction differ so much that the gravest objections to any philosophical doctrine usually pre-exist in the work that declares it. In the *Parmenides* Plato anticipates the argument of the third man which Aristotle will use to oppose him; Berkeley (*Dialogues*, 3) anticipates the refutations of Hume.

Fastball • *Jonathan Williams*

(for WW, Hot for Honorary Installation at Cooperstown)

not just folklore, or
    a tall can of corn (or *Grass* on Cranberry Street)—

to point at the wall and win
       the whole ball of wax . . .

yet
  Walt Whitman

struck out, singing: 'rambled
     all around,
       in & out the town, ram-
     bled til the butchers
        cut him down'

hard from the heels, swung,
     took a notion, had a hankering,
      had good wood, but
        came out—

       a ripple
      in the breeze

bingo!—

    old solitary Whiff-Beard

Autopsy • *Jonathan Williams*

Gentlemen look on this wonder . . .
and wonders within there yet.

"pleurisy of the left side, consumption
of the right lung,

general military tuberculosis
and parenchymatous nephritis . . . a fatty

liver, a huge stone
filling the gall,

a cyst in the adrenal, tubercular abcesses
involving the bones,

and pachymeningitis"

that he was a Kosmos is a piece of news we were hardly prepared for
. . .

good bie Walter dear

Whitman's Song • *Robert Flanagan*

When they tried to catch (to identify and tag) it in clever pens
it rattled and banged, escaped as you on your bed, cagey,
misered one last secret (Traubel scribbling and scribbling), launched
diversionary south and west a troop of wild imaginary bastards.

You and your Self, bodied airs, hugged fiercely together, frightened
boys lost on a raft. When the storm broke, lungs, song-bubbles, collapsed.

Your singing had no more meaning than wind in off the ocean—

less for the curious (the Professor of Gross Morbid Anatomy dissecting)
tracking you down to your last known address.

9.

from "Song of Myself": Intention and Substance

JOHN BERRYMAN

THE ARBITERS of current taste—Pound, Eliot, Auden, others—have generally now declared themselves in favour of Whitman; but always reluctantly
and with a certain resentment or even contempt. I am not able to feel these
reservations myself, but I think I understand their origins and will try
presently to suggest what these are. I like or love Whitman unreservedly;
he operates with great power and beauty over a very wide range, from small
pieces like "A Noiseless, Patient Spider" and "I Saw in Louisiana a Live-Oak
Growing" up through "Out of the Cradle Endlessly Rocking"—a poem in
which a profound experience crucial to the poet's vocation is rendered as
fully as in the Cliff passage in the First Book of *The Prelude* and nearly as
fully as in "Resolution and Independence" (Wordsworth comes first to mind
as being far the greatest poet of his century in England, as Whitman was
here)—up through this range, I say, to *Song of Myself*, which seems to me
easily his most important achievement and indeed the greatest poem so far
written by an American. It is not by any means an easy poem to understand.
It is hard, frequently, to see why the poet is saying what he is saying, and
hard therefore also to see what he is saying. All I mean to do here is to
construct a crude approach that may prove helpful to the discovery of
answers to the questions that these difficulties inspire.

Though I wish so far as possible to avoid the paradoxes that writers on
Whitman too readily indulge in, I note, as an initial problem, that this poem
of fifty pages is the work of a man who agreed with Poe "that (at any rate
for our occasions, our day) there can be no such thing as a long poem" ("The
same thought had been haunting my mind before, but Poe's argument,
though short, worked the sum and proved it to me"—this in 1888). Now
"long" is a relative term, and the author of *The Faerie Queene*, for instance,
may well not have considered *The Rape of Lucrece* (at 1,850 lines) a "long"

152

poem. But clearly this is not what Whitman has in mind. What I think he
does have in mind comes up sharply in another passage: "It is not on 'Leaves
of Grass' distinctively as *literature,* or a specimen thereof, that I feel to dwell,
or advance claims. No one will get at my verses who insists upon viewing
them as a literary performance, or attempt at such performance . . ." He did
not, that is, think of *Song of Myself* as a *long* poem, because he did not think
of it as a poem at all. Our problem has become a question: What then did
he think of it as? The question is quite unanswerable in this form, unless
we say that he thought of it as a work of *life* (as I feel sure he did), but we
can get on by inquiring what it was intended to *do,* what purposes it was
desired to serve. Declared purposes, first; here we have many statements
from him—too many—of which I am going to take four that seem to me
indefeasible. The first is national, the second religious, the third metaphysical, the fourth personal. And although *he* is talking about *Leaves of Grass,*
in quoting him you will understand *me* to be referring to *Song of Myself,* the
epitome of his book, where it stands first.

First: "One main genesis-motive of the 'Leaves' was my conviction (just
as strong today as ever) that the crowning growth of the United States is
to be spiritual and heroic. To help start and favor that growth—or even to
call attention to it, or the need of it—is the beginning, middle and final
purpose of the poems." Nothing could be more comprehensible and explicit, and nothing more incomprehensible or repugnant to most cultivated
readers a century later; though not, as it happens, to me. But in what way
Song of Myself was designed to "favor that growth—or . . . to call attention
to . . . the need of it" is not yet clear.

For the second intention, not less fundamental than the first, I must quote
rather a long passage—in which Whitman had to coin a word, "germenancy," corresponding to "growth" in the first.

When I commenced, years ago, elaborating the plan of my poems, and continued turning
over that plan, and shifting it in my mind through many years, (from the age of twenty-eight
to thirty-five,) experimenting much, and writing and abandoning much, one deep purpose
underlay the others, and has underlain it and its execution ever since—and that has been the
Religious purpose. Amid many changes, and a formulation taking far different shape from
what I at first supposed, this basic purpose has never been departed from in the composition
of my verses. Not of course to exhibit itself in the old ways, as in writing hymns or psalms
with an eye to the church-pew, or to express conventional pietism, or the sickly yearnings
of devotees, but in new ways, and aiming at the widest sub-bases and inclusions of Humanity,
and tallying the fresh air of sea and land. I will see, (said I to myself,) whether there is not,
for my purposes as poet, a Religion, and a sound Religious germenancy in the average
Human Race, at least in their modern development in the United States, and in the hardy
common fiber and native yearnings and elements, deeper and larger, and affording more
profitable returns, than all mere sects or churches—as boundless, joyous, and vital as Nature

itself—A germenancy that has too long been unencouraged, unsung, almost unknown . . .
With Science, the Old Theology of the East, long in its dotage, begins evidently to die and
disappear. But (to my mind) Science—and may be such will prove its principal service—as
evidently prepares the way for One indescribably grander—Time's young but perfect offspring—
the New Theology—heir of the West—lusty and loving, and wondrous beautiful. For
America, and for to-day, just the same as any day, the supreme and final Science is the Science
of God—what we call science being only its minister—as Democracy is or shall be also. And
a poet of America (I said) must fill himself with such thoughts, and chant his best out of
them . . .

You will have observed how intense for Whitman was the despised word
(but not by our political institutions) "average"—a word hardly likely to be
found bearing this exalted stress in Pound or Eliot or Auden. It is clear that
Whitman envisages a post-Christianity (and post-Buddhism, post-Hinduism)
which will serve science and, *eventually* (a dramatic qualification, showing
how little Whitman was taken in by American pretensions), egalitarianism.

Third: as of what I am calling metaphysics, a very short remark: "To the
true and full estimate of the Present both the Past and the Future are main
considerations." It is the second part of this that is startling, and calls in
question the nature of *time;* I suppose being is either associated with, or
precisely dissociated from, time, or is both; this is why I call the present
intention metaphysical. We see that the optimism emotionally visible in the
national and religious intentions is here intellectually asserted. But since we
have come thus so close to what has really to be called doctrine, Whitman's
statement having indeed a dogmatic air, it is time to point out his massive
insistence upon the word "suggestiveness" in all these connections. "I round
and finish little, if anything; and could not, consistently with my scheme."
Again: "I think I have at least enough philosophy not to be too absolutely
certain of anything, or any results." Again: "A great poem is no finish to
a man or woman but rather a beginning."

It is this last quotation that brings him into conflict with current aesthetics, that of the artwork made, finished, autonomous. (Let us concede at once
that *The Waste Land* winds up with various bogus instructions, and so might
be thought to aim at a beginning; but except for the lines about "the awful
daring of a moment's surrender," all this end of that poem is its weakest,
most uneasy, crudest, least inventive, most willed part.) The conflict is
absolute equally in Whitman's formulation of the fourth or *personal* intention. " 'Leaves of Grass' . . ." he says, "has mainly been the outcroppings
of my own emotional and personal nature—an attempt, from first to last,
to put *a Person,* a human being (myself, in the latter part of the Nineteenth
Century, in America,) freely, fully and truly on record." I call your attention
to the incongruity of this formulation with Eliot's amusing theory of the

impersonality of the artist, and a contrast between the mere *putting-on-record* and the well-nigh universal current notion of *creation*, or making things up. You will see that, as Whitman looks more arrogant than Eliot in the Personality, he looks less pretentious in the recording—the mere recording—poet not as *maker* but as spiritual historian—only the history must be, as we'll see in a moment, of the Present—and inquirer (characteristically; Eliot's word in the *Quartets*, "explorer," is more ambitious and charged than "inquirer"). Small wonder—I finish with the arbiters—if they resent Whitman: he has sold the profession short. The poet as creator plays no part in Whitman's scheme at all.

For Whitman the poet is a *voice*. Not solely his own—let us settle this problem quickly: a poet's first personal pronoun is nearly always ambiguous, but we have the plain declaration from Whitman that "the trunk and centre whence the answer was to radiate . . . must be an identical soul and body, a personality—which personality, after many considerings and ponderings I deliberately settled should be myself—indeed could not be any other." I would sorrow over the credulity of anyone who took this account-of-the-decision-as-conscious to be historical; but I am convinced of the reality of the decision. A voice, then, for himself and others; for others *as himself*—this is the intention clearly (an underlying exhibitionism and narcissism we take for granted). What others?—Americans, man. A voice—that is, expressing (not creating)—expressing things already in existence. But what is a voice from?—a *body*. And where?—in America, but this is going to be difficult. And when?—but this is going to be more difficult. And what is in existence? (If anyone doubts that Whitman saw the thing—his intention, his subject— in these apparently abstract but in fact quite literal terms, let him consider these expressions: in Section 23 at the center of *Song of Myself*, "I accept Time, absolutely" and "I accept Reality, and dare not question it"; and as the initial phrase of Section 33, "Space and Time!"—all these capitalized.)

I am going to be most interested in time and existence, but first another word about voice. Other voices in Whitman are regularly metaphors for the human voice, and the voice of the *soul* in Section 5—it must be understood that the "I" in *Song of Myself* often refers only to the body—is metaphorical also, in the exquisite line:

Only the lull I like, the hum of your valvèd voice.

In the light of "lull," the kind of valve here imagined must be a safety valve (compare "loose the stop from your throat" just above): the soul being that which lets the body free a little and then controls it. In the lines immediately following, incest with the soul is dramatized (*by* the body); and that this is not enough we learn from the lines straight after these,

> Swiftly arose and spread around me the peace and
> knowledge that pass all the arguments of the earth,
> And I know that the hand of God is the promise of
> my own . . .

After the New Testament air of the first of these lines, it is clear that "the promise" is a theological allusion, brought over into the New Theology; and suddenly it is also clear that the Johannine *Logos* (God's self-revelation, in Christ—whose name is Word, as His Father's is I AM or Being) influenced Whitman's thought even more than his passion for grand opera, which dominates Section 26:

> The orbic flex of his mouth is pouring and filling me full.

And *when* he is full enough . . . a valve will open. This valve notion, sense of outlet, is crucial to the poem, not only in the fine line discarded in draft (it turned up revised in Section 47)—

> I am your voice—It was tied in you—In me it begins to talk

—but in the marvellous passage in Section 24:

> Through me many long dumb voices
> Voices of the interminable generations of prisoners & slaves,
> Voices of the diseas'd and despairing and of thieves & dwarfs,
> Voices of cycles of preparation & accretion,
> And of the threads that connect the stars, and of
> wombs and of the father-stuff,
> And of the rights of them the others are down upon,
> Of the deform'd, trivial, flat, foolish, despised,
> Fog in the air, beetles rolling balls of dung.

The poet—one would say, a mere channel, but with its own ferocious difficulties—fills with experiences, a valve opens; he speaks them. I am obliged to remark that I prefer this theory of poetry to those that have ruled the critical quarterlies since I was an undergraduate twenty-five years ago. It is as humble as, and identical with, Keats's view of the poet as having no existence, but being "forever in, for, and filling" other things.

Several things have to be said about this passionate sense of identification. In the first place, it supplies the method by which the "I" of the poem is gradually expanded, characterized, and filled with meaning; not until near the end of the poem is the "I" complete—and then it flees. In the second place, the identification is not of course a device adopted for the purposes of the poem; Whitman actually felt thus. Most newspapermen learn to

despise the public; but Whitman wrote in the Brooklyn *Eagle,* shortly after
he became its editor, "There is a curious kind of sympathy (haven't you ever
thought of it before?) that arises in the mind of a newspaper conductor with
the public he serves. He gets to *love* them." These italics are his, and I take
this declaration literally and observe that one always wishes to identify
oneself with the loved object. At the same time we recognize as of psychological origin the profound dissatisfaction (no doubt sexual in character)
that aims at *loss of identity,* in the poem, in two ways, through these
identifications and through death—this is why death is a major subject. But
in the third place, I would deny that this is mystical—indeed, it is the
opposite, as a writer in *PMLA* confessed (in 1955) while producing and
maintaining the monstrous term "inverted mystical." I object to the word
"mystical" in relation to Whitman altogether, as a mere grab-bag term, like
"instinct," for whatever we don't happen to understand, unless it refers to
the perfectly well-known phenomena described in the *Philokalia,* say, and
the works of the English and Spanish mystics. I see no need for a single word
to apply to the complicated phenomenon we are now studying, since none
exists. In the fourth place, this process of identification has limits; it does
not include God. God is envisaged as our lover, first, not very different from
ourselves, except that, second, he provides for us. These roles are important,
certainly, but still leave man very much on his own—though, Whitman
insists, incurious and at peace with this idea. Identification is limited also
within humanity: as against "myself and my neighbors, refreshing, wicked,
real," in Section 42 there are people so despicable, so unreal, that the poet
denies them even personal pronouns, suddenly saying:

> Here and there with dimes on the eyes walking,
> To feed the greed of the belly the brain liberally spooning,
> Tickets buying, taking, selling, but in to the feast
> never once going,
> Many sweating, ploughing, thrashing, and then the chaff
> for payment receiving,
> A few idly owning, and they the wheat continually
> claiming.

It is clear that the allusion to the parable of the Wedding Feast in the third
line has called up the participles in the next line corresponding to "wailing
and gnashing of teeth," and that what the poet is thinking about is the
punishment of the *self-*excluded: the living dead, the sullen, the greedy, the
extortionate. These excepted, all are invited to the identification—the New
Kingdom. . . .

1957

Despair • *John Berryman*

It seems to be DARK all the time.
I have difficulty walking.
I can remember what to say to my seminar
but I don't know that I want to.

I said in a Song once: I am unusually tired.
I repeat that & increase it.
I'm vomiting.
I broke down today in the slow movement of K.365.

I certainly don't think I'll last much longer.
I wrote: 'There may be horribles.'
I increase that.
(I think she took her little breasts away.)

I am in love with my excellent baby.
Crackles! in darkness HOPE; & disappears.
Lost arts.
Vanishings.

Walt! We're downstairs,
even you don't comfort me
but I join your risk my dear friend & go with you.
There are no matches

Utter, His Father, one word

from A Common Ground • *Denise Levertov*

iii

> . . . everything in the world must
> excel itself to be itself.
> —*Pasternak*

Not 'common speech'
a dead level
but the uncommon speech of paradise,
tongue in which oracles
speak to beggars and pilgrims:

not illusion but what Whitman called
'the path
between reality and the soul,'
a language
excelling itself to be itself,

speech akin to the light
with which at day's end and day's
renewal, mountains
sing to each other across the cold valleys.

10.

The Delicacy of Walt Whitman

JAMES WRIGHT

THE PUBLIC MASK, the coarse Whitman, is false. Then what is true? Is there a private Whitman who is delicate, and if there *is* a delicate Whitman, what is his poetry like? Where can we find it? And what does it have to do with those of us who want to read it? Is Whitman's delicacy a power that is alive in American poetry at the present moment? If so, who is displaying it? And is it capable of growth?

The *delicacy* of Walt Whitman. I do not mean to imply that Whitman was delicate as Nietzsche, for example, was in delicate health. Whitman really does seem to have been a strong man, in spite of the public mask's strident insistence on his own vigor. His actions were often modest and yet they demonstrate a physical condition astonishingly robust. When the war began, Whitman was forty-two years old. He went into the war. He did not have to go. I am not concerned with arguing the ethical significance of his relation to the war. I point only to the fact. In an essay published in the *Sewanee Review,* Mr. James M. Cox eloquently describes Whitman's exploit in terms which reveal the abundant physical strength of the man:

Whitman's role in the Civil War stands as one of the triumphs of our culture. That this figure should have emerged from an almost illiterate background to become a national poet, that he should have at the age of forty-two gone down into the wilderness of Virginia to walk across the bloody battlefields ministering to the sick and wounded, that he should have paced through the hospitals and kept a vigil over the mutilated victims on both sides, that he should have created the war in prose and poetry of an extraordinarily high order—that he should have done these deeds shows how truly he had cast himself in the heroic mould.

So the delicacy I have in mind is not an empty gentility, nor the physical frailty that sometimes slithers behind arrogance. It is the delicacy of his *poetry* that concerns me. It has its source in the character of Whitman himself, and it is, I believe, available to American poetry at the present time.

161

Whitman's poetry has delicacy of music, of diction, and of form. The word "delicacy" can do without a rhetorically formal definition; but I mean it to suggest powers of restraint, clarity, and wholeness, all of which taken together embody that deep spiritual inwardness, that fertile strength, which I take to be the most beautiful power of Whitman's poetry, and the most readily available to the poetry, and indeed the civilization, of our own moment in American history.

If what I say is true, then we are almost miraculously fortunate to have Whitman available to us. For some time the features of American poetry most in evidence have been very different from Whitman's: in short, recent American poetry has often been flaccid, obtuse and muddied, and fragmentary, crippled almost. Yet there is great talent alive in our country today, and if the spirit of Whitman can help to rescue that talent from the fate of so many things in America, that begin nobly and end meanly, then we ought to study him as carefully as we can. What is his poetry like?

Let us consider first the delicacy of his music. And since I want to listen to the music closely, a few notes on traditional prosody are in order. At this point Whitman himself is ready to help us. As a stylist, he did not begin as a solitary barbarian (in Ortega's sense of that word). He is many things that are perhaps discomforting and even awkward, but he is not a smug fool—he is not an imitation Dead End Kid pretending that no poet or man of any kind ever existed before he was born upon the earth. Whitman realizes that the past has existed.

He also understands how the past continues to exist: it exists in the present, and comes into living form only when some individual man is willing to challenge it. Whitman dares, like Nietzsche, to challenge not only what he dislikes but also what he *values*. "The power to destroy or remould," writes Whitman in the 1855 Preface to *Leaves of Grass*, "is freely used by him [the greatest poet] but never the power of attack. What is past is past. If he does not expose superior models and prove himself by every step he takes he is not what is wanted."

It seems to me of the gravest importance that Whitman's relation to established traditonal forms of poetry and of society itself be clarified, so that we may free him from the tone of pretentious ignorance that has been associated with his mere name, from time to time, by fools. He knows that the past exists, and he knows that, as a poet and as a man, he has a right to live. His duty to the past is precisely this: to have the courage to live and to create his own poetry.

This is the great way of learning from the noble spirits of the past. And the most difficultly courageous way of asserting the shape and meaning of one's own poetry and one's own life is to challenge and surpass those very traditions and masters whom one can honestly respect. This deep spiritual kinship between a truly original man and the nobility of the past is formulated thus by Goethe: "People always talk of the study of the ancients; but what does that mean, except that it says, turn your attention to the real world, and try to express it, for that is what the ancients did when they were alive" (*Conversations with Eckermann*). And so in Whitman's music we find him turning away from one masterfully delicate verbal musician, Longfellow, toward the real world. Whitman respected Longfellow for his true gifts, as we ought to do. Our own scorn of Longfellow is cant. It is like the scorn of the great Victorian Englishmen that prevailed until recently under the influence of Lytton Strachey; we scurry forth like insects to deface them as soon as a serious, honorable man like Strachey assures us that Dickens, Tennyson, and Florence Nightingale are safely dead. So let us turn, for just a moment, to Longfellow, whose lovely poetry, even in his own time, was in the strict sense a musical embodiment of the European past. In *Specimen Days* ("My Tribute to Four Poets"), Whitman records a visit to Longfellow which unmistakably reveals his true respect for the poet who was almost universally celebrated as the great poet whom Whitman himself would like to be: "I shall not soon forget his lit-up face," says Whitman, "and glowing warmth and courtesy in the modes of what is called the old school." And then Whitman suddenly, and rather startlingly, remarks on his own poetic relation to Longfellow and others (Emerson, Whittier, and Bryant):

In a late magazine one of my reviewers, who ought to know better, speaks of my "attitude of contempt and scorn and intolerance" toward the leading poets—of my "deriding" them, and preaching their "uselessness." If anybody cares to know what I think—and have long thought and avow'd—about them, I am entirely willing to propound. I can't imagine any better luck befalling these States for a poetical beginning and initiation than has come from Emerson, Longfellow, Bryant, and Whittier. . . . Longfellow for rich color, graceful forms and incidents—all that makes life beautiful and love refined—competing with the singers of Europe on their own ground, and with one exception, better and finer work than that of any of them.

Furthermore Whitman's deep humility (an intellectual as well as a moral virtue) appears in his note on the "Death of Longfellow" (*Specimen Days*). There, in the very act of praising Longfellow for his best gift ("verbal melody") he speaks of his radical inadequacy; and thus Whitman inadvertently, almost as an afterthought, identifies his own great strength:

Longfellow in his voluminous works seems to me to be eminent in the style and forms of poetical expression that mark the present age, (an idiosyncrasy, almost a sickness, of verbal melody,). . . . He is certainly the sort of bard and counter-actant most needed for our materialistic, self-assertive, money-worshipping, Anglo-Saxon races, and especially for the present age in America—an age tyrannically regulated with reference to the manufacturer, the merchant, the financier, the politician and the day workman—for whom and among whom he comes as the poet of melody, courtesy, deference—*poet of the mellow twilight of the past* in Italy, Germany, Spain, and Northern Europe. . . . He strikes a splendid average, and does not sing exceptional passions, or humanity's jagged escapades. He is not revolutionary, brings nothing offensive or new, does not deal hard blows. . . . His very anger is gentle, is at second hand, (as in the "Quadroon Girl" and the "Witnesses."). . . To the ungracious complaint-charge of his want of racy nativity and special originality, I shall only say that America and the world may well be reverently thankful—can never be thankful enough—for any such singing-bird vouchsafed out of the centuries, without asking that the notes be different from those of other songsters; adding what I have heard Longfellow himself say, that ere the New World can be worthily original, and announce herself and her own heroes, she must be well saturated with the originality of others, and respectfully consider the heroes that lived before Agamemnon.

The whole passage is moved by an impulse to pass beyond. Not merely to pass beyond what one hates—the phoniness, the counterfeit poetry which is always among us in its thousand blind, mean, sly forms. But to pass beyond what one loves, to open one's ears, to know what one is doing and why. It is a noble statement by a delicate and reverent man.

Let us apply the statement to Whitman's own music. In effect, he tunes his verses toward those very crass and difficult subjects which Longfellow (for whatever reason) avoided. And yet, even so, Whitman's music is not "jagged" like the escapades of that American humanity he often sings of. It is a *delicate* music, a deeper sound than that of Longfellow; it is alive, and it hurts, as men are hurt on the jagged edges of their own lives.

So Whitman respected Longfellow, a traditional prosodist. In spite of his poems like "Evangeline," which we are told to read as though they were written in the classical dactylic hexameter, Longfellow is predominantly an iambic writer. Moreover, he writes the iambic meter with a masterful grasp of its permissive variations: the elisions, the trochaic substitutions, the spondaic effects and their euphonious combination within regular iambic patterns. But Longfellow does not write about American life. He does not write about its externals. And, shunning its externals, he does not penetrate to its spirit. Whitman notices these radical limits in the very act of praising Longfellow for his mastery—mastery of a kind which forces him to turn away from the living world and to sing either of Europe or of the American past.

Whitman also brings a rare technical understanding of prosody to bear on the American present. But in his concern to surpass tradition, he deliberately shuns the iambic measure and all its variations, except in a very few instances (like the notorious "O Captain! My Captain!" and the less frequently quoted "Ethiopia Saluting the Colors") which offer a helpful contrast to the inventive delicacy of music in Whitman's greater poems.

He shuns the iambic measure. He says, in the 1855 Preface, "The rhythm and uniformity of perfect poems show the free growth of metrical laws, and bud from them as unerringly and loosely as lilacs and roses on a bush, and take shapes as compact as the shapes of chestnuts and oranges." Does Whitman mean that "free growth" is aimless? No, he speaks of "metrical laws." Listen to his poem 'Reconciliation":

> Word over all, beautiful as the sky,
> Beautiful that war and all its deeds of carnage must in time
>   be utterly lost,
> That the hands of the sisters Death and Night incessantly
>   softly wash again, and ever again, this soil'd world;
> For my enemy is dead, a man divine as myself is dead,
> I look where he lies white-faced and still in the coffin—I draw
>   near,
> Bend down and touch lightly with my lips the white face
>   in the coffin.

We cannot understand this poem's music in traditional prosodic terms. Still, it's fun to note that Whitman did not write non-iambic verse out of pique at his inability to control its rules. Listen again to Whitman's opening line: "Word over all, beautiful as the sky." The line is a flawless iambic pentameter; he uses a trochaic substitution in the first foot, a hovering spondaic echo between the second and third feet, a daring and yet perfectly traditional inversion; and he successfully runs two light stresses before the final strong stress.

It seems to me wonderful that Whitman should have written that line, which is not only iambic, but as bold in its exploitation of the iambic possibilities as the masters themselves: Campion, Herrick, Wyatt, even Milton. And that is not so strange. In a note on "British Literature" (*Collect: Notes Left Over*), Whitman writes the following: "To avoid mistake, I would say that I not only commend the study of this literature, but wish our sources of supply and comparison vastly enlarged." The trouble is that "the British element these states hold, and have always held, enormously beyond its fit proportions ... its products are no models for us." So he does not hate traditional British prosody, which is of course predominantly iambic. He loves its great craft, and he shows his ability to emulate it. But he is an adventurer; he wants to listen beyond the admittedly rich music of iambic, and to report what he hears.

In prosody, then, Whitman is sometimes a destroyer, but we must see that he knows exactly what he is destroying. He is both theoretically and practically ready to replace it with a new prosody of his own. He begins with a supremely sensitive ear for the music of language; he moves beyond the permissive variations of iambic; and he is not afraid of the new musical possibilities out there, so he brings some of them back with him. Perhaps they were there all the time; perhaps they are the quantitative possibilities of the classical languages that have drifted around in English. In any case, the iambic conventions do not seem to make much provision for them; and yet they can be incredibly beautiful in Whitman. We need only listen:

> Come lovely and soothing death,
> Undulate round the world, serenely arriving, arriving,
> In the day, in the night, to all, to each,
> Sooner or later delicate death.

Whitman really does have something to teach current American poets, in spite of his entering American poetry once again, in Mr. Randall Jarrell's wicked phrase, as "the hero of a de Mille movie about Whitman"—a movie, one might add, which co-stars the Dead End Kids.

To summarize, Whitman can teach us about some possibilities of musical delicacy in our language. He sympathetically understood iambic forms (exemplified by Longfellow) which in his own poems he is trying to break and surpass. He can also teach courage, for he has great rhythmical daring; he seeks constantly for a music which really echoes and fulfills his imaginative vision.

He becomes a great artist by the ways of growth which Nietzsche magnificently describes in the first speech of *Thus Spake Zarathustra:* the Three Metamorphoses of the Spirit. The spirit that truly grows, says Nietzsche, will first be a camel, a beast of burden, who labors to bear the forms of the past, whether in morality or art or anything else; then he will change into a lion, and destroy not merely what he hates but even what he loves and understands; and the result of this concerned and accurate destruction will be the spirit's emergence as a child, who is at last able to create clearly and powerfully from within his own imagination.

Whitman says of the great poet, "He swears to his art, I will not be meddlesome, I will not have in my writings any elegance, or effect, or originality, to hang in the way between me and the rest like curtains. I will have nothing hang in the way, not the richest curtains" (Preface, 1855). And Whitman is well aware of the many curtains that can hang in the way. There is not only the old-world elegance of Longfellow—which may stand for the prosodic traditions of England, beautiful in themselves—but there is also the curtain of aimless destructiveness, which is eventually not even destructive but just trivial. In "After Trying a Certain Book" (*Specimen Days*), Whitman says that the difficulty of explaining what a poem means is not to be taken as evidence that the poem means nothing: "Common teachers or critics are always asking 'What does it mean?' Symphony of fine musician, or sunset, or sea-waves rolling up the beach—what do they mean? Undoubtedly in the most subtle-elusive sense they mean something—but who shall fathom and define those meanings? (*I do not intend this as a warrant for wildness and frantic escapades. . . .*)" (My italics.) Every scholar and every Beat who mentions Whitman ought to read that salutary note beforehand.

Now I want to speculate on the delicacy of Whitman's diction, his choice of words. What is remarkable is not merely his attempt to include new things—objects, persons, places, and events—in his poems. Something more interesting and complex goes on: in the face of this sometimes difficult and prosaic material ("humanity's jagged escapades"), he is able to retain his delicacy, which is a power of mind as well as a quality of kindness. In a crisis, he keeps his head and his feelings alert. He can be as precise as Henry James, as Mr. Jarrell rightly says; but he is sensitively precise about things that are often in themselves harsh, even brutal.

Mr. Jarrell has written one of the liveliest accounts of Whitman's delicacy of diction, and I refer the reader to that essay. Perhaps Mr. Jarrell does not sufficiently emphasize the enormous strength and courage it required even to face some of the horrible things Whitman faced, much less to claim them for the imagination by means of a diction that is as delicate as that of Keats. One of my favorite poems in Whitman is "A March in the Ranks Hard-prest, and the Road Unknown" from *Drum-Taps*. It reveals perfectly what I mean about Whitman's delicate diction: his power of retaining his sensitivity right in the fact of realities that would certainly excuse coarseness, for the sake of self-defense if for no other reason. But Whitman does not defend himself. As he had told us in a Virgilian line, one of the noblest lines of poetry ever written, "I was the man, I suffered, I was there." The line is great because it is not a boast but a modest bit of information, almost as unobtrusive as a stage-direction or perhaps a whispered aside to the reader. (Whitman is always whispering to us—that is another of his musical delicacies.) There he certainly is, gathering the horror into his delicate words, soothing it if possible, always looking at it and in the deepest sense imagining it:

A march in the ranks hard-prest, and the road unknown,

A route through a heavy wood with muffled steps in the
  darkenss,
Our army foil'd with loss severe, and the sullen remnant re-
  treating,
Till after midnight glimmer upon us the lights of a dim-
  lighted building,
We come to an open space in the woods, and halt by the
  dim-lighted building,
'Tis a large old church at the crossing roads, now an im-
  promptu hospital,
Entering but for a minute I see a sight beyond all the pictures
  and poems ever made,
Shadows of deepest, deepest black, just lit by moving candles
  and lamps,
And by one great pitchy torch stationary with wild red flame
  and clouds of smoke,
By these, crowds, groups of forms vaguely I see on the floor,
  some in the pews laid down,
At my feet more distinctly a soldier, a mere lad, in danger of
  bleeding to death, (he is shot in the abdomen,)
I stanch the blood temporarily, (the youngster's face is white
  as a lily,)
Then before I depart I sweep my eyes o'er the scene fain to
  absorb it all,
Faces, varieties, postures beyond description, most in obscurity, some of them dead,
Surgeons operating, attendants holding lights, the smell of
  ether, the odor of blood,
The crowd, O the crowd of the bloody forms, the yard outside
  also fill'd,
Some on the bare ground, some on planks or stretchers, some
  in the death-spasm sweating,
An occasional scream or cry, the doctor's shouted orders or
  calls,
The glisten of the little steel instruments catching the glint of
  the torches,
These I resume as I chant, I see again the forms, I smell the
  odor,
Then hear outside the orders given, *Fall in, my men, fall in;*
But first I bend to the dying lad, his eyes open, a half-smile
  gives he me,
Then the eyes close, calmly close, and I speed forth to the
  darkness,
Resuming, marching, ever in darkness marching, on in the
  ranks,
The unknown road still marching.

I want to draw attention to a single small detail of diction, which becomes huge because of its delicacy. I mean the phrase about the wounded young man's face. He suddenly looms up out of the confusion and darkness; he has been shot in the abdomen; and his face, buffaloed by shock, is "white as a lily."

There have been many poets in America who would compare a white face with a lily. There are also many poets who attempt to deal with a subject matter that is, like Whitman's, very far from the traditional materials of poesy as Longfellow understood them. Moreover, I know that there are many brave American men who write about painful experiences. But what is special about Whitman, what makes his diction remarkable in itself and fertile for us today, is that he does all three of these things at once, and in him they become a single act of creation. Unless we can see the nobility of his courage, then we have neither the right nor the intelligence to talk about the delicacy of his style.

Whitman's diction contains a lesson that can actually be learned, and it does not require the vain imitation of his personal appearance and stylistic mannerisms. It is more spiritually inward than any external accident can suggest. It is this: he deliberately seeks in American life the occasions and persons who are central to that life; he sometimes finds them harsh and violent, as in the war; and he responds to the harshness with a huge effort of imagination: to be delicate, precise, sensitive.

I realize that it is difficult to distinguish between the delicacy of Whitman's diction and his sensitivity as a man. But that is just the point. When a certain kind of diction, like a certain kind of meter, is employed by a coarse man, it automatically becomes a mannerism, or perhaps a stock device, detachable from the body of the poem, like a false eyelash, or a shapely artificial breast. Any concentration upon Whitman's stylistic mannerisms alone betrays an obsession with external, accidental things. Perhaps that is why so many bad poets have claimed Whitman as an ancestor.

I want also to say something about the delicacy of form in Whitman's poems. I think at once of the sentence in the 1855 Preface about rhythm and what he calls "uniformity." Here is the sentence again: "The rhythm and uniformity of perfect poems show the free growth of metrical laws, and bud from them as unerringly and loosely as lilacs and roses on a bush, and take shapes as compact as the shapes of chestnuts and oranges."

This sentence can help us to understand what "form" meant to Whitman and also what it might mean to contemporary poets in America and elsewhere, if they have truly learned from Whitman and still wish to learn from him. The word "form" itself, however, may be ambiguous. So I will shun rhetorical definitions, which often threaten to mislead or oversimplify; and I will discuss a single short poem that, I believe, is a great poem because of the almost perfect delicacy of its form:

> I heard you solemn-sweet pipes of the organ as last Sunday
>   morn I pass'd the church,
> Winds of autumn, as I walk'd the woods at dusk I heard
>   your long-strech'd sighs up above so mournful,
> I heard the perfect Italian tenor singing at the opera, I heard
>   the soprano in the midst of the quartet singing;
> Heart of my love! you too I heard murmuring low through
>   one of the wrists around my head,
> Heard the pulse of you when all was still ringing little bells
>   last night under my ear.

Does this poem have a form? If so, how can I describe it without losing in a general classification the very details that give the poem its life? I can think of at least two possibly helpful ways of answering these questions. First, Mr. Gay Wilson Allen (in his definitive biography of Whitman) supplies us with a crucial bit of textual information. The version of "I heard you solemn-sweet pipes" which I just quoted is not the only one. An earlier version, one of three poems which Whitman published in 1861, is quoted and discussed by Mr. Allen. The revisions are almost all deletions. The earlier version (printed in the New York *Leader*, October 12, 1861) contained apostrophes to "war-suggesting trumpets," to "you round-lipp'd cannons." In the version which Whitman apparently considered final (printed in the "Deathbed" edition of 1892), the references to war are deleted. Whitman also deleted a whole single line, in which he addresses a lady who played "delicious music on the harp."

What is left? A simple poem of five lines. Whitman addresses four different sounds. In these apostrophes and in his arrangement of them we can find the form of his poem.

The form is that of parallelism. But immediately we have to distinguish between the grammatical signification of "parallelism" and Whitman's actual use of it. A grammatical parallelism is primarily concerned with sentence-structure: noun balances noun, verb balances verb, either as repetition or as antithesis. But in Whitman's poem, the appearance of grammatical parallelism is so rare as to be almost accidental. In fact, he almost seems to avoid it. For he uses parallelism not as a device of repetition but as an occasion for development. For this reason, we take a certain risk when we read "I heard you solemn-sweet pipes." After the first two lines, we can know only two things: first, we cannot hope to rest on mere parallel sentence-structure;

second, the poet is probably going to sing about another sound, but it might be the sound of anything. (The possibility is a little scary in a country where, for example, President Coolidge's taciturnity is automatically considered a joke, instead of a great civic virtue. Behind the uneasy joke lies the dreadful suspicion that we talk too much.) There is no way to read Whitman's poem at all unless we yield ourselves to its principle of growth, a principle that reveals itself only in this particular poem, stage by stage.

Whitman first tries to make sure that we will not confuse his poetic forms with the rules of grammar; and then he lets his images grow, one out of another; and finally, we discover the form of the poem as we read it, and we know what it is only after we have finished.

It is this kind of formal growth that, I believe, gives special appropriateness to Whitman's mention of "shapes as compact as the shapes of chestnuts and oranges." These fruits do indeed have "shapes"—delicate shapes indeed. And they are compact, not diffuse. Their life depends on their form, which grows out of the forms of blossoms, which in turn grew out of the forms of trees, which in turn grew out of the forms of seeds. If I followed the changes that overwhelm an orange seed, I should be startled at the unexpected form of each stage of growth; but the form would be there nevertheless, however unexpected: at once undreamed-of and inevitable.

I have avoided the term "organic unity" because I wanted to read Whitman's poem afresh; and I am afraid that we might confuse the philosophical definition of a term in aesthetics with our empirical attempt to pay attention to the form of a poem. Just as bad poets tend to substitute the external accidents of Whitman's personal mannerisms and habits of dress for his poetry, so we readers might tend to substitute a general term for our reading of poetry—any poetry. If you mention the name of Laforgue, for example, it is a rare graduate student who will not immediately say, or think, the phrase "romantic irony," just as certain famous dogs helplessly salivated when a bell was rung. That's a good simile, as W. C. Fields once observed in another connection. Moreover, the simile is horrible; I wish I could make it even more so.

What is "form"? It is not simply the rules of grammar. And it cannot simply be equated with certain conventions of iambic verse. When reviewers of current American verse say that a certain poem is written "in form," they usually mean it is predominantly iambic, either skillful or clumsy. But the form in Whitman's poems is not iambic. Form, in Whitman, is a principle of growth: one image or scene or sound *grows* out of another. The general device is parallelism, not of grammar but of action or some other meaning. Here is a further example of the parallel form, which is delicate and precise

and therefore very powerful but which is not based on the repetition of the
sentence-structure:

> The little one sleeps in its cradle,
> I lift the gauze and look a long time, and silently brush away
> 　flies with my hand.

> The youngster and the red-faced girl turn aside up the bushy
> 　hill,
> I peeringly view them from the top.

> The suicide sprawls on the bloody floor of the bedroom,
> I witness the corpse with its dabbled hair, I note where the
> 　pistol has fallen.
> ("Song of Myself," Section 8)

Form in Whitman is a principle of imagination: the proliferating of
images out of one unifying vision. Every real poem has its own form, which
cannot be discovered through rhetoric, but only through imagination. Whitman can teach current American poets to destroy their own rhetoric and
trust their own imagination. I shudder to think what would happen if every
current versifier in America were to do that. (Is it a shudder of joy? A risky
question.)

I began by asking what Whitman has to do with us, and where he is to
be found. Some great writers of the past continue to exist as objects of
veneration and study. They are no less great for all that. But Whitman is
different, at least for us in America today, scholars and poets alike. Of course
he deserves veneration, and he receives it. But he is also an immediate
presence. He demands attention whether he is venerated or not. His work
is capable of exerting direct power upon some conventional divisions in
American life; and the power can heal the division. For example, in America
today we still suffer from the conventional division between scholarly study
of poetry on one hand and the attempt to practice the living art of poetry
on the other. But consider Mr. Malcolm Cowley's 1959 reprinting of the first
edition of *Leaves of Grass*. The reprinting is a work of the most careful
scholarship: textual, historical, and biographical. It fully deserves the attention of scholars in the most dignified learned journals. It is respected by
scholars who modestly accept their roles as "academics"—men who labor
faithfully by day at the scholarly profession, and are not especially interested
in reading current American verse during their evenings at home with their
families. And yet ... Mr. Cowley's reprinting of the 1855 *Leaves of Grass*

is not only an act of sound scholarship: it is also an act of living poetry. I am sure that Mr. Cowley felt the relevance of Whitman's first edition to any lively interest in current American verse; but I doubt if he could have anticipated the effect of its living presence. The book itself is the newest poetry we have. It is as though the true spirit of Whitman had returned among us in order to rescue himself from the misinterpretations and abuses of his coarse imitators. He is, quite literally, living among us at this very moment; he has just published a new book; his poetry doesn't sound at all like the vast (too vast) clutter of work in two fairly representative anthologies of recent American verse: *The New Poets of England and America* (Meridian Books, 1957) and *The New American Poetry* (Grove Press, 1960). He is newer than both; he is precise, courageous, delicate, and seminal—an abundant poet. I think it would be entirely appropriate to award a prize to Whitman for a beautiful first book; and to Mr. Cowley for a revelation in which scholarship and thrilling poetic vitality are one and the same.

I think Whitman can also be found in other places, and I will mention two of them.

The delicate strength of Whitman was recognized and loved long ago by poets in the Spanish language. It is remarkable how often they speak of him. Often they speak of him in poems. I have in mind Federico García Lorca's magnificent "Ode to Walt Whitman," written in New York City at the end of the twenties. But the spirit of Whitman is everywhere present among Spanish and South American poets: in the form which rejects external rhetoric in order to discover and reveal a principle of growth; in the modesty and simplicity of diction; in the enormously courageous willingness to leap from one image into the unknown, in sheer faith that the next image will appear in the imagination; in the sensitive wholeness of the single poems which result from such imaginative courage; and, above all, in the belief in the imagination as the highest flowering of human life (the phrase belongs to Jorge Guillén), not just a rhetorical ornament. These are all powers of Whitman's spirit. They have been enlivening Spanish poetry for at least fifty years.

Moreover, we are in the midst of a wave of translation in the United States. The September, 1961, issue of *Poetry* (Chicago) is entirely devoted to translation. The poems of Pablo Neruda of Chile, César Vallejo of Peru, and of several great writers from Spain—Juan Ramón Jiménez, Antonio Machado, Jorge Guillén, Miguel Hernandez, and Blas de Otero, to name only a few—are being not only read but also translated by several American writers, and this effort cannot help but lead to Whitman. It is sometimes said that the true spirit of Poe was absorbed into contemporary American literature only after Poe had been truly understood by the French. Perhaps the true Whitman may return to the United States from Spain and South America "through the sky that is below the ground" (Jiménez).

We have spirits capable of welcoming him. Louis Simpson's imagination is obsessed with the most painful details of current American life, which he reveals under a very powerfully developed sense of American history. Several of his latest poems directly address Whitman as a figure who discovers that the Open Road has led to the barren Pacific, to the used-car graveyard, to the earthly paradise of the real-estate agents. Mr. Simpson describes America and Americans in a vision totally free from advertising and propaganda, just as Whitman described the Civil War soldiers, not as "Our Boys" or such like, but rather as startled white faces of youths shot in the abdomen.

Robert Bly's Whitmanesque powers include the ability to write about what he calls "the dark figures of politics." A remarkable sequence describing such "figures" is *Poems for the Ascension of J. P. Morgan*, published in *New World Writing #15*. I want to quote a new poem of Bly's. It is called "After the Industrial Revolution, All Things Happen at Once."

> Now we enter a strange world, where the Hessian Christmas
> Still goes on, and Washington has not reached the other shore;
> The Whiskey boys
> Are gathering again on the meadows of Pennsylvania
> And the Republic is still sailing on the open sea.
>
> In 1956 I saw a black angel in Washington, dancing
> On a barge, saying, Let us now divide kennel dogs
> And hunting dogs; Henry Cabot Lodge, in New York,
> Talking of sugar cane in Cuba; Ford,
> In Detroit, drinking mothers' milk;
> Ford, saying, "History is bunk!"
> And Wilson saying, "What is good for General Motors—"
>
> Who is it, singing? Don't you hear singing?
> It is the dead of Cripple Creek;
> Coxey's army
> Like turkeys are singing from the tops of trees!
> And the Whiskey Boys are drunk outside Philadelphia.

Denise Levertov, an extremely gifted poet, suggests Whitman in several ways: her reverence for the civilization of the past, so deep as to be utterly modest; her willingness to discover the new forms of her imagination; and her nobility of spirit, which knows what is worthy of celebration and is capable of great moral understanding. Two of her recent poems (included in her superb book from New Directions, *The Jacob's Ladder*), "In Memory of Boris Pasternak" and "During the Eichmann Trial," embody this nobility perfectly. The latter sequence includes a cry of pity for Adolf Eichmann; and Miss Levertov sees everyone in the twentieth century caught and exposed in Eichmann's glass cage. The subject is almost unendurably horrible; and it is treated with a tenderness which is in itself an imaginative strength of great purity.

So Whitman is alive; in person, with his own poems; in spirit, among the Spanish writers who long ago understood him; and among certain American writers, in their translations and in their own spiritual courage. Whitman has delicacy; moreover, he dared to subject his delicacy to the tests of the real world, both the external world of nineteenth-century America, with its wars and loud cities and buffaloes vanishing into herds of clouds, and the inner world of his spirit. He loved the human body, he knew that when you kill a man he dies, and he exposed his feelings to the coarsest of wars in order to record its truth. He had nothing against British literature; but he felt that Americans have even greater stores of imagination to draw upon. Here are some of his words, from *Collect: Notes Left Over:*

I strongly recommend all the young men and young women of the United States to whom it may be eligible, to overhaul the well-freighted fleets, the literature of Italy, Spain, France, Germany, so full of those elements of freedom, self-possession, gay-heartedness, subtlety, dilation, needed in preparations for the future of the States. I only wish we could have really good translations. I rejoice at the feeling for Oriental researches and poetry, and hope it will continue.

The man who wrote those words was not only a very great poet. He was also a generous human being, and he rejoiced in the hopes of his fellows. I believe that American poetry at this moment is able to show itself worthy of Whitman's intelligence, his courage, his supremely delicate imagination. At any rate, many living American poets cherish Whitman's best powers; and one cannot love such things without being inwardly changed. We honor Whitman; and we share the happy thought that he would have been delighted and would have wanted to honor us in return. Surely he would have loved another new American poem which occurs to me, for it speaks with his own best voice—uncluttered, courageous, and kind. The poem is Mr. David Ignatow's "Walt Whitman in the Civil War Hospitals," which I quote in its entirety:

Prescient, my hands soothing
their foreheads, by my love
I earn them. In their presence

I am wretched as death. They smile
to me of love. They cheer me
and I smile. These are stones
in the catapulting world;
they fly, bury themselves in flesh,
in a wall, in earth; in midair
break against each other
and are without sound.
I sent them catapulting.
They outflew my voice
towards vacant spaces,
but I have called them farther,
to the stillness beyond,
to death which I have praised.

Communion • *David Ignatow*

Let us be friends, said Walt,
and buildings sprang up
quick as corn and people
were born into them, stock
brokers, admen, lawyers and doctors
and they contended
  among themselves
that they might know
   each other.

Let us be friends, said Walt.
We are one and occasionally two
of which the one is made
and cemeteries were laid out
miles in all directions
to fill the plots with the old
and young, dead of murder, disease,
rape, hatred, heartbreak and insanity
to make way for the new
and the cemeteries spread over the land
their white scab monuments.

Let us be friends, said Walt, and the graves
were opened and coffins laid on top
of one another for lack of space.
It was then the gravediggers slit
their throats, being alone in the world,
not a friend to bury.

Son to Father

DAVID IGNATOW

I SEE MY RELATIONSHIP to Whitman as that of a dissident son to an over-demanding father. He demands, as he does of himself, total allegiance to a transcendental version of existence. I can't see it, especially not on or in his terms. Quite possibly, if he had lived long enough to see the technological advances in space exploration, he would have begun to sense our isolation in the universe which would have given him an altogether different and desolating view of man's relationship to the universe and to himself, the view with which most of us hold, and so while I look on him as a totally affectionate father, one from whom I learned how to free myself from the constraint of given ideas and behavior patterns, not only in poetry but in life too, I cannot accept his acceptance of Nineteenth Century piety in relation to a godhead, nor to a vision of so-called progress, nor a vision of the perfection of man, nor of man's ultimate union in brotherhood. He has lost me there, and yet I deeply regret the loss and sometimes find myself expecting the miracle to happen. Whitman is great because he has given us these issues to debate, to resolve, central to our own existence. His genius as poet all of us now take for granted, even such academicians as Harold Bloom but, of course, with the kind of distortion peculiar to ideologues, which is Bloom's main virtue, and it's not a poetic virtue so that applying his theories to Whitman's work we no longer recognize Whitman as a poet, but this is another story in my "quarrel" with Whitman who now has been taken over by the academicians for their own private literary obsessions.

Waiting Inside • *David Ignatow*

I protest my isolation
but protest is a mark of my defeat,
even as I write.
　　Being a victim,
I am an accuser. Being human,
others feel my fallen weight
upon their thoughts and are oppressed—
as I am, their guilt unlike mine
and unrelated and without hope in it
of change for me.
　　Guilty, my oppressor
and I go separate ways
though we could relieve each other
by going together, as Whitman wrote,
with our arms around each other's waists,
in support.

from The Abyss • *Theodore Roethke*

2

I have been spoken to variously
But heard little.
My inward witness is dismayed
By my unguarded mouth.
I have taken, too often, the dangerous path,
The vague, the arid,
Neither in nor out of this life.

    Among us, who is holy?
    What speech abides?
    I hear the noise of the wall.
    They have declared themselves,
    Those who despise the dove.

Be with me, Whitman, maker of catalogues:
For the world invades me again,
And once more the tongues begin babbling.
And the terrible hunger for objects quails me:
The sill trembles.
And there on the blind
A furred caterpillar crawls down a string.
My symbol!
For I have moved closer to death, lived with death;
Like a nurse he sat with me for weeks, a sly surly attendant,
Watching my hands, wary.
Who sent him away?
I'm no longer a bird dipping a beak into rippling water
But a mole winding through earth,
A night-fishing otter.

Walt Whitman • *Edward Dahlberg*

Sing the Alpha forest gods,
Sorrel, purslane, and the uncured sassafras;
We forsook the soft, doved waters of Venus and Daphne,
And the oaks of Ilium
To quarry our Ghost in the marsh.
Concord was unsown violets and bog-cress,
At Nona the waters smelled of the fox.
Sorrow was our father and hope,
Penury sang in our pockets.
We sowed affliction in rank marl,
And called this Adam's ground.
Then came the cities of Cush and Ham,
And the granaries of shrewd Pul.

The midwest was a Mesopotamian corral for Laban;
Omaha, a stable for the cattle of Asshur,
Roanoke and St. Joseph were as Erech and Calah;
The Missouri was laden with the boats of Tarshish.
Togmarah sold mules and horses to Kansas City,
The mart for the melons and the leeks
That shone as emeralds in Paradise.
Venus came from the bins of Joplin,
Fragrant with rye, oats and papaw.

There was a man named Walt Whitman,
Prophetic goat and Buddha of the states,
An evangelist of the rank gullet,
And the pagan works of Phallus.
An Old Testament Balaam was he,
And as lickerous as the Angels
Who parted the thighs of the daughters of men.
He strode the cities of Shinar,
As though they were the oaks at Mamre.
At Sodom he sat at the gates as Lot.
Strewing his affections as palms and boughs.
Gaza and Akkad comforted his navel.

Every aged man was father Adam;
He went soft upon the ground
Lest he trample Abel's blood.
Among the thorns he grieved anew for Manasseh.
Did the Pharisee he kissed moult the canting hands?
Nimrod has giant laughing shoulders
Which hide the sinews of Cain.

We cannot bear each other,
For we are immense territory
And our malignant folly was to mew us up in cities,
And take away our ocean past.
For the sign of Cain is solitude
And he that goes in the earth apart
Grieves as the worm.

We are still mostly landless,
And a water people,
For we are not yet earth-born children,
And our Abraham, Isaac and Jacob
Are New Mexico, Arizona and Texas,
Residual sand and flood clay,
And the red that came out of it,
Iroquois and Algonquin,
Which means the blood, we slew.
Now the long wastes of flats,
And the terrible inland oceans
Are like our fierce black and gray burial cities.
The country is still more than half whale,

For we go to water quicker than to fire or to blood,
And we are a kinless people
Still suffering for the flood sins.
Whitman, our Adam, has died in our loins.

11.

A Modern Poet • *Howard Nemerov*

Crossing at rush hour the Walt Whitman Bridge,
He stopped at the Walt Whitman Shopping Center
And bought a paperback copy of *Leaves of Grass.*
Fame *is* the spur, he figured; given a Ford
Foundation Fellowship, he'd buy a Ford.

Letters to Walt Whitman • *Ronald Johnson*

V

Earth, my likeness
. . .
I, too, have plucked a stalk of grass

from your ample prairie, Walt,
& have savored whole fields of a summer's hay in it—

I have known your Appalachian length, the heights
of your Sierra
—I have unearthed the roots of calamus
you left at the margin

of many, hidden ponds,
& have exchanged it with the few, select,
lovers.

I have lain in the open night,

till my shoulders felt twin roots, & the tree of my sight
swayed,
among the stars.

I, too, have plucked a stalk of grass

from your ample prairie, Walt.

IX

Landscapes projected masculine,
full-sized and golden...
With floods of the yellow gold of the gorgeous, indolent,

sinking sun, burning, expanding the air.

But are these landscapes to be imagined,
or an actual
Kansas—the central, earthy, prosaic core of us?

Or is the seen always winged, an *eidolon* only to us—& never
the certain capture
of great, golden, unembroidered

slabs?

All is Oz.
The dusty cottonwoods, by the creek,
rustle an Emerald City.

And the mystic, immemorial city

is rooted in earth.

All is Oz & inextricable,

bound up in the unquenchable flames of double suns.

I, Mencius, Pupil of the Master ... • *Charles Olson*

the dross of verse. Rhyme!
when iron (steel)
has expelled Confucius
from China. Pittsburgh!
beware: the Master
bewrays his vertu
To clank like you do
he brings coolie verse
to teach you equity,
who layed down such rails!

Who doesn't know a whorehouse
from a palace (who doesn't know the Bowery
is still the Bowery, even if it is winos
who look like a cold wind, put out their hands
to keep up their pants

       that the willow or the peach blossom
       ...Whistler, be with America
       at this hour

       open galleries. And sell
       Chinese prints, at the opening,
       even let the old ladies in—

       let decorations thrive, when
       clank is let back
       into your song

        when voluntarism
       abandons
       poetic means

Noise! that Confucius himself
should try to alter it, he
who taught us all
that no line must sleep,
that as the line goes so goes
the Nation! that the Master
should now be embraced by the demon
he drove off! O Ruler

in the time of chow,
that the Soldier
should lose the Battle!

that what the eye sees,
that in the East the sun untangles itself
from among branches,
should be made to sound as though there were still roads
on which men hustled
to get to paradise, to get to
Bremerton
shipyards!

II

that the great 'ear
can we no longer 'hear!

o Whitman,
let us keep our trade with you when
the Distributor
who couldn't go beyond wood,
apparently,
has gone out of business
let us not wear shoddy
mashed out of
even the Master's
old clothes, let us bite off Father's
where the wool's
got too long (o Solomon Levi

in your store on Salem Street
we'll go there to buy our ulsterettes,
and everything else that's neat

III

We'll to these woods
no more, where we were used
to get so much, (Old Bones
do not try to dance

      go still
      now that your legs

           the Charleston
           is still for us

                You can watch
It is too late
to try to teach us
      we are the process

         and our feet

              We do not march

We still look

And see

        what we see

               We do not see
               ballads
other than our own.

Introduction to *Whitman Selected by Robert Creeley*

ROBERT CREELEY

ONE OF THE MOST LOVELY insistences in Whitman's poems seems to me his instruction that one speak for oneself. Assumedly that would be the person most involved in saying anything and yet a habit of 'objective' statement argues the contrary, noting the biases and distortions and tediums of the personal that are thereby invited into the writing. Surely there is some measure possible, such would say, that can make statement a clearly defined and impersonal instance of reality, of white clouds in a blue sky, of things and feelings not distorted by any fact of one man or woman's intensive possession of them. Then there would truly be a common possibility, that all might share, and that no one would have use of more than another.

Yet if Whitman has taught me anything, and he has taught me a great deal, often against my own will, it is that the common *is* personal, intensely so, in that having no one thus to invest it, the sea becomes a curious mixture of water and table salt and the sky the chemical formula for air. It is, paradoxically, the personal which makes the common in so far as it recognizes the existence of the many in the one. In my own joy or despair, I am brought to that which others have also experienced.

My own senses of Whitman were curiously numb until I was thirty. In the forties, when I was in college, it was considered literally bad taste to have an active interest in his writing. In that sense he suffered the same fate as Wordsworth, also condemned as overly prolix and generalizing. There was a persistent embarrassment that this naively affirmative poet might affect one's own somewhat cynical wisdoms. Too, in so far as this was a time of intensively didactic criticism, what was one to do with Whitman, even if one read him? He went on and on, he seemed to lack 'structure,' he yielded to no 'critical apparatus' then to hand. So, as students, we were herded past him as quickly as possible, and our teachers used him only as an example of 'the America of that period' which, we were told, was a vast swamp of idealistic expansion and corruption. Whitman, the dupe, the dumb-bell, the pathetically regrettable instance of this country's dream and despair, the self-taught man.

That summation of Whitman and his work was a very comfortable one for all concerned. If I felt at times awkward with it, I had only to turn to Ezra Pound, whom the university also condemned, to find that he too disapproved despite the begrudging 'Pact.' At least he spoke of having 'detested' Whitman, only publicly altering the implications of that opinion in a series of BBC interviews made in the late fifties. William Carlos Williams also seemed to dislike him, decrying the looseness of the writing, as he felt it, and the lack of a coherent prosody. He as well seemed to change his mind in age in so far as he referred to Whitman as the greatest of American poets in a public lecture on American poetry for college students. Eliot also changed his mind, as did James before him, but the point is that the heroes of my youth as well as my teachers were almost without exception extremely critical of Whitman and his influence and wanted as little as possible to do with him.

Two men, however, most dear to me, felt otherwise. The first of these was D. H. Lawrence, whose *Studies in Classic American Literature* remains the most extraordinary apprehension of the nature of American experience and writing that I know. His piece on Whitman in that book is fundamental in that he, in a decisively personal manner, first castigates Whitman for what he considers a muddling assumption of 'oneness,' citing 'I am he that aches with amorous love . . .' as particularly offensive, and then, with equal intensity, applauds that Whitman who is, as he puts it, 'a great charger of the blood in men,' a truly heroic poet whose vision and will make a place of absolute communion for others.

The second, Hart Crane, shared with Whitman my own teachers' disapproval. I remember a course which I took with F. O. Mathiessen, surely a man of deep commitment and care for his students, from which Crane had been absented. I asked for permission to give a paper on Crane, which he gave me, but I had overlooked what I should have realized would be the response of the class itself, understandably intent upon its own sophistications. How would they accept these lines, for example?

> yes, Walt,
> Afoot again, and onward without halt,—
> Not soon, nor suddenly,—no, never to let go
>   My hand
>   in yours,

Walt Whitman—

so—

If they did not laugh outright at what must have seemed to them the awkwardly stressed rhymes and sentimental camaraderie, then they tittered at Crane's will to be one with his fellow *homosexual*. But didn't they hear, I wanted to insist, the pacing of the rhythms of those lines, the syntax, the intently human tone, or simply the punctuation? Couldn't they read? Was Crane to be simply another 'crudity' they could so glibly be rid of? But still I myself didn't read Whitman, more than the few poems of his that were 'dealt with' in classes or that some friend asked me to. No doubt I too was embarrassed by my aunt's and my grandmother's ability to recite that terrible poem, 'O Captain! My Captain!', banal as I felt it to be, and yet what was that specious taste which could so distract any attention and could righteously dismiss so much possibility, just because it didn't 'like' it? Sadly, it was too much my own.

So I really didn't read Whitman for some years although from time to time I realized that the disposition toward his work must be changing. Increasing numbers of articles began to appear as, for one example, Randall Jarrell's 'Whitman Revisited.' But the import of this writing had primarily to do with Whitman's work as instance of social history or else with its philosophical basis or, in short, with all that did not attempt to respect the technical aspects of his writing, his prosody and the characteristic method of his organization within the specific poems.

It was, finally, the respect accorded Whitman by three of my fellow poets that began to impress me as not only significant to their various concepts of poetry but as unmistakable evidence of his basic use to any estimation of the nature of poetry itself. I had grown up, so to speak, habituated to the use of poetry as compact, epiphanal instance of emotion or insight. I valued its intensive compression, its ability to 'get through' a maze of conflict and confusion to some centre of clear 'point.' But what did one do if the emotion or terms of thought could not be so focused upon or isolated in such singularity? Assuming a context in which the statement was of necessity multiphasic, a circumstance the components of which were multiple, or, literally, a day in which various things *did* occur, not simply one thing—what did one do with that? Allen Ginsberg was quick to see that Whitman's line was of very specific use. As he says in 'Notes Written on Finally Recording Howl,' 'No attempt's been made to use it in the light of early XX Century organization of new speech-rhythm prosody to *build up* large organic structures.' The structure of 'Howl' itself and of subsequent poems such as 'Kaddish' demonstrates to my own mind how much technically Ginsberg had learned from Whitman's method of taking the poem as a 'field,' in Charles Olson's sense, rather than as a discrete line through alternatives to some adamant point of conclusion.

In the work of Robert Duncan the *imagination* of the poem is very coincident with Whitman's. For example, in a contribution to *Poets on Poetry* (1966) Duncan writes:

> We begin to imagine a cosmos in which the poet and the poem are one in a moving process, not only here the given Creation and the Exodus or Fall, but also here the immanence of the Creator in Creation. The most real is given and we have fallen away, but the most real is in the falling revealing itself in what is happening. Between the god *in* the story and the god *of* the story, the form, the realization of what is happening, stirs the poet. To answer that call, to become the poet, means to be aware of creation, creature and creator coinherent in the one event. . . .

If one reads the 1855 'Preface' to *Leaves of Grass* in the context here defined, the seeming largenesses of act which Whitman grants to the poet find actual place in that "immanence of the Creator in Creation" which Duncan notes. More, the singular presence of Whitman in Duncan's 'A Poem Beginning with a Line by Pindar' is an extraordinary realization of the *measure* Whitman has given us:

> . . .There is no continuity then. Only a few
>   posts of the good remain. I too
> that am a nation sustain the damage
>   where smokes of continual ravage
> obscure the flame.
>   It is across great scars of wrong
>   I reach toward the song of kindred men
>   and strike again the naked string
>   old Whitman sang from. Glorious mistake!
>   that cried:

> 'The theme is creative and has vista.'
> 'He is the president of regulation.'

> I see always the under side turning,
> fumes that injure the tender landscape.
>   From which up break
> lilac blossoms of courage in daily act
> striving to meet a natural measure.

Louis Zukofsky, the third friend thus to instruct me, recalls and transforms Whitman's *Leaves* again and again, as here:

> The music is in the flower,
> Leaf around leaf ranged around the center;
> Profuse but clear outer leaf breaking on space,
> There is space to step to the central heart:
> The music is in the flower,
> It is not the sea but hyaline cushions the flower—
> Liveforever, everlasting.
> The leaves never topple from each other,
> Each leaf a buttress flung for the other.
>
> (from *'A' 2*, 1928)

I have no way of knowing if those lines directly refer to Whitman's *Leaves of Grass* and yet, intuitively, I have no doubt of it whatsoever. Zukofsky once told me that, for him, the eleventh section of 'Song of Myself' constituted the American *Shih King*, which is to say, it taught the possibilities of what might be said or sung in poetry with that grace of technical agency, or mode, thereby to accomplish those possibilities. *It presents*. It does not talk about or refer to—in the subtlety of its realization, it becomes real.

It is also Zukofsky who made me aware of Whitman's power in an emotion I had not associated with him—a deeply passionate anger. Zukofsky includes an essay called 'Poetry' in the first edition of *'A' 1-12* at the end of which he quotes the entire text of "Respondez!", a poem which Whitman finally took out of *Leaves of Grass* in 1881 but which I have put in this selection, as singular instance of that power and in respect to the man who made me aware of it.

Then, in the late fifties, I found myself embarrassed for proper academic credentials although I was teaching at the time, and so went back to graduate school, to get the appropriate degree. One of the first courses I took in that situation was called 'Twain and Whitman,' taught by John Gerber, who was a visiting professor at the University of New Mexico from the University of Iowa. One thing he did with us I remember very well—he asked us to do a so-called thematic outline of 'Song of Myself.' The room in which we met had large blackboards on all four walls and on the day they were due, we were told to copy our various outlines on to the blackboards. So we all got up and did so. When we finally got back to our seats, we noticed one very striking fact. No two of the outlines were the same—which was Professor Gerber's very instructive point. Whitman did not write with a systematized logic of 'subject' nor did he 'organize' his materials with a logically set schedule for their occurrence in the poem. Again the situation of a 'field' of activity, rather than some didactic imposition of a 'line' of order, was very clear.

At that same time I became interested in the nature of Whitman's prosody and looked through as many scholarly articles concerning it as I could find in the university library. None were really of much use to me, simply that the usual academic measure of such activity depends upon the rigid presumption of a standardized metrical system, which is, at best, the hindsight gained from a practice far more fluid in its own occasion. Sculley Bradley (co-editor with Harold W. Blodgett of the best text for Whitman's poems available to my knowledge: *Leaves of Grass*, Comprehensive Reader's Edition, New York University Press, 1965) did speak of a *variable stress* or *foot*, that is, a hovering accent, or accents, within clusters of words in the line that did not fall in a statically determined pattern but rather shifted with the impulse of the statement itself. This sense of the stress pattern in Whitman's poems was interestingly parallel to William Carlos Williams's use of what he also called 'the variable foot' in his later poems, so that the periodicity of the line, its duration in time, so to speak, stayed in the general pattern constant but the stress or stresses within the unit of the line itself were free to move with the condition of the literal things being said, both as units of semantic information, e.g., 'I am the chanter . . . ,' or as units of sound and rhythm, e.g., 'I chant copious the islands beyond. . . .' It is, of course, impossible ever to separate these two terms in their actual function, but it is possible that one will be more or less concerned with each in turn in the activity of writing. More simply, I remember one occasion in high school when I turned a 'unit' primarily involved with sounds and rhythm into a 'unit' particularly involved with semantic statement, to wit: 'Inebriate of air am I . . .' altered in my memory to read, 'I am an inebriate of air. . . .' My teacher told me I had the most unpoetic ear he'd yet encountered.

Remember that what we call 'rhyming' is the recurrence of a sound sufficiently similar to one preceding it to catch in the ear and mind as being the 'same' and that such sounds can be modified in a great diversity of ways. In the sounding of words themselves the extension seems almost endless: *maid, made, may, met, mad, mate, wait, say,* etc. Given the initial vowel with its accompanying consonants and also its own condition, i.e., whether it is 'long' or 'short,' one can then play upon that sound as long as one's energy *and* the initial word's own ability to stay in the ear as 'residue' can survive. In verse the weaving and play of such sound is far more complex than any observation of the rhymes at the ends of lines can tabulate.

This kind of rhyming is instance of what one can call *parallelism,* and the parallelism which similarity of sounds can effect is only one of the many alternate sources of 'rhyming' which verse has at hand. For example, there is a great deal of syntactic 'rhyming' in Whitman's poetry, insistently parallel syntactic structures which themselves make a strong web of coherence.

There is also the possibility of parallelism in the nature of what is being thought and/or felt as emotion, and this too can serve to increase the experience of coherence in the statement the poem is working to accomplish.

The constantly recurring structures in Whitman's writing, the insistently parallel sounds and rhythms, recall the patterns of waves as I now see them daily. How can I point to *this* wave, or *that* one, and announce that it is *the* one? Rather Whitman's method seems to me a process of sometimes seemingly endless gathering, moving in the energy of his own attention and impulse. There are obviously occasions to the contrary to be found in his work but the basic pattern does seem of this order. I am struck by the fact that William Michael Rossetti in the introduction to his *Poems of Walt Whitman* (1868) speaks of the style as being occasionally 'agglomerative,' a word which can mean 'having the state of a confused or jumbled mass' but which, more literally, describes the circumstance of something 'made or formed into a rounded mass or ball.' A few days ago here, walking along the beach, a friend showed me such a ball, primarily of clay but equally compacted of shells and pebbles which the action of the waves had caused the clay to pick up, all of which would, in time, become stone. That meaning of 'agglomerate' I think particularly relevant to the activity of Whitman's composition, and I like too that sense of the spherical, which does not locate itself upon a point nor have the strict condition of the linear but rather is at all 'points' the possibility of all that it is. Whitman's constant habit of revisions and additions would concur, I think, with this notion of his process, in that there is not 'one thing' to be said and, that done, then 'another.' Rather the process permits the material ('myself' in the world) to extend until literal death intercedes. Again, it is interesting to think of Zukofsky's sense that any of us as poets 'write one poem all our lives,' remembering that Whitman does not think of his work as a series of discrete collections or books but instead adds to the initial work, *Leaves of Grass,* thinking of it as a 'single poem.'

The implications of such a stance have a very contemporary bearing for American poets—who can no longer assume either their world or themselves in it as discrete occasion. Not only does Whitman anticipate the American affection for the pragmatic, but he equally emphasizes that it is space and process which are unremittingly our condition. If Pound found the manner of his poems objectionable, he nonetheless comes to a form curiously like *Leaves of Grass* in the *Cantos*, in that he uses them as the literal possibility of a life. Much the same situation occurs in Williams's writing with *Paterson,* although it comes at a markedly later time in his own writing. Charles

Olson's *Maximus Poems* and Louis Zukofsky's *'A'* are also instances of this form which proposes to 'go on' in distinction to one that assumes its own containment as a singular case.

Another objection Rossetti had concerned what he called 'absurd or ill-constructed words' in Whitman's writing. One distinct power a poet may be blessed with is that of *naming* and Whitman's appetite in this respect was large and unembarrassed. One should read a posthumously published collection of notes he wrote on his own sense of words called *An American Primer* (City Lights, 1970), wherein he makes clear his commitment to their power of transformation. Whitman's vocabulary moves freely among an extraordinarily wide range of occupational terminologies and kinds of diction found in divers social groupings. Frequently there are juxtapositions of terms appropriate to markedly different social or occupational habits, slang sided with words of an alternate derivation:

> I chant the chant of dilation or pride,
> We have had ducking and deprecating about enough. . . .

Whatever the reader's response, such language permits Whitman to gain an actively useful diversity of context and tone. The toughness of his verse—what Charles Olson referred to as its *muscularity*, giving as instance 'Trickle Drops'—can sustain the tensions created in its movement by these seeming disparities in diction. It is, moreover, a marked characteristic of American poetry since Whitman, and certainly of the contemporary, to have no single source for its language in the sense that it does not depend upon a 'poetic' or literary vocabulary. In contrast, a German friend once told me that even a novelist as committed to a commonly shared situation of life as Günter Grass could not be easily understood by the workmen whose circumstance so moved him. His language was too literary in its structures and vocabulary, not by fact of his own choice but because such language was adamantly that in which novels were to be written in German. An American may choose, as John Ashbery once did, to write a group of poems whose words come entirely from the diction of the *Wall Street Journal,* but it is his own necessity, not that put upon him by some rigidity of literary taste.

Comparable to this flexibility of diction in Whitman's writing is the tone or mood in which his poems speak. It is very open, familiar, at times very casual and yet able to be, on the instant, intensive, intimate, charged with complexly diverse emotion. This manner of address invites, as it were, the person reading to 'come into' the activity and experience of the poems, to share with Whitman in a paradoxically unsentimental manner the actual texture and force of the emotions involved. When he speaks directly to the reader, there is an uncanny feeling of his literal presence, physically.

I have avoided discussion of Whitman's life simply because I am not competent to add anything to the information of any simple biography, for example, Gay Wilson Allen's *Walt Whitman* (Evergreen Books, London, 1961). I am charmed by some of the details got from that book. Apparently Mrs. Gilchrist, the widow of Blake's biographer, Alexander Gilchrist, was very smitten upon reading Whitman's poems and wrote accordingly:

> Even in this first letter (3 September, 1871) Mrs. Gilchrist made it plain that she was proposing marriage. She hoped, she said, to hear, 'My Mate. The one I so much want. Bride, Wife, indissoluble eternal!' And, 'Dear Walt. It is a sweet & precious thing, this love: it clings so close, so close to the Soul and Body, all so tenderly dear, so beautiful, so sacred. . . .'

It is simple enough to make fun of this lady and yet her response, despite Whitman's very careful demurring, is one that his poems are unequivocally capable of producing. It would be sad indeed if books could not be so felt as entirely human and possible occasion.

More to the point, Whitman's life is a very discreet one, really. John Addington Symonds so pestered him concerning 'the meaning of the "Calamus" poems,' that Whitman finally answered, 'Though unmarried, I have six children. . . .' But whether or not that was true, or untrue, or whether Whitman was homosexual, bisexual, or heterosexual, has not primarily concerned me. In other words, I have been intent upon the writing and what there took place and that, literally, is what any of us have now as a possibility. We cannot haul him back any more than we can Shakespeare, just to tell us who he was. It would seem that he *had,* with such magnificent articulation one is almost persuaded there can be no end to him just as there is none to the genius of his writing.

Nor have I been able to do more than gloss the multiplicity of uses I find in the work itself. I wish there were time to think of Whitman as instance of what Allen Ginsberg pointed out as a great tradition of American poets, that of the *crank* or true eccentric. Surely his contemporaries often felt him to be. There is a lovely letter which Gerard Manley Hopkins wrote Bridges, in which he says that Whitman is closer to him in technical concerns than any other poet then writing—but also, that he is a veritable madman, so what does that make poor Hopkins? Or I would like to consider a suggestion of Duncan's, that possibly Williams's uneasiness with Whitman's writing had in part to do with the fact that Williams uses *enjambment,* or 'run-over' lines, very frequently whereas Whitman uses it not at all—wherein he is very like Ezra Pound. Or to trace more carefully the nature of Whitman's influence on American poetry—an influence I find as clearly in Frank O'Hara's poems as I do in Crane's or Ginsberg's.

Undertaking any of this, I felt a sudden giddiness—not at all self-humbling. This man is a *great* poet, our first, and it is unlikely indeed that his contribution to what it literally means to be an *American* poet will ever be equalled. But I do not want to end this note with such blatant emphasis. As Duncan says, Whitman is a deeply gentle man and, humanly, of great, great reassurance. If our America now is a petty shambles of disillusion and violence, the dreams of its possibility stay actual in Whitman's words. It is not 'democracy' that, of itself, can realize or even recognize the common need. It is only, and literally, people themselves who have that choice. So then, as Lawrence said: 'Ahead of all poets, pioneering into the wilderness of unopened life, Whitman. . . .'

Bolinas, California, 30 January, 1972.

Populist Manifesto • *Lawrence Ferlinghetti*

Poets, come out of your closets,
Open your windows, open your doors,
You have been holed-up too long
in your closed worlds.
Come down, come down
from your Russian Hills and Telegraph Hills,
your Beacon Hills and your Chapel Hills,
your Mount Analogues and Montparnasses,
down from your foot hills and mountains,
out of your tepees and domes.
The trees are still falling
and we'll to the woods no more.
No time now for sitting in them
As man burns down his own house
to roast his pig.
No more chanting Hare Krishna
while Rome burns.
San Francisco's burning,
Mayakovsky's Moscow's burning
the fossil-fuels of life.
Night & the Horse approaches
eating light, heat & power,
and the clouds have trousers.
No time now for the artist to hide
above, beyond, behind the scenes,
indifferent, paring his fingernails,
refining himself out of existence.
No time now for our little literary games,
no time now for our paranoias & hypochondrias,
no time now for fear & loathing,
time now only for light & love.
We have seen the best minds of our generation
destroyed by boredom at poetry readings.
Poetry isn't a secret society,
It isn't a temple either.
Secret words & chants won't do any longer.

The hour of *om*ing is over,
the time for keening come,
time for keening & rejoicing
over the coming end
of industrial civilization
which is bad for earth & Man.
Time now to face outward
in the full lotus position
with eyes wide open,
Time now to open your mouths
with a new open speech,
time now to communicate with all sentient beings,
All you 'Poets of the Cities'
hung in museums, including myself,
All you poet's poets writing poetry
about poetry,
All you poetry workshop poets
in the boondock heart of America,
All you house-broken Ezra Pounds,
All you far-out freaked-out cut-up poets,
All you pre-stressed Concrete poets,
All you cunnilingual poets,
All you pay-toilet poets groaning with graffitti,
All you A-train swingers who never swing on birches,
All you masters of the sawmill haiku
in the Siberias of America,
All you eyeless unrealists,
All you self-occulting supersurrealists,
All you bedroom visionaries
and closet agitpropagators,
All you Groucho Marxist poets
and leisure-class Comrades
who lie around all day
and talk about the workingclass proletariat,
All you Catholic anarchists of poetry,
All you Black Mountaineers of poetry,
All you Boston Brahmins and Bolinas bucolics,

All you den mothers of poetry,
All you zen brothers of poetry,
All you suicide lovers of poetry,
All you hairy professors of poesie,
All you poetry reviewers
drinking the blood of the poet,
All you Poetry Police—
Where are Whitman's wild children,
where the great voices speaking out
with a sense of sweetness and sublimity,
where the great new vision,
the great world-view,
the high prophetic song
of the immense earth
and all that sings in it
And our relation to it—
Poets, descend
to the street of the world once more
And open your minds & eyes
with the old visual delight,
Clear your throat and speak up,
Poetry is dead, long live poetry
with terrible eyes and buffalo strength.
Don't wait for the Revolution
or it'll happen without you,
Stop mumbling and speak out
with a new wide-open poetry
with a new commonsensual 'public surface'
with other subjective levels
or other subversive levels,
a tuning fork in the inner ear
to strike below the surface.
Of your own sweet Self still sing
yet utter 'the word en-masse'—
Poetry the common carrier
for the transportation of the public
to higher places
than other wheels can carry it.

Poetry still falls from the skies
into our streets still open.
They haven't put up the barricades, yet,
the streets still alive with faces,
lovely men & women still walking there,
still lovely creatures everywhere,
in the eyes of all the secret of all
still buried there,
Whitman's wild children still sleeping there,
Awake and walk in the open air.

Face on the Daguerreotype • *Norman Rosten*

For Walt Whitman

In the beginning, we had to deny you.
Cities of whores and builders, we had no time
For your prophecies. Your light blinded us.
We hid our nakedness, pursued money.

Now you are more alien to us than ever,
With your haunted face and rather foolish stance,
And those catalogues of names and occupations
Growing over your pages like weeds.

Lord, how you exaggerate, your embrace
Drowning us in the milk of human virility.
Men, women, animals, stones, trees—
You anoint all with your seminal bragging.

In a way, you've been destructive,
Forever tieing us to objects and geography,
Whereas poetry, to survive, must somehow cut free,
Blossom in a timeless air.

The truth is, I tell myself, we've outgrown you
As an older athlete his once powerful stride.
The younger men are clever, all turned pro,
With an eye not on beauty but getting ahead.

After all is said, and you put publicly in place,
Publicly unsolved, I am moved to a secret reverence.
I see your largeness, our own diminution,
Our people, generals, explorers, poets:
How small in prophecy, how big in wars—
And I see you plain, though flickering,
And finally accept you, blowzy and barnacled,
With your one-stringed instrument, our desperate glory.

Over Colorado • *Derek Walcott*

When Whitman's beard unrolled like the Pacific,
when he quit talking
to prophesy the great waggons

the dream began to lumber to delirium.
Once, flying over Colorado
its starved palomino mountains

I saw, like ants, a staggering file
of Indians enter a cloud's beard;
then the cloud broke on

a frozen brave, his fossil
a fern-print on the spine of rock,
his snow-soft whisper

Colorado, rust and white;
the snow his praise, the snow
his obliterator.

That was years ago,
in a jet crossing to Los Angeles,
I don't know why it comes now,

or why I see only this
through those democratic vistas
parting your leaves of grass.

Hopkins to Whitman: From the Lost Correspondence
• *Philip Dacey*

"I always knew in my heart Walt Whitman's mind to be more
like my own than any other man's living."—GMH, 1882

So at ease, so American, so at home in the world
In that portrait you look out from. At me?
You say so. "I am with you. I am as good
As looking at you." I would like
To believe you. Would like to think that pose
is addressed to me, the collar unbuttoned,
The hand on the hip (the other democratically deep
In a pocket), and the soft hat tilted carelessly
O so carefully that I, looking and wondering, might hear,
"Comrade."
        Comrade. I am lonely. (You see,
I shall never send this and therefore can tell
The most outrageous lies. For I have my Christ,
My only lover, for whose sake I left behind
Your book, touching I did indeed touch a man, at Bridges'.
That's Robert. You'd like him. Athletic. Rowed for Eton.
Until last year a physician but now devotes
All his time to poetry. Destined for great things.
Like yourself, Walt.)
        I like to say your name:
Walt. Walt. Walt. Walt. Walt.
You would have less love of mine. I do.
And less love of my garb than I feel for your
Open dress, roomy and airy, a type
Of the American land itself. I am a black-robe.
Worse. A Jesuit. I know what you say of priests.
I am your reversed image, as you are mine.
I still remember the shock when my Uncle George,
Who took up photography immediately it crossed from France,
First showed me my other self: all my shadows
Blazed white, all my sunniness gone black.

That same shock again, when I encountered you,
Though this time gradual, reviews in *The Academy, Athenaeum,*
Rosetti's edition, then everything, in Bridges' library—
The difference between Paul's conversion, at a flash
On the road to Damascus, and Austin's, sweet a-building.
You so robust, manly, a prophet of good cheer;
I but animated dust, Manley, mere. And I, too,
Write poetry. But write it in a dark corner
And leave it there. For the God of Dark Corners.
You take yours out-of-doors and it expands
Ever rarer, ancient aether, to the stars.
Your gab a gas; my words a web. And I wait.
For prey. Pray to catch Christ. Fast. To eat.
How could any two be so different?
We each must be the other's Hyde.
(Do you know Stevenson over there? The book,
No doubt too heavily shadowed for such as
You and your countrymen, has caught on here.)
I mounting a cross, you laughing at loss:
The counter-colored squares of a harlequin.

Yet. Yet. The point of the horrible fable
Is they are one. Bridges tells me someone
Wrote of you as a modern Christ. Years
In the hospitals. The sick lifted
To your breast. Not that I myself
Am fixed at any cross-point. No, my Self
Is too much indulged. I am one of your
Naked swimmers. I splash and roll.
My belly, for all its thinness, glints.
Or perhaps I am the twenty-ninth. Perhaps I am
The lady herself, behind the curtain, careful,
Indulging herself in restraint. In touching them
Nowhere, she touches them everywhere.
The sun is so hot upon the water.
I must give it up. I write to tell you
I shall not, will not, touch you anymore.
The sun is too hot upon the water.

I must kill my Hyde, lest he kill me.
He wants love, and he is not my Lord.
But how kill him, and miss my own heart?
Walt, who does not hear me now,
Help me. May your brotherly love,
Be it earth- or heaven-begot,
Enfold one hard upon his dark way.
Yours, and not,
       Gerard M. Hopkins, S.J.

For You, Walt Whitman • *William Stafford*

Here is a message for you—the whole world sent it,
or maybe a ghost on radar, maybe lichen
growing on a stone. I'll try to read it—
it says there's a storm out there, there's a larger world
more gray than this one, and the storm is coming. I read
the message carefully: some day, and soon, not even
the lichen may speak, and even the ghost be gone,
and maybe even the large gray world you were standing on.

The Good Grey Poet • *Theodore Weiss*

Look to your words, old man,
for the original intelligence, the wisdom
buried in them. Know however that it
surfaces when it will. Perfect comrades
words have been, constant like few others
in your loneliness. But they too have a life,
a time, of their own to mature. Experiencing
the slow, essential music of their natures,
they must go their ways as you go yours.

After so many throes, so many convulsions,
not only a war that threatened to tear
your world to pieces, the world you had
most ambitiously dreamed, all the pieces
of bodies you had seen stacked under a tree,
the maggots working overtime, but deaths
accumulating of those dearest to you,
politics, conviviality, love, the rest
at last exhausted, do you not hear hints
from the vantage point of what you've become?

Your ideal, you wrote a healthy time ago
to guide yourself, was Merlin: "strong
& wise & beautiful at 100 years old."
Strong & wise since "his emotions &c are
complete in himself. . . . He grows, blooms,
like some perfect tree or flower, in Nature,
whether viewed by admiring eyes or in
some wild or wood entirely unknown."

For your liver fattening, the cyst ripening
in your adrenal, the left lung collapsed,
the right perhaps an eighth suitable
for breathing, a big stone rattled round

in your gall bladder (righter than you knew,
you were—and even at the time you wrote,
rock-bottom feelings under you, your poems—
truly incorporating gneiss!), the ball
of string tangled in the gut like a clue
to knit up all contrarieties, you must be
more and more yourself.

      Often, leaning
against a ferry rail, the sea your company,
your words beat out a rhythm so continuous
inside your body that you hardly noticed it,
content to let its current carry you along,
wherever it took you your place.
      Now
you, who thought—sufficient stores laid in—
that your awareness had already pierced
the distant future, view these phrases
and that rhythm, still pursuing its course,
as any stranger might.
      Your doubt does not
surprise. Who can miss the unexpected things
emerged to startle you, even waking shame
and fear?
      But then you surely realize
how lucky you are, not only to have them,
these words, striking out on their own,
bearded with faces you scarcely recognize,
refusing to bend to your wishes or regrets,
refusing to acknowledge you in any way,
but to be able to use them—most because
they refuse—to measure that essential music
as it, and at its own sweet pace, moves on
to find the latest version of the truth
in the changes it is making.

Beyond that,
your words work, and work for you, by what
they do to others, bringing you—this
from far-off continents—reports of pleasure,
love, the tender might your poems go on
gathering as they inspire it.
And those,
the first breezy verses informing the winds,
your words in all their youthful innocence,
become so different, yet so much themselves,
like fruits more and more are bearing, bearing
out their father tree.

For Whitman • *Diane Wakoski*

I have observed the learned astronomer
telling me the mythology of the sun.
He touches me with solar coronas.
His hands are comets with elliptical orbits, the
excuses for discovering planet X.

Lake water shimmering in sunset light,
and I think of the whitewashed dome of discovery
hovering over the landscape
wondering what knowledge does for us
in this old and beautiful un-knowing world.
     Yes,
       I would
rather name things
than live with wonder
or religion.

What the astronomer does not understand about poetry
is the truth of disguise.
That there are many names for the same phenomenon.
Love being
the unnamed/
the unnameable.

Whitman's Indicative Words

GALWAY KINNELL

WHITMAN KNEW THAT in its own time *Leaves of Grass* was a failure. But he belonged to that little era which had the dream of progress, and he could believe that one day the book would come into its glory. He tells poets to come:

> I myself write but one or two indicative words
>   for the future,
> I but advance a moment only to wheel and hurry
>   back in the darkness.
>
> I am a man who, sauntering along without fully
>   stopping, turns a causal look upon you and
>   then averts his face,
> Leaving it to you to prove and define it,
> Expecting the main things from you.

It has turned out as he hoped, but his rise from obscurity to mastery took a very long time. It took so long because, excepting Thoreau and Emerson, most American literati of the nineteenth century suffered from snobbery and anglophilia and thought of Whitman as a queer cultist or a blethering yokel. In the twentieth century this neglect persisted among the New Critics and their poets, who, being of a technological cast of mind, took a stern, cerebral approach to poetry and tended to patronize this poet who claimed to live on instinct.

A few American poets did feel attracted to Whitman—Vachel Lindsay and Carl Sandburg, and perhaps in a perverse, or reverse, way Robinson Jeffers too. But not until Hart Crane do we find an American poet who was drawn to Whitman's essential enterprise. In Crane's case, however, the temperamental differences were extreme, and also Crane was always being lectured on Whitman's faults by his literary friends. In the end Whitman's influence is not very visible in Crane's work. As far as I can see, except here and there and in "The River" section of *The Bridge,* Crane was not very deeply affected by that most affecting element, Whitman's musical line.

A few foreign poets, notably Lawrence and Neruda, absorbed Whitman's influence long before our own poets did. For Pound, Eliot, Frost, and Williams, Whitman meant very little. Whitman's return to American poetry, if we can set a date, did not come until 1956, one hundred and one years after the appearance of *Leaves of Grass,* with the publication of Ginsberg's *Howl.*[1] Other American poets were turning to Whitman about the same time, and some few, such as Tom McGrath and Robert Duncan, had begun as much as a decade earlier to retrieve Whitman's music.[2] But only very recently has Whitman been widely accepted as our greatest native master, the bearer of the American tradition.

In these notes I want to try to describe some of the attraction Walt Whitman holds for me—and I trust for others—to make out if I can one or two of his indicative words, to catch something of the casual gaze he turns towards us.

* * * * *

What first strikes me when I read Whitman is the music, what I can only call the mystic music, of his voice. There are debts to Shakespeare and the King James Bible, but Whitman was an original. No one before him had thrust his presence and actual voice so boldly onto the written page. This voice, so unmistakably personal, is also universal: while it is outgoing and attaches itself to the things and creatures of the world, it speaks at the same time of a life far within. In this double character, of intimacy and commonality, it resembles prayer.

This music flows from a source deeper than its words. If you croon to a baby in iambs, the baby will laugh, for helpless creatures find control of nature amazing. A woman who has nursed many babies, however, croons to the infant in Whitmanesque lines, and the infant croons back also in Whitmanesque lines. They communicate perfectly, yet use no words, only that music the words themselves will also have when their time comes. The rhythms of Whitman's lines are not merely ornamental but an essential expressive element.

It is true that the nursery rhyme, which often uses countable meter, appeals to little children too, and not just because of its power to control nature. The iambic beat seems embedded in our language, and Whitman does not ignore it. His free verse speaks in iambs almost as much as do many passages in Shakespeare's blank verse or much of seventeenth-century syllabic poetry. But his iambic flow, which is never counted out, connects seamlessly to surrounding non-iambic passages. This music, which profoundly affected him, D. H. Lawrence compares to the flight of birds, now flapping, now soaring, now gliding, as opposed to that of counted meter, which in his analogy is like the plod of earthbound creatures.

Whimsical as it must strike a sensible person, I believe that long before Whitman came on the scene, ever since Milton in fact, poets writing in English unconsciously hungered for such a music as Whitman was to discover. It may have been heroic for the post-Miltonic poets, all of them brought up on the King James Bible and on Shakespeare, nevertheless to swear fealty to counted meter, in the faith that this was loyalty to poetry itself, but it is possible to imagine that more was lost than gained. Ginsberg's revival of Whitman's line was long overdue; but Whitman's discovery of his own line may have also been long overdue.

His music exerts a power on words, drawing from them both pre-historic and infantile resonances, these deepest sub-meanings. Most nineteenth-century poetry relies on overtones, which are superficial and usually nostalgic. In Whitman's poetry, the words seem spoken for the first time, whereas in Longfellow or Tennyson words appear to have spent all their force already—spent it putting into the reader, in other poems, emotions they try to elicit from the reader in these. Whitman knew that for the voice which loves it every word is virginal. There are "archaic" things, which may drag words along with them into the past, and there are archaic phrases, but very likely there is no such thing as an archaic word.

* * * * *

In the history of literary criticism, tracts have been written on practically every subject there is—as well as on many subjects there aren't—but as far as I know only Whitman has written on this primary subject, the original music of the human voice, how it rescues words and makes them fresh. Since words form in the poet's throat and mouth, they can be said to come out of his very flesh. And since the reader's throat and mouth must form the words, the words enter the reader's very flesh. Poetry goes not merely from mind to mind, but from the whole being to the whole being. Whitman understood this.

Given the great public voices of Theodore Roethke and Dylan Thomas, it is true that Whitman's specific prescriptions occasionally appear to be in error:

Drinking brandy, gin, beer, is generally fatal to the perfection of the voice;—meanness of the mind the same;—gluttony in eating, of course the same; a thinned habit of body, or a rank habit of body—masturbation, inordinate going with women, rot the voice.

But Whitman was the first to grasp the basic truth, that the music of the voice releases the word's secret life, just as being loved makes plain people brighten.

The charm of the beautiful pronunciation of all words, of all tongues, is in perfect flexible vocal organs, and in a developed harmonious soul.—All words, spoken from these, have deeper sweeter sounds, new meanings, impossible on any less terms.—Such meanings, such sounds, continually wait in every word that exists—in these words—perhaps slumbering through years, closed from all tympans of temples, lips, brains, until that comes which has the quality patiently waiting in the words.

Whitman's language is as fresh as if spoken today—or for that matter tomorrow.

Whitman's love of words was not, as was Pound's, literary, referential, and etymological. Whitman loved words as physical entities. But entities can become physical only through attachment to reality. For it is curious with words: they can't be loved for themselves alone. Like our human lovers, words attach to a deeper life than their own, and are loved for their own particular qualities, yes, but loved supremely because in them flowers that which we more deeply love. In these few passages, picked nearly at random, it is obvious that what entrances Whitman is not words as such but what they render luminous. In return for his love, his carnal desire, reality seems to lay these words freely and unasked for on his tongue.

> The brisk short crackle of the steel driven
>   slantingly into the pine,
> The butter-color'd chips flying off in great
>   flakes and slivers . . .

> Evening—me in my room—the setting sun,
> The setting summer sun shining in my open
>   window, showing the swarm of flies,
>   suspended, balancing in the air in the
>   centre of the room, darting athwart, up
>   and down, casting swift shadows in specks
>   on the opposite wall where the shine is . . .

> I too many and many a time cross'd the river
>   of old

> Watched the twelfth-month sea-gulls, saw them high
>   in the air floating with motionless wings,
>   oscillating their bodies,
> Saw how the glistening yellow lit up parts of
>   their bodies and left the rest in strong
>   shadow,
> Saw the slow-wheeling circles and the gradual
>   edging toward the south,
> Saw the reflection of the summer sky in the water,
> Had my eyes dazzled by the shimmering track of
>   beams,
> Look'd at the fine centrifugal spokes of light
>   round the shape of my head in the sunlit
>   water . . .

> She sits in an armchair under the shaded porch
>   of the farmhouse,
> The sun just shines on her old white head . . .

These examples of Whitman's novelistic virtuosity are, more than that, loving acts which rescue things and creatures from time and death.

Such adjectives as "butter-color'd," which is photographically descriptive, belong, it's true, to the realm of prose. At his best Whitman goes far beyond photographic description. His adjectives do not merely try to categorize, give colors, shapes, likenesses. They try to bring into language the event or the creature itself, however unspeakable. So his descriptions may sometimes almost detach themselves from a visible surface.

> Hefts of the moving world at innocent gambols
>   silently rising, freshly exuding.
> Scooting obliquely high and low.

> Something I cannot see puts upward libidinous
>   prongs,
> Seas of bright juice suffuse heaven.

A powerful sympathy flows from Whitman toward the thing. He loves the thing; he goes out to it, enters it; he becomes its voice and expresses it. But to enter a thing is also to open oneself and let the thing enter oneself. So that when Whitman speaks for a leaf of grass, the grass also speaks for him. The light from heaven which shines in Whitman's poetry is often a consequence of these loving unions. At the end of "Crossing Brooklyn Ferry" Whitman tells the appearances of things, "We use you, and do not cast you aside—we plant you permanently within us," in his offhand way coming close to describing the resurrection of the world within us which Rilke strains his whole being to describe at the end of the Ninth Elegy.

* * * * *

Whitman says that in *Leaves of Grass* his aim was to set forth "uncompromisingly, my own physical, emotional, moral, intellectual, and aesthetic personality ... in a far more candid and comprehensible sense than any hitherto poem or book." He doesn't quite do that. It is impossible not to feel in this man who always proclaims his health, this good gray poet who writes constantly about himself yet about whom we know very little, something unavowed, a trouble, perhaps even a sickness, at least an intense loneliness and a more than ordinary fear both of sex and of death.

He protests too much, to begin with; no healthy person could generate that much energy merely to announce that he is healthy. Sometimes Whitman almost suggests the nature of his troubles, the source of those wounds, still unhealed, which were inflicted on an exceptionally indulged child when it confronted the "reality principle," in this case an exceptionally puritan society.

He says, for instance:

> I keep as delicate around the bowels as around
> the head and heart.
> Copulation is no more rank to me than death is.

The explicit content is unexceptional. Yet something in the way it comes out isn't quite right. The first line makes one think of people who, appalled by their own excrement, perform enemas on themselves daily. And I can imagine Whitman trying the comparison in the second line the other way around—"Death is no more rank to me than copulation is"—before, still vaguely bothered, settling on the line as it is, although its use, even in the negative, of "rank" to link sex and death suggests unresolved sexual anxieties.

Whitman did not like us to see his troubled side. He wanted us to see him as he wished to be. His confessions of having experienced base emotions are merely concessions, claims to common humanity, and they have a patronizing tone. His poems, therefore, rarely contain struggles of any kind. They begin in the same clarity in which they end. This is often their weakness. It is what spoils, for instance, "When Lilacs Last in the Dooryard Bloom'd," in which the grief is too thoroughly consoled before the first line is uttered. One of the exceptions is the curious "This Compost," which begins with Whitman's telling us how frightened he is of the earth, since in it have been buried so many diseased carcasses.

> Something startles me where I thought I was
>   safest,
> I withdraw from the still woods I loved,
> I will not go now on the pastures to walk,
> I will not strip the clothes from my body to
>   meet my lover the sea,
> I will not touch my flesh to the earth as to
>   other flesh to renew me.
>
> O how can it be that the ground itself does not
>   sicken?
> How can you be alive you growths of spring?
> How can you furnish health you blood of herbs,
>   roots, orchards, grain?
> Are they not continually putting distemper'd
>   corpses within you?
> Is not every continent work'd over and over
>   with the sour dead?
>
> Where have you disposed of their carcasses?
> Those drunkards and gluttons of so many
>   generations?
> Where have you drawn off all the foul liquid and
>   meat?
> I do not see any of it upon you to-day, or perhaps
>   I am deceiv'd.
> I will run a furrow with my plough, I will press
>   my spade through the sod and turn it up
>   underneath,
> I am sure I shall expose some of the foul meat.

At the end of the poem, of course, he comes around and blesses the earth, as healthy after all, but along the way he exhibits an ultra-fastidiousness which would sound hysterical if we were able to take it quite seriously.

Nevertheless, when Whitman does affirm his own health I believe him, even as I disbelieve him. The truth of prose is usually imponderable, for in prose to be persuaded one has to follow all the steps of its argument. Poetry verifies itself, telling us by the authenticity of its voice how true it is, in this respect resembling actual speech. I don't fully believe Thoreau, for example, when he says with just a touch of elegant cleverness, 'we need pray for no higher heaven than the pure senses can furnish, a purely sensuous life . . . ," a skepticism which may have grounds, for Thoreau elsewhere remarks, this time in response to *Leaves of Grass:*

> There are 2 or 3 pieces in the book which are disagreeable to say the least, simply sensual. He does not celebrate love at all. It is as if the beasts spoke. I think that men have not been ashamed of themselves without reason.

I am able to believe in Whitman's declarations of health because, being spoken in poetry, I hear the tone in which he speaks them, I listen carefully, I note the authentic music, the energy of the language—the hum, I could say, of his valvèd voice. What he says is raised to the level of truth by the aliveness of his words. Is it absurd to say that even the passages that betray his sickness are convincing statements of health?

Leaves of Grass set out not only to rescue the things and creatures of the world; it also tried, more seriously from Whitman's viewpoint, to redeem in the flesh this nineteenth-century American puritan: to transform him from one who felt ill toward himself into one who exuberantly loved himself, to make him into "one of the roughs, a kosmos, disorderly, fleshy and sensual"—which, of course, in some way he must have been all along. The energy which made me feel his declarations of health to be false overflows; the surplus energy that remains in the poems gives them life; and it is this surplus, this life, that convinces. We see the sickness; in the same moment we see the sickness healed. On Whitman's face, as it turns briefly towards us, there is both radiance and amazement: it is a face almost confident of its light and yet surprised by it, still trying to get used to this radiance that is all the more startling for coming from within, from an extremely unstable source.

* * * * *

In certain incandescent passages Whitman's poetry approaches a vision, in Norman O. Brown's sense of the phrase, of the "resurrected body." In the following passage Whitman feels his way back into an infant's joy in the body: he fondles himself, adores himself, revels in that lot of him which is all, he discovers with one of his all too rare flashes of humor, totally luscious, that sweet fat sticking to his own bones:

> If I worship one thing more than another it
>   shall be the spread of my own body, or any
>   part of it,
> Translucent mold of me it shall be you!
> Shaded ledges and rests it shall be you!

Firm masculine colter it shall be you!
Whatever goes to the tilth of me it shall
    be you!
You my rich blood! your milky stream pale
    strippings of my life!
Breast that presses against other breasts it
    shall be you!
My brain it shall be your occult convolutions!
    nest of guarded duplicate eggs! it shall
    be you!
Mix'd tussled hay of head, beard, brawn, it
    shall be you!
Trickling sap of maple, fibre of manly wheat,
    it shall be you!
Vapors lighting and shading my face it shall be
    you!
You sweaty brooks and dews it shall be you!
Winds whose soft-tickling genitals rub against
    me it shall be you!
Broad muscular fields, branches of live oak,
    loving lounger in my winding paths, it
    shall be you!
Hands I have taken, face I have kiss'd, mortal
    I have ever touch'd, it shall be you!

The infantile narcissism opens outward in the last line. In this line Whitman recrosses the reality principle, the frontier which once damaged him so severely, recrosses it this time with tenderest words of outgoing and freely given love.

Perhaps the supreme sexual moment in Whitman comes in the fifth section of "Song of Myself." The passage may be about the self and the body and the soul, but to begin with, it is about a man and his lover. If in the previous passage Whitman succeeds in transforming self-love into love for another person, here he transforms love for another person into sacred relationship with all creation. It is true, as Thoreau said, more eloquently than he knew, "It is as if the beasts spoke"; in poetry there are not many higher tributes.

Loafe with me on the grass, loose the stop
    from your throat,
Not words, not music or rhyme I want, not
    custom or lecture, not even the best,
Only the lull I like, the hum of your valvèd
    voice.

I mind how once we lay such a transparent
summer morning,
How you settled your head athwart my hips
and gently turn'd over upon me,
And parted the shirt from my bosom-bone,
and plunged your tongue to my bare-script
heart,
And reach'd till you felt my beard, and
reach'd till you held my feet.

Swiftly arose and spread around me the
peace and knowledge that pass all the
argument of the earth,
And I know that the hand of God is the elder-hand
of my own,
And I know that the spirit of God is the
brother of my own,
And that all the men ever born are also my
brothers, and the women my sisters and
lovers,
And that a kelson of the creation is love,
And limitless are leaves stiff or drooping
in the fields,
And brown ants in the little wells beneath
them,
And mossy scabs of the worm fence, heap'd
stones, elder, mullein, and poke-weed.

In this last passage Whitman climbs down the Platonic ladder. The direction
is perhaps Blakean, or Rilkean—but mostly Whitmanesque—a motion from
the conventionally highest downward toward union with the most ordinary
and the least, the conventionally lowest, the common things of the world.

It is the same at the very close of *Song of Myself*, where Whitman
disintegrates before us and bequeaths his flesh and spirit not to heaven but
to the ground and the air:

I depart as air, I shake my white locks at the
runaway sun,
I effuse my flesh in eddies, and drift it in
lacy jags.

I bequeath myself to the dirt to grow from
the grass I love,
If you want me again look for me under your
boot-soles.

You will hardly know who I am or what I mean,
But I shall be good health to you nevetheless,
And filter and fibre your blood.
Failing to fetch me at first keep encouraged.
Missing me one place search another,
I stop somewhere waiting for you.

Had Whitman been less secretive, it is possible he might have grown more and changed more through the rest of his life. As it was, after this re-invention and salvation of himself, he seems to have concentrated on establishing the personage perhaps only flimsily created. In this light, I know, his work can be regarded as nothing but an elaborate act of wishful thinking. But perhaps "wishful thinking" is a disparaging term for what might be called "vision"—and the vision of glory more than the possession of it produces art. Whatever the case with Whitman, we should not ask everything of those whose gift may have been achieved at severe cost in other areas of life and art.

I know of only one account of Whitman written by someone who knew him both before and after the publication of *Leaves of Grass*. It describes a person rather different from the rapt and garrulous hero of the poems.

Walt Whitman had a small printing office and book store on Myrtle avenue, Brooklyn, where after his return from the South he started the *Freeman* newspaper, first as a weekly, then as a daily, and continued it a year or so. He always earned his own living. I thought him a very natural person. He wore plain, cheap clothes, which were always particularly clean. Everybody knew him; everyone, almost, liked him. We all of us [referring to the other members of his family—brothers, sisters, father and mother] long before he published *Leaves of Grass*, looked upon him as a man who was to make his mark in the world. He was always a good listener, the best I ever knew—of late years, I think, he talks somewhat more. In those early years (1849-54) he talked very little indeed. When he did talk his conversation was remarkably pointed, attractive, and clear. When *Leaves of Grass* first appeared I thought it a great book, but that the man was greater than the book. His singular coolness was an especial feature. I have never seen him excited in the least degree; never heard him swear but once. He was quite gray at thirty. He had a look of age in his youth, as he now has a look of youth in his age.

It is not surprising that Whitman was a listener. Ezra Pound's silence during his last years was perhaps his own tribute, paid too late (but paid), to that one law he had overlooked—that the mother of poetry is silence. Whitman gathered the world into his silence. His poetry is that receptive consciousness turned inside out: the listener has become the speaker, magnetism has changed to radiance.

I am fascinated by that observation about Whitman's altered appearance.

"We poets in our youth begin in gladness / Whereof in the end come despondency and madness." The curse is often quoted. But to achieve his exemplary self-portrait—a self-portrait which would also portray everyone—Whitman had to lift the curse. He had to set against his despondency all his gratefulness. He had to clarify his madness and find in it possibilities of joyful health—and do this, moreover, as a work of supererogation: the surplus would be the poems. *He was quite gray at thirty. He had a look of age in his youth, as he now has a look of youth in his age.* If Whitman's poetry in some sense consists of wishes, it is useful for our faith in his enterprise to know that they came true in his own flesh.

* * * * *

Speaking in New York in the Spring of 1972, Pablo Neruda acknowledged Whitman to be his greatest master. He said:

> For my part, I, who am now nearing 70, discovered Walt Whitman when I was just 15, and I hold him to be my greatest creditor. I stand before you feeling that I bear with me always this great and wonderful debt which has helped me to exist.
>
> I must start by acknowledging myself to be the humble servant of a poet who strode the earth with long, slow paces, pausing everywhere to love, to examine, to learn, to teach and to admire. The fact of the matter is that this great man, this lyric moralist, chose a hard path for himself: he was both a torrential and a didactic singer—qualities which appear opposed, seeming also more appropriate to a leader than a writer. But what really counts is that Walt Whitman was not afraid to teach—which means to learn at the hands of life and undertake the responsibility of passing on the lesson!

Whitman not only saved himself, not only resurrected himself in his body, but, being, as Neruda says, also a teacher, he bravely undertook that most difficult role, of trying to lead others to do the same for themselves. He indicated to poets to come—and to everyone—that, like a poem, a life is not to be a timid, well-made, presentable, outward construction. It is the consuming enterprise, leading to intensified life, possibly to self-transfiguration. He indicated, too, that the great poem may or may not be set down on paper, but first it shall be written by the power of existence in the flesh of a man or woman.

> This is what you shall do: Love the earth and sun and the animals, despise riches, give alms to every one that asks, stand up for the stupid and crazy, devote your income and labor to others, hate tyrants, argue not concerning God, have patience and indulgence toward the people, take off your hat to nothing known or unknown or to any man or number of men, go freely with powerful uneducated persons and with the young and with the mothers of families, re-examine all you have been told at school or church or in any book, dismiss

whatever insults your own soul . . . and your very flesh shall be a great poem and have the richest fluency not only in its words but in the silent lines of its lips and face and between the lashes of your eyes and in every motion and joint of your body.

NOTES

1   Of course Whitman was not the only influence on the music of *Howl*. It may be that Ginsberg owes even more to Christopher Smart. But the lessons of *Leaves of Grass* are clearly present as well. It is possible that, along with *Jubilate Agno,* the model for *Howl* is Whitman's "Poem on the Proposition of Nakedness" (later titled "Respondez," and in 1881 dropped from *Leaves of Grass*).—G. K. 1980.

2   My own discovery of Whitman happened also in 1956. While teaching at the University of Grenoble, I was asked to give a course on *Leaves of Grass* for the French students majoring in English and American literature. During that time, almost all my conversations took place in French, as did most of my reading, so that Whitman came to me especially intensely, being my main contact with the mother tongue. The following fall, in New York City, living on East 5th Street, around the corner from Avenue C, I continued to read Whitman, and at the same time I undertook a rereading of the King James Bible. Just as Walt Whitman had wandered through market places and peered into shops from thresholds, so I loitered gazingly up and down my more desolate Avenue. My ambition became to sing the place into the music which "Song of Myself" and the Bible had both set flowing within me.—G. K. 1980.

12.

1980s

13.

Allen Ginsberg on Walt Whitman: Composed on the Tongue

ALLEN GINSBERG

THERE WAS A MAN, Walt Whitman, who lived in the nineteenth century, in America, who began to define his own person, who began to tell his own secrets, who outlined his own body, and made an outline of his own mind, so other people could see it. He was sort of the prophet of American democracy in the sense that he got to be known as the good gray poet when he got to be an old, old man because he was so honest and so truthful and at the same time so enormous-voiced and bombastic that he sounded his "barbaric yawp over the roofs of the world." As *he* said: "I sound my barbaric yawp over the roofs of the world," writing in New York City probably then, thinking of the skyline and roofs of Manhattan as it might have been in 1883 or so. He began announcing himself, and announcing person, with a big capital P, Person, self, or one's own nature, one's own original nature, what you really think when you're alone in bed, after everybody's gone home from the party or when you're looking in the mirror, shaving, or you're not shaving and you're looking in the mirror, looking at your long, white, aged beard, or if you're sitting on the toilet, or thinking to yourself "What happened to life?" "What happened to your Mommy?" or if you're just walking down the street, looking at people full of longing.

So he wrote a book called *Leaves of Grass*. (The text referred to here is the Modern Library edition: *Leaves of Grass and Selected Prose*, New York: Modern Library, Random House, Inc., 1950.) And the very first inscription, at the beginning of *Leaves of Grass*, was "One's-Self I Sing":

> One's-Self I sing, a simple separate person,
> Yet utter the word Democratic, the word En-Masse.

231

> Of physiology from top to toe I sing,
> Not physiognomy alone nor brain alone is worthy for the Muse, I
>   say the Form complete is worthier far,
> The Female equally with the Male I sing.

> Of Life immense in passion, pulse, and power,
> Cheerful, for freest action form'd under the laws divine,
> The Modern Man I sing.

Well, that's kind of interesting. He starts with the female equally with the male, so he begins in the middle of the nineteenth century to begin saying "women's lib," actually, "The Female equally with the Male I sing." But he's going to talk about the body he says, of physiology from top to toe, so he's going to sing about the toes and the hair: modern man. This is on the very first page of his book *Leaves of Grass*.

Then, the next page, he has a little note, "To Foreign Lands":

> I heard that you ask'd for something to prove this puzzle the New
>   World,
> And to define America, her athletic Democracy,
> Therefore I send you my poems that you behold in them what you
>   wanted.

An "athletic Democracy," so that was an idea. But what did he mean by that? He means people who are able to get up off their ass and get out and look up at the blue sky in the middle of the night and realize how big the universe is and how little, tiny America is, or, you know, how vast our souls are, and how small the state is, or the Capitol building, magnificent and glorious as it is, it's rendered the size of an ant's forefoot by the immensity of a cloud above it. And so, the soul that sees the cloud above the Capitol or the universe above the cloud, is the giant athletic soul, you could almost say. So, it's democracy, though, that is the key, which for him is meaning, in the long run, the love of comrades, that men will love men, women love women, men love women, women love men, but that there be a spontaneous tenderness between them as the basis of the democracy. "Athletic" probably ultimately for him means "erotic," people having sports in bed.

So he goes on, "To the States," announcing:

> To the States or any one of them, or any city of the States, *Resist*
>   *much, obey little,*
> Once unquestioning obedience, once fully enslaved,
> Once fully enslaved, no nation, state, city of this earth, ever
>   afterward resumes its liberty.

Well, that's a warning to America, much needed later on, when as Eisenhower, once President a hundred years later, warned, "Watch out for the military-industrial complex which demands unquestioning obedience and slavery to military aggression." Fear, nuclear apocalypse, unquestioning obedience like "Don't ask, maybe they know better than you do." So this is a warning from Whitman about the difficulties of democracy. Then he, like a Bodhisattva, that is to say, someone who has taken a vow to enlighten all beings in all the directions of space and in all the three times—past, present, and future—has a little poem or song to his fellow poets that would be born after him, that, like myself, will sit in a recording studio reading his words aloud to be heard by ears through some kind of movie/television/theater: "Poets to come! orators, singers,"—that must be, "orators," now who would that be, as "Thou shalt not crucify mankind upon a cross of gold," that was William Jennings Bryan, a great political orator; "singers," that must be Bob Dylan; "musicians to come," that must be Mick Jagger; "Poets to come! orators, singers, musicians to come . . ." "orators," that must be Kerouac.

> Poets to come! orators, singers, musicians to come!
> Not to-day is to justify me and answer what I am for,
> But you, a new brood, native, athletic, continental, greater than
>   before known,
> Arouse! for you must justify me.

> I myself but write one or two indicative words for the future,
> I but advance a moment only to wheel and hurry back in the
>   darkness.

> I am a man who, sauntering along without fully stopping, turns a
>   casual look upon you and then averts his face,
> Leaving it to you to prove and define it,
> Expecting the main things from you.

Ah, he wants somebody to pick him up in the street and make love to him. But he wants to give that glance, so that you know he's open, but what kind of love does he want?

He wants a democratic love, and he wants an athletic love, he wants a love from men, too, and he also wants a love in the imagination. He wants an expansiveness, he wants communication, he wants some kind of vow that everybody will cherish each other sacramentally. So he's going to make the first breakthrough, which is what he's saying. So he's got another little poem following that, "To You":

> Stranger, if you passing meet me and desire to speak to me, why
> should you not speak to me?
> And why should I not speak to you?

Well, I don't know why not except everybody's too scared to be generally walking down the street, they might get hit for being a fairy or something. Or, you know, be trying to pick you up or be a nut talking in the subway, or somebody babbling to himself walking in the street. So there's all these bag ladies and bag men, old Whitmans wandering around with dirty white beards eating out of the garbage pail wanting to talk to nobody actually. Those are the people that won't talk to anybody, they just go around mumbling to themselves, they talk to themselves. But he was willing to talk to anybody, he said. Of course he was living in a time when there weren't too many people to talk to anyway, in the sense of nineteenth-century America. Population was growing but there were still lots of farms. There was still some sense of sport in the cities. Not a total fear of being mugged by a junkie, I guess. I wonder what he would've done with a junkie going along, "Hey, Mr. Whitman, you got some smash? Got some spare change?" Or maybe he would have been the one going around asking for spare change. Well why not? Spare, he's looking for spare love, actually. Or spare affection. Or just spare openness, spare democracy. "You got any spare democracy, Mister?" Some enthusiasm, a little bit of vitality, a little bit of that hard, gem-like flame that artists burn with.

So, his major work is known as "Song of Myself." "Song of Myself" is a long thing, about thirty-two pages of not such big type; he wrote a lot. And this was a major statement, this was his declaration of his own nature. Now, what is a declaration of nature for a guy? In the nineteenth century, everybody was writing closed verse forms. They all went to Germany for their education, like Longfellow, they went to Heidelberg University, and they studied esoteric sociology and epistemology and linguistics and ancient Greek and they thought back on the United States romantically and wrote long poems about Hiawatha and the Indian maidens under the full moon near the Canadian lakes. Whitman actually just stated America and slugged it out with the beer carts along the Bowery and wandered up and down and sat afternoons in Pfaff's. Pfaff's was a bar he used to go to, a Bohemian hang-out, a downstairs beer hall, sort of like a German *bierstuben*. Bohemian friends used to meet there, probably like a gay gang, plus a newspaper gang, plus a theatrical gang, and the opera singers, and some of the dancers, a Broadway crowd sort of, way down, downtown though. And that was his hang-out. Probably down around the Bowery I think it was.

There he'd meet his friends, there he'd sit around and try to pick up people I guess or he'd write his articles. He was very naive at first. A young guy, he started out writing temperance novels and editing the *Brooklyn Eagle*, or some such newspaper from Brooklyn. Then, something happened to him in his thirties, about thirty-four, well, you know, crucifixion time, he realized he was going to die some day maybe, or that America was weird, or that he was weird, or maybe some kind of breakthrough of personal affection, maybe some kind of gay lib thing, anyway, he discovered his own mind and his own enthusiasm, his own expansiveness is the thing. The fact that his mind was so expansive that it was completely penetrant. That it penetrated through curiosity and inquisitiveness into every crevasse and nook, every tree, bowl, every vagina, every anus, every mouth, every flower stamen, every exhaust pipe, every horse's ear and behind that he met, penetrated through the clouds; notice he wandered, he thought a lot, he wandered in his mind and he wasn't ashamed of what he thought.

So, Whitman was probably the first person in America who was not ashamed of the fact that he thought things that were as big as the universe. Or that were equal to the universe, or that fitted the universe. He wasn't ashamed of his mind or his body. So he wrote "Song of Myself," and it began tipping off where he was coming from and where he was going, saying that you, too, needn't be ashamed of your thoughts: "I celebrate myself, and sing myself [quotes Part 1] . . . with original energy," Wow, what a thing to do!

So that's nineteenth century, and he's threatening to speak Nature without check, with original energy. Well, who's willing to pick that one up? What does that mean, anyway? Means, born here from parents the same, so you can't accuse him of being un-American, he's 4th, 5th, 6th generation so he can say whatever he wants, on his own soil, on his own land, nobody can intimidate him, nobody can say "You didn't think that thought how dare you make up a thought like that and say you thought it." He just said what he actually thought.

So, Part 2 of "Song of Myself," going on with his original mind that he is presenting, and then he looks out at the drawing rooms of Brooklyn and lower Manhattan and the rich of his day, and the sophisticated culture of his day, and he sees that it's pretty shallow: "Houses and rooms are full of perfumes . . ." [quotes Part 2]. So, what he's done here is he has completely possessed his own body, he's gone over and realized he's breathing, that his heart is beating, that he has roots that go from his crotch to his brain, he begins to sniff around him and extend his thought around him to the sea, to the woods, to the cities, recognizes his emotions, going all the way out to the millions of suns, then realizing that most of the time he and most everybody else is taking things second- and third-hand from television, from *Time, Newsweek, New York Times,* from the *Boulder Camera,* from the *Denver Post,* from the *Minneapolis Star,* from the *Durham Gazette,* from the *Raleigh News of the Dead,* from *Las Vegas Sporting Spectator,* from the *Manhattan Morbid Chronicle,* but who actually looks out of their own eyes and sees the revolutions in the trees in the fall or the bursting forth of tiny revolutions with each grass blade? Well, Whitman looked that way and recommended that everybody else look at the actual world around them rather than the abstract world they read about in the newspapers or saw as a pseudo-image/event, screened dots on television: "You shall listen to all sides and filter them from yourself."

So, then what is he going to do now? What is he going to say next about where we all come from, where we are going?

> I have heard what the talkers were talking, the talk of the begin-
>   ning and the end,
> But I do not talk of the beginning or the end.

> There was never any more inception than there is now,
> Nor any more youth or age than there is now,
> And will never be any more perfection than there is now,
> Nor any more heaven or hell than there is now.

That's a great statement, very similar to what some of the Eastern, Oriental meditators, transcendentalists, or grounded Buddhists might say. Their no-tion is the unborn, that is to say, everything is here already, it wasn't born a billion years ago and slowly developed, it isn't going to be dead a billion years from now and slowly undevelop, it's just here, like a flower in the air. There's never going to be any more hell than there is now and never be any more understanding of heaven than there is right now in our own minds, with our own perception. So that means you can't postpone your accepta-tion and realization, you can't scream at your own eyes now, you've got to look out through your own eyes as Whitman said, hear with your own ears, smell with your own nose, touch with your own touch, fingers, taste with your own tongue, and be satisfied. ". . . I see, dance, laugh, sing . . ." [reads rest of Part 3].

So he's not interested in that kind of invidious comparison and competi-tion. In the midst of "Song of Myself" he does come to a statement of what is the very nature of the mind, what is the nature of the human mind, his mind as he observed it in himself and when the mind is most open, most expanded, most realized, what relation is there between human beings and between man and nature. So I'll just read these little epiphanous moments showing, for one thing, his meditative view, this is the fourth part of "Song of Myself," and then an epiphany or ecstatic experience that he had. First of all, does he doubt himself? So, he says: "Trippers and askers surround me . . ." [reads Part 4]. Now that's a real classical viewpoint, the last poet to really announce that was John Keats, who said he had a little idea about what made Shakespeare great. He said that was "negative capability," quote negative capability unquote. Which is to say, the possibility of seeing contending parties, seeing the Communists and Capitalists scream at each other, or the Buddhists and non-Buddhists, or the Muslims and Christians, or the Jews and the Arabs, or the self and the not-self, or your mommy and daddy, or yourself and your wife, or your baby and yourself. You can see them all screaming at each other, and you can see as a kind of comedic drama that you don't get tangled and lost in it, you don't enter into the daydream fantasy of being right and being one side or the other so completely that you go out and chop somebody's head off. Instead you just sort of watch yourself, you watch them in and out of the game at the same time, both in and out of the game, watching and wondering at it. That is to say, the ability to have contrary ideas in your head at the same time without it freaking out, without "an irritable reaching out after fact" or conclusions. Without an irritable reaching out. Naturally, you reach out and want to know more, but you don't get mad, crazed, say "I gotta know the answer, there is one answer and I, me, I have to have the one answer, me, my answer, me, answer answer." Well, you don't have to go through all that. Because maybe you don't know the answer, maybe there is no answer, maybe the question has no answer, maybe there is not even a question, though there may be perturbation and conflict. So, you could apply that, say, to the present Cold War situation where everyone wants to destroy the world in order to win victory over the Wrong (either side). Here, "apart from the pulling and hauling stands what I am," which is actually what we are, in the sense of nobody really believes all the stuff they talk, you know, you say it to hear what it sounds like most of the time. Even Whitman, I think, is just saying to hear what it sounds like because it's sort of the sound you might make when you're talking more frankly to yourself, or to friends. "Apart from the pulling and hauling stands what I am/ Stands amused, complacent, compassionating," compassionating because both sides are right, and they don't even know it, both sides are wrong and they don't even know it. "Idle," he's not going to act on it, he's going to observe it, maybe go fry an egg. "Unitary," unitary is one thing, it is not divided up into this half of me is right and this half of me is wrong. "Looks down," well, you have to be looking down. "Is erect," straightens up, "bends an arm on an impalpable certain rest," maybe puts his arm down on the library desk, and thinks a little bit more, or spaces out. "Looking with side-curved head curious what will come next," come next out of his own mind he means, or who will come into the door of the library. What plane, or when Mt. St. Helens will explode. Both in and out of the game, watching and wondering at it which is the best we can do actually. The best thing we can do is wonder at everything, it's so amazing. So, then what happens? If you take that attitude and open yourself up and allow yourself to admit everything, to hear everything, not to exclude, just be like the moon in the old Japanese haiku: "The autumn moon/ shines kindly/ on the flower-thief," or like Whitman's sun which shines on the common prostitute in his poem "To A Common Prostitute"—"Not till the sun excludes you do I exclude you." His mind is there, he's aware of her, she's aware of him and everybody's sitting around and internally scratching their head. So there is an epiphany out of this, or a rise, or a kind of exquisite awareness that intensifies.

Part 5 of "Song of Myself": "I believe in you my soul . . ." [reads Part 5]. So just out of that one experience of a touch with another person, of complete acceptance, his awareness spread throughout the space around him and he realized that that friendly touch, that friendly awareness was what bound the entire universe together and held everything suspended in gravity.

So given that, where could he go from here? Well, a long survey of America, which he did in "Song of Myself," in which he extended his own awareness to cover the entire basic spiritual awareness of America, trying to make an ideal America which would be an America of comradely awareness, acknowledgment of tenderness, acknowledgment of gentleness, acknowledgment of comradeship, acknowledgment of what he called adhesiveness. Because what he said was that if this country did not have some glue to keep people together, to bind them together, adhesiveness, some emotional bond, there was no possibility of democracy working, and we'd just be a lot of separate people fighting for advantage, military advantage, commercial advantage, iron advantage, coal advantage, silver advantage, gold, hunting up some kind of monopoly on molybdenum. On the other hand, there was a total democracy of feeling around, so in Part 11 of "Song of Myself": "Twenty-eight young men bathe by the shore . . ." [reads Part 11].

Well, so he pointed out the longing for closeness; erotic tenderness is of course implicit here, his own as well as in empathy, the spinster lady behind her curtains looking at the naked bathers. He pointed to that as basic to our bodies, basic to our minds, basic to our community, basic to our sociability, basic to our society, therefore basic to our politics. If that quality of compassion, erotic longing, tenderness, gentleness, was squelched, repressed, pushed back, denied, insulted, mocked, seen cynically, then the entire operation of democracy would be squelched, debased, mocked, seen cynically, advantaged, poorly made into a paranoid, mechano-megalopolis congregation of freaks afeard of each other. Because that may have been the very nature of the industrial civilization, that by the very roboting of work and homogenization of talk and imagery, unlike Whitman, people not speaking for themselves but talking falsely, as if they represented anything but themselves, like as if a President could represent anybody but his own mind, then there was going to be trouble. So, at one point he says human society is kind of messed up; so, Part 32 of "Song of Myself,"

> I think I could turn, and live with animals, they are so placid
> and self-contain'd,
> I stand and look at them long and long.

> They do not sweat and whine about their condition,
> They do not lie awake in the dark and weep for their sins,
> They do not make me sick discussing their duty to God,
> Not one is dissatisfied, not one is demented with the mania of
> owning things,
> Not one kneels to another, nor to his kind that lived thousands
> of years ago,
> Not one is respectable or unhappy over the whole earth.

Not one animal is respectable, in all of creation. All these human beings want to be respectable, but he's pointing out that not one elephant in Africa would ever dream of considering himself respectable. So, they ". . . show their relations to me and I accept them,/ They bring me tokens of myself, they evince them plainly in their possession."

Then, what does he do in the city? He's lonesome, so there's a little one-line description of himself in the city, "Looking in at the shop-windows of Broadway the whole forenoon, flatting the flesh of my nose on the thick plate-glass." But then, also he can get out in his mind: "I go hunting polar furs and the seal, leaping chasms with a pike-pointed staff, clinging to topples of brittle and blue." He empathizes with everybody: "I am an old artillerist, I tell of my fort's bombardment,/ I am there again." And in Part 34: "Now I tell what I knew in Texas in my early youth," and then he goes on with a long anecdote. Or, Part 35: "Would you hear of an old-time sea-fight," and he went on and on to that, telling about old-time sea-fights, and "Toward twelve there in the beams of the moon they surrender to us,"—the moony imagination. Then, maybe he's a sea fighter, or he's an Arctic explorer, or maybe he's a jerk. Part 37: "You laggards there on guard! look to your arms!/ In at the conquer'd doors they crowd! I am possess'd!" He wasn't afraid of that, see: "Askers embody themselves in me and I am embodied in them,/ I project my hat, sit shame-faced, and beg." That's like Bob Dylan in his film *Renaldo and Clara*, walking down the street and all of a sudden the camera catches him and stares him in the eye and he stares the camera in the eye and all of a sudden he shivers and puts out his right hand held by his left palm out, "Some change? Spare change of love? Spare change?" And so you have, "Enough! enough! enough!/ Somehow I have been stunn'd. Stand back! . . . That I could look with a separate look on my own crucifixion and bloody crowning." Ah, so he has suffered a bit here, he does empathize with all the beggars, the monstrous convicts with sweat twitching on their lips, but his point here is that everybody so suffers, everybody is everybody else, in the sense of having experienced in imagination or in real life all of the non-respectable emotions of the elephants and the ants. So he says, "It is time to explain myself—let us stand up . . ." [reads Part 44], and "I am an acme . . . Now on this spot I stand with my robust soul." So that's great, so he's here, he recognizes he's here:

> My rendezvous is appointed, it is certain,
> The Lord will be there and wait till I come on perfect terms,
> The great Camerado, the lover true for whom I pine will be there.

So he says:

> I have no chair, no church, no philosophy,
> I lead no man to a dinner-table, library, exchange,
> But each man and each woman of you I lead upon a knoll,
> My left hand hooking you round the waist,
> My right hand pointing to landscapes of continents and the public
>   road.

> Not I, not any one else can travel that road for you,
> You must travel it for yourself.

> It is not far, it is within reach,
> Perhaps you have been on it since you were born and did not
>   know,
> Perhaps it is everywhere on water and on land.

Shoulder your duds dear son, and I will mine, and let us hasten
    forth,
Wonderful cities and free nations we shall fetch as we go.

If you tire, give me both burdens, and rest the chuff of your hand
    on my hip,
And in due time you shall repay the same service to me,
For after we start we never lie by again.

On the road, Walt Whitman, 1883 probably, prophesying what would happen to America 100 years later.

So he comes to his conclusions at the end of the poem. He wants to tell
finally what he can get out of it all. Part 50 of "Song of Myself," approaching
the end of the poem: "There is that in me—I do not know what it is—but
I know it is in me . . . It is not chaos or death—it is form, union, plan—it
is eternal life—it is Happiness." And Part 51: "The past and present wilt—
. . ." [reads Part 51]. Finally, Part 52, the last section, he'll make his last
prophecy, dissolve himself into you the listener, the reader, and his poem
will become a part of your consciousness: "The spotted hawk swoops by
. . . [reads Part 52] . . . I stop somewhere waiting for you." That's a very
tearful, deep promise, "I stop somewhere waiting for you," so he's going
to wait a long, long, long time, and have to go through a great deal of his
own loves and fears before he actually finds a companion. What kind of
companion does he want, what does he look for? "The expression of the
face balks account . . ." and this is in the poem called "I Sing the Body
Electric," in which he begins to describe his own body and other peoples'
bodies in an intimate way, numbering all the parts, numbering all the
emotions, and naming them and actually attempting to account, and give
an accounting and itemization of all men. There is a little four or five lines
of, just about, well, what does he look for?

The expression of the face balks account,
But the expression of a well-made man appears not only in his
    face,
It is in his limbs and joints also, it is curiously in the joints
    of his hips and wrists,
It is in his walk, the carriage of his neck, the flex of his waist
    and knees, dress does not hide him,
The strong sweet quality he has strikes through the cotton and
    broadcloth,
To see him pass conveys as much as the best poem, perhaps more,
You linger to see his back, and the back of his neck and
    shoulder-side.

Well, everybody's done that, man or woman to each other, who is interesting, who's got something going there. "Spontaneous me," he says, and so he keeps walking around, "has native moments."

Finally he has a little short poem, "Native Moments," actually, defining what they are, when some authentic flash comes to him: "Native moments— when you come upon me— . . ." [reads "Native Moments"]. Well he is really declaring himself, declaring his own feelings, he's not scared of them, like born for the first time in the world, recognizing his own nature, recognizing the world. The last of the poems in the first part of *Leaves of Grass* is "As Adam Early in the Morning":

> As Adam early in the morning,
> Walking forth from the bower refresh'd with sleep,
> Behold me where I pass, hear my voice, approach,
> Touch me, touch the palm of your hand to my body as I pass,
> Be not afraid of my body.

Well, there is some false note there I guess, he really wants someone to love him, and he's not quite able to say it right. Still he does want to make democracy something that hangs together using the force of Eros, so, "For You O Democracy," in the "Calamus" section of *Leaves of Grass:* "Come, I will make the continent indissoluble . . . [reads] . . . With the life-long love of comrades," Beatles, Rolling Stones, beatniks, the life-long love of comrades, "I will plant companionship as thick as trees . . . [reads the rest of "For You O Democracy"] . . . For you, for you, I am trilling these songs." Well, that's his statement of politics, actually, and, however, you never can tell, maybe he's just a big fairy egotist.

So he's got a little poem "Are You the New Person Drawn toward Me?" in the "Calamus" section of *Leaves of Grass,* "Calamus," that is a section of *Leaves of Grass;* calamus has a forked root, oddly enough, it is a marsh plant, calamus grows, lives in marshes in the northeast, around Manhattan, in the old days on Long Island up near Cherry Valley where I live in the bogs. It has a somewhat manlike forked root, and its root is said to contain elements of LSD according to the *Encyclopedia of Hallucinogens* by Humphrey Osmond and Abraham Hoffer, the standard encyclopedic scholarly work in the subject. Odd title, "Calamus."

The "Calamus" section of *Leaves of Grass* was that describing erotic pleasure and parts of the body, which when Whitman sent them to Ralph Waldo Emerson shocked the elder American prophet Emerson a bit, and he suggested that Whitman leave it out when he published the book because it was perhaps that people were not ready for it, America was not ready for it. Whitman, however, persisted and felt that that was an integral part of his message that if he was going to talk about honesty and frankness and openness and comradeship he did have to say the un-sayable, did have to talk about people's bodies, did have to describe them with beauty and Greek levity and healthiness and heroism. So he did have to make heroes out of our private parts. So "Calamus" does include that but it's actually, nowadays reading, very tame. However, because he was so intent on his purpose, he was a little worried. So: "Are you the new person drawn toward me? . . ." [reads "Are You the New Person Drawn toward Me?"]. I guess he's talking to himself. However, he's willing to trust his senses. So he says, "Behold this swarthy face . . ." [reads "Behold This Swarthy Face"]. Okay, so he's proposing that the dear love of comrades and the unabashed affection between citizens be acknowledged as it stands rather than mocked. And then, of course, not to get people upset, so: "I hear it was charged against me . . ." [reads "I Hear It Was Charged against Me"]. And that includes like the prairie grass everyone equal, so that there are ". . . those that look carelessly in the faces of Presidents and governors, as to say *Who are you?*," that's a little line from a poem called "The Prairie-grass Dividing." So what's the big thrill like our big thrill nowadays? Well, here's my big thrill, here's Whitman's big thrill:

> A glimpse through an interstice caught,
> Of a crowd of workmen and drivers in a bar-room around the stove
> late of a winter night, and I unremark'd seated in a corner,
> Of a youth who loves me and whom I love, silently approaching and
> seating himself near, that he may hold me by the hand,
> A long while amid the noises coming and going, of drinking and oath
> and smutty jest,
> There we two, content, happy in being together, speaking little,
> perhaps not a word.

So that's a recognizable emotion between friends.

But there may be things that he doesn't want to say even, so he says: "Earth, my likeness . . ." [reads from "Earth, My Likeness"]. So there's more to come and it'll come out of Whitman as he goes forward in his life, renouncing all formulas ". . . O bat-eyed and materialistic priests," (that's from "Song of the Open Road ").

So his next long poem is called "Salut au Monde!," saying, 'Come on, let's go out, let's explore life, let's find out what's going on here. Let's look at the tents of the Kalmucks and the Baskirs, let's go out and see the African and Asiatic towns, go to the Ganges, let's go to the groves of Mona where the Druids walked and see the bodies of the gods and wait at Liverpool and

Glasgow and Dublin and Marseilles, wait at Valparaiso, Panama, sail on the waters of Hindustan, the China Sea, all the way around the world, on the road.' So it began: "O take my hand Walt Whitman!/ Such gliding wonders! . . ."—he's going to guide everybody around the world, spiritual trip around the work, like fuck in bed, but it will be in the spirit.

Then there's this very famous poem where he realizes, yeah, sure, but all that's transitory, it's going, there's not much, you know, like 20 years, 50 years, 70 years, then zap it's gone. So there is this great poem, in the middle of Manhattan looking over at Brooklyn on the Brooklyn ferry, called "Crossing Brooklyn Ferry," realizing, okay, he's had these feelings, everybody has these kinds of feelings, everybody rarely has the chance to experience them, much less say them aloud, much less propose them as politics, much less offer to save the nation with feeling and at the same time it's in the appearances of life even though it was very rare for people to understand that, except that at the deepest moment of their life they do understand that. And, looking at the vast apparition of Manhattan and the masts of ships around it and the sunset and the seagulls, what more does he have to ask than the immensity of universe around him and the river on which he's riding and the feelings which he's aware of and the ability he has to call these feelings out to other people from his time to the future. He says:

> We understand then do we not?
> What I promis'd without mentioning it, have you not accepted?
> What the study could not teach—what the preaching could not
>   accomplish is accomplish'd, is it not?

[Reads from first half of Part 9.] That's very subtle, you see from the sunshine halo, aureole, aura around the hair in the sunshine reflected in the water. He's even noticing, his noticing is so exquisite and ethereal and fine that he's got massive masts of the aureole of the light of the sun reflected shining in water and reflected in people's hair around him. [Reads second half of Part 9.]

So, he needs from that, after "Crossing Brooklyn Ferry," he needs someone to answer him, so his next long poem is "Song of the Answerer," in which he imagines the answerer, he is the answerer, what can be answered he answers and what cannot be answered he shows how it cannot be answered and that goes on and on and on and praises the words of true poems of the true poets which do not merely please: "The true poets are not followers of beauty, but the august masters of beauty. . . ."

Well, he'll go on and then there's a great tragedy coming up ahead. He's passed through California and he's written about lonesome Kansas and he's written about birds of passage and a song of the rolling earth and he's written about the ocean and then back to his birthplace in Long Island looking at the city, a vision of birth continuous and death continuous. Again, sort of an ecstatic acknowledgment of the continuity of feeling from generation to generation as the continuity of birth that no matter what the appearances, there always is a rebirth of delight, of feeling of acknowledgment, of the spaciousness of glittery sunlight on the ocean. And that's the famous poem "Out of the Cradle Endlessly Rocking" [reads first stanza]. Of course, the form there is a classical form: "Of Man's First Disobedience, and the Fruit/ Of that Forbidden Tree, whose mortal taste/ Brought Death into the World, and all our woe . . . Sing Heav'nly Muse," that's John Milton's opening of *Paradise Lost*. Or the opening of Homer's *Iliad:* "Sing O Goddess of the wrath of Achilles, Peleus' son, the ruinous wrath that brought down countless woes upon the heads of the Achaeans and sent many brave souls hurrying down to Hades and many a hero left for prey to dogs and vultures . . ." or something like that. Again, in that same long, long, long breath of realization that ends with an accomplished trumpet call, almost to sing the personal, I mean, ". . . a reminiscence sing," and then it's a reminiscence of a whisper of death, when he was young at the oceanside. "Sea-Drift," "Tears," "On the Beach at Night Alone," "The World Below the Brine," "Song for All Seas, All Ships," those are some of the titles of the poems of that era—that was up until about 1854. Then, a few prophecies of the presidents, and some patriotic songs, and more awareness of the problems of America as it was going into the Civil War. Then, in the Civil War he himself following his instincts, followed the soldiers, went to Washington, worked in hospitals, took care of dying men, was out on the battlefields as a nurse and then in the hospitals in Washington, D.C. as a nurse, saw a link in walking around Washington likely enough at 4 A.M.; as Whitman was walking around on his own mission of mercy or mercies of mission, he wrote a lot of poems, like "A Sight in Camp in the Daybreak Gray and Dim"—this is a little, say, a snapshot, the same theme of human divinity in the midst of the degradation of horror and war: [reads from "A Sight in Camp in the Daybreak Gray and Dim"].

So, he worked as a wound-dresser, taking care of the wounds of the injured and the dying in the Civil War. Having the same delicate, emotional relationships with the people he met as:

> O tan-faced prairie-boy,
> Before you came to camp came many a welcome gift,
> Praises and presents came and nourishing food, till at last among
>   the recruits,

> You came, taciturn, with nothing to give—we but look'd on each
>   other,
> When lo! more than all the gifts of the world you gave me.

Funny, his idea of America, "tan-faced prairie-boy," full of feeling and awareness, not at all a stereotyped television Barbie doll.

Then, in the midst of the tragedies of the war and the visions of death he had, the actual dying, memories of President Lincoln who was shot, and so his great old elegy for Lincoln, which most every kid in America knew back in the 20s and 30s, with its very beautiful description of the passing of Lincoln's coffin on railroad through lanes and streets, through the cities and through the states and with processions, seas of silence, seas of faces and unbared heads, the coffin of Lincoln mourned and in the middle of this poem a recognition of death in a way that had not been proposed in America before. Just as he had accepted the feelings of life, there was the appearance and feelings of death, the awareness of death that he had to tally finally. So there's this great italicized song in Part 14 of "When Lilacs Last in the Dooryard Bloom'd," from "Memories of President Lincoln."

Actually, the whole of "When Lilacs Last in the Dooryard Bloom'd" is so beautiful that it would be worth reading, but it's so long that I can't do it and also it's so beautiful that I'm afraid I'll cry if I read it. "When Lilacs Last in the Dooryard Bloom'd,"—which is a very interesting title because I visited Whitman's house in Camden, New Jersey, and in the back yard in the old brick house on Mickle Street where he lived the last years of his life, though not likely where he wrote this poem, there were lilacs blooming in the back yard, blooming by the outhouse which was right outside the back door in the garden. "When lilacs last in the dooryard bloom'd . . ." [reads Parts 1, 2, 3, 5, 6 & "Hymn to Death" in Part 14].

Then Whitman grew older, traveled, extended his imagination to blue Ontario shore, began to see the declining of his own physical body in a series of poems called "Autumn Rivulets." He wrote about the compost, as Peter Orlovsky did a hundred years later. So Whitman wrote:

> Behold this compost! behold it well!
> Perhaps every mite has once form'd part of a sick person—yet
>   behold!
> The grass of spring covers the prairies,
> The bean bursts noiselessly through the mould in the garden,
> The delicate spear of the onion pierces upward, . . .

So, after the carol to death there is a realization of the recycling in the compost, the recycling of soul, the recycling of body, the inevitability of passage, transitoriness, of things entering the earth and emerging from the earth, and he wrote poems about the city dead-house, too. So these were all autumn rivulets. He wrote his poem to the singer in prison, and "Outlines for a Tomb."

Incidentally, he took his own tomb at that point, made up a little drawing of a tomb for himself which he took from the opening page of William Blake's last great prophetic book "Jerusalem," of a man entering a stone, open door, stone pillars on each side, stone floor, stone arch, a triangular arch on top with a great stone door opened, a man carrying a great globe of light. A consciousness entering into this dark, he can't see what's in it, he's going in like passing through with a big black cat. Whitman designed this tomb for himself, which is now standing in Camden, New Jersey, in exactly the same image as the Blake. He wrote little poems to his own tomb then and to the negative and began to consider the negative, how do you recompost the negative?

So, the line I was quoting from "To a Common Prostitute," that line occurs here: "Be composed—be at ease with me—I am Walt Whitman, liberal and lusty as Nature,/ Not till the sun excludes you do I exclude you . . ." [reads all of "To a Common Prostitute"]. That's a good way to be kind to your neighbor, and to acknowledge the varying vocations.

He took a trip out to Kansas and wrote funny little poems about the encroaching civilization that was beginning to cover the prairies. There is a little tiny poem that I've quoted, "The Prairie States":

> A newer garden of creation, no primal solitude,
> Dense, joyous, modern, populous millions, cities and farms,
> With iron interlaced, composite, tied, many in one,
> By all the world contributed—freedom's and law's and thrift's
>   society,
> The crown and teeming paradise, so far, of time's accumulations,
> To justify the past.

So, that was ambitious and hopeful thought, he might have had some change of mind if he saw Kansas during the Vietnam War, with army bases and airplane bases and "iron interlaced" above the plains there, horrific iron.

He wrote a great poem now beginning to go into a recognition of the Orient and recognition of the ancient wisdoms of death that were understood there, that is, the acceptance of death as well as the acceptance of life, seeing an identity between his own extended empathy and sympathy and compassion, and the ancient empathies and sympathies and compassions of the meditators of the Himalayas.

There's a very interesting section in "Passage to India," interesting to those of us who already made that passage ourselves, either mentally or physically. Remember, in the nineteenth century lots and lots of poets and philosophers in America were interested in transcendentalism and oriental wisdom and Brahma and the Hindus and the romantic, glamorous wisdom of the East, the Brook Farm experiment, many people and Bronson Alcott were interested in Western gnosticism, and Bronson Alcott went to England to buy up the neo-Platonic and hermetic translations of Thomas Taylor, the Platonist, translations which were from Greek Orphic mysteries and Dionysian mysteries, that were also read by the great British transcendental mystic poets like Coleridge, Shelley, William Blake, those same books were brought to Brook Farm and then translations by Thomas Taylor of ancient hermetic Greek texts were circulated by Bronson Alcott to Emerson and to Thoreau and Hawthorne. So there was this movement of transcendentalism and a recognition of the exotic East, there was the opening of Japan around that time. There was Lafcadio Hearn, maybe thirty years later, going to Japan and making great collections of Japanese art to bring to Boston to impress the New Englanders in the second wave of Oriental understanding thirty years later, but even in Europe at that time, Japanese prints by Hiroshige were circulating and were eyed by Gauguin and Van Gogh, who began imitating their flat surfaces and their bright colors. So, a whole new calligraphy of the mind was beginning to be discovered by the West—in the same time that the West was peddling opium in China, oddly enough, that was the trade exchange, opium for meditation.

However, Whitman reflected that in "Passage to India": "Lo soul, the retrospect brought forward ..." [reads next 15 lines of Part 6]. So he acknowledged that transcendent, and like D. H. Lawrence a hundred years later, wrote about the great ship of death that goes forward to explore: "O we can wait no longer,/ We too take ship O soul, ..." Talking about going through the soul as well as going through the world.

However he sees that most of the world is asleep. Alas, so there's this long poem "The Sleepers." This is like middle age now, it's really getting deeper on him now and death is coming a bit into his mind as he gets into his 50s and 60s. Also the fact that most of the living on the world are the living dead or the sleepers:

> I wander all night in my vision,
> Stepping with light feet, swiftly and noiselessly stepping
>   and stopping,
> Bending with open eyes over the shut eyes of sleepers,
> Wandering and confused, lost to myself, ill-assorted,
>   contradictory,
> Pausing, gazing, bending, and stopping.

> How solemn they look there, stretch'd and still,
> How quiet they breathe, the little children in their cradles. . . .

Well, they all sleep, so he moves on, and says at the end of all these sleepers, "I too pass from the night . . ." [reads conclusion of "The Sleepers"]. So he's now beginning to think of the future, what's going to happen to him.

Then the next set of poems in *Leaves of Grass* is called "Whispers of Heavenly Death," very interesting, beginning to get more and more close to the grand subject of all poetry. "Quicksand Years" is a very charming little statement on that. Now he's beginning to doubt himself a little bit:

> Quicksand years that whirl me I know not whither,
> Your schemes, politics, fail, lines give way, substances mock and
>   elude me,
> Only the theme I sing, the great and strong-possess'd soul, eludes
>   not,
> One's-self must never give way—that is the final substance—
>   that out of all is sure,
> Out of politics, triumphs, battles, life, what at last finally remains?
> When shows break up what but One's-Self is sure?

Well, how does he know that? That one's self is even sure, well, he's going to get older, we'll see what happens next.

That's an interesting thing, because now he realized that it is the notion of an unconquerable self or soul that all along has sustained him, but that, too, will dissolve and as a great poet he's going to let it dissolve. He has a few thoughts about the dissolution, also, incidentally, just as of his soul, of the soul of the nation, the dissolution of democracy, and in those days, of public opinion. Well, here's what he's got to say, "Thoughts," he's not going to give it a title, you know. It's all about Watergate basically: "Of public opinion . . ." [reads from "Thoughts"]. So that prophesied way in advance, even the President of the United States someday must stand naked, by Bob Dylan.

"So long!" finally he says to all these thoughts. It's toward the end of *Leaves of Grass*, in fact, I think it's the last great poem in *Leaves of Grass*, salutation and farewell and summary, conclusion, triumph, disillusion, giving up, taking it all on, giving it all over to you who are listening. "So Long!": "To conclude, I announce what comes after me . . ." [reads "So Long!"].

But he wasn't dead yet, actually, he was only 70. So now he's got to go through the actual dying, so how does he do that? How does he take that?

What has he got to say about that? Well, there are some really interesting "Sands at Seventy" thoughts, giving out, he was quite ill and old in his 70s, in the sense of old in the body, gallstones, paralysis, uremia probably, emphysema, great many of his heart difficulties. I think his autopsy, according to a poem by Jonathan Williams I once read, showed him to have been universal in his illnesses near death as he was in his healths in life. So, little poems, then, just whatever he could write now, his great major work over, and yet the little trickle drops of wisdom of a man of 70 are exquisite and curious.

> As I sit writing here, sick and grown old,
> Not my least burden is that dulness of the years, querilities,
> Ungracious glooms, aches, lethargy, constipation, whimpering
> *ennui,*
> May filter in my daily songs.

And he's got a little poem to his canary bird, he's stuck in his little bedroom up in Camden, on Mickle Street, in a little house with low ceilings, visited by many people including Edward Carpenter, the tutor to Queen Victoria's children who abandoned his official role and went out as one of the first six revolutionists, humanists, visited Walt Whitman and Whitman told him to go to India. He studied, probably with Ramakrishna or one of the other sages. Edward Carpenter left behind a testament of his sleeping with Whitman, in the form of a conversation with Gavin Arthur, one of the gentlemen of the old school, the grandson of President Chester A. Arthur, who was living in San Francisco, and told me one day the story of his sleeping with Edward Carpenter, and Carpenter's account of his sleeping with Whitman, so I asked Gavin before he died to write me an account of that which he did, which was published in *Gay Sunshine Interviews*.[1] And since the later Whitmanic hero Neal Cassady slept with Edward Carpenter, there is a straight transmission from Whitman on down through the present day.

So, he's sitting there talking to his canary bird, "Did we count great, O soul, to penetrate the themes of mighty books. . .?" Then "Queries to My Seventieth Year": "Approaching, nearing, curious,/ Thou dim, uncertain spectre—bringest thou life or death?" Well, everything wasn't bad, he had his first dandelion, springtime:

> Simple and fresh and fair from winter's close emerging,
> As if no artifice of fashion, business, politics, had ever been,
> Forth from its sunny nook of shelter'd grass—innocent, golden,
>   calm as the dawn,
> The spring's first dandelion shows its trustful face.

So he had that same witty awareness, even lying in his sickbed.

Then people began exploring the North Pole, and he was amazed at that: "Of That Blithe Throat of Thine . . ." [reads this poem]. Well, that's what wisdom brings, he's no longer dependent on that youthful self, in fact the self is dissolving as it will in these last poems. "To Get the Final Lilt of Songs," he says in "Sands at Seventy": "To get the final lilt of songs,/ To penetrate the inmost lore of poets—to know the mighty ones/. . . Old age, and what it brings from all its past experience." So, you need that, otherwise you ain't gonna learn nuttin' if you don't grow old and die, you just know what you have in your mind when you think you've got the world by the crotch.

So, an odd lament for the aborigines, an Iroquois term "Yonnondio," the sense of the word is *lament for the aborigines,* Whitman has a little note here, ". . . an Iroquois term; and has been used for a personal name." It's an odd little political poem at the end, warning us of Black Mesa, of the Four Corners, of the civilization's destruction of the land and the original natives there. "A song, a poem of itself . . ." [reads from "Yonnondio"]. So he's also saying as he dies, so may all the machinery of the civilization, so there's nothing for anybody to get too high and mighty about.

But he's got to give thanks in old age. For what? [Reads "Thanks in Old Age."] But there is also "Stronger Lessons"—is everything thanks for the memories and thanks for the good times, and thanks for the gifts and thanks for the loves? "Stronger Lessons":

> Have you learn'd lessons only of those who admired you, and
>   were tender with you, and stood aside for you?
> Have you not learn'd great lessons from those who reject you,
>   and brace themselves against you? or who treat you with
>   contempt, or dispute the passage with you?

That's a good piece of advice of how to alchemize fear to bliss, how to alchemize contrariety to harmony, how to ride with the punches, so to speak. But what is it all about? So he's got finally, twilight, not quite sure about that old self. "Twilight":

> The soft voluptuous opiate shades,
> The sun just gone, the eager light dispell'd—(I too will soon be
>   gone, dispell'd,)
> A haze—nirwana—rest and night—oblivion.

But there are still a few thoughts left in his mind before he goes off into that rest and night. [Reads from "You Lingering Sparse Leaves of Me."]

Well, what has he done, he wonders, with his life? So he says farewell to
all of his earlier poems. [Reads from "Now Precedent Songs, Farewell."]
Then, having summed up his life, well, just waiting around, "An Evening
Lull":

> After a week of physical anguish,
> Unrest and pain, and feverish heat,
> Toward the ending day a calm and lull comes on,
> Three hours of peace and soothing rest of brain.

Then, "After the Supper and Talk" is the last of the poems of "Sands at
Seventy," and perhaps his last. [Reads from "After the Supper and Talk."]
So, that was goodbye my fancy, but that wasn't his last word, no, because
he lived on. So he's got, what, "Good-Bye My Fancy," "Second Annex,"
"Preface Note to the Second Annex," where he says:

Reader, you must allow a little fun here—for one reason there are too many of the following
poemets about death, &c., and for another the passing hours (July 5, 1890) are so sunny-fine.
And old as I am I feel to-day almost a part of some frolicsome wave, or for sporting yet
like a kid or kitten—. . .

Still there are a couple of little last poems. [Reads "My 71st Year."] Then
at last he'll have another comment on his work: "Long, Long Hence":

> After a long, long course, hundreds of years, denials,
> Accumulations, rous'd love and joy and thought,
> Hopes, wishes, aspirations, ponderings, victories, myriads of
>   readers,
> Coating, compassing, covering—after ages' and ages' encrus-
>   tations,
> Then only may these songs reach fruition.

Well, that's actually what happened to him in the sense that his work was
little famous, not much read and a bit put down in the years after his death,
to the point of . . . or to the situation that when I went to Columbia College
in 1945, between '44 and '49, by scholars and academic poets and by
professors and their ilk and by the Cold War soldiers and warriors of those
days, Whitman was considered some lonesome, foolish crank who'd lived
in poverty and likely Bohemian dis-splendor, having cantankerous affairs
with jerks of all nations, in his mind. Not to be considered a major
personage like the witty dimwits of mid-town Manhattan who worked for
Time, Life, CIA, *Newsweek,* and their own egos.
   Whitman, still clinging on, recognized what it was that was his victory,

the commonplace, ordinary mind, as it is known around the world. [Reads "The Commonplace."] So he knew what the basis was where everybody could stand, which was where we all actually are, and was recognizable in our own bodies in our own thoughts in our own work in our own nation, in our own local particulars. A wisdom that was inherited by Ezra Pound and William Carlos Williams and whole generations of poets after Walt Whitman who had discovered that common ground of self and dissolution of self, common ground of his own mind and the common ground of city pavement he walked on with his fellow citizens and the common ground of their emotions between them.

At the end, there is a rounded catalogue complete, he says, [reads "The Rounded Catalogue Divine Complete."] Okay, so he says, finally, in the "Purport" to *Leaves of Grass*, his entire book, "Not to exclude or demarcate, or pick out evils from their formidable masses (even to expose them,)/ But add, fuse, complete, extend—and celebrate the immortal and the good. . . ." So what was there unexpressed, actually, in his life? He has a little poem, almost his last here, "The Unexpress'd": "How dare one say it? . . . Still something not yet told in poesy's voice or print—something lacking,/ (Who knows? the best yet unexpress'd and lacking.)"

So, if there is yet unexpressed form, there'll be unseen buds for the future. His next-to-the-last poem: "Unseen Buds": "Unseen buds, infinite . . ." of course he's garrulous to the very last, as he's said, "Unseen buds, infinite, hidden well . . ." [reads rest of "Unseen Buds"].

So he can with good conscience say farewell to his part, to his own fancy, to his own imagination, to his own life's work, to his own life, "Good-Bye My Fancy!": "Good-bye my Fancy!/ Farewell dear mate, dear love! . . ." [reads from the rest of "Good-Bye My Fancy!"]. And that's counted as almost his last poem, but then he didn't die, he had to go on, there's more. He had to keep going, poor fellow, thinking, putting it all out, *Old Age Echoes*. To be at all, he's amazed at it, and he's there, so what can you do? Remember all the dirty deeds he did? "Of Many a Smutch'd Deed Reminiscent":

> Full of wickedness, I—of many a smutch'd deed reminiscent
> —of worse deeds capable,
> Yet I look composedly upon nature, drink day and night the
> joys of life, and await death with perfect equanimity,
> Because of my tender and boundless love for him I love and
> because of his boundless love for me.

Well, that's something fine to figure on, but his actual last poem after writing something about death's valley, and there are poems about death's valley and "Nay Tell Me Not Today the Publish'd Shame," he's got an account of the horrible politics going on there as he was dying. Last: "A Thought of Columbus," it's a forward-looking thing about exploration, navigation, going on into worlds unknown, unconquered, etc. "A Thought of Columbus," not his most moving poem, not his greatest poem, but on the other hand his last poem as listed, and so maybe his last thoughts: "The mystery of mysteries ..." [reads from "A Thought of Columbus"].

So, he ended on a heroical historic note, congratulating the explorer, himself really, or the Columbus in himself, and the Columbus in all of us for seeking outward in our spiritual journey looking for not even truth, because it wasn't truth he was proposing, except the truth of the fact that we are here with our lusts and delights, our givings up and grabbings, growings into trouble and marriage and birth and growings into coffins and earth and unbirth. Good character, all in all, the kind of character that if a nation were composed of such liberal, large-minded gentlemen of the old school or young, large-bodied persons with free emotions and funny thoughts and tender looks, there might be the possibility of this nation and other nations surviving on the planet, but to survive, we'd have to take on some of that large magnanimity that Whitman yawped over the roof tops of the world.

NOTES

1   See end notes in *Gay Sunshine Interviews*, Vol. I, Gay Sunshine Press, San Francisco, 1978. Page 126—Gavin Arthur document.

Walt Whitman at Bear Mountain • *Louis Simpson*

"... life which does not give the preference to any
other life, of any previous period, which therefore prefers
its own existence ..."—Ortega Y Gasset

Neither on horseback nor seated,
But like himself, squarely on two feet,
The poet of death and lilacs
Loafs by the footpath. Even the bronze looks alive
Where it is folded like cloth. And he seems friendly.

"Where is the Mississippi panorama
And the girl who played the piano?
Where are you, Walt?
The Open Road goes to the used-car lot.

"Where is the nation you promised?
These houses built of wood sustain
Colossal snows,
And the light above the street is sick to death.

"As for the people—see how they neglect you!
Only a poet pauses to read the inscription."

"I am here," he answered.
"It seems you have found me out.
Yet, did I not warn you that it was Myself
I advertised? Were my words not sufficiently plain?

"I gave no prescriptions,
And those who have taken my moods for prophecies
Mistake the matter."
Then, vastly amused—"Why do you reproach me?
I freely confess I am wholly disreputable.
Yet I am happy, because you have found me out."

A crocodile in wrinkled metal loafing ...

Then all the realtors,
Pickpockets, salesmen, and the actors performing
Official scenarios,
Turned a deaf ear, for they had contracted
American dreams.

But the man who keeps a store on a lonely road,
And the housewife who knows she's dumb,
And the earth, are relieved.

All that grave weight of America
Cancelled! Like Greece and Rome.
The future in ruins!
The castles, the prisons, the cathedrals
Unbuilding, and roses
Blossoming from the stones that are not there. . . .

The clouds are lifting from the high Sierras,
The Bay mists clearing.
And the angel in the gate, the flowering plum,
Dances like Italy, imagining red.

Honoring Whitman

> He most honors my style who learns under it how to
> destroy the teacher.
>
> "Song of Myself"

I BEGAN READING WHITMAN seriously around 1959. I had read him before
that out of curiosity, but in 1959 I was changing from writing in regular
meters and forms to writing in irregular meters and forms, and Whitman
was one of the poets I read to see how they did it.

I liked the pictures in Whitman's poems: cavalry crossing a ford, a tree
standing by itself. I liked his idea of a "Muse install'd amid the kitchenware,"
i.e., making poetry out of common things. This seemed useful in view of
the part played by machinery in our lives a hundred years later.

On the other hand, his whooping it up over the chest-expansion of the
United States didn't do a thing for me. His wish for young men to throw
their arms about his neck struck me as incomprehensible. I was put off by
his use of big-sounding words or French words. He was capable of writing
long passages naming countries he'd read about or heard about, the names
of mountains and rivers, the races of men, et cetera.

> I see the Brazilian vaquero,
> I see the Bolivian ascending mount Sorata. . . .

I don't see how anyone could ever have read these passages in Whitman with
pleasure.

At times, however, he was capable of a surprising compression of thought
and style—he was almost epigrammatic: "The nearest gnat is an explanation," "Trippers and askers surround me."

257

On the whole I found Whitman exhilarating. His freedom of line and style, and his interest in pots and pans, bringing them over into poetry, were what I needed at the time.

So far I haven't mentioned Whitman's "philosophy." It consists of two or three ideas. One, it is possible to merge in your feelings with others, and it is possible for others to merge in their feelings with you. Two, if this occurs over a distance, or over a span of time, it seems to annihilate space and time. This is a kind of immortality. Three, in order to convey your feelings to others you must, by a process of empathic observation, using all your senses, take things into yourself and express them again. The senses are "dumb ministers" of feeling . . . through them we know one another. The poet is the manager of this process—he puts what we feel and see into words.

These ideas, which can be found in "There Was a Child Went Forth" and "Crossing Brooklyn Ferry," are the substratum of Whitman's thinking. This is quite enough for a poet to go on. Poets don't have to be philosophers on the scale of Kant—they need only have ideas that enable them to make sense out of their experience and make it seem worthwhile to go on writing. They don't need to be original—the first ambition of those who are profoundly unoriginal. It isn't so hard to be original—it's a sight harder to say something true and useful.

It may appear that I've overlooked Whitman's mystical, visionary side. I haven't overlooked it, but Whitman doesn't strike me as mystical or visionary—he is a naturalist first and last. He wills to see things—even "The Sleeper" is laid out and proceeds according to plan. His most ecstatic passages are descriptions of sexual intercourse or frottation.

> I mind how once we lay such a transparent summer
>   morning,
> How you settled your head athwart my hips and gently
>   turn'd over upon me . . . .

These lines are addressed to his soul, but can there be any doubt as to what is actually happening? Sex may be the link with a mystery, but at least let us see that it is sex and not rush to find an alternative explanation. There is the kind of reader who, having no knowledge of religion, is always looking in books for the secret of the universe. For such a one, Whitman will be mystic, together with Kahlil Gibran and the authors of pamphlets on astrology.

In so far as Whitman enthuses over "a great round wonder rolling in space" he is a rudimentary poet, the eternal sophomore enthusing over "the great ideas" and neglecting his physics lesson and his French. In so far as Whitman talks about the universe he is not worth the attention of a grown person.

On the other hand, when he looks at what he sees, he is certainly a great American poet (though he cannot stand comparison with Dante, Chaucer, or a dozen others). These are the passages to look for:

> The little one sleeps in its cradle,
> I lift the gauze and look a long time, and silently
>   brush away flies with my hand.

> The youngster and the red-faced girl turn aside up
>   the bushy hill,
> I peeringly view them from the top....
>   "Song of Myself"

* * *

> Through the ample open door of the peaceful country barn,
> A sunlit pasture field with cattle and horses feeding,
> And haze and vista, and the far horizon fading away.
>   "A Farm Picture"

I don't want to suggest that Whitman is only a picture-artist. "When Lilacs Last in the Dooryard Bloom'd" and "Out of the Cradle Endlessly Rocking" hold our attention through rhythm and sound as well as imagery. But as rhythm and sound are operating just as audibly in his empty, monotonous, forgettable poems, I do not think that Whitman's impressiveness depends on rhythm and sound. It is what he describes that makes him a poet. Rhythm and sound are only an aid to this.

Critics who wish to pore over a phrase in Whitman, or the structure of a line, and show how perfectly suited it is to his purpose, should choose a banality and show why the meter and phrasing are perfect. This is the trouble with criticism that concentrates on technique—it is an *arrière-pensée*. We know that the poetry is fine, and set about finding reasons why the meter and the syntax had to be just so. But these things in themselves do not make fine poetry. If nothing worthwhile is being said, meter, syntax, and the rest of the prosodist's and the grammarian's bag of tricks are so much useless baggage.

There are ranges of poetry that lie beyond Whitman. Of situations such as occur in people's lives he appears to have known very little, and these are our main concern. He is good at describing shipwrecks, which are infrequent, but does not show affections, attachments, anxieties, shades of feeling, passions ... the life we actually have. The human appears in his poems as a crowd or as a solitary figure ... himself, looking at others.

In recent years there has been talk by American poets of developing new kinds of consciousness which would, presumably, enable us to advance beyond the merely human. But it is self-evident that if we are to continue to exist it will be as human beings, not some other species. Our poets are trying to be like stones ... another way of saying that they would rather be dead. Paul Breslin made the point clearly in an article ("How to Read the New Contemporary Poem," *The American Scholar,* Summer, 1978) but the thought had occurred to me independently. According to Breslin, our poets of darkness and stones are trying to escape the consequences of being human. They are trying to cast out the ego and live in a Jungian universe of archetypes.

Readers of this kind will find Whitman reassuring—he never becomes involved. "I am the man," he states, "I suffer'd, I was there." The passage may be so well known because it is so refreshing, in the wasteland of his usual detachment. He is a stroller, an onlooker, a gazer, and has nothing to say about what goes on in the houses he is passing, or behind office or factory windows, or in the life of the man turning a plough. He does not seem to know what people say to each other—especially what men say to women, or women to men. Reading Whitman's poetry one would think that the human race is dumb—and indeed, as he tells us, he would rather turn and live with animals.

His poetry is about a spectacle ... a crowd on the ferry, "the fine centrifugal spokes of light round the shape of my head in the sunlit water." But the actualities of human society are a closed book to him. It isn't the "proud libraries" that are closed to him—indeed, at times we could wish they were. What is closed is the life of the individual, and the lives of two, and three.

Whitman has plenty to say about man *"En-Masse."* His optimism about the common man reflects the optimism of the bankers and railroad-builders in the Gilded Age. Man *"En-Masse"* provided them with labor and then with a mass-market. But optimism about the masses seems out of place in our century. The masses elect mass-murderers—if we survive it will not be due to the good nature of the common man. Whitman's view of mankind is of no use at all—it doesn't help when it comes to understanding one another and building a community.

As he has so little to say about actual circumstances, Whitman is not among the very great, realized poets. There is hardly any drama or narration in his poetry—ideas aren't realized in action. We rise from reading Whitman with the feeling that he has talked about life rather than created it.

Building on his achievement we may hope to do much better, as he himself, in one of his generous moods, said that we would.

Pacific Ideas—A Letter to Walt Whitman •
Louis Simpson

When the schooners were drifting
Over the hills—schooners like white skulls—
The sun was the clock in that parlor
And the piano was played by the wind.

But a man must sit down,
And things, after all, are necessary.
Those "immensely overpaid accounts,"
Walt, it seems that we must pay them again.

It's hard to civilize, to change
The usual order;
And the young, who are always the same, endlessly
Rehearse the fate of Achilles.

Everyone wants to live at the center,
"The world of the upper floors."
And the sad professors of English
Are wishing that they were dead, as usual.

But here is the sea and the mist,
Gray Lethe of forgetfulness,
And the moon, gliding from the mist,
Love, with her garland of dreams.

And I have quarrelled with my books
For the moon is not in their fable,
And say to darkness, Let your dragon come,
O anything, to hold her in my arms!

With Walt Whitman at Fredericksburg •
Dave Smith

after Louis Simpson

I have brought the twittering flags old bear-hug,
the swaying noose you admired at the end
of the 13th Brooklyn muskets sashaying
down Broadway, everybody's intended girl
swooning, Jesus, for the grandeur of it.

I have brought a tumbler of spring water
for the sipping if your brother George lives.

I see you and Simpson stepping carefully through
wreckage, the hacked-off arms, useless with Masonic
rings, for God's sake, shining like used-car lots.
The arms are so American, like parts junked
before the expiration of their longevity.
This is no joke for Velsor Brush to peddle.

I have brought a red handkerchief
for our mouths. Godalmighty, the stink grows.

I've come here like you to pick a way to the heart
of the business, tracing out what ripples I can,
skirting blood pooled like knocked-over
coffee on my own sunny backporch. But
I see you and Simpson arm wrestling
in a lantern's moon, sighing out
the lonely words of America's losses.

I wish I could say it was December 13, 1862,
but the faces of young men I see aren't Christ,
dead and divine, and brother of all, though
they wear the green clothes of Park Rangers,
the polite smile of Toledo, and one
thinks you sold him a Buick.

Isn't it for them we threw the noose in a can?
I gave George's water to a small boy found
by his mother in time, the life saved
he thought lost, which he will lose again.

If you lay your body down in this Virginia green,
you feel the quick shadows of tourists, the whispers
that zing in your stomach like miniballs or
knee-high bees. Loafing like this
you can hear the freeway moaning under ground
dry and beige as free-shrunken coffee,
or look up into the drained, tossing leaves
of October. Alone on a stolen Army blanket

I've stretched out a long time here
to dig from a bright afternoon the glazed eyes
of anyone whose temple, as I touch it to clean
away the smear of ice, breaks my heart.

At dusk I may be the only one left to drift
down Marye's Heights where the Rappahannock mist rolls
over rocks humped like bodies, little dunes
inside which a black tide I cannot see
goes on rising and falling. I want

to tell you how progress has not changed us much.
You can see breaking on the woods the lights
of cars and the broken limbs glow
in the boomed rush of traffic that chants
wrong, wrong, wrong, wrong.

Essay Beginning and Ending With Poems for Whitman

I

The Traffic

Red lights pulse and weave in
toward an accident ahead.
Trying to leave Smithtown,
I'm stopped dead,

here, where Whitman trooped
to tally the eighth-month flowers' bloom.
Diesels jam their bumpers together in a long line,
gas and rubber heat wafts in like soup.

A truck's exhaust curves up beside me
like a swan's neck. I sigh,
make a mistake, and breathe deep.
Concrete, signs, and cars cloud:

Lilacs utter their heart-shaped leaves,
locusts spell their shade. The Jericho's air
creaks with cartwheels, a carriage
moves with the certainty of mirage.

The Widow Blydenburgh flows to church,
stoops to admire an iris, and to smell.

A pigeon bends the slim branch of a birch.
The Widow plucks the iris for her Bible.

Horns soon blare me out of this.
Trailing a plume of smoke,
the trucker grunts his rig ahead.
I accelerate past a cop

directing traffic around the wreck.
He asks if I'm all right. I nod
and close the lane. Glass sparkles,
a splash of blood still shines

on the pavement, and time's itself again.
Pressed against the porch of Whitman's school,
the Dairy Freeze is booming, winks
its windows tinted green, and cool.

II

WALT WHITMAN WAS BORN on Long Island, moved with his family to Brooklyn when he was four, attended public schools there, worked from 1830 to 1836 at various jobs in Brooklyn and New York, and then returned to Long Island to teach and work on Island newspapers for several years before returning to Brooklyn. "In 1851," says Gay Wilson Allen, "he was operating a small printing office and bookstore on the first floor of the three-story house he had built at 106 Myrtle Avenue."

I was born in Brooklyn, spent my first years in a house on Myrtle Avenue. We then moved to Woodhaven (which was anything but wooded), near Jamaica, then to the wilds of Hauppauge in Suffolk County when I was four or five, and then further east outside Smithtown to Nesconset where I began, I believe, third grade. "O World so far away! O my lost world!" says Theodore Roethke. But Roethke knew, as did Whitman, that those worlds would always live inside him, that poems would flow out of those "lost" worlds.

Long Island to Brooklyn in Whitman's case, Brooklyn to Long Island in mine, both of us children of carpenter fathers. Now and then, I tremble with connections. It's an ongoing privilege for me to feel so close, physically close, to the great world poet. At the same time, in any case, time and space avail not, as he says, and that New Jersey country pond he bathed in and wrote so beautifully about (and even gave credit to his recovery for), in *Specimen Days,* is one of the ponds of his old Island, too.

By school bus, or riding with my parents, or hitchhiking, or, as a senior in 1957 driving my brother's Plymouth—he was in the service—to high school on New York Avenue in Smithtown, I would pass through Smithtown Branch, under the huge locusts, past the Blydenburgh house. The Smithtown schoolhouse where Whitman taught in 1837-38 is just off the Jericho Turnpike in the area across from the old Presbyterian Church where 25A begins its winding to St. James, and Route 111 angles left to Hauppauge. Though it is half hidden by a drive-in dairy food store, you can see it from the Jericho. Last I knew, it housed a lawyer's office. When I think of Smithtown, I first think of that place, that confluence.

I didn't know anything about Whitman. When I remember myself as I was, I picture a boy wading Gibbs Pond in Nesconset, and other ponds in Lake Grove, St. James, Hauppauge, Ronkonkoma, the natural world bending in to him, as it did. I spent so much time at ponds, that this is the most enduring image I have of myself as a youngster, and now I know that Whitman saw me, and now I know that the *presence* I felt when I was otherwise alone at a pond or walking through woods or, later, clamming at St. James Harbor, was his, as he is abiding spirit, as he is the miraculous confluence of space and time within a human voice.

Working on my poem "The Traffic," I was thinking of that busiest block of Bull Smith's town—in 1660 the Nissequogue Indians gave Smith, in exchange for trinkets and cattle and guns, as much land as he could encircle between sunrise and sunset while riding bareback on a bull. My speaker, "Trying to leave Smithtown," is stuck in traffic, "here, where Whitman trooped / to tally the eighth-month flowers' bloom." He is dizzied by a truck's fumes, and falls back into the past world of this same place:

> Lilacs utter their heart-shaped leaves,
> locusts spell their shade. The Jericho's air
> creaks with cartwheels, a carriage
> moves with the certainty of mirage.

> The Widow Blydenburgh flows to church,
> stoops to admire an iris, and to smell.
> A pigeon bends the slim branch of a birch.
> The Widow plucks the iris for her Bible.

At the end of the poem, his head clear again, he glances to his right:

> . . . and time's itself again.
> Pressed against the porch of Whitman's school,
> the Dairy Freeze is booming, winks
> its windows tinted green, and cool.

What is the true traffic? I am far from this poem now. It is as much any reader's as mine, as I try to hear it.

The irony seems heavy, and intended, but I wonder if I was writing more than I knew. Earlier in the poem the speaker had compared a truck's exhaust pipe to a "swan's neck," and now, it seems to me, the Dairy Freeze windows, "green and cool," remind him bitterly of another world, the world of the sea and of ponds that we know is a part of his sensibility, in this one poem, or in the book *Long Island Light* in which this poem appears. But I wonder if the poem, with its lines juxtaposing Whitman's school and the Dairy Freeze pressed against it, isn't more, doesn't, somehow, find a kind of solace in the present traffic, doesn't, somehow, trust the "booming" future, as Whitman did. I notice, now, the cop's concern, the healing influence of the speaker's vision of the past, his humor, the blood-like *body* of the experience ("Red lights pulse and weave in"). I see now that "Glass sparkles," and now know—I don't know if I did when I wrote the poem—Whitman's poem "Sparkles from a Wheel" "Where the city's ceaseless crowd moves on the livelong day" with "Myself effusing and fluid, a phantom curiously floating. . . ." On Island ground, having been everywhere, part of the traffic river flowing up against and through Whitman's world, my speaker may be curiously at home with himself.

III

As a child and young man, I had heard Whitman's name in grade school and high school. I remember that about the same time that we were reading Longfellow's "Evangeline" in seventh or eighth grade, we also read "O Captain! My Captain!," and it was from this same time that "I Saw in Louisiana a Live-Oak Growing" embedded itself behind my eyes. But, in general, I didn't read Whitman, but knew him, as any Island resident (even someone who has not read him) when alone but feeling, in Whitman's word, some "impalpable" presence ("The impalpable sustenance of me from all things at all hours of the day" of "Crossing Brooklyn Ferry") must know him. Sometimes Whitman says, as he does here in "Whoever You Are Holding Me Now in Hand," that we must be alone with him to know him:

> (For in any roof'd room of a house I emerge not,
>   nor in company,
> And in libraries I lie as one dumb, a gawk, or unborn,
>   or dead,)
> But just possibly with you on a high hill, first
>   watching lest any person for miles around
>   approach unawares,

> Or possibly with you sailing at sea, or on the beach
> of the sea or some quiet island,
> Here to put your lips upon mine I permit you. . . .

But alone or with others, impalpable, but tending toward him, all earthly
things suffuse the power that sustains him, the physical world not only an
emblem of benevolent spirit presiding and blessing, but spirit itself, indwell-
ing, undivided soul and body of all being.

It seems to me that sometimes Whitman protests too much, tries in
strained keys to "show that there is no imperfection in the present, and can
be none in the future" ("Starting from Paumanok")—that overwhelming
well-being I recently felt in the room in the Old Manse in Concord where
Emerson, at white heat, wrote *Nature*. There is a bloated, declarative, Santa
Claus quality in the unrealized work. But I care for Whitman all the more
for this, his great humanity breaking through as he yearns to comfort and,
often with sweep and subtler music, does. What he turns to, the force that
will integrate all, solve all, resolve the knots of contrariety is, of course, love.

> (Were you looking to be held together by lawyers?
> Or by an agreement on a paper? or by arms?
> Nay, nor the world, nor any living thing, will so cohere.)
>   "Over the Carnage Rose Prophetic a Voice"

Not "any living thing" will cohere without love, he says, in so many ways.
Cells at the centers of things, atoms at the centers of cells, whole nations
at the centers of cells are held together by love. Whether or not this is true,
great poetry has never depended on literal, empirical Truth, but on a
rhythmical and imagistic passion of voice that involves us in and makes us,
at least while we are in its presence, believe its truth. *Leaves of Grass* itself
coheres because the poet's love—variously diffuse, teasing, specific, all-
encompassing, wrenching, erotic, quietly transfiguring, pounding, disguised,
blatantly passionate—draws it together, despite our ignorance, despite contrary aesthetics coming toward it to tear it apart, despite the singer's heartbreak or even his beloved nation's Civil War. Whitman never wrote a poem
that was not, at its center, a poem of love.

IV

Whitman is the poet, finally, who comes full circle, who includes everything, but he will not be forced. I think of *Leaves of Grass* as a necklace
gradually becoming visible for me as I grow older, the necklace of "The
glories strung like beads on my smallest sights and hearings" of "Crossing

Brooklyn Ferry," each poem, perhaps, a bead of a different size on the necklace, the necklace and the beads themselves, of course, shifting shapes in time and changing light.

No single bead will be forced. Its facets and lines gradually impress themselves on me. I stare at them as Yeats in "Lapis Lazuli" stares at the stone, "Every discoloration of the stone, / Every accidental crack or dent," until he sees "a water-course or an avalanche, / or lofty slope where it still snows. . . ." When I think of a single Whitman line, and repeat it to myself, one like "Fog in the air, beetles rolling balls of dung" of that fathomless bead "Song of Myself" (a line prophesying the modern world, a line the angelic forefather of Eliot's dolorous "Her drying combinations touched by the sun's last rays" in "The Waste Land"), I can only shake my head in amazement and gratitude. When I roll one of the great shorter beads on my tongue, I know it will give of itself for as long as I live. When I think of *Leaves of Grass*, the necklace itself . . .

V

Just northeast of the confluence I've described is/was an estate of 37 acres, the Rockwell estate. Bull Smith obtained the land three centuries ago, and it was passed down through nine generations to Charles Embree Rockwell, sixty-one as of June 12, 1978, the date of a *Newsday* article sent me by a friend.

Unable to afford twentieth-century property taxes, Rockwell sold 26 acres to The Point of Woods Construction Co. of Massapequa. He donated one and one-half acres to the Town of Smithtown. And then he signed a contract of purchase for the remaining nine and one-half acres with Gordon and Jack Real Estate and Developers of Huntington. He plans to leave Long Island.

Rockwell once came into my father's woodworking shop on the Jericho with a walnut log from one of his trees fallen in a storm. Rockwell loved his trees, my father told me. He could tell this by the man's eyes and voice. Rockwell wanted to know what could be made out of the walnut log. It turned out that much of it was rotten, but my father pieced together enough of it for a table pedestal.

Rockwell's son Charles, asked how he felt when he was told that the land had been sold, said, "Well, it's as if I had been told someone in the family had died."

I don't know the details of what is happening/will happen to that land. The two-story family house, built about 1750, is on the plot donated to the town. Near it is a large red barn built in 1850, and next to it a carriage house where "rows of cobwebbed carriages lie under decaying white dust covers."

The *Newsday* article says that the town plans to move the family house but that the Smithtown Historical Society is against it, maintaining that its original site is the town's most historically important. Widow Blydenburgh's tavern stood on this land, too, and it was here that George Washington, on April 21, 1790, stopped, to feed his horses and to thank Island residents for their support during the Revolution. The town may build a parking lot for the town library, if the Rockwell home is moved. It's interesting to think that people wanting to check out a book by Whitman, of course, will need a parking space. Says Town Historian Virginia Malone, "I consider that to turn into a blacktop parking lot the place where the first president of the United States once greeted the residents of Smithtown, [would be] a desecration of the land."

This complex story goes/will go on and on. Its repetition across America does not make it any easier to understand. No one knows what it means, not Rockwell or the Town Historian or the lawyers in Whitman's school. But as the farms are lost, as the maples, elms, walnut, oak, locust, hickory are lost, the blackberry brambles and honeysuckle and laurel, the dogwoods and lilac and wild roses, the deer and smaller animals, those of us in the traffic flow in the intersections of new and old Island, that Island that is everywhere, bear witness with the center of our lives. There is no answer. I am not sure of the question. But we will come away from the Island with what we need for eternity. The undiminished poet insists that we open ourselves to the new day, and that we are forever able to reciprocate, to conduct the current. "Dazzling and tremendous how quick the sunrise would kill me / If I could not now and always send sunrise out of me." Despite whatever deaths we suffer, there will be compensation, in our knowledge of Whitman and Whitman's light.

VI

Witness

We'd walked into the small warm shed
where spring lambs lay in straw
in the half-dark still smelling of their birth,
of ammonia, the damp grass, dung,
into this world in the middle of a field
where lambs bleating soft songs lifted
their too-heavy heads toward their mothers,
gentle presences within their wool clouds.
Later, outside, as I watched,
Wenzel wrapped his left arm around a sheep's neck
and struck her with the sledge in his right hand.

The dying sheep, her forehead crushed, cried out,
past pain, for her mortal life. Blood flowed
from her burst skull, over her eyes, her black nose.
Wenzel dropped her to the grass.
When I ran home, I struck my head
on a blossoming apple-bough.
Where was the dead sheep?
What did I hear?
Where is the witness now?

I was nine or ten.
Her cry was terror,
so I lay awake to hear her,
to wonder why she didn't seem to know
her next manger, her golden fields.
Her odors drifted through my screen—
the hay at the roots of her wool,
her urine, the wet graindust under her chin,
her birth fluids hot and flecked with blood.
I could hear her bleat
to her last lamb, hear her heartbeat
in the black air of my room.
Where was the dead sheep?
Why did she cry for her loss?
Where is the witness now?

Not to accept, but to awaken.
Not to understand, to cry terror, but to know
that even a billon years later, now,
we breathe the first circle of light,
and the light curves into us, into the deer's back,
the man's neck, the woman's thigh,
the cat's mouse-mossed tongue, all the ruby
berries ripening in evening air.
The dead elms and chestnuts are of it, and do not
break the curve. The jeweled flies sip it,
and do not break the curve.
Our homes inhabit, and ride the curve.
The mountains, its children, do not break the curve.
Our moon, our rivers, the furthest stars blinking blue,
the great named and nameless comets do not break the curve.
The odorous apple-blossom rain does not break the curve.
The struck ewe's broken brainpan does not break the curve.
Wenzel nor this witness breaks the curve.

In the shed's dusk where spring lambs
sang to their mothers, in my dark room

where the dead ewe's odors drifted my sleep,
and now, within these cells where her forehead blood
flows once more into recollection,
the light curves. You and I bear witness, and know this,
and as we do the light curves into this knowledge.
The struck ewe lives in this light,
in this curve of the only unbroken light.

To Love the Earth: Some Thoughts on Walt Whitman

Joseph Bruchac

I HAVE NO DOUBTS about what pieces of Whitman's are my favorites. They are his "Preface" to the 1855 edition of *Leaves of Grass* and that long and most famous of his poems which was untitled in its first printing and later entitled "Song of Myself."

Quoting a few of my favorite statements from that Preface may show why I am so drawn to it. In speaking of the United States he says, "Here is not merely a nation but a teeming nation of nations." It is a simple phrase, but one to be often quoted and seen as more and more accurate each year. And that recognition of America's diversity of voices is even further augmented in a statement which prefigures the current—and to me significant—rise of "regional" poetry in the United States when he says of the American poet that "his spirit responds to his country's spirit. . . he incarnates its geography and natural life and rivers and lakes. Mississippi with its annual freshets and changing chutes, Missouri and Columbia and Ohio and Saint Lawrence with the falls and beautiful masculine Hudson. . . ." It is, I suppose, true that Whitman was talking of himself, viewing himself with his massive egoism as *the* one poet whose voice would speak for all regions and all nations within this nation, but I feel that his advice is so sound in the Preface, so true to this continent, that it serves, perhaps, an even greater purpose than Whitman imagined it would.

Whitman is such a namer of names, too. He sees the natural world as no other American of European ancestry before him has ever seen it—at least any who wrote lasting poetry. Here is another passage from that Preface: "On him rise solid growths that offset the growths of pine and cedar and hemlock and liveoak and locust and chestnut and cypress and hickory and limetree and cottonwood and tuliptree and cactus and wildvine and tama-

274

rind and persimmon. . .with flights and songs and screams that answer those of the wildpigeon and highhold and orchard-oriole and coot and surf-duck and redshouldered-hawk and fish-hawk and white-ibis and indian-hen and cat-owl and water-pheasant and qua-bird and pied-sheldrake and blackbird and mockingbird and buzzard and condor and nightheron and eagle." Similar catalogues of plants and animals and birds appear in "Song of Myself." Here are just a few of the plants whose names are called in that poem: elder, mullein, pokeweed, violet, stonecrop, cedar, lilac, sweet-flag, maple and liveoak. I think that it would be very difficult for anyone to find another poet of the nineteenth century—or indeed of much of the first half of the twentieth—who has such an intimacy with nature to be able to name so many things with such precision—rather than just referring to amorphous nature, to trees as "trees" and birds as background.

Kofi Awoonor, a fine African poet from Ghana, once told me that he saw a similarity between my work and that of Whitman. Why? Because, like Whitman, the natural world is an integral part of my poems. Whitman, Awoonor went on to say, was the one American poet who recognized the soil, who "went back to the earth to listen to the footbeats of earlier sojourners." And, for Awoonor and many other non-western writers, Whitman was and remains the foremost American poet thus far. As Whitman put it, and again I quote from that Preface, "The land and sea, the animals fishes and birds, the sky of heaven and the orbs, the forest mountains and rivers, are not small themes." That statement, for me, ranks with one which I have on the wall of my study. Written many centuries ago by Tu Fu, the T'ang poet, it glows with the same sort of energy as I find in those words of Whitman's. "The ideas of a poet should be noble and simple." It is not an easy path to follow. Yet I think it worth following, even as I think that Whitman's charge—to himself and to future poets of the United States—is worth following: "This is what you shall do: Love the earth and sun and the animals, despise riches, give alms to every one that asks, stand up for the stupid and crazy, devote your income and labor to others, hate tyrants, argue not concerning God, have patience and indulgence toward the people, take off your hat to nothing known or unknown or to any man or number of men, go freely with powerful uneducated persons and with the young and with the mothers of families, re-examine all you have been told at school or church or in any book, dismiss whatever insults your own soul. . . ." And where does the poet go to for his work and his inspiration? "He shall go directly to the creation."

Gary Snyder, Ted Kooser, Wendell Berry—those are a few of the contemporary poets whose poems bear witness to Whitman's influence, whose lives, too, bear that witness. Whitman in his hay loft in "Song of Myself" is so much like Snyder out there under the stars reading Milton. "Love the earth and sun and the animals. . . ." What a wonderful phrase! It is as wonderful as his speaking of "the perfect equality of the female with the male"—another concept which seems so out of step with the middle of the nineteenth century, so much an idea whose time *still* has not come round at last. I see Whitman's spirit, too, in the poems of Leslie Silko and Simon Ortiz, two of the finest of the new generation of Native American writers—though Whitman's influence may be less important in the formation of their voices than their having a direct connection with that same source from which Whitman drew the best of his strength.

There were, of course, other voices which sang the rhythms of this continent's soil before Whitman. Yet it in no way belittles his accomplishment to say that he was only the first of those whose traditions stemmed from Europe to truly come to terms with the nature and the reality of the American earth, with its spirit of place. Only Thoreau can be compared with him. Almost unconsciously—despite his huge self-consciousness—Whitman has heard the songs of the black slave, of the native (dimly, yet still heard) and finally, after four centuries of occupation, a European has become something new, has sounded a note which can lead to a new, an "American" literature. My own divided ethnic heritage, Slovak, English, American Indian, draws me to Whitman, to his mongrel voice, the voice which was needed for the plurality of the new experience.

There is much in Whitman which reminds me of the American Indian way of looking at the world, of *being* in the world and not just *observing* it. Many writers, I know, have linked Whitman with East Indian mysticism, with ideas stemming from Buddhism. There is no doubt that those links are there, that Whitman makes use of words absorbed from somewhere or other which are of East Indian origin. Yet the deeper influence, the influence less known by those writers—who are always looking at distant hills and tripping over the anthills in front of their own feet—is a native one. If it is not the actual oral literature of Native American people it is the *force* which those traditions draw their energy from, the connection. Whitman's celebration of the earth and natural things, his precise namings, are very much like Native American song. The healing way chants of the Dineh—those we call the Navajo—remind me of sections of "Song of Myself." Here is a very small section of the Night Chant:

> Beauty all around me, with it I wander.
> In old age travelling, with it I wander.
> I am on the beautiful trail, with it I wander.

And here is a small section from "Song of Myself":

> The moth and his eggs are in their place
> The suns I can see and the suns I cannot see are in their place
> The palpable is in its place and the impalpable is in its place. . . .

The same qualities of wonder, of appreciation, are in both. There is also that quality of incantation which repetition brings in both. For American Indian people, poetry is not just for entertainment. It changes lives, it restores the balance. I am certain Whitman would have deep sympathy for that idea. I know that I do.

How often it has happened that I have been influenced by a writer—Pablo Neruda, for example—only to find that one of his deep influences was Walt Whitman. The Latin American poets have loved Whitman better, perhaps, than most American writers have. Neruda certainly has so many Whitmanic traits—those long lines, those rhythms, those connections to the natural world, real and impure as it truly is, even some—unfortunately—of Whitman's self-indulgent stances turn up in Neruda.

Although Whitman tried to be the poet of a whole vast continent, he is, for me, always best when his focus is most limited. When his poems reflect the city and country places of that Long Island he knew so well, Whitman comes most alive for me, when the things he felt, touched, smelled, come into his poems. Here is one of the finest examples of that focus:

> Do you guess I have some intricate purpose?
> Well I have. . . for the April rain has, and the mica
>   on the side of a rock has.
>
> Do you take it I would astonish?
> Does the daylight astonish? or the early redstart
>   twittering through the woods?
> Do I astonish more than they?

It has always been my belief that the "universal" can often, in poetry, best be found in the particular. It is in those particulars, not in his sweeping generalizations and his sometimes fuzzy mysticism, that Whitman speaks most truly to my own soul. It was that voice which I heard when I wrote a poem acknowledging some of my debt to Whitman a number of years ago:

CANTICLE

Let others speak
of harps and
heavenly choirs

I've made my decision
to remain here
with the Earth

if the old grey poet
felt he could turn and
live with the animals
why should I be too good
to stay and die with them

and the great road of the Milky Way
that Sky Trail my Abenaki ancestors
strode to the last Happy Home
does not answer my dreams

I do not believe
we go up to the sky
unless it is
to fall again
with the rain

"I Teach Straying from Me—Yet Who Can Stray from Me?"

Alvaro Cardona-Hine

WHEN WE WERE ABOUT to come to the United States (in 1940, when I was twelve years old), my father warned me about life here. "They have bad manners," he said, "they put their feet on the furniture." He had guided my reading from the beginning, using Defoe, Jules Verne and Kipling, and, after I had learned the language, some three years later, he seems to have suggested Whitman, for I ended up perennially exploring the then sparsely populated Hollywood hills with an ubiquitous volume of the Modern Library's *Leaves of Grass*. It was only much later that I understood why that volume wasn't Twain or Emerson or even Thoreau.

Each generation of Latin American intellectuals is baffled—frightened even—by the nearly angelic yet immensely crude, satanic, mechanized, land-devouring Yankee (American) apparent, if not often enough in his own literature, then always in the flesh. The only comfort in a rather Nordic array of dispositions has been Walt Whitman. Walt Whitman could be said to be the only pre-twentieth-century figure in American letters sensed a brother by men of different culture and coloration. He has the careless and forgiving odor of someone who will let you live . . . (live your own way. And of who else could that be said?).

I think that that explains why Whitman and not the more urbane Emerson fell into my hands. Of course, historicity of any kind is at best a frame of reference; at worst, a frame-up of reality. Walt Whitman became immediately important to me not because he wore a less formidable mask than, say, Melville, but because his rambling acceptance of the world was so willing to be river bottom to the feet of a half-drowning Hispanic teenager.

Perhaps others have had an easier time shedding childhood skin. For me, before becoming an adult, existence was a harmful and often petulant concoction of abandoned Catholicism, Marxism of the Red Dean of Canterbury variety, and a nihilism most likely due to the hormonal imbalances characteristic of youth. I floated in this amalgam of world views and emotional depression without an integrated personality. The lack of frontiers and skin made life seem particularly harsh and meaningless. Without friends, I sought the solitude of those hills that sprawl above Hollywood Boulevard. They are covered with brush, manzanita, sage; and the soil is a broken-down, sun-drenched pebbly material that hasn't had the geologic decency to mature into rock. Ants and lizards, bees, flies, and a few birds would join me with their own particular emptinesses. I used to flee from home because it was always hot there; it seemed as if Los Angeles could never muster a breeze strong enough to waft the curtains inward into our rooms. Los Angeles doesn't have a weather of rage or elegance but in those hills there was enough space to make up for air.

The book *was* Whitman himself (I was child enough to know that without his confirmation in the "Songs of Parting") and therefore it should not appear strange if I say that I seldom opened it or that I seldom read more than a few lines when I opened it. A few lines could last me a week; what was most important were the transformations that his message took. Because it went so deep it had to assume a form natural to me; it had to be included in my life with all of its own ongoing details. At the time I had no idea that I would take up writing as a lifetime pursuit so the reading was not critical; there was no scanning to see what I could get out for my own use. The chaotic mysticism was what went to feed my psyche. There was a constant homage in his poetry to labyrinths of joy and that was a challenge because joy (love without cause) was the most appealing of the impossibilities presented by life.

The book, the man present, had a certain impenetrability. Large portions were of no interest to me. When he started to talk of democracy, or occupations, he left me as cold as a friend who suddenly develops interests I don't share. Democracy and progress were not real issues in my life when I needed a soul and its patience, a sexless expectancy that is sex's way of maturing and providing cover to meaning. And also, even then, I had the feeling that Whitman believed in the causes of his time but was not their poet; he was the poet of the formless, internal freedoms. Nor was he a creature that could long endure in a world where money is more tenable than soul. This will be borne by the following bitter quote.

A friend in Los Angeles, researching in the main library, found it once. Apparently, Whitman had been queried for a symposium to be entitled "What Are the Attributes of Perfect Manhood." He replied, writing from Camden, New Jersey, in 1891:

The answer to such questions ought to be the thoughts and results of a life time & w'd need a big volume. Seems to me, indeed, the whole varied machinery, intellect, & even emotion, of the civilized universe, these years, are working toward the answer. (My own books, poems and prose, have been a direct and indirect attempt at contribution.) No doubt what will be sent you will be salutary & valuable, & all fit in. Though the constituents of "perfect manhood" are much the same all lands & times, they will always be sifted & graduated a good deal by conditions, and especially by the United States. Then I sh'd say, with emphasis, we c'd not have (all things consider'd) any better chances than mainly exist in these States today—common education, general inquiry, freedom, the press, Christianity, travel, &c. &c. But perhaps I may vary and help by growling a little as follows: For one thing out of many, the tendency in this Commonwealth seems to favor & call for & breed specially *smart men*. To describe it (for reasons) extra sharply I sh'd say we New Worlders are in danger of turning out the trickiest, slyest, 'cutest, most cheating people that ever lived. Those qualities are getting radically in our business, politics, literature, manners, and filtering in our essential character. All the great cities exhibit them—probably New York most of all. They taint the splendid & healthy American qualities, & had better be well understood like a threatening danger, & confronted & provided against.

In my formative years then I would wait till those moments when something we had in common could come into being, when he addressed himself to the pure and mysterious essence of consciousness:

> Who goes there? hankering, gross, mystical, nude;
> How is it I extract strength from the beef I eat?

I would close the book immediately, moved but curiously uncurious about what came next. Any kind of concentrated reading was impossible, the thought that he might explicate anything too much for my raw nerves. It was a time, paradoxically, for a singular kind of creature laziness and this wonderful virtue demanded timelessness of time, the way a slow Haydn movement demands it. Whitman's vastness of anchorage itself called for patience, wait-and-see-ness. In retrospect, I can see how nothing was as remedial for me as that aspect of his singing. His words, just as a stick or a rock I might have picked up as companion for a while, were medicinal and not to be taken in large doses once the book had been opened at random.

In the daily shapelessness of my life then, Whitman was happiness by prediction. And he had the unmatched American language for that innate and numinous nervousness and unexpectedness of the moment in life when one is awash with questions and the questions turn happy. Sometimes they can even turn into perfume (that fantastic something which, as we become more and more civilized, we associate only with expensive women): his groupings of words, his bunches of thoughts, were directly comparable in their ability to gesture to consciousness as the night-blooming jasmine growing in the gardens of the houses at the base of the hills, a jasmine so potent that one could smell it a block away.

The responsibility one has towards questions is that of living them. I do not exaggerate when I claim that Whitman allowed me to live; he made room in his work for one like myself to come and see his anguish reflected honestly, affirmed and transcended. By showing me that words are what we have to say he also *prepared* me for becoming a writer.

A few years later, the prospect of a career in science drove me from my textbooks and into the bookstacks of the library of Los Angeles City College. If someone had told me that by doing that I was going to discover what *singing* is I would have been very surprised. Stanley Kurnik, the same friend who provided me with the Whitman quote, showed me a volume of García Lorca's *Poet in New York* asleep in those library stacks. From that moment on I began to see poetry as the means by which to externalize (finally!) and give life to one's inner world. Reality did not have to be understood *beforehand* (!!! as the academician undoubtedly believes). In fact, it had the same devious terrain as dream. Surreal yet populist imagery, as in a great deal of twentieth-century Spanish poetry, manufactures the reality that it purports to address out of the myth substance of dream (including hope). In the process of developing the tools by which to become reality in just that way, I came to realize how much I owed Whitman and essayed his style in youthful poems such as the following:

> Landscape of Antiquity
> (In the style of Walt Whitman)
>
>
> Thought of the horizon—of its harpstrings
> —its Greek grace.
>
>
> Thought of caverns—echoes
> —animal hearts
>
> (1949)

Or addressed him turbulently, in very personal terms, the way one always seems to address the hero-inhabitants of one's youthful mind:

> I am a young blade like you, Walter:
> the happiest helium of the sun,
> the proudest jasmine of the night,
> the milkiest way of any mule team in the West.
>
> (from "Bivoac")

And so, even though I would follow a different path in my own writing, at nineteen and twenty I was writing (by retrograde influence) a poetry touched by the Whitman of the small poems, the Whitman I had read as testament years back:

Mater

You are the soft tiger skin that, furred around me,
produces this thing called I.

You come from nowhere, from the wind, from the air
that surrounds us.

You are the terrible sadness
of the brown, of the green, of the things that concern us.

Even today, something of Whitman's language pervades some of the things I write. A poem written this year can exemplify this:

For E.C.L.

I was idly mulling over my life the other day
the past (its few distinctive moments) unfolded before me in
  its entirety
there you were at the start of that painful decade
somewhat aloof from friend or family
beautiful/ diffident/ complete/ a suicide
alone possessed of the clarity and compassion of true rage

It would be many years before what Whitman instilled in me could bloom as assurance. Cottonwoods bordering a river bank take as long to begin being more than just a bush. What is most wonderful is that having been prepared to dislike the crudeness of this enormous land, it was its most carefree spokesman who gave my soul leave to plant its feet anywhere (and like a drunk) on the body of my work.

Whitman • *Larry Levis*

"I say we had best look our times and lands searchingly in the
face, like a physician diagnosing some deep disease."
—*Democratic Vistas*

"Look for me under your bootsoles."

On Long Island, they moved my clapboard house
Across a turnpike, then
Named a shopping center after me!

Now that I'm required reading in your high schools,
Teen-agers call me a fool.
Now what I sang
Stops breathing, like the daughter too high on drugs
To come back, in your arms. Her white dress
So hopeful, & beside the point.
And yet

It was only when no one could believe in me
That I began living again—
In the thin whine of Montana fence wire,
In the transparent, cast off garments hung
In the windows of the poorest families,
In the glad music of Charlie Parker.
At times now,
I even come back to watch you
From the eyes of a taciturn boy at Malibu.
Across the counter at the beach concession stand,
I sell you hot dogs, Pepsis, cigarettes—
My blond hair long, greasy, & swept back
In a vain old ducktail, deliciously
Out of style.
And no one notices.

Once, I even came back as myself,
An aging homosexual who ran a Tilt-a-Whirl
At country fairs, a Mardi Gras tatoo on my left shoulder;
And the chilled paint on each gondola
Changing color as it picked up speed, made me smile.
I thought you caught the meaning of my stare:
Still water, merciless
As my laughter.

A Cosmos. One of the roughs.

And Charlie Parker's grave in Kansas City
Covered with weeds.

Leave me alone.
A father who's outlived his only child.

To find me now will cost you everything.

Walt's Waltz • *Anselm Hollo*

for Alice Notley

who knows when this'll get to you

    main thing now don't know what is but urgent

or just another silly moment in life

    says semi-sensible person
in head as opposed to or rather conjoined
  if crazily
  with heart

doesn't mind commas well both of us here boss
  just wanted to say hello

let's get together before they sound the all-aboard

where did i go well she was here
  that while ago
    her hand
      her her

    (what does "take" mean?)

old songs of tribes:

  cowards cowards

  ancient garbage

how to go on loving
　how to survive in this lot

all of which gone & ancient time but now
　who knows when this'll get to you

main thing now to say:

　love her his her him he she

　[she-hee he-shee]

who to save but the ones that move ?

Some Intricate Purpose

MICHAEL KINCAID

SPEAKING OF RIMBAUD, René Char has said that he was "the first poet of a civilization which does not yet exist." He has also said that if he knew what Rimbaud meant to him, he would know what poetry itself meant, and would have no need to continue writing his own poems. I could say something similar of Whitman.

Of all my poetic models and sources, Whitman embodies for me the purest and most challenging idea of what poetry is about. Yet of all poets, he also inspires the gravest doubts and reservations. The essay that follows represents a long-term inner argument, my pro and con struggle over Whitman's work. It is an argument that is never quite finished, perhaps because it is involved with a deeper argument concerning poetic principle and practice, at the center of which is my own "intricate purpose."

I

Whitman announced early his intention of being the poet of "these democratic States," and of using his Personality as a medium to chronicle and embody the life and times he shared with his country. "The direct trial of him who would be the greatest poet is today," he wrote, and the success of some of his poems on contemporary matters testifies that it was no miscarriage of self-confidence that made him accept that trial.

But to be a poetic chronicler of current history is one thing; to be the national poet of your country is another—and Whitman decided to be both. When Homer and Shakespeare composed the national poems of their respective countries, those countries had already had long histories, which had pretty much formed their respective characters and myths. What was needed was a touch of genius, to crystallize their myth- and character-substance into classical language. But as poet of a country less than a century old, Whitman lacked the stock of myth and history which a national poet characteristically weaves into epic or dramatic form.

So Whitman resorted to prophecy, and devised a poetry of oracular promise. But what *could* he promise, on such thin credit as his country offered him? All he had in the bank, nationally speaking, was a Constitution of eighteenth-century European ideals, and a hectic democracy, waywardly spilling westward. The solution, then, was the proposition that America, yet nothing in itself, was to become the fulfillment of ages; was to incorporate and transcend all the best which the Old World had accomplished: a myth made to order for a hypothetical country.

At its easiest, poetry is a difficult occupation, but the promissory poet lays burdens on himself above and beyond the call. The poet who sees his country as the promise of the future must also see its unfolding history as a messianic fulfillment, or as an Apocalypse. When such a poet writes and perceives in a lyric mode, he takes the stresses of that history directly on himself. Where the epic or dramatic poet distances himself from his material by resolving it into character and plot, the lyric-prophetic poet may experience history's conflicts as no less than a crucifixion. Whitman's identification with his Promised Land was so complete that the Secession and ensuing war amounted to a personal dismemberment—the symbolic value he attached to the Civil War far exceeding its political significance.

The rest is history: how Whitman's grueling work in the war hospitals, "binding his country's wounds," and his exhausting attentiveness to the progress and setbacks of the Union cause, led to a series of strokes, and the progressive invalidism of his later years. It is in the nature of prophecy that the word becomes flesh. Whitman sacrificed his flesh to the words of his prophecy, and lived to inherit his reward: a broken body, and the squalor of Reconstruction.

* * * * *

When a poet makes a fundamental artistic error of such grand proportions as Whitman's, and with such dire personal consequences, and when that poet is as important to me as Whitman is, I feel moved to look into the circumstances behind that error.—To examine, in short, the personality Whitman so generously put on display in his writings.

Poetry is at least partially a means of transcending the bounds of one's personal ego, and identifying with conditions other than one's own. Such means give the poet leave from his personal actuality on rare and fortunate occasions, and return him to himself with a refreshed sense of his limited identity. But the imperatives of Whitman's makeup were such that he had to be *more* than himself, all of the time. He had to be not only the United States of America, past, present and future, but, as D. H. Lawrence pointed out, everything he had ever seen, heard of, or read about. When Whitman claims identity with criminals, firemen, Hottentots and Parsees, he is fantasizing, substituting ego-insistence for poetic realization.

Looking for the origin of this consuming need to identify with the macrocosm, I find between the lines of *Leaves of Grass* a pathetic sense of loneliness and isolation.—A sense that may have been symptomatic of the country and the times; of a vast, expanding nation, which, in the exuberant centrifugal energies of its expansion, left the inner person isolated and unregarded. Perhaps a deep national need for human touch and contact, left unsatisfied by an external-materialist society, surfaced in Whitman's compulsion to merge with everything around him—as if, to confirm his existence in the world, he had to have the world in *him*.

Looking closer still, I see an individual who possibly rather early in life felt himself defeated by the whole radical otherness of the world; for whom the very fact that there were things in the universe *that were not him* posed a major problem. I would guess further, that woman was part and parcel of the world's defeating Otherness; that what constituted for Whitman the baffling and central problem of existence began and ended with woman.

* * * * *

Woman, as symbol, has a central place in Whitman's writing. Sometimes she appears as the ideal mother or grandmother, a figure generalized from Whitman's own mother (whom he revered above all beings except, perhaps, Lincoln). At other times she is the Muse of Democracy, a fecund but demanding spirit hardly distinguishable from Nature, teaching the young nation hard lessons through war and turbulence. Yet again, she is the poet's hypothetical partner in procreation, a sort of ovarian athlete, upon whom he jets the stuff of nimbler babes and prouder republics. But always she is an ideal; despite the poet's account of the effect "the female form" has on him, and his fiction of himself as divine stud horse, doing its prophetic work, woman never takes on an erotically tangible presence in his writings. Whitman's capacity for eroticized responses of tremendous power and diversity is everywhere evident; it is the basis of his ecstatic sympathy with nature, and the score upon which his greatest poetry is written. But—it stops short at woman, who becomes through this default Woman, an abstraction.

Yet she is an abstraction, or absence, of overbearing importance in Whitman's scheme of things. For he relegated woman to abstraction in the same motion with which he made his own ego identical with the world. It is impossible to know whether, for example, it was some experience with a woman which threw him back upon the infantile order of himself, a fictive self which *includes* the injurious world and is therefore not subject to it—or whether, from within the established walls of his ego-fiction, the poet looked out and saw woman as the symbol of release from his self-created prison, an object of both longing and terror: for to allow his erotic current to breach the wall would mean the destruction of his fictive world-self. Between longing and terror, he remained.

D. H. Lawrence, Whitman's aptest critic, once exclaimed in disgust, "Everything was female to him—even himself." This provides a clue to the operation I've described above: again, the infantile process of conquest through identification. In a world of threatening otherness, which for Whitman was identified with woman, Whitman became woman also, to short-circuit her dangerous otherness, and to seal himself in a narcissistic communion with the cosmos of Himself. So that all that remained of woman outside that cosmos was an abstraction, an ideal, a hope beyond hope.

Having thus, in effect, occluded sex from his world, he was like a God safe in his own universe—and tragically alone. For the world he had made was a mirror, and the one human direction left for his erotic impulse was the one the mirror showed him. And as in the case of Narcissus, procreation with his reflection produced a flower: the calamus.

* * * * *

The *Calamus* poems are the Sargasso of Whitman's psychic voyage, the swamp of despondency where he found himself becalmed. In this secluded setting nature is rank, and communes with herself in an enigmatic stillness. It is the place where man arrives when he has cancelled the mystery of sex, and is faced with a mystery far more cruel and exacting. It is the cul-de-sac of monopolistic maleness, of the exclusive male ego that would reign supreme. In a similar place Jesus cried out in despair to his all-promising father, and it was here that Whitman dreamed his manly lovers, Camerados to redeem his loneliness.

The despair of the *Calamus* poems is pathetic and deeply touching. Lawrence noticed—and it would be hard not to notice—that the erotic longing expressed in them is very close to a longing for death.

Yet you are beautiful to me, you faint-tinged roots, you make me

> think of death.
> Death is beautiful from you . . .
> O I think it is not for life I am chanting here my chant of lovers,
>   I think it must be for death . . .
> Indeed O death, I think now these leaves mean precisely the same
>   as you mean, . . .

Having cancelled, or assimilated, the reality of woman, death becomes the poet's only resort. Having effectively nullified the generative principle of sex, this poetic incarnation of the Western Male Rocket can only crash on the moon, without issue. In "Scented Herbage of My Breast," from which the above lines are quoted, and which is surely the greatest and most disturbing of the poems in the *Calamus* group, Whitman embraced his fate.—Did so with a bravery and clarity which, as Lawrence rightly noted, helped make him the great poet that he was.

Yet the clarity of unmitigated despair was not for Whitman, and as he drank his bitter cup, he characteristically sweetened it with a far-fetched hope. It was here, among the "faint-tinged roots" that grew at the dead end of his masculine Open Road, that Whitman proclaimed his wistful doctrine that the "dear love of comrades," man for man love, would form the spiritual basis of the new democratic order. For was not his Self the world's Self as well? It had to be. And was not his own necessity, however tragically twisted, equally the rule by which the world must be ordered? So it must be, or his own world would collapse.

II

Perhaps it shouldn't seem odd that a dandified journalist from Long Island should proclaim himself our national poet. What is strange and a bit unsettling is that the Whitman described above *is* our national poet, without even a remote competitor for the role. What is more unsettling is Lawrence's view of him as "our one pioneer poet, blazing the way ahead . . . fearfully mistaken."—This is in reference not just to America, but to the whole of Western culture.

For Whitman's private pathology, or rather the cultural artifact he made of it, is among other things the decaying flower of a gone-to-seed patriarchy, and the virulent last-stand insistence of something about to die. He not only embodies the idealist-absolutist tendencies of the patriarchal West—his enthusiasm for the Hegelian fallacy is part and parcel of this—but carries them a step further, by his reflexive exclusion of woman from his erotic cosmos, and his subsumption of the feminine into himself. At its worst—as, say, in "Pioneers! O Pioneers!"—Whitman's poetry is the final, apocalyptic expression of the masculine ego-machine, broken loose from its rootedness in sexual life.

What, then, of the "other" Whitman, the pagan priest and compassionate initiator, usher to the mysteries? The profound and sweet singer, preternaturally sensitive to the cosmic pulse and the hum of being, who first gave voice to the native New World cadence, grand yet infinitely subtle? D. H. Lawrence, helpful once again, has provided the lens that brings the two Whitmans into focus:

> ... the rhythm of American art-activity is dual.
> 1. A disintegrating and sloughing off of the old consciousness.
> 2. The forming of a new consciousness underneath.

Whitman became easier for me to see when I recognized two things going on at once in his work, a death and a birth. Certain of his poems become clearer if we hear them as simultaneous death-throes and birth-pangs—and if his readers are often confused, think how confused Whitman must have been about who it was that was dying and who was being born.

I think this explains his strange hymns to ". . . death, death, death," so anomalous in this less-than-middle-aged poet, singing the life of an infant republic. It also accounts for the coexistence in one poet of the authentic American pagan and the puritan idealist Lawrence saw, "driving a car with a very powerful headlight, the car of the One Idea." And it reconciles Whitman's magnetic animal health with the "post-mortem effects" and machine-like insistence Lawrence pointed out.

For in Whitman's poems two worlds crossed currents on their ways to their separate destinies, and the focus of that cross was his agony and sacrifice. The ideal ship of the West had run aground on the coast of a female continent, but the "captain" had the genius to survive, and make his camp among the wreckage. The New-World consciousness that took form inside the disintegrating chrysalis of the old was the reverse Janus-face of the European quest, that of the archetypal poet, baffled and terrorized by the Feminine, but also empowered by it, and blessed beyond measure.

III

I have gradually come to believe that what took place in Whitman's poetry was not merely an artistic revolution, of the kind that occurs every fifty or a hundred years, but a world revolution, wrought by artistic means. It is easy to imagine that once, perhaps in matriarchal times, the poet was a priest of the life-more-abundant-here-and-now, a servant of that Goddess whose kingdom was the realm of the senses, organic nature. But devotees of the growing cult of the father-god insisted their deity was *superior* to nature, outside it, not available to the senses—and when they won out in the spiritual power-struggle that ensued, poets were in effect stripped of their power and consigned to the role of entertainers.

By Whitman's time, the primal function of poetry had been sleeping in the West for many centuries, supplanted by religion, which is metaphor frozen into dogma. Religion, with its creeds and observances, mystified poetic truths and put them out of reach, so that only dispensation from above, rewarding faith, or mediation by the church, could afford believers a glimpse of the Fountainhead.

Yet all the time poetry was asleep, it had dreams—was, in fact, the medium in which the Goddess dreamt her comeback. This dreaming expressed itself in individuals as dichotomous torments and irresolvable conflicts: Donne, for example, couldn't reconcile the rich sensuous life of his earlier poems with a religious life, which he finally opted for. The tortured, self-divided quality of Donne's poetry made him the first Modernist poet—Modernism defined here as the poet's more or less self-conscious embrace of his state of "sin," that is, his alienation from the glory he was created to celebrate, the mind-body unity which is the realm of the Goddess.

As the authority of religion declined, from the Reformation onward, the stage was being set for a new spiritual principle to take effect in the life of Western peoples. There were signs that poetry was stirring in its sleep: the "prophetic" vocations of Milton and Blake, and the respiritualizing of nature in the poetry of Goethe and others.

Enter Walt Whitman, singing the authentic message of the New World Muse. Through him she announces that spiritual life and the life of the senses are one, that what is promised in the spirit shall be fulfilled in the flesh and vice versa; that no longer shall priests and institutions mediate between us and what is beyond, rather we shall explore the beyond here and now, through the medium of our lives, enhanced by poetic means. For what use are creeds and dogmas to beings whose real life is lived on the brink of mystery where the gods come into being?

This, I think, is something like the "religion" of poetry, which had moved like a sleepwalker through the entranced words of poets during the period of their "exile," the centuries of abstract religion. The substance of this creedless creed—disciplined and informed by the long dream of exile—is what Lawrence rightly called "the bravest doctrine man has ever proposed to himself." For it is predicated on the highest possible estimate of human capability. All "previous religions" have seen the human being as a rather weak, sheeplike creature, in need of illusion and shepherding. And now Walt Whitman tells this same creature,

> Long enough have you dreamed contemptible dreams,
> Now I wash the gum from your eyes,
> You must habit yourself to the dazzle of the light and of every
>   moment of your life.

The burden of Whitman's work is this deep, artistically realized conviction that the human race is ready for poethood, life lived in full acknowledgment of mystery, but without mystification.—Life lived from its source, for its own sake, enhancing itself through the arts and sciences. Life lived "close to the quick," in Lawrence's phrase; the life more abundant lived here and now, with wide open senses.

IV

I am grateful to Whitman for helping me to realize that this "religion" is also my own, and stands at the center of my life and poetic practice. Yet this is only part of the gratitude I feel in the presence of Whitman's poems—for finally they *are* poems, above and beyond all the foregoing analysis, and it is through the alchemy of language that Whitman works his magic and bestows his great gifts. If he is a great spiritual teacher, it is through his adherence to the indirect medium of language and its potential for saying the unsayable—as through the ingenious rightness of his *measure*, the technical rectitude which Williams mistakenly thought Whitman lacked. The weird, incalculable delight of those enigmatic passages that incant the ineffable and glide off into mystery, carries every bit as much of his "message" as his direct exhortations. And the "didactic" parts, in turn, can't be reduced to their content; so much of their authority resides in their surging and falling rhythms, and in the manner of the speaking voice.

For me, "Song of Myself" is Whitman's greatest poem, a banquet for a lifetime. Outside of Shakespeare and the King James Bible, I know of nothing in English to compare with it, both for minute rightness and grandeur of orchestration. With its evanescent moods, haunting modulations, spine-tingling chants and pagan profusions—as well as its profound authority, its solid yet slippery wisdom, and the "wild soft laughter" Carl Sandburg noticed running between the lines—it is everywhere true to Whitman's "religion of poetry," which insists on freedom, eluding creeds and defying formulation.

Do you guess I have some intricate purpose?
Well I have, for the Fourth-month showers have, and the mica
    on the side of a rock has.
Do you take it I would astonish?
Does the daylight astonish? Does the early redstart twittering
    through the woods?
Do I astonish more than they?

This hour I tell things in confidence,
I might not tell everybody, but I will tell you.

"There," Whitman might have said, "try building a church on *that*."

V

... I have arrived,
To be wrestled with as I pass for the solid prizes of the universe,
For such I afford whoever can persevere to win them.

For the sake of a semi-coherent focus, I have narrowed and simplified the record of my long wrestling match with Whitman. In so doing, I've slighted many interesting questions—such as that of the meaning he attached to Democracy, and the relation it bears to his poetic principles and his vision of America.—In regard to which I find myself wondering if he was so "mistaken" as I've made him out to be in the first part of my essay. For his power is such that I have to reconsider every negative appraisal—just as my pleasure in *Leaves of Grass* is repeatedly interrupted by the pathological rhythms of his poetic Doomsday Machine.

Such alternation of assent and revolt is as Whitman would have wanted it. For he wished above all for his "disciples" to be independent of him, to work things out for themselves, even refute him. I have been reading Whitman for fifteen years, and would have been deluding myself if I thought I would settle the argument he provokes by writing this essay. The bond that connects me to Whitman, as to poetry, is an enigmatic faith, or a question beyond discussion. The proof and resolution of what Whitman did must finally be poetic, the work of many lifetimes.

For Walt Whitman • *Patricia Goedicke*

Whatever it was to you,
   Finally I think I am only one blade of it,
   Tiny, infinitesimally

Also I think there is nothing very unusual about my life
   Or most people's:

Climbing the steepest face of the mountain
   Struggling to go up

Even as the dirty seesaw tips
   Slowly, irrevocably
     Down

Any one of the world's giants could step on me
   And never notice

Even if I cried out, in a cracked voice
   Under the rubble of the earthquake
     Among the dying cattle who would hear?

Not that there is anything so unextraordinary, either
   About my comings and goings:

It is just that there are so many of us,
   Each sword single,
     Each miniscule life . . .

Therefore to my mind it is more a matter
   Of quiet roots, of connections,

Of speaking out, loud
   Or just soft enough
     For a few friends to hear

The beautiful names of all those
Who eventually will but must not
Entirely disappear.

14.

The Mayflower Moment: Reading Whitman During the Vietnam War

PATRICIA HAMPL

for Sherman Paul

IN 1968, BELIEVE IT OR NOT, you blushed when you asked your doctor for birth control pills. You were twenty-two and unmarried, and were wearing the angular paper garment which, about that time, doctors began to issue for examinations instead of crisply laundered cotton gowns (cheaper, no doubt, although the nurse, starchy herself, had said, "More sanitary"). You wondered briefly if this change had put somebody out of a job: economics were strangely powerful though you rarely considered the subject; you were arty, as your brother frequently said. Then you moved on to the small but definite humiliation of asking for the key to personal freedom from a man wearing a $200 suit while you were dressed in a large blue Kleenex.

He was a nice man. You remembered from a previous visit that he was bald as a cue-ball; this time his head was a fetching riot of dark curls. A toupée, and the vanity relaxed you a lot. It made him somehow more like you, more feminine, someone who understood the gloss we are required to put on reality to get through. He handed over the pills as easily as if you'd asked for a Life-saver (Ah, you had). He was so nice maybe you found yourself saying you were getting married—"next month sometime"—so he would not think evil thoughts about you. Or maybe you didn't say that because you had rehearsed the scene heavily the night before with your girlfriends (as you still, though not for long, called them): *You* were not going to lie; you were going to march right in there and *tell* the doctor to give you the goods. And you did, sort of. Then you blushed.

That is what I did. Afterwards, I went across the street to the Brothers Delicatessen in downtown Minneapolis and ordered a Reuben sandwich ("Big Enough to Feed Two!"), a piece of five-layer chocolate cake, a pot of tea, and a glass of water. The glass of water was business; the rest was glee. I put my purse beside me, along with the book I was carrying. I held the plastic circle in my hand, the prayer wheel of the month's pills. Enlightenment welled up in me, the hilarity of revelation: it's so *simple*. The little pill—I marvelled at its tininess, I bowed to medical science—popped, almost eagerly it seemed, out of its Day 1 slot. Imitating the motion, I popped Day 1 itself lightly into my mouth, took a swallow of water, and let technology course through me. Today is the first day of the rest of your life, right?

I settled into the Reuben sandwich which, though big enough for two, was going to feed just one and no doubt about it now. I picked up the book (always bring a book to the doctor's office; they always make you wait: the wisdom of my mother—who didn't know about *this* doctor's appointment) and propped it between the sugar dispenser and the plate, and I read and ate and was happy in my new high-tech body. The book was the Modern Library edition of *Leaves of Grass*. I had just taken care of personal life neatly. Now I could move on to America which, at the time, seemed to present more unsettling troubles even than sex did. Where was the pill for that?

The idea of America. The idea of friendship as a model for sexual relations and for citizenship. The very idea of ideas, the allure of speculation, the satisfaction of considering the Big Questions, of mapping things out. And always, the reassuring (because I was just beginning to write) elevation of the role of the "poet and literatus." These, for me, were Whitman's initial appeal. It seems now as if I read Whitman all that year and the next two, 1969 and 1970; as if I read no one but Whitman. Or—this is it—I read others as footnotes or responses to the main text which was always his.

For it was also the time when I began to read contemporary American poetry. The poets I read then will probably always people my private roster of our national poetry, and the ones I happened not to read then are figures I sketched in lightly later; they are ghosts with no power to spook me. I didn't happen to read Robert Lowell then (except for a few anthology pieces) and so, although people say he is more important than, say, Louis Simpson, I can't feel it. I was reading Simpson's *At the End of the Open Road* in 1968, neatly writing "image," "surrealism," "metaphor," "irony" next to particular lines, as if accurate labeling would assure me a place in the kingdom. I wanted to be a poet too.

I read with the hunger of my Victorian novel reading in high school. It was a second childhood of passionate reading, only this time the books were modern, minimal and austere even in their physical aspect: the lean volumes of living poets. It was easy to cart ten of them home from the library at a time. And—ominous good luck which I rued later when my own first book was published—nobody else seemed to be checking out the skinny books, so I always had my pick. I was, in my way and for my own satisfaction (I was about to write: for my consolation), trying to make a believable picture of my country and my times through my reading of poetry.

I was consoled by these contemporary poets and by Whitman not simply because their world view mirrored my own less articulate, formless one; in fact, as feminism claimed more territory in my mind and heart, my heroes often disappointed me (although Whitman had the good habit of often writing "men and women," rather than just "men"). My fascination was of another sort. The consolation they provided may seem at first abstract, barely recognizable as passion. Yet it was fiercely passionate: I loved Whitman and the poets I saw as his heirs because they addressed the question of "a national self." They pondered the American identity—did it exist? What was it? Would such an identity help? It was the Vietnam War era and, like a lot of people, I felt desperate about being an American, an identity which until then had seemed attractive and had been associated in my mind (as poetry itself was) with idealism and a radiant goodness.

At the Brothers Delicatessen I had swallowed the lozenge of personal revolution; I was an earnest communicant—at last—at the modern altar after long tarrying in the vestibule of Catholic girlhood. But still, all was not well. I waited for "experience" to claim me, for "personal life" to happen—and I was ready. Nothing bad can happen to me, I truly thought. The pill instantly became metaphorical and represented not only freedom but safety. But I was already nursing a broken heart. And nothing had even happened to me yet. I felt jilted by the country. It seemed I didn't *know* my own people, the way one feels when a friend acts in a completely uncharacteristic, appalling way. I had an overpowering desire to analyze this American self.

As far as I could tell, the national self had either never existed or if it had, was now grotesquely ravaged by our role in Vietnam. I did not feel American. Or rather, I felt terribly, grievously American, but I didn't know what to do about it or what that meant. I registered shame as a national emotion, and a powerful sense of having been cheated, but mainly I was confused. Who *were* we, anyway? I felt I knew who *I* was: a modern woman with a body that ticked now not like a bomb planted in a locker but like a tightly wound porcelain clock painted with flowers, as feminine as you please but a reliable machine. But I didn't know who *we* were. And that drove me, as it did many others, to a passion for analysis, looking for explanations and discussions of the American self. Beyond my protest of the War, I was impelled by a need to consider the larger issue of the national identity, much as a woman who goes into therapy because her marriage is on the rocks and she's unable to eat solid food or brush her teeth without weeping, but who stays to unravel a much denser, more ancient skein of yarn that may go back to childhood and the chancy cards dealt at birth: the fact of being a woman, or a Catholic, or a Jew. In this case, the fact of being an American.

Beyond my personal ambition and desire to be a poet, I *trusted* poetry. I had always known I wanted to write, but I had assumed I would be a reporter or some kind of journalist. I hadn't considered "being a poet," although I had always written poems. But I turned to poetry in a more complete way at this time, as reader and as a young writer, because it was one of the places I recognized American voices speaking with candor. It was a time when, like so many of my generation, I trusted little I read or heard. That may be why I have the sense that I read poetry for consolation. Also for the news, even though it was usually bad news. But at least the poets I was reading or whom I heard at the anti-war readings (Kinnell, Bly, Snyder, Wright, Levertov, to name a few) were able to indicate a relation between the current national trauma and the past. "Folks expect of the poet to indicate . . . the path between reality and their souls," Whitman wrote. "Men and women perceive beauty well enough . . . probably as well as he." I believed that and looked for "the path," or a desire for it, in the poets I read.

These contemporary poets had a sense of the national self, an ethical and psychological instinct, which radical political commentators, with whom I basically agreed, often lacked. (As for the mainstream press and our elected leaders—the lying, the subterfuge and cowardice were choking the voice of the land. It is so much accepted today as part of the national myth that "Vietnam was a mistake" that it is hard to recapture the genuine anguish and loneliness many people felt as they protested not only against the war but against people and institutions they would otherwise have trusted.) I recognized in contemporary poetry a voice, quite a few voices, I could trust. I cannot think of Whitman without thinking of these contemporary poets. They are part of the same book I was trying to read: the story of the self in the nation.

Louis Simpson said the open road led to the used car lot and I was not only shocked but subtly thrilled, as if I'd arrived at the denouement of a compelling story. James Wright said he could not bear

To allow my poor brother my body to die

> In Minneapolis.
> The old man Walt Whitman our countryman
> Is now in America our country
> Dead.
> But he was not buried in Minneapolis
> At least.
> And no more may I be
> Please God.

Minneapolis—not, for me, the name of a city, but Minneapolis *where I lived.* I shivered the provincial shiver, the unfamiliar glamour of significance. It hardly mattered that in the poem my town was the metaphor for everything crummy and worthless: our name was on the paper, we were part of the story, in direct (if negative) relation to Whitman himself. Maybe the end of the open road was Minneapolis.

These poems were new at the time and I took them personally, which is the only way to take poetry, to know something *is* poetry. I was dazzled by the ferocious disappointment of these poets of the generation immediately preceding my own. I took in their disillusion in heavy draughts at the same time that I was reading Whitman's theoretical rhapsodies (especially in the preface to the 1855 edition of *Leaves of Grass* and the long essay, "Democratic Vistas."). I felt, in reading these contemporary poets, like a sneak who turns to the last page of a thriller but who still goes diligently back to find out how the puzzling crime began. Whitman, for me, was the beginning. He was there along with Emily Dickinson. I liked the idea that our literary history—my version—began with these two poised above us like an icon of sexual equality, proof of an even-handed distribution of genius. Two odd ducks, she with her spectral virginity and brief, rectitudinous metric lines, acute and strange; and Whitman cramming the page with his radically long lines, practically jabbering at times, transfiguring his sexuality, which bewildered him, into a vision of democracy—"the dear love of comrades." I was entirely satisfied with Mother and Father.

But I chose Father, as girls often do. I would have become a Whitmanian, had it been possible, the way Russians became Tolstoyans. Whitman advised against this sort of thing:

> Are you the new person drawn toward me?
> To begin with take warning, I am surely far different from
>   what you suppose;
> Do you suppose you will find in me your ideal?
> Do you think it so easy to have me become your lover?
> Do you think the friendship of me would be unalloy'd satisfaction?
> Do you think I am trusty and faithful?

> Do you see no further than this facade, this smooth and tolerant
> manner of me?

But I paid no heed. I suppose I wanted to find a gorgeously optimistic voice
to reassure me that, in spite of the evidence (those ears dangling from a
string on a GI's belt in a *Life* magazine picture), the national self could be
saved, that my life—just beginning as I felt—would not be indentured to
the guilt of appalling crimes, but could continue to tick along in its flower-
painted clock, as free in spirit as my toupée-wearing gynecologist had made
me in body.

I clung to Whitman because he had a theoretical bent, which I read as
entirely sunny: he was not the poet of death and lilacs for me, but the man
who said things like, "Of all nations the United States with veins full of
poetical stuff most need poets and will doubtless have the greatest and use
them the greatest." He said we were a spiritual and poetic people. On the
other hand, I read Bly and Wright, Kinnell and Levertov because they
expressed the immediate horror and grief and kept the moral pulse beating.
I read them and Whitman in a sort of balancing act: bad news, good news.
But I was glad Whitman's book was fat and endless like an ancient sacred
text to which I could turn at any time, and that these others were thin and
immediate. The contemporary verdict was grave, but these living poets also
turned to Whitman for the prophetic gleam. Reading him was like touching
base in some way. For there, in Whitman, the national self—what he called
"the American stock personality"—held its head high and looked out at the
world guilelessly, like the poet he said we were meant to be.

It made a great difference to me that Whitman wrote prose as well as
poetry: it actually heightened his authority as a poet. The poetry and the
essays, taken together (and I did take them together), made him a bard
because he sang but he also speculated, prophesied, admonished. The prose
also made him more accessible, gave range and intimacy to anything he
touched. I had wanted to be a writer and had been drawn more deeply into
poetry than I had expected, and so maybe it was natural that I felt especially
kindred to a poet who, like me, had been a working journalist and to whom
prose was not an alien genre but another way of speaking.

Whitman might sing of love in his poems, but he also thought about it,
speculated about it, in his essays. My favorite of his love poems, I suppose
my single favorite of his short lyrics, was this one from "Children of Adam":

> I heard you solemn-sweet pipes of the organ as last Sunday
> morn I pass'd the church,

Winds of autumn, as I walk'd the woods at dusk I heard your
    long-stretch'd sighs up above so mournful,
I heard the perfect Italian tenor singing at the opera, I
    heard the soprano in the midst of the quartet singing;
Heart of my love! you too I heard murmuring low through one
    of the wrists around my head,
Heard the pulse of you when all was still ringing little
    bells last night under my ear.

I went from reading this sheer lyric grace with its lucidity of passion, to his speculations in the essays about "the dear love of comrades" which he proposed as the basis of a genuine American democracy. We weren't going to be a nation based on hierarchy as the old feudal world had been; we were not even going to settle for the correct comfort of being a nation of laws. We were going to be pals, a nation of buddies. This vision delighted me.

For one thing, it was warm and attractive: I was glad of the family feeling. As it was, my own family and I were enacting the classic Vietnam-era battles and arguments, ornamented in our baroque Catholic way. Sometimes I wasn't sure whether my father and I were fighting about the War, my boyfriend's long hair, my long hair, the smoking of marijuana by me or by "the nation's youth" ("Do you want to become an *addict*? Your brother says it could lead to addiction." My brother was a dentistry student and had the authority of science; I was on the student newspaper and was arty. I could never win an argument).

All the arguments in our family, in everybody's family, seemed to lead to or from Vietnam and yet Vietnam was not the entire point. The desire for personal identification with a larger-than-self heritage was the point. In "Democratic Vistas" Whitman said "democracy . . . ever seeks to bind all nations, all men into a brotherhood, a family." I wanted to believe this—as an American but also as the troubled and troublesome (I started the dinner table arguments) member of a real family. One Sunday while my father was changing a lightbulb in the dining room chandelier, standing on top of the very table we fought across, I announced I wasn't going to Mass anymore, ever. Period. He said nothing, just continued screwing in the new lightbulb, looming above me like a silent giant, as powerfully mysterious as an electrical charge, no matter what rebellion I visited upon him with my gnat-like persistence, my protests and arch refusals.

So. I didn't belong to the Church. Nor to a happy family. And I didn't stand up for the national anthem at ball games. The only thing I belonged to was my generation—hardly a permanent address, although I tried to make it home for a long time. But reading Whitman I belonged: to what I felt was the true nation, to those who lived in the magic of the possible, in mourning for America, the pure idea.

Here, in Whitman, America shimmered for me in its refracted identity, the only truly innocent identity it has ever had: America as an idea. As Whitman put it

> ... the true nationality of the States, the genuine union, when we come to a mortal crisis, is, and is to be, after all, neither the written law, nor (as generally supposed,) either self-interest, or common pecuniary or material objects—but the fervid and tremendous IDEA ...

I could dream the American idea over again with Whitman even though air-conditioned, transistor radio-equipped American helicopters were dropping napalm on green villages at that very moment. I could escape American history which was a bad dream and enter the dream of America which I wished could be history. A sleight of hand, a last ditch attempt to return to the purity of abstraction, to the Mayflower moment, the arrival in paradise before anything had happened. Before history. Whitman, as I read him, was an invitation to innocence.

If the gospel means "good news," I read Whitman as gospel. He had had his war, calamitous and divisive of the national self, and now we had ours. He had his aberrant sexuality and we (American women) had our sudden "sexual liberation." Out of the ashes of the Civil War and out of his ambivalence about his own sexuality, Whitman fashioned the most beautiful (or at least most appealing) American conception, fusing together sex and nationhood, envisioning a country full of charmed lovers with arms around each others' waists. We would be friends. Our relation as a nation would be chosen and free, affectionate and "adhesive," as he put it. The sad American patrimony, the inheritance of alienation under the mantle of individualism, was, in Whitman's vision, transfigured into a rich and radiant conception of nationhood.

If, after his war, Whitman could dream such a dream, why couldn't we? We weren't the first American generation saddled with disillusion and rancor. I forgot, of course, that Whitman felt his war had been won and disaster averted. I'm not sure, even now, that any victory, any sense of transcendence, was possible for my generation once Vietnam became our focus. When the War finally ended in 1975 (it did end, didn't it?), there was a curious lack of joy. No dancing in Times Square, no elation. The word wasn't "Peace" but the lackluster phrase, "The troops pulled out." We hadn't won, we hadn't even lost. It was just over—sort of.

A heritage is usually, for most nations, a sort of goulash of history and legend and shared values. In our case, it seemed, history was bypassed, replaced by the utopic reliance on the future. "America," Whitman writes at the beginning of "Democratic Vistas," counts, as I reckon, for her justification and success (for who, as yet, dare claim success?) almost entirely on the future. Nor is that hope unwarranted. Today, ahead, though dimly yet, we see, in vistas, a copious, sane, gigantic offspring. For our New World I consider far less important for what it has done, or what it is, than for results to come. Sole among nationalities, these States have assumed the task to put in forms of lasting power and practicality, on areas of amplitude rivaling the operations of the physical kosmos, the moral political speculations of ages, long, long deferr'd, the democratic republican principle, and the theory of development and perfection by voluntary standards, and self-reliance.

I read Whitman ahistorically, as if "Democratic Vistas" had not been written in 1871 but yesterday. The dream was alive, the idea was possible—it all lay ahead, it was all in the future. Here I was, 100 years later, two world wars into history, bored by the inevitable pioneer imagery of the country (The New Frontier, the "frontiers of space"), not recognizing that the boredom masked yet another shame, the plain fact of massacre which is the underbelly of the pioneer spirit, of "settling the country." I wanted, in a self-righteous way as well as helplessly, the only American birthright I could imagine: to step off the Mayflower onto undefiled land, unlimited possibility, unwritten history. I suppose I was truly American in that desire, and entirely conceptual: I was consoled by the *idea* of America. I thought I was seeking—and finding in Whitman—a national identity. But I think now that I was looking for something else. I wanted to find America innocent. Innocence was the only "national self" I was prepared to acknowledge and pledge allegiance to. Whitman provided that—or my reading of him did. We might be untrue to this self—as the poets at the anti-war readings reminded us—but at least the self existed. I think Whitman saved me from a paralyzing self-hatred. He fixed my mind on a vision.

My best friend's husband went to prison as a draft resister. Then my own boyfriend went in 1970, having bewildered his Illinois draft board with a letter that explained that because Walt Whitman had said, "Dismiss whatever insults your own soul," he was dismissing his draft card (see enclosed, etc., etc.). This struck me as heroic, Whitmanian, wonderfully independent: a patriot. I am still loyal to that act, even though I think at the time I was more thrilled by the romance of it than by the correctness. But of course the slow, annoying and dull details of courts and incarceration blunted the dagger of the initial gesture. What about dismissing the judge, the prison, the War itself, the whole rotten business? Didn't they insult the soul too? At the trial I was dismayed to realize that, unlike a courtroom scene on Perry Mason, it was impossible from the visitors' gallery to hear a single thing either judge or defendant was saying. The grand dismissal was a mumble and then my patriot was in handcuffs and leg-irons and the whole thing was over. One dismissal made for a raft of acceptances, for suddenly the body, unlike the soul, could not do much dismissing. My God, I thought as they led him away, they're really going to put him in *prison*. As if that had never been a possibility, when in fact it had always been the only possible result of his action and I had known that—or thought I had.

The beautiful directive had been followed: an insult to the soul had been dismissed. But I think for many people who made such decisions, who responded to the Whitmanian vision, or who were affected by the decisions of others close to them, the real lesson and effect came later. For it turned out that the initial dismissal caused one to live in an environment (either in actual prison or in the reflected life of acts with consequences) where insulting things could not be dismissed. The first dismissal was important— because it was a genuine act, one with consequences. But the acceptances that followed were the real melting pot of character. For it is in those things which cannot be dismissed or chosen but which must be acquiesced to and assimilated that "identity" of self or of nation begin to take on authenticity. Vision is necessary—and our literature is rich with the power of dream. But there must be a moment when one is no longer just stepping ashore onto the unmarked New World, eyelashes aflutter like an ingenue in her first glittering ballroom, waiting for something to happen, something wonderful. The future is here, now, and the past is full of actual deeds, some good, a lot awful. But actual deeds, real history. Utopias hardly have the meat on their bones to sustain a people in grave times.

I saw a number of letters that young men sent to their draft boards during those years. Whitman was quoted frequently: "Dismiss whatever insults your own soul." "The soul has that measureless pride which consists in never acknowledging any lessons but its own." But it was acting on the vision, taking the utopic idea seriously into history, and then living with the consequences, which finally gave the idea dignity. Many of the young men who went to prison felt they ruined their lives. Their wives left them or they found themselves mired in terrible depressions, nursing dark nights of the soul and growing fatally ironic about their own grand gestures. All of a sudden there was nothing left to dismiss; they could only endure. Hanging in there lacks the élan of dismissing whatever insults your own soul. I wonder how many of those young men—not young anymore—ended up dismissing Whitman or dismissing themselves, or simply hating the tender idealism which they took with them into prison.

Recently at a party I overheard a conversation between an ex-draft resister and a woman who said to him, "Well, I suppose you feel pretty good about how you handled yourself during the War. I mean, you were right."

He laughed. "Oh, I just had to prove I was a hero." Said without rancor, no bitterness. He seemed amused with himself. There was a long-ago-and-far-away quality to his relation with his own protest. The woman was a little put off, and did not like his lightness, although there was no self-hating irony to it. The self-mockery was gentle. But then maybe she had never dismissed what had insulted her own soul and didn't know how foolish that makes you feel. Foolish and full to the brim with contradictions, as Whitman knew. The test of dismissing whatever insults your own soul turned out to be the ability to hold in balance all the foolishness and contradictions that followed in the wake of a real gesture.

And then there was the fact of charm. Whitman charmed me. Charm is entirely powerful in normal human relations, in conversation, for instance, when being boorishly right is *merely* being right. Oddly enough, charmlessness is not only a form of aggression but of dishonesty, a revocation of an essential part of candor. For in human relations to dispense with charm is to dispense with the other person. It is a kind of psychological nudity—not lovely but belligerent as it is on certain public beaches, "nude beaches," where people are pompously aware of their honest flesh, freed of the lie of cloth.

To speak, to write, without charm is to make utterances without reference to a reality outside oneself. It is an act of self-absorption, devoid of the playfulness of art, without the attractive humility of one who knows absolutely that others exist and therefore feels drawn to charm them, because to charm is to acknowledge their existence. And if Whitman often admonished, it is a mark of his genius that even his strictures managed to charm, even as they struck comfortably close to the bone. I might snort when I read Whitman carrying on—his "America *ma femme!*" or his "man-balls and man-root." But he gave me a relish for nerviness, for declaration and a personal re-naming of even the simplest facts of existence which I value still. Even a contorted phrase like "the perennial health-action of the air we call the weather" charmed me—not because it was beautiful ("No one will get at my verses who insists upon viewing them as a literary performance, or attempt at such performance, or as aiming toward art of aestheticism"), but because it attested to Whitman's personal inspection of the universe, down to the last detail. The first rule was to take nothing for granted; the second rule was, however, to *take* everything—to take every detail in his own hand and look at it: "Who knows the curious mystery of the eyesight?"

Whitman's greed appealed to me, too. "I contain multitudes." And just on the other side of that statement was the irrepressible avidity that was crying, More, more! I loved his catalogues partly for the serenity to be found in any litany; there is something religious about a list. But also I loved them for the proprietary, almost housekeeperly tabulation: he was counting up the national silver, listing rivers, toting up the states, nationalities, regions, fields and forests. It was another, more concrete, way of stalking the national identity. Our features went on and on; we had a shape, we could be named.

As a reader I was charmed to be addressed directly ("dear, earnest reader"), to be appealed to:

... the reader is to do something for himself, must be on the alert, must himself or herself construct indeed the poem, argument, history, metaphysical essay—the text furnishing the hints, the clue, the start or frame-work. Not the book needs so much to be the complete thing, but the reader of the book does.

He even flirted:

Camerado, this is no book,
Who touches this touches a man,
(Is it night? Are we here together alone?)

He gave instructions about where to read his book (outside, if possible, under a tree), he practically cozied up on the reader's lap. Is there anyone who has insisted so strenuously that he *is* his book and who has as nearly accomplished that magic trick? The real camerado he succeeded joining his life with was his book. No wonder there is, then, "the book," not many books. The self, if it is healthy, does not divide but contains its multitudes, its contradictions within easy grasp and range. Whitman, paradoxically then, who is often cited as the source of the loose, even sloppy, American poetic diction, is in fact the father of greatest, most immaculate form: there is room for everything. Another of his contradictions. Another charm.

By 1973 I wasn't reading Whitman anymore. I wasn't taking the pill either. Technology had let me down. There were ominous findings about blood clots and other side effects from "long-term reliance on the pill as a form of contraception." Long term reliance! I'd planned to pop those little numbers till kingdom come. Then my mother got breast cancer (she recovered) and my very nice gynecologist thought it best "in your case, given the high risk situation," that I "discontinue use."

He mentioned an IUD. But my honeymoon with modern science was over. The pill had been pristine and almost abstract, a metaphor right from the start. But this other gadget looked like a pop-tab from a can of Pepsi. Later, one of my friends, who was rendered infertile by the IUD, financed her graduate school education with a court settlement she made with the Dalcon Shield people.

I went back to the diaphragm. I tried to be cheerful about it, but that old contraceptive magic was gone. The pill had popped out of its little slot almost eagerly, but the diaphragm, lathered correctly with its goo, had a habit of springing wildly, perversely, out of my hand, across the room, behind the radiator where, when I retrieved it, it was covered with a soft fur of dust like a mushroom feathered with fresh mold. When someone told me that the diaphragm had been invented in 1890, I felt the humiliation was complete—back to the nineteenth century with us. We hadn't even had the vote then.

I had stopped reading Whitman. Personal life, sexual life certainly, could not be so easily regulated as I had thought in 1968. My friends were out of prison but the War still went on. I didn't believe anymore—how could I?—that a "national self," no matter how deeply desired (and I still felt the desire), could be chosen or synthesized by an act of will. Not even by an act of the imagination.

America was not an idea, not anymore. It was not a matter of the future. We had not all arrived on the Mayflower, blinking at the New World's brightness, grasping an irreproachable Idea. There had been slave ships and steerage passages too. Soon there would be "boat people," as if the most recent arrivals were named for us and were not emblematic of their own country's history but of our own: Americans as eternal new arrivals, just disembarking. America wasn't an idea. It was a country, and its national self—that personality Whitman tried to identify so passionately—was emerging as national identity always does: out of history, out of circumstance and experience.

I had leaned too hard on Whitman, had not read his contradictions into him though I'd paid lip service to all that. I had gone to him for a package deal, for the pill. He even looked like a guru—he looked like Tolstoy. I don't blame myself. He certainly had his "dear, earnest reader" in me, and he wouldn't like apologies. What can you do? We all contain multitudes, not just Whitman.

But I realize, as I've been going through my Modern Library edition of *Leaves of Grass* (how soft the pages are from use, how frequent my underlinings, how diligent the margin notes where I indicated "the roles of the poet," "the democratic ideal"), in this re-reading, I see how much Whitman has mattered to me in ways I hadn't been aware of. It's so *simple*, I find myself saying, some frail echo of that enlightened glee at the Brothers Delicatessen—Whitman matters because he made *himself* a book. The magic, the genius, is that although he says he sings himself, that is a "kosmos," even so these assertions are the opposite, in fact the denial, of self-absorption. Whereas in my earlier reading, I always saw his cheer, his invitation, his constant insistence on relation, now I seem to see his vast privacy, that his invitation was really to my own self, my own book.

I would not even be writing this in the way I am—as a personal memoir— if Whitman had not written "Song of Myself," if he had not done that astonishing thing: pose for his own portrait and call it America. He poised himself between the personal and impersonal—he saved himself. And perhaps that fact, the fundamental courage of it, explains why in his book which is such an embrace, perhaps the fondest embrace between writer and reader in world literature, that in this book of love and comrades, there are the stern farewells and admonitions to go to our own work, our own life. My guru is running us out of the ashram. He is a Father who—lucky us—really wants us to grow up, even to bid the old camerado farewell:

> For it is not for what I have put into it that I have
>   written this book,
> Nor is it by reading it you will acquire it,
> Nor do those know me best who admire me and vauntingly praise me,
> Nor will the candidates for my love (unless at the most a very
>   few) prove victorious,
> Nor will my poems do good only, they will do just as much evil,
>   perhaps more,
> For all is useless without that which you may guess at many times
>   and not hit, that which I hinted at;
> Therefore release me and depart on your way.

Reaching Around • *Judith Moffett*

for Walt Whitman

I have perceiv'd that to be with those I like is enough . . .
To pass among them or touch any one, or rest my arm ever so
   lightly round his or her neck for a moment, what is this then?
I do not ask any more delight, I swim in it as in a sea.

1972 We're all uproarious, Philip and I and his
       preposterously pregnant wife who can't get up,
       their sofa's sagged too low, just since yesterday
       she's too immense—or tired, it's late,
       I should think about rising, but for me as well
       that's hard. Harder each time in fact
       to leave this house, though on the carpet I'm
       dissembling more and more: for the past hour
       I've been aware, as mercifully they're not
       yet, of the slow ache secretly uncoiling
       down the long inner muscles of my arms,
       clamped round me for safe-keeping. I can visualize
       these muscles, as in a Ben-Gay ad,
       spangled to show the pain. The pain bears lengthwise
       down, bears down, bears down; my elephantine
       friend, hilarity-weakened, tries again to heave
       herself out of her seat, it's her they want
       mostly, she's great, who wouldn't? Shhh don't don't
       Driving home I sober up at once.
       The outlook's awful, instinct says not a prayer.
       At arm's length sure, they like me, I can feel it,
       but the least whiff of serious weirdness—oh,
       damn the damn thing! clumsily complicating
       what should be unaffected, plain . . . poor arms,
       they want to reach around, that's all, an impulse
       so natural it's cruel to have to inhibit,
       so mulish it's exhausting to, and so
       imperative it's freakish. Don't I know.

1955   Scout camp at twelve. Through sunburned weedfields
        my group of girls kicks tentward. Grasshoppers
        explode about us, our shirts and shorts, and limbs,
        accumulate those smaller leaf-green hopping
        things that live in tall weeds in Ohio.
        A prickly walk, I like it, glad to be
        one among them at this ugliest age
        of inch-thick glasses, nose and sailor hat
        and mammoth chest, and so forth. So I've got
        my copious third period now—so what!
        To my mind I'm no Girl, I'm just plain Scout.

        We're telling what we're going to be; I volunteer
        "A missionary to Africa." Touched by this,
        our nicest counselor, Margie, slides a half-hug
        round my stiff shoulder. For me to shrug
        from under growling "Mush!" is automatic,
        I really have to, yet in a trice I'm dying
        to take back both: her arm, my churlish gesture—
        unthinkable. We both feel bad.
        I scuff on, blazing trail through prickly heat,
        Queen Anne's lace, bugs on springs, all trussed up tight
        in a self-image, Billy Goat Gruff's own Kid.

1968   A stone-cold toad-hideous
        gargoyle squats on a sofa croaking croaking
        warts all blood . . .
        aghast, my friends strip beds,
        pile covers on, but nothing warms
        or comforts, or shuts me up: *Be physical*
        with kids, obsessively. The parents
        behold my state in wonderment, confer in whispers;
        their little boy, who's two,
        runs in circles endlessly,
        hollering till nerve-ends
        squirm gibbering through lumpy skin, while I

don't stop and don't stop
hoarsely warning his macho dad: hold him, cuddle him.
Often as I've since been thanked
for this advice, or order, I still marvel
it was heeded. "You
kidding? The envoy from the brink of doom? My God,
that shaking voice, those cold thin fingers
clutching every blanket in the house
around you—you had authority,
believe me, I *believed* you."

1963   Classic Hall, mid-evening and mid-May.
I'm nominally reading in "my" office
but concentration's poor. Far down along
the dark corridor, light squares through a doorframe—
my teacher-mentor-"father," working late.
How soon can I go calling? Wait.
Don't crowd. Studying him closer than Shakespeare,
his ease, warmth, gentleness, his . . . anti-Gruffness,
I've glimpsed some happier ways to be not spineless
than Dad's. A mild and passive missionary
he thinks I *go at* things too hard. (He would.)
Well, fine—I'll be his auto-convert
        Light
snaps out, spatter of rubber footsteps—*wait!*
Slam book, grab notes and pen, pelt headlong down
the black stairs, catch him up too breathless—Hi!
I just this minute finished *Henry the Fifth!*
Isn't that last act awful? Courtly love—
Katharine—"God of battles"—Falstaff/Hal—
The door; revealing racket muted against
a close, soft, honeysuckle-hyperbolic
Hoosier spring night. Between two breaths I'm offered
a lift back to the dorm. "Sure, thanks a lot!"
On flows and flows the babbling brook of language,
undammable we're halfway to the car

his sudden warm enclosing hand his voice
a chuckle mine a plug-jerked radio

1979   Whitman, when I read over what you wrote
        I have to wonder. Takes one to know one, right?
        You doted on yourself, there was that lot of you
        and all so luscious; you found no sweeter fat
        than stuck to your own bones. Oh yeah?
        No doubts then? It's our weakness to confuse
        wish and conviction, ought-to-be with is,
        and something in your voice . . . but if I'm wrong
        and you aren't bluffing, Walt, how happy you were
        in that belief. I'm mired, I'm pretty sure,
        in doubt for keeps. It creeps and creeps along,
        a glacial progress I extrapolate
        will have me hugging friends, age 68,
        in 2010; I don't call that a cure.

The touch that heals? The laying on of hands?

When (in 1970) on the Delaware
I was the Scout camp counselor,
not for the first time nor the last, we had
this problem child. Obnoxious fat complainer,
she hated camp, crafts, swimming, cookouts, hikes—
Ready to brain the brat, I overheard
Margaret, my assistant, remark offhand
as if to state the obvious, "That kid
just needs to be held and held." Dumb stare: she did?
I of all people had the least excuse
not to sense that. The change in the little wretch
amazed us all. And hugging her felt *good*,
how can I put this right? almost as though
that thistly girl were me at her age, ten—
as though my reflex fendings-off had been
taken for what they were, and been ignored.

Balky, sulky, stiff in my arms as wood,
what was her name? *She*'d be in college now,
that camper who alone could tell us what
came of our cuddling—anything? If not
enduringly for her, to me it's meant
ever since then—that no child's need
gnarl into mine unmet—I've been released
to reach toward children every way one can,
help them be certain, clear to the marrow-lattice,
the fat that sticks to their bones is sweeter than sweet,
self-evident as weight and sight, so they
may never in their lives endure self-loathing
or self-constraint because of "a few light kisses,
a few embraces, a reaching around of arms"
that didn't happen. Otherwise no—except
as, clustered in a beaten space between
peaked huts, Kikuyu watch a white fanatic's
kind, sweaty, earnest face, or classroomful
of undergraduates sits forward rapt—
for who's the missionary *alias*
professor now, who strains to touch and change
minds with a mind? (I never saw this, strange—
language as sublimated touch, ideas
as sublimated—something . . .) Yet despite
that half-truth, and how stirring it can be
to touch a book and seem to touch a man,
flesh that embraces flesh still satisfies
our childish fat-and-bones' avidity
better than "Crossing Brooklyn Ferry" can
—though he was right.

Envoi

Whoever I am holding you now in hand
Has understood how much that luscious lot
You rightly said you were would understand
This long hug made of words that say I'm not.

Revolutionary Frescoes—the Ascension • *Thomas McGrath*

in memory of Walter Lowenfels

On that morning when the Unknown Revolutionary rises
From his bed in the Veterans' Hospital in Fargo, North Dakota
There will be free cigarettes for everyone and no lumps in the porridge!
Trumpets will sound and resound from the four corners of the world!
The four blue-blowers and commissars of the vagrant and workless winds,
Standing at the round earth's blazing corners, in arms,
Will organize the demonstration: Marx, Engels, Lenin,
Che—the last and youngest at the western corner with machine gun.

Then, in the hospital corridors the walking wounded will fly
As a Blakean column of pure spirit toward the operating room
And the rotting flesh, bed-bound will rise up in song!
The walking delegates with wooden legs will race through the halls
And the wheel-chairs, now winged—the wheels within wheels of
   Fellow-worker Ezekiel—
Will sport it in the very whiskers of Marx as he beams from his plinth
Near the ceiling of the north corner! And all four commissars will
sound
The timbrel and the fraternal harp and the mouth organ and the guitar,
And the heavenly host will chant, led by Woody and Cisco:
Everything or Nothing, Comrades! All of us or none!

Then the rolling tomb will arrive blazing with slogans and flowers!
But *no gardenias*, dear Comrades! Damn all bourgeois conventions!
Let us have something simpler instead. Geraniums, maybe—
From the window-boxes of the poor. And, from the woods,
   red cardinals—and trillium!
To stand for the flowering unity of theory and practice and daring—
But leave it to the Mexican and Italian sections to organize:
   they *know!*
Finally the heavenly cadres have all in hand—no more
To do but fly up in a great hosting of real and hallucinatory
Light!

They fly up . . .
   Farewell, Comrade!
      You did your share.

And now, in the pause that follows, I remember walking with you
And your other comrade, Walt Whitman, beside the Jersey shore
While he talked of news of these states and the foiled revolutionaires
Out of an earlier time; and we run to keep up with his stride.
Himself with his beard full of butterflies, you with the moon
   on your forehead!
Midnight ramblers and railers! By the cradle, endlessly rocking,
Of a fouled contaminant sea you both saw clean and young . . .
Father of the dream, you said he was; father of poets.
I see you now in the Shades, old Double Walt, dear outlaws.

And now we must straighten the chairs in the meeting room.
A few need dues-stamps to fill out their Party Books.
A few buy the works of the Lost Poet at the Literature table—
A bit dubious for all that the young Lit-comrade says.
Finally we divide the left-over cigarettes,
Cutting some in half so that everything comes out even.
All squared away. All in good proletarian order,
We leave the place ship-shape for the next delegation to use—
Though such uprisings don't happen every day . . .

What Whitman Did Not Give Us

ROBERT BLY

I THINK OF WHITMAN and Frost as two co-fathers of American poetry. Each left many gifts behind, and what one poet doesn't give, the other gives. I don't mean they together make up a full 360-degree circle, but they are strangely complementary, the one standing for public speech, for example, the other for private. I think it is important to examine the strengths and weaknesses of each poet so that we don't isolate either in the position of good, unread father. Even in his lifetime Whitman suffered from peoples' tendency to make him a remote good: the good, grey poet.

Many contributors to this volume will, justly, speak to Whitman's greatness as a poet, opener of the Road, and as rescuer of the feminine soul for men. I have decided to go the other way mainly to set down some thoughts about what is missing in his legacy—what he did not give us.

Whitman's influence has been very strong on my generation. One cannot imagine Galway Kinnell's work appearing without Whitman in the background: one cannot think of *Howl* without Whitman nor Simpson's *At the End of the Open Road:* one cannot imagine *The Teeth Mother* appearing without Whitman beforehand. So when I write of Whitman's legacy I am thinking also of my own experience as a poet so far, that is: what I received from his example—or what I took in, at least—and what I did not receive or did not take in. To talk of a writer's inheritance is not the same thing as to talk of his work; the subject is not so concrete, we have to pick, to some extent, his "inheritance" out of the air. A writer's inheritance is everything that has gathered around him, the fragrance that flows out of people when they are touched; and thinking of Kierkegaard's inheritance, we realize that what is not present in his books has had as much influence as what is present.

I'll suggest then seven areas in which Whitman's example—among those

321

of us who have used him as a master—has proved to be a narrow example. I'll mention Pushkin and the Russians sometimes for contrast. One reason I chose Russia is because like the United States it had not much poetry before the nineteenth century, then suddenly a massive poet, in this case Pushkin, as in ours Whitman, set a stamp on the developing poetry-substance. South American poetry developed later and their poetry is influenced by Whitman—Neruda deeply so; as contrast I looked for a poetry like the Russian, without influence from Whitman.

The seven areas I'll mention are: care for male masters, the problem of pain, the emphasis on audience, care for small sounds, care for pauses, the problem of observation vs. participation, and the question of whether private or public speech is appropriate to poetry.

The matter of the fathers is a problem in Whitman. Justin Kaplan's new biography makes clear how many European and American writers he draws from: how many men said in prose what he managed to say, in his own way, in poems later. When Whitman was nearly seventy, he wrote a biographical piece on Elias Hicks, who had influenced him tremendously; but in Whitman's poetry we don't get any sense of spiritual fathers. He pretends all this has come to him spontaneously. Thoreau, in the opening pages of *Walden*, said "I have lived some thirty years on this planet, and I have yet to hear the first syllable of valuable or even earnest advice from my seniors. They have told me nothing, and probably cannot tell me anything to the purpose." This is a disgraceful statement and we feel that when we realize that Emerson was fourteen years older than Thoreau, and Thoreau had read his essay on "Nature" many times. Thoreau in fact wrote this in 1847, and had by that time already lived several months in Emerson's house, and written love poems to his wife. The generation of Thoreau and Whitman had a longing, it seems, to cast off fathers, and so they hide the influence and refuse to praise.

By contrast Rilke gives many pages of his work to praise of those he learned from—Hölderlin, Jens Peter Jacobsen, Gespara Stainpa, Mariana Alcoforado, Baudelaire, Goethe, and Rodin, in whose house he lived for a while.

An interesting story has recently come out of Russia: Pasternak's religious poems suddenly appeared in print, a few months ago, after years of official silence on their existence. It turned out that Andrei Voznesensky had spent four to five years secretly working for their publication, which meant visiting bureaucratic offices and engaging the bureaucracy at some risk to himself. By this act he makes clear that Pasternak was his master. That's the way it goes in poetry. Voznesensky's generous act is an act Thoreau did not take.

Thoreau and Whitman wanted a clean sweep: "Take no illustrations whatsoever from the ancients or classics," Whitman said to himself in his journal.
In differing ways Thoreau and Whitman each wanted to make a clean slate.
And I think their refusal to praise spiritual fathers has thrown many American poets off in their relationship to the past; some poets do not look
creatively or productively to the past but choose one hero only. Rilke makes
clear what his lineage is, and so does Voznesensky. When a writer insists
that he is unique, he never makes clear what his lineage is.

Mentioning Rilke reminds us of his preoccupation with pain, and that
reminds us that we ask of every poet: "What does one do with pain?" One
of our greatest sources of pain is that we are who we are, and not someone
else. We feel that pain often around college age, when we become ashamed
of our parents, or angry at them, and long to have a different accent perhaps,
or belong to a different class; and so naturally we turn and attack our own
class. But certain parents gave birth to us, and certain parents bore them,
and so certain positive energies are built into our natures, and certain dark
energies, making a peculiar heaviness the alchemists call "lead"; moreover,
our social group adds detail to our character, and even the few square miles
where we spent the major part of our childhood makes us particular. Rilke
faces this inheritance in his "Self-Portrait from the Year 1906." For example:

> Der Mund als Mund gemacht, gross und genau,
> nicht überredend, aber ein Gerechtes
> Aussagendes.

(The mouth is made as a mouth, large and defined, not very persuasive, but
it says something about justice.)

And we remember all the self-portraits that Rembrandt painted, with the
pain very clear. Whitman wants to say something quite different:

> I am of old and young, of the foolish as much as the wise,
> Regardless of others, ever regardful of others,
> Maternal as well as paternal, a child as well as a man,
> Stuffed with the stuff that is coarse, and stuffed with
>   the stuff that is fine,
> One of the great nation, the nation of many nations,
>   the smallest the same, and the largest the same,
> A southerner soon as a northerner, a planter nonchalant
>   and hospitable,
> A Yankee, bound my own way, ready for trade, my joints the
>   limberest joints on earth and the sternest joints on earth,
> A Kentuckian, walking the vale of the Elkhorn in my
>   deer-skin leggings. . . .

I won't quote all of it, but it ends:

> Of every hue, trade, rank, caste and religion,
> Not merely of the New World, but of Africa, Europe,
>   Asia—a wandering savage,
> A farmer, mechanic, artist, gentleman, sailor, lover, Quaker,
> A prisoner, fancy-man, rowdy, lawyer, physician, priest.

This really is quite mad: it is a drastic solution to the problem of pain, too drastic, I think. He wasn't all these things, but rather a son and grandson of Dutch and English farmers and slave-owners, from Long Island, with an idiot brother, several disturbed siblings, and a deep culture, laboriously taken in from Western sources. He is not of every hue or religion. And yet we understand him, in the passage I've quoted, to say that he doesn't mean that he *is* all of these beings, a planter, a savage, a lawyer, a priest. He is rather Being itself. But that is the most dangerous solution of all.

In the *New York Quarterly,* John Ashbery remarked, "I find it very easy to move from one person in the sense of a pronoun to another and this again helps to produce a kind of polyphony in my poetry which I again feel is a means toward greater naturalism." Helen Vendler went on to say, " 'A crowd of voices' as Stevens called it, is spoken for by the single poet; as we feel ourselves farther and farther from uniqueness and more and more part of a human collective, living, as Lowell said, a generic life, the pressure of reality exerts a pressure on style—a pressure to speak in the voice of the many. . . ."

Drew K. Martin said, referring to the "twenty-eight young men" passage: "Anonymous sexuality is an important way station on the path to the destruction of distinctions of age, class, beauty *and* sex. Whitman loves all being and will love, and be loved by all being." I feel then that Whitman often evades his own pain, and by doing that evades his own reality, and allows the pain of his family—his idiot brother for example—to disappear in the mush of Being.

It is a sort of Asian solution, and all of us who lived through the sixties felt a longing to adopt this solution: the way to solve pain is to transcend pain, simply declare yourself healthy; but that has not worked out. Whitman's legacy is not helpful here.

I've mentioned that I want to set American poetry against a background of Russian poetry, so as to see certain traits more clearly. There is always in art the question of whether to pay attention, as artist, to the audience or to the work of art. Pushkin helped Russian poets to love the work of art itself. He taught it as something that could float in its own silence, as a beautiful vase moves; and it has to be constructed using cunning, sound and rhythm in a conscious way. He also taught that every true work of art is made somehow against the grain of nature, that sacrifice and discipline are essential. One is reminded of Machado's remark about handwriting: "Making the letters well is more important than making them."

Akhmatova's poems are often masterpieces of sound, made with tact, cunning and great respect for elegance and briefness. And Russians memorize poem after poem of Pasternak's because of his equal care for sound and his ability to keep some interior heart-mystery alive inside the net of sound.

I don't mean that Whitman doesn't write well. Let's take a really fine passage:

> I understand the large hearts of heroes,
> The courage of present times and all times,
> How the skipper saw the crowded and rudderless
>   wreck of the steam-ship, and Death chasing it up
>   and down the storm,
> How he knuckled tight and gave not back one inch, and was
>   faithful of days and faithful of nights,
> And chalked in large letters, on a board, *Be of good cheer,*
>   *We will not desert you;*
> How he followed with them, and tacked with them—
>   and would not give it up,
> How he saved the drifting company at last,
> How the lank loose-gowned women looked when boated from
>   the side of their prepared graves,
> How the silent old-faced infants, and the lifted sick,
>   and the sharp-lipped unshaved men,
> All this I swallow—it tastes good—I like it well—it becomes mine,
> I am the man—I suffered—I was there.

It is magnificent. And yet we don't memorize a passage like this, magnificent as it is. Americans, of course, do not memorize as much poetry as Russians, but there is also something collective about Whitman's passage; it's not clear if the private heart is there or not.

Whitman tends to turn attention toward the audience more than toward the work of art. He said, "To have great poets we must have great audiences." All of us who wrote in the fifties and sixties read this sentence hundreds of times, since *Poetry* magazine printed it on their cover for many years. Whitman said many other things too, and yet to quote this sentence is not totally unjust; something of him is in it. I think the American poet's concern with numbers, with how many people attend poetry readings, how many people buy poetry books, how one could widen the audience for poetry—all of these reverberate to Whitman's concern with audience. Of course European poets are concerned with numbers and audience too, but not quite in the same way. The Russian poet constructs his poem even when not allowed to publish.

Whitman's genius included an enormous intuitive grasp of sound's relation to mood, a natural grasp of the intensity of the operatic solo, and he learned how to tell a story wonderfully well. But we don't hear him say much about the work of art or what has to be sacrificed for it. Not every writer has to talk about art, and yet the omission is odd. Robert Frost wrote brilliantly about sequences of pitches, about the essence of art as "saying one thing and meaning another" and about the human things given up for art.

Alexander Glatkov, who was with Pasternak during the War, mentions that Pasternak loved this passage from Victor Hugo:

> To give every object as much space as it needs—neither more, nor less; that is simplicity in art. To be simple means to be fair. That is the law of true taste. Each thing must be given its due place and expressed by the right word. And if we assume there is a certain hidden balance in the work of art, a certain mysterious proportion has been preserved, then the most sophisticated complexity in style or form may prove to be this simplicity....

Pasternak draws his love of tact and art from Pushkin and I quote this paragraph on tact to suggest how different the Russian inheritance is from ours: Hugo's and Pasternak's care for art is not a part of the inheritance we get from Whitman.

I want to talk about care for sound, and here we'll have to stay within the English language for comparisons. I'll set down a passage of Whitman's I love, and always have;

> I sit and look out upon all the sorrows of the world,
>   and upon all oppression and shame,
> I hear secret convulsive sobs from young men, at anguish
>   with themselves, remorseful after deeds done;
> I see, in low life, the mother misused by her children,
>   dying, neglected, gaunt, desperate,
> I see the wife misused by her husband—I see the
>   treacherous seducer of the young woman,
> I mark the ranklings of jealousy and unrequited love,
>   attempted to be hid—I see these sights on the earth,
> I see the workings of battle, pestilence, tyranny—I
>   see martyrs and prisoners,
> I observe a famine at sea—I observe the sailors casting lots
>   who shall be killed, to preserve the lives of the rest,
> I observe the slights and degradations cast by arrogant
>   persons upon laborers, the poor, and upon negroes,

and the like;
All these—All the meanness and agony without end,
  I sitting, look out upon,
See, hear, and am silent.

I'll make a suggestion of my own now about a poem. In a poem that is a true work of art, every sound is accounted for. I mean that no sound is insignificant, or drops out of consciousness, or is there because "it has to be"—each sound, whether it belongs to a rising syllable or a sinking syllable, takes its place, and *has* a place, in the pattern of sound moving through the passage. A sober quality penetrates a poem when the poet cares for each sound.

I think of Joyce, writing about his small son:

> From whining wind and colder
> Grey sea I wrap him warm
> And touch his trembling fineboned shoulder
> And boyish arm.

Synge's *Prelude* goes this way:

> Still south I went and west and south again,
> Through Wicklow from the morning till the night,
> And far from cities and the sight of men
> Lived with the sunshine and moon's delight.
> I knew the stars, the flowers, and the birds,
> The grey and wintry sides of many glens,
> And did but half remember human words,
> In converse with the mountains, moors, and fens.

The sounds here resemble notes in a string quartet: each sound is loved. But I don't feel that in Whitman's lines beginning "I sit and look out upon all the sorrows of the world." Whitman's flow of syllables is lively, his music is charming, there is firm repetition of sound, and yet some dampening occurs. Something muffles the sound.

What is it that muffles the sound? I'll set down a few possibilities and make a few speculations. Somehow the presence of the "ai" sound, appearing mostly at the beginning and middle of lines, regularly, dominates this line, and does not allow the other sounds to resonate with each other.

It's possible too that Whitman is including too many unstressed syllables in this passage; perhaps we could even call them unaccounted for. English, by nature, has an initial problem in producing crisp sound, in that it needs phrases that embody essentially dull sounds: "of the" . . . "on the" . . . "and upon" . . . "and the" . . . "upon all" . . . "with." The word "the," appearing obsessively in English sentences, dampens sound a lot. Latin poets did not have to deal with "the," nor did Chinese poets, nor do either have to make place for words like "into" or "toward."

> I sit and look out upon all the sorrows of the world, and
> upon all oppression and shame.

The little words here are tying the vivid sounds down with thin ropes; the sounds in "sorrow" and "shame" can at most get to their knees, but they cannot stand upright or lift their feet. The little sounds that tie down the big sounds, and become noticeable doing that, are moreover not the sounds important for grasping the frustration and injury that he is singing of.

No poet in English can get rid of these little words that dampen sound, but it is a question of degree. Whitman uses them too much. Emily Dickinson, uninfluenced by Whitman, has very few wasted sounds, and H. D. follows her in that. Carl Sandburg, following Whitman, has many. In our time, it is often the poets who resist Whitman—Robert Creeley is an example—who face, in their best poems, the threat of the little words.

Poetry in Old English shows no trace of giving in to a flood of unstressed sounds. I'll quote the opening lines of *Beowulf* and though no one is positive about pronunciations of sound, there is enough general agreement to be confident we have the gist of it. I'll write out the words using our modern way of indicating sounds:

> Hwaht! Wee Gahr-dana
> in geahr dagum,
> They-od kinninga,
> Thrym ya froonan—
> Hoo thah athelingas
> ell-en frem-a-don.

Even those who haven't studied Anglo-Saxon can experience the sound of this passage by saying the words aloud. The passage means roughly: "All right, all right! Our tribe has strong memory, we think about what strength is, how the leaders got so strong."

The critics of *Beowulf* so far, except for Bessinger, have short-changed the art of it by emphasizing alliteration, as if that were all. The vowels interweave with each other, also, and make a pattern not unlike the interweaving of snakes in their wood carvings. In this passage, we hear the most marvellous *in-an-on* work, which reminds us of Wallace Stevens's work with *n's*, and we hear *ah* resonating to itself, and *ooh* resonating in *ya froonan* and *hoo*. I know the rhythm also affects the sounds, but that issue is so complicated we can only mention it here.

Yeats often shows great care for individual sounds, even those not stressed. One of his masters was Landor. We might set down a passage by Landor in which all sounds work together:

> Rose Aylmer, whom these wakeful eyes
> May weep, but never see,
> A night of sorrows and of sighs
> I consecrate to thee.

We feel similar care for each sound in "That time of year thou mayst in me behold," and in "I placed a jar in Tennessee." We find it also in Milton's early poems, in the odes and epodes of Horace, in Dante's sonnets, and in Akhmatova and Pasternak. Among contemporary poets in English, often in James Wright, Ted Hughes, and many others.

We might say that Whitman is setting up a kind of drone in the background through his unaccounted-for syllables; and yet I don't think the drone works as music. We get from him instead the habit of allowing uncared-for sounds to enter, out of concern for meaning. I believe that a true work of art does not allow that. To choose an analogy from painting, the Turner canvas hanging in the National Gallery, showing coal-burning ships floating on the Thames at night, has no spot of color that does not contribute to the central grief of the painting. Turner knows what every inch of the painting is doing.

Next I'd like to touch on the problem of pauses. When one mentions Horace, one remembers that he wrote in stanzas invented by Sappho and by Alcaeus, among others, and that those stanzas carry in their structure respect for pauses. A strong pause breaks each line.

Whitman says very little about the pause, and his lines do not show much respect for it. Even in his best poems, such as "When Lilacs Last in the Dooryard Bloom'd," a line will often go for sixteen syllables without a pause:

> In the dooryard fronting an old farm-house near the
> white-wash'd palings. . . .

The sorrow and shame passage quoted above has few pauses:

> I sit and look out upon all the sorrows of the
> world, and upon all oppression and shame,
> I hear secret convulsive sobs from young men,
> at anguish with themselves, remorseful after deeds done.

The opening line goes on for fourteen syllables without pause, or with a very light pause after "out," and continues then for nine more syllables without pause. The later line:

> I observe the slights and degradations cast by
> arrogant persons upon laborers, the poor, and
> upon negroes, and the like. . . .

carries for thirty-three syllables or so without major pause.

As contrast, we could set down Wyatt's stanza:

> They flee from me, that sometime did me seek,
> With naked foot stalking in my chamber.
> I have seen them, gentle, tame, and meek,
> That now are wild, and do not remember
> That sometime they put themselves in danger
> To take bread at my hand; and now they range,
> Busily seeking with a continual change.

He uses syntax to create a pause when he wants one, usually every four to seven syllables; and then, when he wants an unbroken line, as he wanted it at the end, the line comes through with great beauty and surprise.

If we look back at the *Beowulf* passage, we see that the poet there will rarely go more than six syllables without a deep pause. The pauses we experience in *Beowulf*, which we truly experience only when we memorize and say the lines, are long, amazingly long: and this length is surely significant. The pause enables us to hold our ground against the poet, to think, to have some time for ourselves.

We see the deep pause in Joyce's lines, already quoted, and in Synge:

> Still south I sent and west and south again.

Whitman in general ignores the pause, which is a way of not allowing the reader to interrupt: it could be considered a part of oratory. We notice that the American poets who follow Whitman in my generation do not include the pause consciously; Ashbery virtually ignores the pause. Ginsberg has few pauses, and my own poetry does not do much conscious work with the pause. Occasionally a poet not in the Whitman tradition will create a poem with marvellous pauses. The poem that follows by Robert Creeley has pauses that Horace would have adored:

> Love comes quietly,
> finally, drops

about me, on me,
in the old ways.

What did I know
thinking myself
able to go
alone all the way.

When this poem is memorized and spoken, we feel grand and deep pauses and during these pauses we come to ourselves, and there is a silence for us to say something to the poet if we want to.

So the pause helps us to participate in the poem, rather than simply observing. The poet himself faces a similar choice when writing the poem: shall he observe the moment, or participate in it? If we look back at the passage beginning:

I sit and look out upon all the sorrows of the world,
    and upon all oppression and shame,

it is clear that Whitman, here at least, is coming down on the side of observing, and the lines carry the unbroken flow of observation.

As a contrast to that, we might refer to the *Beowulf* passage, which begins "we people of the Bar-Dana Tribe remember what strength is." The poet is not watching from a vantage point, but is using "we" in a different way than Whitman does.

There's an interesting story about the way the Anglo-Saxon meter came into daily use. The old Norwegian parliament, called The Thing, involved much free discussion of issues, and there were compliments or insults spoken in public. If one man confronted another in public, the man spoken to was given three or four minutes of silence: the hearers expected his answer to appear in lines that were insertable, so to speak, in *Beowulf*—that is, a few lines, composed in a five- or six-syllable unit, with a long pause, alliterative consonants, and the resonating vowels, woven together by certain rhythms we haven't discussed here. Ancient Anglo-Saxon poetry had some connection with talking to a person face to face.

When we read the lines about shame and sorrow, we see at once that Whitman is not participating in a conversation; he is not defending himself, nor replying to a compliment, he is not attacking another or reaching out to any one person—he is observing, and observing many people from a vantage point, a hidden point. By contrasting participation and observation, I don't mean that all poetry must be answers to questions, nor directed at another person, nor that introverted watching is unfruitful or wrong. I am saying that respect for the pause has something to do with speaking firmly, clearly, to another human being in a tense situation charged with meaning.

In Sappho's poems we find ourselves in an Eros situation; she speaks to one person, and the pauses carry Eros, and allow the feelings between two people to resonate. Horace's odes and epodes are often comparable. In Sappho the syntax creates the pause. Perhaps Whitman's syntax is too elementary to keep him aware of the pause. But it is not only syntax that creates a pause, as this stanza from Yeats makes clear:

> I will arise and go now, and go to Innisfree,
> And a small cabin build there, of clay and wattles made;
> Nine bean-rows will I have there, a hive for the honeybee,
> And live alone in the bee-loud glade.

Yeats achieves his pauses sometimes by putting long vowels together.

To concentrate so much on the pause may seem eccentric to some readers of this essay, but I feel the pause is not eccentric, but central. We hear the pause in poets who have kept their link either to the Anglo-Saxon line, or to the Greek and Latin line. Sir Thomas Wyatt stands in a meeting place of both: the Greek and Latin line came down to him through Latin studies in general, and French influence specifically, and the old *Beowulf* line through Anglo-Saxon speech in general, and Langland specifically. Both traditions preserve the pause and both preserve the tradition of face to face conversation in poetry. I'll quote here the second stanza of "They flee from me," so beautiful in both respects.

> Thanked be Fortune it hath been otherwise,
> Twenty times better; but once in special,
> In thin array, after a pleasant guise,
> When her loose gown from her shoulders did fall,
> And she me caught in her arms long and small,
> And therewith all sweetly did me kiss
> And softly said, "Dear heart, how like you this?"

I have one last point to make about those qualities in Whitman's inheritance that tend to narrow poets who follow him. The inheritance from him does not make clear the distinction between private speech and public speech. He has deep alliances to oratory and spoken language. But when we puzzle over the multitude of little words and the relative absence of the pause, we see that a key to both has to be the printed page.

It cannot be an accident that Whitman was a printer. His poems declare themselves to be personal, but in some way they are actually public speech, even collective speech, intended for the printed page.

If we contrast *Leaves of Grass* with *Beowulf,* we see further paradoxes. *Beowulf,* which scholars have taught us to imagine as always being delivered to a crowd, has the quality, in *sound,* of passionate conversation between one person and another, no sound wasted, no rhythm flattened, plenty of deep pauses. Wyatt's poems have that quality also. And *Leaves of Grass,* which Whitman declares to be non-collective, a new discovery of what is deeply personal, an infinitely hopeful appearance of closeness, achieved without the distancing habitual to institutions and institutionalized European culture, has the quality of collective speech intended for the printed page, which cannot be interrupted, and is addressed to faces he does not recognize and to whom he is not looking. I exaggerate, but the collective social world is in it.

Robert Hass, to whom I read an early draft of this essay, remarked that the long Whitman line requires a deep breath. What it does physiologically is to breathe in more of the world than the short line. He remarked also that the long line without pauses may be modeled on the prayer. I like that idea very much, but we still feel ourselves caught in a confusion, or contradiction, between public and private speech. The long line, if prayer, is presented to us as social in intent. So that becomes an additional paradox.

I am a student of Whitman's and I think he is a genius several times over. But as many poets of my generation sense, his influence carries us only part way—either part way through our lives, or part way toward the great poem. Why is that?

Kaplan's biography, and Gay Wilson Allen's, makes clear that Whitman belonged to an unlucky family, with tremendous grief in it, psychic confusion and obsession with death. But he pretended that he was one of the lucky ones; we hear him say that a new era has come, that we are all lucky now, and we can transcend inner pain by moving toward general Being.

We hear him say that it is not only possible to make that leap in one's own life, but it is the best way to defeat pain. It is also the best way to create a great work of art. It is not only possible to do that, but easy, if one ignores the pain of one's own identity and family, and cancels all the works that have come before. If a poet ignores separate beings and thinks only of Being, it will happen. But this habit of mind is precisely what William James warned Wallace Stevens about in his philosophy class: and Wallace Stevens took in the warning. If we ignore separate beings and think of Being; ignore separate truths and think of Truth, we come into what William James called the fallacy of "the one."

We tend to think, after reading Whitman a long time, of Being rather than of separate beings, of Transcendent Spontaneity rather than the long lineage of fathers and mothers through which spiritual truths have come to us. We think of Audience rather than of one or two listeners whom we recognize, and who can talk back to us if they want to, and we think of the flow of creativity after reading Whitman rather than the shape and weight of a jar. "I placed a jar in Tennessee." "Nuns fret not at their convent's narrow room." All artists love art, but we miss sometimes in Whitman reminders of what a triumph the intensely worked poem can be, and how much a human being can justly sacrifice to create a single work of art.

Sometimes I feel that Whitman skips over the pause and the sort of rhythm possible to us through syntax somewhat as he smooths over pain. Whitman is wonderfully fair to human feelings, but I'm not sure he is always fair to the non-human elements that make up a work of art—for example, sound, which he uses well sometimes and sometimes not, variety of rhythm, which animals have and had long before human beings wrote poetry, and the pause, which is a part of silence, also in the world long before us. When Pushkin urges poets to love the work of art, he is not being elitist, he is pointing to the responsibility the artist has to these three elements, as fundamental as earth, air, fire, and water to an alchemist. Art resembles alchemy then more than a treatise on Being, and Whitman in different poems at different times embarks on each, but we don't learn much in the second effort about the difficulty of the first. The discipline of art concentrates on the responsibility to honor sound, silence, and rhythm, and it calls the artist to this difficulty and this joy.

Whitman Exilado

C. W. TRUESDALE

SOMEWHERE IN MY LIBRARY, I have a volume of Whitman's *Leaves of Grass* translated into Spanish. It was given to me in Mexico in 1966 by the Ecuadorian poet and political exile, Miguel Donoso Pareja. "This is my text," he said. "This is my only Bible. Your country is very fortunate to have had such a great poet. Without Whitman, there is no Neruda. Without Neruda, there is no poetry. Without poetry, there is no culture."

Such a frank and open passion for any sort of poetry was something almost entirely foreign to my own experience, as was Miguel's political commitment to a revolutionary cause and his association of Whitman, and poetry, with that cause. Except for one five-year period when I was a part-time cattle farmer in Virginia, my life experience had been thoroughly academic. And everyone knows that in American colleges and universities, enthusiasm and passion of Miguel's sort, however intelligent and justified, are looked upon with something what smells like embarrassment. Except in a very private way, I had not experienced at all, until Mexico, the Great Awakening that had been taking place, mainly in California and mainly out on the streets and coffee houses. I knew, and loved, and I even taught some of Ginsberg's poems from the *Howl* and *Kaddish* years, and it was very obvious to me what a thing he had going for Whitman, but I was still saturated, then, by a more traditional—and English—literary background, and I tended to read Ginsberg against that background, seeing his lovely "Sunflower Sutra" poem, for instance, as a kind of funky and quirkish parody (which it is!) of poems like Keats's "Ode to a Nightingale." What I didn't really see, then, was that Ginsberg had a unique and important voice that would do much more to reshape American poetry than most of my earlier heroes like James Wright, W. S. Merwin, and James Dickey, and that he would have an even more profound influence in reshaping the social and political culture of this

335

great, conservative nation, since he gave new voice, as Whitman had tried to do, to that whole wave of energy for change and growth we came to call in the seventies the Counter Culture. No poet, not even Whitman, had ever achieved that kind of stature in this country before.

Mexico City, Spring 1966

It is useful, I believe, to read Whitman again through the eyes of Latin American poets like Neruda and Miguel Donoso Pareja, just as it is instructive to view America from inside another culture with political, geographical, and economic ties to this country that are not quite as wonderful as we would like to think. I can't pretend ever to have been a real exile—not in Miguel's sense of that word. For Miguel, it was either political exile or the firing squad, and pure necessity, yet Ecuador lived on in him and in his poetry like a terrible obsession, a mistress who had spurned and humiliated him for the likes of some fat, rich corporate lover like the United Fruit Company.

Unlike Miguel, I was free to come and go, but I lived long enough in Mexico—six months—to get into a daily routine of writing and studying and thinking, endlessly, about what my country was doing—again—in Vietnam, about what there was in our history and culture that led us down that imperial highway, again and again, and always in the name of some mockery of Freedom and Justice and the Open Society.

Unlike many of the revolutionaries I came to know in Mexico—unlike even Meg Randall, my first publisher, for instance—Miguel was never strident or single-minded, and he never knowingly provoked my conscience or sense of social guilt. But he talked a great deal about the pernicious character of American Corporations like Coca-Cola and United Fruit, unrestrained as they are in most Latin countries by legal machinations and blatantly on the side of the oppressors. (It is easy to see how Miguel arrived at his Marxism— it was as natural to him as bread and water and his identification with the poor and the oppressed. He was one of them. He was simply their articulated suffering.) But Miguel did not, even for the sake of argument (where such sallies are commonplace), try to make me personally responsible for such atrocities. Miguel was kindness itself and warmth; he was affection, humor, and worldliness. In fact, he radiated unthinkingly those qualities of humanity, compassion, and camaraderie he probably knew could flourish only in exile or under a radically different political order. Although he had suffered some dreadful losses and deprivations, had been tortured and sentenced to death, Miguel was not an unhappy man.

For he understood, I believe, something that few Americans, especially white, middle-class midwesterners like myself, really understand: that existence itself is always a struggle towards the unaccomplished, undertaken with grace and humor, and that the ideal is sometimes, perhaps, worth dying for but unlikely ever to be attained. He would gladly give up his life but never his humanity. And Whitman, along with a handful of other great poets, spoke this common tongue.

It was the visionary and transcendent qualities in Whitman's work that spoke to Miguel Donoso—Whitman's faith in the ability of Man to shape his society and environment along compassionate and humanitarian lines—a faith that, in the twentieth century, to most American intellectuals, seems at best naive because it seems to demand a kind of assent, even a submission, to an ideology that squares with no reality they know or particularly want to deal with.

It is not surprising that Whitman has never had the great audience here in America that his work commands elsewhere—in Latin America, in Russia, in Yugoslavia, and, for all I know, in Zaire. Perhaps the reason for this, or one of them, is that the idiom of the Transcendentalist Movement—scarcely more than a brief flurry in American history, a futuristic dream which has slender bases in reality—translates easily and naturally into the rhetorical flourishes and rhythms of Spanish and Latin American poetry. In this respect, the very fact that Whitman's poetry—unlike Twain's prose, for example—is not particularly rooted in American folk traditions is an advantage. He can gain an immediacy and universality in another tongue that not even greater poets like Shakespeare can ever hope to attain. Shakespeare's work is so rooted in English folk traditions and a vernacular no longer current that any would-be translator must be baffled. I suspect that something like this may also be true of some of the best things in Twain's work—those subtleties of sub-text his language gives rise to and the particular feel he had for an adolescent's unconscious struggle to identify himself in the words of his own limited, narrow-minded, bigoted community, those subtleties of language and character which are perhaps more than anything else the strength of *Huckleberry Finn*—are almost untranslatable and might even sound pretty silly in another tongue. Whitman, on the other hand, in Spanish, sounds as if that were his native language. And this is true of some of his most memorable lines. This paradox, if true, can lead us to some rather interesting observations. If Twain seems more "American" to us and more in tune with the realities of American history and some of its absurdities,

Whitman is probably seen by other cultures as more characteristically "American," as embodying *in himself* a vision of the New Man in the New World, the sleeping giant of humanity awakened by the touch of song, man's ancient, unrealized dream of his own greater destiny. We Americans tend to see Whitman as one of the most dynamic products of a short-lived (if influential) movement called Transcendentalism—which means little or nothing to an Ecuadorian poet like Miguel Donoso. We see him as living through a period (prior to the Civil War) when optimism, idealism, and even naiveté seemed viable alternatives to the exhausted, inertia-ridden political and social regimes of the Old World. They see him as offering an "American solution" (consistent with Marxism) to the dreadful problems of oppression and exploitation (fostered, ironically, by United States corporations), problems they are faced with, still, on a day-to-day basis, and they respond as literally to his summons to greatness, compassion, and openness as Whitman intended us to—to that revolution of the spirit that, in reality, could never flourish very long at all in the face of the basically conservative temperament of the American people. Whitman's summons fell on deaf ears in America, and, except for one brief flowering in the heady days of the counterculture, Whitman never has been, here, the national poet he knew he was meant to be and is, in fact, elsewhere.

St. Paul, Minnesota, December 1980

Most of the really lovely and important things in my life, I've come to very late, including Whitman. I seem to be able to accept something—a person, a relationship, an idea—only by living it through, trying it on, so to speak, which means feeling out how it relates to the immense range of things and events I've experienced, much of which (thanks in part to a very rich dream life) is almost continually present.

What that something is in Whitman is the way he, uncannily, in poems like "Crossing Brooklyn Ferry," "The Sleepers," and in parts of "Song of the Open Road," establishes a dramatic involvement with the reader, so that you know his presence is talking directly with you and that you are, just as much, a real presence to him. It is this *double journey*, this two-way street, that is uncanny to me and fascinating. He comes on in these poems as if he knows something about me that usually I hardly know about myself or wouldn't care to discuss with most people. At such times, I find myself, unthinkingly, giving my assent to this and talking back at him—sometimes with affection and sometimes with all the feistiness I have at my command, and always with what I feel at the moment is the best that I have and the truth as I perceive it. There aren't too many people in the whole wide world I can talk with on that level—without feeling some kind of power loss, without feeling I've given something of myself away, irrevocably. Maybe he *knows* that—talking his way out of his own shadows into my shadows—there's no way I am going to make *that* kind of submission!

We are schooled these days to value specificity at any cost. Witness the tedious recent biographical works about Faulkner and Hemingway, or the dryly detailed and boring novels of Robbe-Grillet. Whitman gains the effect I am talking about by *not* being laboriously detailed, by taking a few simple facts about his life and our lives and relating us to them in a different way. In "Song of the Open Road," for instance, he is primarily concerned about the walls and barriers we construct between us and about breaking down or through these walls. The actual walls in the poem have nothing on them, nothing like the late Emmeline Grangerford's lugubrious paintings (in *Huckleberry Finn*)—like a good old-fashioned radio show, he lets us decorate those walls with whatever is familiar to us and then starts hacking away at them. Because I've read Whitman now in so many different circumstances and in so many different studies and bedrooms, he comes on like an almost sacred text and relates to whatever reality or location I am preoccupied with at the moment.

And the way he comes on is always the same, as though he had made an alliance or treaty with the darker self of me, with the subconscious, with dreamings and musings that don't always have a lot to do with the workaday world and that he knows I have been neglecting lately because I have gotten myself into being so fucking busy, with publishing, or construction, or teaching. And he just wants me to come full awake, to let my consciousness be flooded by these other, neglected things.

But he is no father. More a brother. Not conscience, but challenge, gentle but ever so strong.

The best myths I know of about this kind of experience are Menelaus wrestling with Proteus in *The Odyssey* and Jacob wrestling with his angel in the Bible. In both instances, it is not just a matter of submitting to a difficult process in order to gain a specific piece of knowledge or a blessing or whatever, but rising to the challenge of it, which is a commitment of power and imagination—that may fail—and not a submission.

I think this is what Allen Ginsberg picked up on in his great poem called "A Supermarket in California," where he is literally turning the tables on the Whitman of "Crossing Brooklyn Ferry" to reach back, to invoke (read *seduce* in this instance) the eccentric and possibly abnormal spirit of his dead master. Probably he does this because he feels that Whitman in his own time had set himself loose on the same kind of risky and adventurous and lonely voyage that Ginsberg himself was just getting started on.

There are many, many things I like about this poem, not the least being its wonderful and surprising mix of feelings. But it is the *challenge* of it that concerns me now, challenge in the best sense of that word. It's like he's saying to Whitman and his other dead masters, "I dare you to come back and let me do my thing with you. And Walt, old buddy, let's clear up right away this ambiguity about whether you are really gay or not."

The difference between *commitment* or *commission* and *submission* is that with the latter you're looking around for someone to tell you what to do and this is likely to produce *imitation* in your own work (if you can call it that), unless there's a healthy amount of parody in it. With *commitment* you're putting yourself on the line in full consciousness of what that self is, so that in this case you see and feel a hell of a lot about Ginsberg—his youthful promiscuity, his "delight in disorder," his posturing, his loneliness and alienation, his reverent/irreverent feelings about his masters like Whitman and Lorca, and it's like he's giving his target (or his lover)—who happens in this case to be Whitman—all his personal qualifications, *as if* he were risking, literally, a big rejection.

The difference between this and what Whitman's doing to the reader in "Crossing Brooklyn Ferry"? Not very big—except for the wonderful humor in the Ginsberg piece. Just a reversal. Whitman is coming on to future readers and being "a living presence" to them; Ginsberg is coming on to a dead poet and master and, maybe, indirectly coming on to now and future readers and trying to get Whitman to come along for the ride.

When you consider that Allen Ginsberg was doing all this back in the early and academical fifties when most of the rest of us were writing new critical essays analyzing the ironies of T. S. Eliot's style, Ginsberg's achievement in restoring to American poetry not just Whitman but some very basic and primary qualities of all fine lyrical poetry is very considerable. He's taught us all how to use our Whitman—and by extension, other fine writers of the past—without in any way submitting or enslaving ourselves to a dead past or a demeaning present.

St. Paul, Minnesota, May 1981

He wanted to be President. For a brief time that Monday afternoon in

March when Reagan was shot, many of us were under the delusion that he was President. He certainly sounded like it. He has the kind of mouth that slaughters language with authority. His eyes have the hard, fixed glare of the Congressional Medal of Honor. He is contemptuous of politicians and might not have tolerated Speaker Tip O'Neill if the Vice-President's jet had fallen out of the sky over Dallas or Amarillo. Although he was never President of Vietnam or Japan, the ghostly eminence of General Douglas MacArthur breathes in him and comes rumbling stentoriously out of that mouth. And like MacArthur he would probably cross the Rubicon of Constitutional Authority, if he could, and bring down the Republic in the name of the Republic, if he could.

Miguel Donoso Pareja would have recognized him immediately. "Ah, my friend," he would say, "your General Haig is what poetry is all about. He is the School I attended and the University of my most awesome dreams. He is 'el Angel de la Guerra' and for him the apples fall down out of the trees and the birds are afraid to sing."

15.

For the Sake of a People's Poetry: Walt Whitman and the Rest of Us

JUNE JORDAN

IN AMERICA THE FATHER is white: It is he who inaugurated the experiment of this republic. It is he who sailed his way into slave ownership. It is he who availed himself of my mother: the African woman whose function was miserably defined by his desirings, or his rage. It is he who continues to dominate the destiny of the Mississippi River, the Blue Ridge Mountains, and the life of my son. Understandably, then, I am curious about this man.

Most of the time my interest can be characterized as wary, at best. Other times, it is the interest a pedestrian feels for the fast-traveling truck about to smash into him. Or her. Again. And at other times it is the curiosity of a stranger trying to figure out the system of the language that excludes her name and all of the names of all of her people. It is this last that leads me to the poet Walt Whitman.

Trying to understand the system responsible for every boring, inaccessible, irrelevant, derivative, and pretentious poem that is glued to the marrow of required readings in American classrooms, or trying to understand the system responsible for the exclusion of every hilarious, amazing, visionary, pertinent, and unforgettable poet from N.E.A. grants and from national publications, I come back to Walt Whitman.

What in the hell happened to him? Wasn't he a white man? Wasn't he some kind of a father to American literature? Didn't he talk about this New World? Didn't he see it? Didn't he sing this New World, this America, on a New World, an American scale of his own visionary invention?

It so happens that Walt Whitman is the one white father who shares the systematic disadvantages of his heterogeneous offspring trapped inside a closet that is, in reality, as huge as the continental spread of North and South America. What Whitman envisioned we, the people and the poets of the

343

New World, embody. He has been punished for the political meaning of his vision. We are being punished for the moral questions that our very lives provoke.

At home as a child I learned the poetry of the Bible and the poetry of Paul Laurence Dunbar. As a student, I diligently followed orthodox directions from *The Canterbury Tales* right through *The Waste Land* by that consummate Anglophile whose name I can never remember. And I kept waiting. It was, I thought, all right to deal with daffodils in the seventeenth century on an island as much like Manhattan as I resemble Queen Mary. But what about Dunbar? When was he coming up again? And where were the Black poets altogether? And who were the women poets I might reasonably emulate? And wasn't there, ever, a great poet who was crazy about Brooklyn or furious about war? And I kept waiting. And I kept writing my own poetry. And I kept reading apparently underground poetry: poetry kept strictly off campus. And I kept reading the poetry of so many gifted students when I became a teacher myself, and I kept listening to the wonderful poetry of the multiplying numbers of my friends who were and who are New World poets until I knew, for a fact, that there was and that there is an American, a New World, poetry that is as personal, as public, as irresistible, as quick, as necessary, as unprecedented, as representative, as exalted, as speakably commonplace, and as musical, as an emergency phone call.

But I didn't know about Walt Whitman. Yes: I had heard about this bohemian, this homosexual even, who wrote something about The Captain and The Lilacs, but nobody ever told me he was crucial to a native American literature. Not only was Whitman not required reading, in the sense that Wordsworth and Robert Herrick are required reading, he was, on the contrary, presented as a rather hairy buffoon suffering from a childish proclivity for excercise and open air. Nevertheless, it is through the study of all the poems and all the ideas of this particular white father that I have reached a tactical, if not strategic, understanding of the racist, sexist, and anti-American predicament that condemns most New World writing to peripheral/small press/unpublished manuscript status:

Before these United States, the great poems of the world earned their luster through undeniable forms of spontaneous popularity: Generations of a people chose to memorize and then to further elaborate and then to impart these songs to the next generation. I am talking about people: African families and Greek families and the families of the Hebrew tribes and all that multitude to whom the Bhagavad-Gita is as daily as the sun! If these poems were not always religious, they were certainly moral in motive, or in accomplishment, or both. None of these great poems could be mistaken for the poetry of another country, another time; you do not find a single helicopter taking off or landing in any of the sonnets of Elizabethan England, nor do you run across Jamaican rice and peas in any of the psalms! Evidently, one criterion for great poetry used to be the requirements of cultural nationalism.

But with the advent of the 36-year-old poet Walt Whitman, the phenomenon of a people's poetry, or great poetry and its spontaneous popularity, could no longer be assumed. The physical immensity and the far-flung population of this New World decisively separated the poet from the suitable means to produce and to distribute his poetry. Now there would have to be intermediaries—critics and publishers—whose marketplace principles of scarcity would, logically, oppose them to populist traditions of art. In place of the democratic concepts, elitist Old World concepts would, logically, govern their policies; in the context of such considerations, an American literary establishment antithetical to the New World meanings of America took root. And this is one reason why the pre-eminently American white father of American poetry is practically unknown outside the realm of caricature and rumor in his own country.

As a matter of fact, if you hope to hear about Whitman, your best bet is to leave home: Ignore prevailing American criticism and, instead, ask anybody anywhere else in the world this question: As Shakespeare is to England, Dante to Italy, Tolstoi to Russia, Goethe to Germany, Agostinho Neto to Angola, Pablo Neruda to Chile, Mao Tse-tung to China, and Ho Chi Minh to Vietnam, who is the great American writer, the distinctively American poet, the giant American "literatus"? Undoubtedly, the answer will be *Walt Whitman*. He is the poet who wrote:

> A man's body at auction,
> (For before the war I often go to the slave-mart and watch the sale,)
> I help the auctioneer, the sloven does not half know his business.

> Gentlemen look on this wonder,
> Whatever the bids of the bidders they cannot be high
>   enough for it . . .
>   "I Sing the Body Electric"

I ask you today: Who in America would publish those lines? They are all wrong! In the first place, there is nothing obscure, nothing contrived, nothing an ordinary straphanger in the subway would be puzzled by! In the second place, the choice of those lines is intimate and direct at once: It is the voice of the poet who assumes that he speaks to an equal and that he need not fear that equality; on the contrary, the intimate distance between the poet and the reader is a distance that assumes there is everything important, between them, to be shared. And what is poetic about a line of words that runs as long as a regular, a spoken idea? You could more easily imagine an actual human being speaking such lines than you could imagine an artist composing them in a room carefully separated from other rooms of a house, carefully separated from other lives of a family: This can't be poetry. Besides, these lines apparently serve an expressly moral purpose! Then is this didactic/political writing? This cannot be good poetry. And, in fact, you will never see, for example, *The New Yorker* publishing a poem marked by such splendid deficiences.

Consider the inevitable, the irresistible simplicity of that enormous moral idea:

> Gentlemen look on this wonder,
> Whatever the bids of the bidders they cannot be high
>   enough for it . . .
> This is not only one man, this the father of those who shall be
>   fathers in their turns,
> In him the start of populous states and rich republics,
> Of him countless immortal lives with countless embodiments and
>   enjoyments.

"I Sing the Body Electric"

This is not an idea generally broadcast in America. It is an idea to violate the marketplace: The poet is trying to rescue a human being while even the poem cannot be saved from the insolence of marketplace evaluation!

Indeed Walt Whitman and the traceable descendants of Whitman, those who follow his democratic faith into obviously New World forms of experience and art, they suffer from the same establishment rejection and contempt that forced this archetypal American genius to publish, distribute, and review his own work—by himself. The descendants I have in mind include those unmistakably contemporaneous young poets who base themselves upon domesticities such as disco, Las Vegas, McDonald's, and forty-dollar running shoes. Also within the Whitman tradition, Black and Third World poets traceably transform, and further, the egalitarian sensibility that isolates that one white father from his more powerful compatriots. And I am thinking of those feminist poets who are evidently intent upon speaking with a maximal number and diversity of other American lives. And I am thinking of such first-rank heroes of the New World as Pablo Neruda and Agostinho Neto. Except for these last two, New World poets are overwhelmingly forced to publish their own works, or seek the commitment of a small press or else give it up entirely. That is to say, the only peoples who can test or verify the meaning of America as a democratic state, as a pluralistic culture, are the very peoples whose contribution to a national vision and discovery meet with general ridicule and disregard. A democratic state does not, after all, exist for the few, but for the many. A democratic state is not proven by the welfare of the strong but by the welfare of the weak. And unless that many, that manifold constitution of diverse peoples, can be seen as integral to the national art/the national consciousness, you might as well mean only Czechoslovakia when you talk about the U.S.A., or only Ireland, or merely France, or exclusively white men.

The fate of Pablo Neruda differs from the other Whitman descendants because Neruda was born into a sovereign New World country where a majority of the citizens did not mistake themselves for Englishmen or long to find themselves struggling, at most, with cucumber sandwiches and tea. He was never European. His anguish was not aroused by three-piece suits and rolled umbrellas. When he cries, toward the conclusion of *The Heights of Machu Picchu*, "Arise to birth with me, my brother," he plainly does not allude to Lord or Colonel Anybody At All. As he writes, earlier, in that amazing poem:

> I came by another way, river by river, street after street,
> city by city, one bed and another,
> forcing the salt of my mask through a wilderness;
> and there, in the shame of the ultimate hovels, lampless and fireless,
> lacking bread or a stone or a stillness, alone in myself,
> I whirled at my will, dying the death that was mine.

Of course Neruda has not escaped all of the untoward consequences common to Whitman descendants. American critics and translators never weary of asserting that Neruda is a quote great unquote poet despite the political commitment of his art and despite the artistic consequences of that commitment. Specifically, Neruda's self-conscious decision to write in a manner readily comprehensible to the masses of his countrymen and his self-conscious decision to specify outright the United Fruit Company when that was the instigating subject of his poem become unfortunate moments in an otherwise supposedly sublime, not to mention surrealist, deeply Old World and European but nonetheless Chilean case history. To assure the validity of this perspective, the usual American critic and translator presents you with a smattering of the unfortunate, ostensibly political poetry and, on the other hand, buries you under volumes of Neruda's early work that antedates the Spanish Civil War or, in other words, that antedates Neruda's serious conversion to a political world view.

This kind of artistically indefensible censorship would have you perceive chasmic and even irreconcilable qualitative differences between the poet who wrote:

> You, my antagonist, in that splintering dream
> like the bristling glass of gardens, like a menace
> of ruinous bells, volleys
> of blackening ivy at the perfume's center
> enemy of the great hipbones my skin has touched
> with a harrowing dew
>
> "The Woes and the Furies"

and the poet who wrote, some twenty years later, these lines from the poem entitled "The Dictators":

> lament was perpetual and fell, like a plant and its pollen,
> forcing a lightless increase in the blinded, big leaves.
> And bludgeon by bludgeon, on the terrible waters,
> scale over scale in the bog,
> the snout filled with silence and slime
> and vendetta was born.

According to prevalent American criticism, that later poem by Neruda represents a lesser achievement precisely because it can be understood by more people, more easily, than the first. It is also denigrated because it attacks a keystone of the Old World, namely dictatorship, or, in other words, power and privilege for the few.

The peculiar North American vendetta against Walt Whitman, against the first son of this democratic union, should be further fathomed: Neruda's eminence is now acknowledged on international levels; his work profoundly affects many North American poets who do not realize, because they have never been shown, the North American/the Walt Whitman origins for so much that is singular and worthy in the poetry of Neruda. You will even find American critics who congratulate Neruda for overcoming the "Whitmanese" content of his art! This perfidious arrogance is as calculated as it is common. You cannot persuade anyone seriously familiar with Neruda's life and art that he could have found cause, at any point, to disagree with the tenets, the analysis, and the authentic New World vision presented by Walt Whitman in his essay "Democratic Vistas," which remains the most signal and persuasive manifesto of New World thinking and belief in print.

Let me define my terms in brief: New World does not mean New England. New World means non-European; it means new, it means big, it means heterogeneous, it means unknown, it means free, it means an end to feudalism, caste, privilege, and the violence of power. It means *wild* in the sense that a tree growing away from the earth enacts a wild event. It means *democratic* in the sense that, as Whitman wrote:

> I believe a leaf of grass is no less than the journey-work
>   of the stars ...
> And a mouse is miracle enough to stagger sextillions of infidels.
> > "Song of Myself"

New World means, in Whitman's words, "I keep as delicate around the bowels as around the head and heart." New World means, again, *to quote* Whitman, "By God! I will accept nothing which all cannot have their counterpart of on the same terms." In "Democratic Vistas," Whitman declared,

As the greatest lessons of Nature through the universe are perhaps the lessons of variety and freedom, the same present the greatest lessons also in New World politics and progress ... Sole among nationalities, these States have assumed the task to put in forms of history, power and practicality, on areas of amplitude rivaling the operations of the physical kosmos, the moral political speculations of ages, long, long deferr'd, the democratic republican principle, and the theory of development and perfection by voluntary standards, and self-reliance.

Listen to this white man; he is so weird! Here he is calling aloud for an American, a democratic spirit, an American, a democratic idea that could morally constrain and coordinate the material body of U.S.A. affluence and piratical outreach, more than a hundred years ago. He wrote:

The great poems, Shakespeare included, are poisonous to the idea of the pride and dignity of the common people, the lifeblood of democracy. The models of our literature, as we get it from other lands, ultra marine, have had their birth in courts, and bask'd and grown in castle sunshine; all smells of princes' favors ... Do you call those genteel little creatures American poets? Do you term that perpetual, pistareen, paste-pot work, American art, American drama, taste, verse? ... We see the sons and daughters of The New World, ignorant of its genius, not yet inaugurating the native, the universal, and the near, still importing the distant, the partial, the dead.

Abhorring the "thin sentiment of parlors, parasols, piano-song, tinkling rhymes," Whitman conjured up a poetry of America, a poetry of democracy that would not "mean the smooth walks, trimm'd hedges, poseys and nightingales of the English poets, but the whole orb, with its geologic history, the Kosmos, carrying fire and snow that rolls through the illimitable areas, light as a feather, though weighing billions of tons."
Well, what happened?
Whitman went ahead and wrote the poetry demanded by his vision. He became, by thousands upon thousands of words, a great American poet:

> There was a child went forth every day,
> And the first object he look'd upon, that object he became,
> And that object became part of him for the day or a certain part
>   of the day,
> Or for many years or stretching cycles of years.
>
> The early lilacs became part of this child,
> And grass and white and red morning-glories, and white and red
>   clover, and the song of the phoebe-bird, . . .
>   "There Was a Child Went Forth"

And elsewhere he wrote:

> It avails not, time nor place—distance avails not,
> I am with you, you men and women of a generation, or ever so
>   many generations hence,
> Just as you feel when you look on the river and sky, so I felt,
> Just as any of you is one of a living crowd, I was one of a crowd,
> Just as you are refresh'd by the gladness of the river
>   and the bright flow, I was refresh'd,
> Just as you stand and lean on the rail, yet hurry
>   with the swift current, I stood yet was hurried,
> Just as you look on the numberless masts of ships and the
>   thick-stemm'd pipes of steamboats, I look'd . . .
>   "Crossing Brooklyn Ferry"

This great American poet of democracy as cosmos, this poet of a continent as consciousness, this poet of the many people as one people, this poet of a diction comprehensible to all, of a vision insisting on each, of a rhythm/a rhetorical momentum to transport the reader from the Brooklyn ferry into the hills of Alabama and back again, of line after line of bodily, concrete detail that constitutes the mysterious, the cellular tissues of a nation indivisible but dependent upon and astonishing in its diversity, this white father of a great poetry deprived of its spontaneous popularity/a great poetry hidden away from the ordinary people it celebrates so well, he has been, again and again, cast aside as an undisciplined poseur, a merely freak eruption of prolix perversities.

In 1978, the *New York Times Book Review* saw fit to import a European self-appointed critic of American literature to address the question: Is there a great American poet? Since this visitor was ignorant of the philosophy and the achievements of Walt Whitman, the visitor, Denis Donoghue, comfortably excluded every possible descendant of Whitman from his erstwhile cerebrations: Only one woman was mentioned. (She, needless to add, did not qualify.) No poets under fifty, and not one Black or Third World poet, received even cursory assessment. Not one poet of distinctively New World values, and their formal embodiment, managed to dent the illiterate suavity of Donoghue's public display.

This *New York Times* event perpetuates American habits of beggarly, absurd deference to the Old World. And these habits bespeak more than marketplace intrusions into cultural realms: We erase ourselves through self-hatred, we lend our silence to the American anti-American process whereby anything and anyone special to this nation state becomes liable to condemnation because it is what it is, truly.

Against self-hatred there is Whitman and there are all of the New World poets who insistently devise legitimate varieties of cultural nationalism. There is Whitman and all of the poets whose lives have been baptized by witness to blood, by witness to cataclysmic, political confrontations from the Civil War through the Civil Rights Era, through the Women's Movement, and on and on through the conflicts between the hungry and the fat, the wasteful, the bullies.

In the poetry of The New World, you meet with a reverence for the material world that begins with a reverence for human life, an intellectual trust in sensuality as a means of knowledge and of unity, an easily deciphered system of reference, aspiration to a believable, collective voice and, consequently, emphatic preference for broadly accessible language and/or "spoken" use of language, a structure of forward energies that interconnects apparently discrete or even conflictual elements, saturation by quotidian data, and a deliberate balancing of perception with vision: a balancing of sensory report with moral exhortation.

All of the traceable descendants of Whitman have met with an establishment, an academic, reception disgracefully identical: Except for the New World poets who live and write beyond the boundaries of the U.S.A., the offspring of this one white father encounter everlasting marketplace disparagement as crude or optional or simplistic or, as Whitman himself wrote, "hankering, gross, mystical, nude."

I too am a descendant of Walt Whitman. And I am not by myself struggling to tell the truth about this history of so much land and so much blood, of so much that should be sacred and so much that has been desecrated and annihilated boastfully.

My brothers and my sisters of this New World, we remember that, as Whitman said,

> I do not trouble my spirit to vindicate itself or be understood,
> I see that the elementary laws never apologize.
>> "Song of Myself"

We do not apologize because we are not Emily Dickinson, Ezra Pound, T. S. Eliot, Wallace Stevens, Robert Lowell, or Elizabeth Bishop. If we are nothing to them, to those who love them, they are nothing to us! Or, as Whitman exclaimed: "I exist as I am, that is enough."

New World poetry moves into and beyond the light of the lives of Walt Whitman, Pablo Neruda, Agostinho Neto, Gabriela Mistral, Langston Hughes, Margaret Walker, and Edward Brathwaite.

I follow this movement with my own life. I am calm and I am smiling as we go. Is it not written somewhere very near to me:

> A man's body at auction . . .
> Gentlemen look on this wonder,
> Whatever the bids of the bidders they cannot be high
>   enough for it. . . .

And didn't that weird white father predict this truth that is always growing:

> I swear to you the architects shall appear without fail,
> I swear to you they will understand you and justify you,
> The greatest among them shall be he who best knows you, and
>   encloses all and is faithful to all,
> He and the rest shall not forget you, they shall perceive that you
>   are not an iota less than they,
> You shall be fully glorified in them.
> "A Song of the Rolling Earth"

Walt Whitman and all of the New World poets coming after him, we, too, go on singing this America.

Jelly Roll

MERIDEL LESUEUR

WALT WHITMAN AND BESSIE SMITH made the best American Jelly Roll. Emerson didn't like either one of them.

Emerson didn't like American Jelly Roll.

He told Walt not to print "I Sing the Body Electric," to murder the body and destroy it right there. Walt went out in the park and thought for a while and decided Emerson was wrong, the transcendentalists were wrong and he would keep the body. The transcendentalists did a lot to destroy the American body . . .

Walt Whitman printed *Leaves of Grass* himself.

Bessie Smith died on the grass in front of a white hospital that would not take her in. The Body bled to death.

I would have become a midwest Christian ghost without Walt Whitman. He gave me the courage to demand and get a body.

When I was fifteen and first read Whitman before World War I, he was considered by the Christian culture to be pornographic because he was for the body on this earth with all the senses and life now without waiting for some far-off heaven.

The Socialists were often Puritans but they often loved and certainly circulated *Leaves of Grass*, because of Whitman's passionate democracy, love of Lincoln and poems about European revolutionists and his love of the common people and occupations.

The IWW [Industrial Workers of the World] loved Whitman more for they had a pagan streak and did believe in "free love" or that love was free.

He was read at the agrarian picnics where reading poetry out loud was always part of the program. The IWW learned "When Lilacs Last in the Dooryard Bloom'd" to read in jail especially in winter. I learned and read "O Captain! my Captain! our fearful trip is done,/ The ship has weather'd every rack, the prize we sought is won . . ."—the poem about the death of Lincoln.

Sometimes in Arkansas a hill-billy farmer would accompany me with guitar or zither or jew's harp, making sad music. The popular poets to be recited were James Whitcomb Riley and Eddie Guest and Service because they rhymed and many learned them by heart. Bill Haywood and Debs liked to recite poetry in the saloons. Whitman didn't rhyme but he sounded like talking, which had a virtue of making everyone think they might write if they could speak. Anna Louise Strong wrote free verse in the early IWW papers and freed a flood of such poetry coming out of jails and summer freight cars as they went to the North Dakota harvest.

I recited "Dalliance of Eagles" once in a rowdy crowd who thought it was a swell poem on mating in the air.

It has not been studied how much Whitman reflected the democratic free speech of burgeoning and growing industrial America. As a newspaper man, he undoubtedly read the country papers of his day and, if you look into his writing, you will find it full of the poetry of occupations, poems that are long lists of tools and the praise of work, and the common doings (as they were called) of fraternity, brotherhood, love of comrades—"liberty is the last to go out of this place." He expressed the love of the land, of men and women, of children, of communality, of common grief and social and political rebellion, and above all, which in the established culture was unheard of, a passionate and bold break with European culture, effetism, alienation, and hierarchy. It is not appreciated now, I think, the long and hard struggle to break away from European thought and culture. Plato had a terrible grip on our schools. In 1930, you had to be a "European" writer to speak at the University of Minnesota. I heard them hiss Sandburg—a midwestern guitar-playing yokel out of the cornfields.

It was not merely a provincial distrust that made Americans so often hate the foreign culture of Europe. With a wonderful and dogged instinct they rooted into their own culture, their own experience, their passion for a purely indigenous democratic race that Whitman sings about. It's amazing to go through *Leaves of Grass* and find how it reflects the deepest instinctive American native. He was resonant to the new American being created, the most fragile tendencies and as yet unspoken declarations.

This was reflected not only in the use of the vernacular of the street and countryside, but also in the rhythm, the long line, the walking stanzas, tonal to a man's body, walking, striding, going forward not in gloom and pessimism of an elite England, but the plunging prairie movement into an apocalyptic age—into amazing structures and landscapes, and a people tenderly breasted and aflame with a new concept of solidarity and fraternity. These feelings were very deep, carried from the revolutions of Europe and bred in a new scape, 160 acres of free land and every man as good as the next and even a little better.

I cannot make it clear how much Whitman meant before World War I, in the grip of the white puritan, the Wasp, the Bible belt—the severe and terrible trashing of the body . . .

I remember when the Little Blue Books first published Whitman. They were published by Emanuel Haldeman-Julius and the newspaper *The Appeal to Reason*, which could circulate a million copies in a crisis because there were no consumers as such. Everyone was a distributor. It was the publication of the workers and farmers. Most books were expensive and hard to get. *Leaves of Grass* was one of them. These little books were blue and made to fit in the overall pocket so you could pull them out at work or at the plow and read. Thousands of titles eventually were published. A generation of American workers got their education from these. And they published some of *Leaves of Grass* to carry in your overall pocket. Walt should have been there, striding across Kansas, hearing the "Open Road" shouted from freight cars and cattle towns . . . and lonely farmers in the years of drought and ruin. Who can measure the wonder of such a thing?

Once I was reading Neruda and Whitman, who go together fine, in a schoolhouse in North Dakota with a swinging kerosene lamp casting light and shadow over the gnarled and drouthy faces. As I read, a stalwart old farmer slowly rose and came toward me holding out his hands. "Let me touch that book," he said.

Another time I was sitting beside a country road in Missouri, reading from a small edition of *Leaves of Grass*. In the long light of late afternoon, in a bright dust, a flock of sheep came down the road herded by an old patriarch with a long white beard. I didn't move and the sheep encircled me and his prophetic face looked down at me in the motes and baaing of the sheep. After greeting and small talk he said, "Is that a book you are reading? Is that one of them?" he said. "I never learned the reading," he said almost proudly. "What is in that book? What does it say?" "I'll read you some," I said, and he eagerly sat down beside me and I read the "Song of Occupations." He listened as if lighted. He stood up and caressed the book. "Why," he said, "I might write that if I could write. I didn't know anyone wrote about such things as what you are doing all the days of your life. I didn't know that was poetry. What's his name?" "Walt," I said, "Walt Whitman." Then he shouted and threw back his head laughing. "Walt," he cried, "why it's my own name! It can't be a poet in a book printed by the name of Walt!

Ho—you're lying to me girl. You must be lying! If he's a poet then I've been a poet all along." I gave him the book and he walked down amongst the sheep with the book open as if he was reading. He was matching it with his own occupations and the poetry he lived.

An old lumberjack on the St. Croix one snowy night when we were snowed in at the tavern listened to the "Lilacs Last in the Dooryard Bloom'd," and became amorous, and full of memory of a forest love in his youth which he had never told before.

What an honor to be a poet like this, bringing up from deep down the unknown images of a birthing nation. Singing the body electric amidst the ghostly, desecration of the puritans. Printing it yourself, rewriting, even criticizing bitterly the growth of Capitalism and the danger to the masses and the singing of America.

He gave us a body and taught us to sing in our own voice.

During the McCarthy period you could not write your dissertation in Minnesota on Whitman. The southern agrarians made him a bad word, at best a naive yokel of the mob. Their fierce animosity showed how good he was for us, how dangerous, how alive.

16.

17.

The Poets Respond: A Bibliographic Chronology

ED FOLSOM

WHITMAN'S 'POETS TO COME' have been exceedingly generous in the frequency of their response to Whitman. In essays, poems and books, from his time to ours, year by year, poets and novelists have talked back to him. The bibliography that follows is the most comprehensive charting, to date, of this vast and varied response. I have not attempted to list every essay about Whitman written by a poet; instead, I have listed only those essays which genuinely seem a part of the long tradition of carrying on the conversation that Whitman began—those essays that read as 'poet talking back to poet.' I have listed letters about Whitman only in rare cases when they seem extensive and original enough to be important in tracing out that conversation. While I have included most poems about Whitman that I have found, I have not included all the 'parodies' of Whitman's poems; they are included here only when they were written by poets well enough known that they take on interest and resonance beyond the simple act of parody. (Nearly a hundred parodies, from 1860 to 1920, are available in Henry S. Saunders, ed., *Parodies on Walt Whitman* [1923; rpt. New York: AMS, 1970], abbreviated PAR in this bibliography.)

This is not a bibliography of Whitman's 'influence' on other poets, although it clearly relates to and supplements such studies. There is no end, of course, to studies on Whitman's influence: we already have book-length studies of his relationship to particular poets (see Sydney Musgrove's *T. S. Eliot and Walt Whitman* [New York: Haskell House, 1966] and Diane Middlebrook's *Walt Whitman and Wallace Stevens* [Ithaca: Cornell University, 1974]), as well as numerous shorter studies of his influence on American poets and writers as diverse as Emily Dickinson, Edgar Lee Masters, Eugene O'Neill, Carl Sandburg, William Carlos Williams, Hart Crane, Robert Frost, Ezra Pound, Henry Miller, Robinson Jeffers, Theodore Roethke, Robert

Duncan, Lawrence Ferlinghetti, Gary Snyder, Robert Creeley, W. S. Merwin, Allen Ginsberg, Adrienne Rich and Anne Sexton, to name a few. A valuable study of Whitman's growing fame and influence in America is Charles B. Willard's *Whitman's American Fame* (Providence: Brown University, 1950); his chapter on 'The Creative Writers' offers a brief overview of the reactions of late nineteenth and early twentieth century poets to Whitman.

Whitman's influence and reputation in other countries are investigated in books like Harold Blodgett's *Walt Whitman in England* (Ithaca: Cornell University, 1934); Betsy Erkkila's *Walt Whitman Among the French* (Ithaca: Cornell University, 1980); Gay Wilson Allen, ed., *Walt Whitman Abroad* (abbreviated WWA below) (Syracuse: Syracuse University, 1955), which contains essays on Whitman's influence in Germany, France, Scandinavia, Russia, Italy, Spain and Latin America, Israel, Japan, and India; and Roger Asselineau and William White, eds., *Walt Whitman in Europe Today* (WWE) (Detroit: Wayne State University, 1972), with essays on Whitman's stature in Spain, Germany, Belgium, France, Italy, Czechoslovakia, Yugoslavia, Denmark, Sweden, Iceland, and Russia. Gay Wilson Allen's *The New Walt Whitman Handbook* (New York: New York University, 1975), contains an excellent overview of 'Walt Whitman and World Literature,' as well as a valuable bibliography of translations of Whitman, and Roger Asselineau's bibliographic essay, 'Walt Whitman,' in *Eight American Authors* (New York: Norton, 1971), has a full examination of the material written about Whitman's 'Fame and Influence,' pp. 267-71.

There are several other books that closely relate to ours: James E. Miller, Jr., Karl Shapiro, and Bernice Slote, *Start with the Sun: Studies in the Whitman Tradition* (Lincoln: University of Nebraska, 1960) is a book with essays on the relationship of Whitman to Lawrence, Hart Crane, Dylan Thomas, Henry Miller and W. C. Williams, and a helpful overview called 'Walt Whitman and the Secret of History'; Ronald Hayman's brief *Arguing with Walt Whitman* (London: Covent Garden, 1971), offers some suggestions of poets' ongoing discussions with Whitman; and James E. Miller, Jr.'s recent *The American Quest for a Supreme Fiction: Whitman's Legacy in the Personal Epic* (Chicago: University of Chicago, 1979), contains thoughtful analyses of Whitman's pervasive and often surprising presence in the longer works of Robert Lowell, John Berryman, Ezra Pound, T. S. Eliot, W. C. Williams, Hart Crane, Charles Olson, and others.

Some previous volumes have collected poems about Whitman: Henry Eduard Legler's *Walt Whitman: Yesterday and Today* (WWYT) (Chicago: Brothers of the Book, 1916), prints a selection of early poems, often severely edited; *The Beloit Poetry Journal*, 5, 1 (1954), consists of a special chapbook edited by David Ignatow called *Walt Whitman: A Centennial Celebration* (WWCC), and collects nearly twenty poems relating to Whitman; Didier Tisdel Jaén edited *Homage to Walt Whitman* (HWW) (University: University of Alabama, 1969), a collection of poems about Whitman from Spanish poets. A few journals have 'specialized' in Whitman-inspired poems; *The Conservator* (CON), in the late years of the nineteenth and first years of the twentieth centuries, printed numerous poems about Whitman, and the *West Hills Review* (WHR) and *The Mickle Street Review* (MSR) do so now. (Both WHR and MSR began in 1979 and are published yearly; not all the poems and essays from these periodicals are listed below.) *American Dialog* (AD), 5 (Spring-Summer, 1969), was a special issue devoted to Whitman, with several poems and essays dealing with him.

There are several excellent collections of criticism about Whitman, and most of them print a few responses by other poets: Edwin Haviland Miller, ed., *A Century of Whitman Criticism* (Bloomington: Indiana University, 1969); Milton Hindus, ed., *Walt Whitman: The Critical Heritage* (New York: Barnes & Noble, 1971); Francis Murphy, ed., *Walt Whitman: A Critical Anthology* (Baltimore: Penguin, 1970); and Sculley Bradley and Harold Blodgett, eds., *Walt Whitman: Leaves of Grass: A Norton Critical Edition* (New York: Norton, 1973), all print several essays by poets and novelists, so some of the essays listed below can be found reprinted in these collections. Horace Traubel edited *Camden's Compliment to Walt Whitman* (Philadelphia: David McKay, 1889), a record of the celebration of Whitman's seventieth birthday; it contains many addresses by and letters from writers (e.g., Mark Twain, W. D. Howells, John Greenleaf Whittier, William Morris, Hamlin Garland, Julian Hawthorne), but most of the comments are very brief and all are purely occasional pieces; they are not included below.

The interest in poems about Whitman is not just a recent phenomenon; in fact a reader queried *The Critic* on October 17, 1885 (p. 180): "Will you please inform me whether any verses commendatory of Walt Whitman and his poetry have ever been written by American poets, and where I shall be able to find them?" *The Critic*'s answer—six poems appearing mostly in newspapers (by J. C. Hagen, Richard Watson Gilder, Kate A. Taylor, Linn B. Porter, Walter R. Thomas, and J. N. Matthews)—might well represent the germ of this bibliographic study. Since then, there have been several bibliographies with brief listings of poems about or to Walt Whitman. The 1902 edition of *The Complete Writings of Walt Whitman* (New York: G. P. Putnam's Sons) has a listing of poems to Whitman in volume X, pp. 231-33, but the longest listing of early poems about Whitman is in the *New York University Index to Early American Periodical Literature*, No. 3: Whitman

(New York: Pamphlet Distributing Co., 1941), pp. 17-18; most of the entries are for poems published in Horace Traubel's *Conservator,* his journal of Whitman items and ideas. *Walt Whitman: A Catalogue Based Upon the Collections of the Library of Congress* (Washington: Library of Congress, 1955) has a very brief listing of 'Whitman in Fiction and Poetry' and of 'Parodies' on pp. 125-26. Evie Allison Allen's 'A Check List of Whitman Publications: 1945-1960,' in Gay Wilson Allen, *Walt Whitman as Man, Poet, and Legend* (Carbondale: Southern Illinois University, 1961), pp. 243-44, lists twelve 'Poems about Whitman' and one fictional work. The invaluable current bibliography in the *Walt Whitman Review* occasionally lists poems, and Jeanetta Boswell's recent *Walt Whitman and the Critics: A Checklist of Criticism, 1900-1978* (Metuchen: Scarecrow, 1980), indexes a handful of entries under 'Poems [written to honor Whitman].' Roberts W. French offers a more complete bibliography in 'Whitman as Poetic Subject,' *Walt Whitman Review,* 26 (1980), 69-70, in which he lists around forty 'poems in which Whitman appears, either by name or by clear allusion, and in which he serves as a thematic focal point.' French wants 'to make the first step toward compiling an extensive list of those poems that somehow present Whitman in significant ways.' With around three hundred poems and over one hundred and twenty-five essays, this bibliography is offered in the same spirit, step two.

Note on Arrangement: Entries are arranged in chronological groups, the same that are used for our selections in this volume. Within groups, entries are arranged chronologically by date of earliest publication or, when it can be determined, date of composition. All entries in any one chronological group for a single author are listed immediately after the earliest entry for that author. A crosshatch (#) appears by the names of authors who have entries under more than one chronological grouping (Borges, for example, wrote essays on Whitman during the 1905-1955 period, the 1955-1980 period, and during the 1980s, so he appears under all three groups). An asterisk (*) appears by the titles of all works that appear in this volume, and essays and poems attributed simply to WMS are works which are published for the first time in *Walt Whitman: The Measure of His Song.*

1855-1905

RALPH WALDO EMERSON, Letter to Walt Whitman,* in Whitman, *Leaves of Grass* (Brooklyn: [Fowler & Wells], 1856), appendix.

JAMES RUSSELL LOWELL, Letter to C. E. Norton (1855), *Letters of James Russell Lowell,* ed. Charles Eliot Norton (New York: Harper, 1894), I, 242-43.

EDWARD EVERETT HALE, "Leaves of Grass," *North American Review*, 82 (Jan., 1856), 275-77. Essay.

HENRY DAVID THOREAU, Letter to Harrison Blake (1856),* in F. B. Sanborn, ed., *The Writings of Henry David Thoreau* (Boston: Houghton Mifflin, 1906), VI (Familiar letters), 295-96.

HENRY JAMES, Review of *Drum-Taps, Nation,* 1 (Nov. 16, 1865).

——, Review of *Calamus, Literature,* 2 (April 16, 1898), 453.

WILLIAM DEAN HOWELLS, "Review of *Drum-Taps,*" *The Round Table* (November, 1865), 147-48.

——, "Editor's Study," *Harper's Monthly,* 78 (Feb., 1889), 488-92.

——, "My Impressions of Literary New York," *Literary Friends and Acquaintance* (New York: Harper, 1900), 73-76; printed as "Walt Whitman at Pfaff's," CON (June, 1895), 61-62.

MONCURE CONWAY, "Walt Whitman," *The Fortnightly Review,* 6 (Oct. 15, 1866), 538-48. Essay.

MATTHEW ARNOLD, Letter to W. D. O'Connor (1866),* quoted in Harold Blodgett, *Walt Whitman in England* (Ithaca: Cornell, 1934), 167-68.

——, "Theodore Parker," *Culture and Anarchy,* ed. R. H. Super (Ann Arbor: University of Michigan, 1965), 78-84. Essay, 1867.

WILLIAM MICHAEL ROSSETTI, "Prefatory Notice," *Poems by Walt Whitman,* ed. Rossetti (London: John Camden Hotten, 1868), 1-27.

ALGERNON CHARLES SWINBURNE, *William Blake,* in Edmund Gosse and Thomas James Wise, eds., *The Complete Works of Algernon Charles Swinburne* (London: Heinemann, 1926), XVI, 342-46. Essay, 1866.

——, "Under the Microscope," *Works,* XVI, esp. 411-20. Essay.

——, "To Walt Whitman in America,"* *Works,* II, 184-88. Poem, 1876.

——, "Whitmania," *Works,* XV, 307-18. Essay, 1887.

ALFRED AUSTIN, "The Poetry of the Future," *The Poetry of the Period* (London: Richard Bentley, 1870), 192-223. Essay.

RODEN NOEL, "A Study of Walt Whitman," *Essays on Poetry and Poets* (1886). Essay.

R. H. NEWELL ("Orpheus C. Kerr"), "Aeriform America, By W-lt Wh-tm-n," *New York Daily Graphic* (August 2, 1873), rpt. PAR, 23. Parody.

BAYARD TAYLOR, "Walt Whitman on Oxford," rpt. PAR, 24. Parody, 1874.

——, "Camerados," "Walt Whitman," *The Echo Club,* (Boston: James R. Osgood, 1876), 157-58, 169. Parodies.

JAMES THOMSON ("B. V."), *Walt Whitman, the Man and the Poet* (New York: Haskell House, 1971; orig. pub., 1910). Essays, 1874, 1881-82.

ROBERT BUCHANAN, "Walt Whitman," "Socrates in Camden," and "Walt Whitman,"* *The Complete Poetical Works of Robert Buchanan* (London: Chatto & Windus, 1901), I, 425; II, 395-98. Poems, 1876, 1885, 1892.

JOAQUIN MILLER, "To Walt Whitman,"* *The Galaxy,* 23 (Jan., 1877), 29. Poem.

——, "The Passing of Tennyson," *The Complete Poetical Works of Joaquin Miller* (San Francisco: Whitaker & Ray, 1897), 225-26. Poem.

ARRAN LEIGH, "They Say Thou Art Sick," in Richard Maurice Bucke, *Walt Whitman,* (1883; rpt. New York: Johnson Reprint, 1970), 215. Poem, 1870s.

LEONARD WHEELER, "O Pure Heart Singer," in Bucke, *Whitman,* 213. Poem, 1870s.

SIDNEY LANIER, Lecture III, *The English Novel,* in Clarence Gohdes and Kemp Malone, eds., *Sidney Lanier: The English Novel and Essays on Literature* (Baltimore: Johns Hopkins, 1945), IV, 42-63. Essay, 1881.

H. C. BUNNER, "Home, Sweet Home, with Variations," part VI, *Airs from Arcady* (New York: Scribner's, 1884), 68-73. Parody.

RICHARD WATSON GILDER, "When the True Poet Comes," *Century Magazine,* 23 (n.s., I: November, 1881), 64. Poem.

LINN PORTER, "I Knew There Was an Old White-Bearded Seer," in Bucke, *Whitman,* 223. Poem, 1881.

GERARD MANLEY HOPKINS, Letter to Robert Bridges (1882),* *The Letters of Gerard Manley Hopkins to Robert Bridges,* ed. Claude Abbott (London: Oxford, 1935), 154-58.

RICHARD GRANT WHITE, *The Fate of Mansfield Humphreys* (Boston: Houghton Mifflin, 1884), 102-111. Parody.

WILLIAM WATSON, "LXXXII," *Epigrams of Art, Life, and Nature* (Liverpool: Gilbert G. Walmsley, 1884), n.p. Poem.

LIONEL JOHNSON, Letter to Whitman (1885), in Traubel, *With Walt Whitman in Camden* (New York: Mitchell Kennerley, 1914), II, 180-81.

A. T. QUILLER-COUCH, "Behold! I Am Not One That Goes to Lectures," *The Oxford Magazine,* 1885, rpt. PAR, 61. Parody.

#SADAKICHI HARTMANN, "To Walt Whitman," in George Knox, *The Whitman-Hartmann Controversy* (Frankfurt: Peter Lang, 1976), 104-105. [Also contains other "Whitman Imitations" by Hartmann]. Poem, 1886.

LOUIS SULLIVAN, Letter to Whitman (1887),* in Horace Traubel, *With Walt Whitman in Camden,* III, 25-26.

RENNELL RODD, "To Walt Whitman," in Horace Traubel, *With Walt Whitman in Camden,* III, 392-94. Poem, 1887.

OSCAR WILDE, "The Gospel According to Walt Whitman," in Richard Ellmann, ed., *The Artist as Critic: Critical Writings of Oscar Wilde* (New York: Random House, 1969), 121-25. Essay, 1889.

#ERNEST RHYS, "To Walt Whitman,"* in Horace L. Traubel, ed., *Camden's Compliment to Walt Whitman* (Philadelphia: David McKay, 1889), 6. Poem.

OLIVER WENDELL HOLMES, Paper X, *Over the Teacups* (Boston: Houghton, Mifflin, 1891), 231-38. Essay.

RUBEN DARIO, "Walt Whitman,"* *Azul* (1890), rpt. HWW, 12-13.

[NATHAN HASKELL DOLE], "To Walt Whitman," *Literary World Fortnightly*, 22 (May, 1891), 160. Poem.

MERLIN [pseud.], "To Walt Whitman," *The Week, Toronto* (Jan. 16, 1891). Poem.

#HARRIET MONROE, "A Word about Walt Whitman," *The Critic*, 20 (April 16, 1892), 231. Essay.

EDMUND CLARENCE STEDMAN, "Good-Bye Walt," CON, 3 (1892), 26; appears as "W. W." in Stedman, *Poems Now First Collected* (Boston: Houghton Mifflin, 1897), 124. Poem.

ALBERT EDMUND LANCASTER, "To Walt Whitman," in Horace L. Traubel, et. al., eds., *In Re Walt Whitman* (Philadelphia: David McKay, 1893), 212. Poem.

ANDRE RAFFALOVICH, "Not since some mariners," *The Critic*, 20 (April 23, 1892), 245 (rpt. from *The Hawk*). Poem.

ANONYMOUS, "Walt Whitman," in Traubel, *In Re*, (rpt. from *Punch*, 1892). Poem.

ANONYMOUS, " 'The good grey poet' gone," *The Critic*, 20 (April 23, 1892), 245 (rpt. from *Punch*). Poem.

HARRISON S. MORRIS, "Poem to Walt Whitman," CON, 3 (1892), 26. Poem.

JOHN JAMES PIATT, "To Walt Whitman, the Man," *The Cosmopolitan*, 14 (November, 1892), 118. Poem.

#EDMUND GOSSE, "Walt Whitman,"* *Critical Kit-Kats* (New York: Dodd, Mead, 1896), 95-111. Essay.

JOHN ADDINGTON SYMONDS, *Walt Whitman: A Study* (London: John C. Nimmo, 1893). Book.

——, "Love and Death: A Symphony," in Traubel, *In Re*, 1-12. Poem.

#HAMLIN GARLAND, "A Tribute of Grasses,"* *Prairie Songs* (Cambridge: Stone and Kimball, 1893), 116. Poem.

LOUIS J. BLOCK, "Walt Whitman," *Poet-Lore* 5 (Aug.-Sept., 1893), 422-23. Poem.

GEORGE HORTON, untitled, in Traubel, *In Re*, 22. Poem.

FRANCIS HOWARD WILLIAMS, "Walt Whitman," in Traubel, *In Re*, 436; rpt. in *The Flute Player & Other Poems* (1894). Poem.

——, "Before I Knew the Leader," CON, 18 (June, 1907), 53-4. Poem.

SAM WALTER FOSS, "Walt Whitman," CON, 6 (Oct., 1895), 116. Poem.

ROWLAND THURNAM, "To Walt Whitman," CON, 6 (June, 1895), 55. Poem.

LAURENS MAYNARD, "For Whitman's Birthday—1895," CON, 6 (June, 1895), 53. Poem.

——, "The Walt Whitman Fellowship," CON, 5 (Dec., 1894), 147. Poem.

JOHN HERBERT CLIFFORD, "Fellowship of Whitman," CON, 6 (June, 1895), 51. Poem.

JULIAN HAWTHORNE, "Walt Whitman," CON, 7 (1896), 153-54. (Rpt. from Hawthorne, *American Literature*). Essay.

WILLA CATHER, "Whitman," in Bernice Slote, ed., *The Kingdom of Art: Willa Cather's First Principles and Critical Statements 1893-1896* (Lincoln: University of Nebraska, 1966), 350-53. Essay, 1896.

WILLIAM GAY, "To Walt Whitman, In His Own Spirit," CON, 6 (Jan., 1896), 168. Poem.

J. WILLIAM LLOYD, "Mount Walt Whitman," *Windharp Songs* (Buffalo, 1896). Poem.

——, "Written at Whitman's Grave," CON, 13 (Jan., 1903), 165. Poem.

#HORACE L. TRAUBEL, "The Master Came to the Earth," CON, 7 (Dec., 1896), 151. Poem.

EDWIN ARLINGTON ROBINSON, "Walt Whitman,"* *The Children of the Night* (New York: Scribner's, 1897; rpt. 1921), 85. Poem.

JOHN HENRY BROWN, "To Walt Whitman," CON, 8 (July, 1897), 77, and in *Poems Lyrical and Dramatic* (1897). Poem.

MARY STODDART, "Walt Whitman," CON, 8 (1897), 20. Poem.

TUCKER, "To Walt Whitman," CON, 9 (1898), 25. Poem.

GUSTAV P. WIKSELL, "To Walt Whitman," CON, 10 (June, 1899), 52. Poem.

GRACE ELLERY CHANNING, "The Voiceless Syllables of Grass," CON, 10 (June, 1899), 61. Poem.

C. F. GOSS, "An Ode to Old Chronics," CON, 9 (Jan., 1899), 168-69. Parody.

WILLIAM VAUGHN MOODY, "An Ode in Time of Hesitation," section 7, in Robert Morss Lovett, ed., *Selected Poems of William Vaughn Moody* (Boston: Houghton Mifflin, 1931), 21-23. Poem, 1900.

ROBERT LOUIS STEVENSON, "Walt Whitman," *Familiar Studies of Men and Books* (New York: Scribner's, 1901), 104-36. Essay.

#WILLIAM STRUTHERS, "Walt Whitman," CON 12 (June, 1901), 52-3. Poem.

——, "To Walt Whitman," CON, 15 (Aug., 1904), 84. Poem

ADALENA DYER, "Recent Study and Criticism of Whitman," CON, 12 (Sept., 1901), 108. Poem.

ELIZABETH PORTER GOULD, "To Walt Whitman," *Gems from Walt Whitman*, rpt. WWYT, 70. Poem, c. 1900.

GEORGE CABOT LODGE, "To W. W.,"* in *Selected Fiction and Verse*, ed. John W. Crowley (St. Paul: John Colet, 1976), 202. Poem, 1902.

JOSEPH LEWIS FRENCH, "To the Spirit of Walt Whitman," CON, 13 (Nov., 1902), 132. Poem.

RAY CLARKE ROSE, "Walt Whitman," *Sign of the Ginger Jar* (Chicago, 1902), rpt. WWYT, 55. Poem.

EDWIN A. BRENHOLTZ, "To Leaves of Grass," CON, 14 (May, 1903), 36. Poem.

#G. K. CHESTERTON, "Conventions and the Hero," *Lunacy and Letters* (New York: Sheed & Ward, 1958), 62-5. Essay, 1904.

HERMAN HESSE, "Walt Whitman: *Leaves of Grass*," in Hesse, *My Belief*, ed. Theodore Ziolkowski (New York: Farrar, Straus and Giroux, 1974), 312-13. Essay.

ELSA BARKER, "To Walt Whitman," CON, 15 (June, 1904), 52-4. Poem.

ALBERTA MONTGOMERIE, "A Birthday Month," CON, 16 (May, 1905), 36-7. Poem.

——, "The Wound Dresser," CON, 16 (Aug., 1905), 84. Poem.

HENRY L. BONSALL, "All Hail to Thee! Walt Whitman!," WWYT, 66-67. Poem, c. 1900.

JOSEPH W. CHAPMAN, "One Master Poet," WWYT, 64. Poem, c. 1900.

EDWARD S. CREAMER, "Thou Lover of the Cosmos," WWYT, 65. Poem, c. 1900.

MAX J. HERZBERG, "He Passed Amid the Noisy Throngs," WWYT, 71. Poem, c. 1900.

HARRISON S. MORRIS, "He Was in Love with Truth," WWYT, 48. Poem, c. 1900.

1905-1955

EDWARD CARPENTER, *Days with Walt Whitman* (London: George Allen, 1906). Book.

MAY MORGAN, "To Walt Whitman," *The Critic*, 49 (August, 1906), 148. Poem.

HYACINTH SMITH, "Insight: To Walt Whitman," CON, 17 (Aug., 1906), 84. Poem.

HENRY BRYAN BINNS, "The Divine Man," CON, 17 (June, 1906), 52-3. Poem.

GEORGE M. HARTT, "Walt Whitman," CON, 18 (June, 1907), 52. Poem.

ESTELLE DUCLO, "Walt Whitman," CON, 18 (April, 1907), 29. Poem.

ELLEN GLASGOW, Letter to Whitman Fellowship, CON, 19 (June, 1908), 56.

L. CONRAD HARTLEY, *The Spirit of Walt Whitman: A Psychological Study in Blank Verse* (Manchester: J. E. Cornish, Ltd., 1908). Long poem.

EZRA POUND, "What I Feel About Walt Whitman,"* *Selected Prose: 1909-1965*, ed. William Cookson (New York: New Directions, 1973), 145-46. Essay.

——, ["Whitman is the Voice of One Who Saith"], *The Spirit of Romance* (New York: New Directions, 1929), 168-69. Parody.

——, "A Pact,"* "L'Homme Moyen Sensuel," *Personae* (New York: New Directions, 1971), 89, 238-46. Poems, 1913, 1915.

——, LXXX, LXXXII, *The Cantos* (New York: New Directions, 1970), 493-516, 523-27. Poems, 1948.

#WILLIAM STRUTHERS, "Dear Walt," CON, 20 (March, 1909), 4-5. Poem.

——, "Of Walt," CON, 29 (1918), 101. Poem.

HARRY WEIR BOLAND, "Walt Whitman," CON, 21 (April, 1910), 21. Poem.

JOHN REED, "The Tenement Clothes Line," *Boston Evening Herald* (April 25, 1912), rpt. PAR, 122. Parody.

#ERNEST RHYS, "Walt Whitman's *Leaves of Grass*," *Everyman*, 1 (Feb. 28, March 7, 1913), 623; 656-57. Essay.

——, "Walt Whitman," *The Bookman* (London), 56 (May, 1919), 66-68. Essay.

JOHN COWPER POWYS, "Walt Whitman," *Visions and Revisions* (New York: G. A. Shaw, 1915), 281-89. Essay.

WILLIAM ROSE BENET, "After Hearing John Cowper Powys Lecture on Walt Whitman," reprinted in Christopher Morley, *Essays* (Philadelphia: J. B. Lippincott, 1927), 703. Poem, c. 1915.

FERNANDO PESSOA, "Salutation to Walt Whitman,"* in Edwin Honig, trans., *Selected Poems by Fernando Pessoa* (Chicago: Swallow Press, 1971), 56-71. Poem, 1915.

EDGAR LEE MASTERS, "Petit the Poet,"* *Spoon River Anthology* (New York: Macmillan, 1915), 78. Poem.

——, *Whitman* (New York: Scribner's, 1937). Book.

WITTER BYNNER, *The New World,* section 4, (New York: Mitchell Kennerley, 1915), 29-31. Poem.

——, "Whitman,"* *A Canticle of Pan and Other Poems* (New York: Alfred A. Knopf, 1920), 154-55. Poem.

#WILLIAM CARLOS WILLIAMS, "America, Whitman, and the Art of Poetry," *The Poetry Journal,* 8 (November, 1917), 27-36. Essay.

——, "Choral: the Pink Church," *Selected Poems* (New York: New Directions, 1969), 122-25. Poem, 1949.

COLIN CUTHBERT ALEXANDER, CON, 27 (Feb., 1917), 165. Poem.

BENOY KUMAR SARKAR, "Walt Whitman," CON, 28 (1917), 116. Poem.

VIRGINIA WOOLF, "Visits to Walt Whitman," *Granite and Rainbow: Essays by Virginia Woolf* (London: Hogarth, 1960), 229-31. Essay, 1918.

VALERY LARBAUD, "Development of the Poet," WWA, 61-75. Essay.

SHERWOOD ANDERSON, "Song of Industrial America," *Mid-American Chants* (New York: John Lane, 1918), 15-18. Poem.

——, "Walt Whitman,"* *Leaves of Grass* (New York: Thomas Y. Crowell, 1933), v-vii. Essay.

CARL SANDBURG, "Interior," *The Complete Poems of Carl Sandburg* (New York: Harcourt Brace, 1969), 112-13. Poem, 1918.

——, "Introduction,"* *Leaves of Grass* (New York: Modern Library, 1921), iii-xi. Essay.

——, "The People, Yes," Section 67, *The Complete Poems of Carl Sandburg,* 544-48. Poem, 1936.

#HORACE L. TRAUBEL, "As I Sit at Karsner's," CON, 30 (1919), 37. Poem.

——, "A Common Nuisance," CON, 30 (1919), 21-22. Poem.

JAMES D. LAW, "Walt Whitman," CON, 29 (Oct., 1918), 117-19. Poem.

FRANK HARRIS, "Walt Whitman," *Contemporary Portraits* (Third Series), (New York: Privately printed, 1920), 211-33. Essay, 1919.

PADRAIC COLUM, "Poetry of Walt Whitman," *New Republic,* 19 (June 14, 1919), 213-15. Essay.

#HARRIET MONROE, "Walt Whitman," *Poets & Their Art* (New York: Macmillan, 1926), 179-84. Essay, 1919.

CHRISTOPHER MORLEY, "Walt Whitman Miniatures," *Mince Pie* (New York: George H. Doran, 1919), 272-91. Essay.

——, "Walt on Market Street," *Travels in Philadelphia* (Philadelphia: David McKay, 1920), rpt. PAR, 156. Poem.

——, "Preface," PAR, v-ix. Essay.

——, "Fulton Street and Walt Whitman," *Plum Pudding* (Garden City: Doubleday and Page, 1921), 57-62. Essay.

——, "Moby Walt," *Forty-Four Essays* (New York: Harcourt Brace, 1925), 204-07. Essay.

——, "Whitman Centennial," *Essays* (Philadelphia: J. B. Lippincott, 1927), 435-41. Essay.

——, "Preface to 1855 *Leaves of Grass,*" *Essays,* 694-707. Essay.

——, "Notes on Walt," *Streamlines* (Garden City: Doubleday, Doran, 1936), 284-90. Essay.

——, "The Atom Splitter," *The Ironing Board* (Garden City: Doubleday, 1949), 179-86. Essay.

EMANUEL CARNEVALI, "Walt Whitman,"* *Poetry,* 14 (May, 1919), 60. Poem.

JOHN RUSSELL MCCARTHY, "Come Down Walt," *Poetry,* 14 (May, 1919), 59-60. Poem.

LOUIS UNTERMEYER, "Walt Whitman Rhapsodizes About It," *Including Horace* (New York: Harcourt, Brace, 1919), 22-3. Poem.

FRANZ KAFKA, Comments on Whitman, in Gustav Janouch, *Conversations with Kafka* (New York: New Directions, 1971), 167-68. Comments, c. 1920.

JAMES OPPENHEIM, "The Mystic Warrior," *The Sea* (New York: Knopf, 1924), 5-139 (esp. 16-17, 25-28), and *passim.* Poem, 1920.

——, "Memories of Whitman and Lincoln," *The Sea,* 438-42. Poem, 1924.

——, "Whitman," in John Macy, ed., *American Writers on American Literature* (New York: Liveright, 1931), 258-73. Essay.

JOHN GOULD FLETCHER, "Walt Whitman's Beginnings," *The Freeman,* 3 (May 4, 1921), 188. Essay.

——, "Whitman," *Selected Poems* (New York: Farrar & Rinehart, 1938), 127. Poem, 1928.

——, [Whitman and Tolstoy], *The Two Frontiers* (New York: Coward-McCann, 1930), 230-45. Essay.

#G. K. CHESTERTON, "Old King Cole," *New Witness* 16, (Dec. 10, 1920), 577. Parody.

D. H. LAWRENCE, "Whitman,"* *Nation & Athenaeum,* 29 (July 23, 1921), 616-18. Essay.

——, "Whitman," *Studies in Classic American Literature* (New York: Viking, 1964), 163-77. Essay, 1923.

——, Preface to the American Edition of *New Poems,* and "Democracy," in E. D. McDonald, ed., *Phoenix* (New York: Viking, 1936), 218-22, 699-718. Essays, 1920, 1930.

——, "Bibbles," "The Evening Land," "Retort to Whitman,"* in Vivian de Sola Pinto and Warren Roberts, eds., *The Complete Poems of D. H. Lawrence* (New York: Viking, 1964), I, 394-400, 289-93, II, 653. Poems, 1928-32.

THOMAS MANN, "Letter to Hans Reisiger," in WWA, 16. Letter, 1922.

VACHEL LINDSAY, "Walt Whitman," *The New Republic,* 37 (Dec. 5, 1923), (Supplement: "Views of American Poetry"), 3-5. Essay.

——, Letter to Elizabeth Mann Wills (1923), in Marc Chénetier, ed., *Letters of Vachel Lindsay* (New York: Burt Franklin, 1979), 296-300.

——, "The Loneliness of Walt Whitman, Statesman-Poet," *The Litany of Washington Street* (New York: Macmillan, 1929), 54-64 (with references throughout book). Essay.

CONRAD AIKEN, "Henry James (and Walt Whitman)," *Collected Criticism* (New York: Oxford, 1968), 230-233. Essay.

——, "The Kid," Section VII ("The Last Vision"), *Collected Poems* (New York: Oxford, 1970), 859-62. Poem, 1947.

WILLIAM BUTLER YEATS, "Phase Six," *A Vision* (New York: Collier, 1967), 113-14. Essay, 1925.

WALTER HART BLUMENTHAL, "The Miracle in Camden Town," "Walt Ruminates," *Winepress: A Vintage of Verse* (New York: Vail-Ballou, 1925), 157-59, 162-63. Poems.

#HAMLIN GARLAND, "Walt Whitman," in Donald Pizer, ed., *Hamlin Garland's Diaries* (San Marino: The Huntington Library, 1968), 196-97. Essay, 1926.

——, "Walt Whitman Old and Poor," *Roadside Meetings* (New York: Macmillan, 1930), 127-43. Essay.

AMY LOWELL, "Walt Whitman and the New Poetry," *Yale Review,* n.s., 16 (1926-7), 502-19; rpt. in Lowell, *Poetry and Poets* (Boston: Houghton Mifflin, 1930), 61-87. Essay.

T. S. ELIOT, "Whitman and Tennyson,"* *The Nation & Athenaeum,* 34 (December 18, 1926), 426. Essay.

#EDMUND GOSSE, "Walt Whitman," *Leaves and Fruit* (New York: Scribner's, 1927), 203-211. Essay.

#SADAKICHI HARTMANN, "Salut au Monde: A Friend Remembers Whitman," in George Knox, *The Whitman-Hartmann Controversy* (Frankfurt: Peter Lang, 1976), 131-34. Essay, 1927.

#JORGE LUIS BORGES, "El Otro Whitman," *Discusion* (Buenos Aires: M. Gleizer, 1932), 65-70. Essay, 1929.

——, "Note on Walt Whitman,"* *Other Inquisitions, 1937-1952* (Austin: University of Texas Press, 1964), 66-72. Essay, c. 1950.

——, "Matthew XXV: 30," *Selected Poems, 1923-1967,* ed. Norman Thomas DiGiovanni (New York: Delacorte Press, 1972), 92-3. Poem, 1954.

EZEQUIEL MARTINEZ ESTRADA, "Walt Whitman,"* *Humoresca* (1929), HWW, 14-15. Poem.

FEDERICO GARCIA LORCA "Ode to Walt Whitman,"* *Poeta en Nueva York* (1929), HWW, 20-29. Poem.

MIGUEL DE UNAMUNO, "Adamic Song," WWA, 220-23. Essay, 1930.

EDWIN MARKHAM, "Walt Whitman,"* *New Poems: Eighty Songs at Eighty* (New York: Doubleday, 1932), 95-98. Poem, 1931.

CESARE PAVESE, "Interpretation of Walt Whitman, Poet," in *American Literature: Essays and Opinions* (Berkeley: University of California, 1970), 117-41. Essay, 1933.

——, "Whitman—Poetry of Poetry Writing," WWA, 189-97. Essay, 1951.

HART CRANE, "Cape Hatteras,"* *The Bridge* (New York: Liveright, 1933), 37-47. Poem.

MARK VAN DOREN, "Walt Whitman, Stranger," *American Mercury*, 35 (July, 1935), 277-85. Essay.

——, "Introduction," *The Portable Walt Whitman* (New York: Penguin, 1973), ix-xxvii. Essay, 1945.

——, "The Poet: Walt Whitman," William Claire, ed., *The Essays of Mark Van Doren* (Westport, Conn: Greenwood, 1980), 76-100. Essay, 1955.

#MURIEL RUKEYSER, "The Lynchings of Jesus," *The Collected Poems* (New York: McGraw-Hill, 1978), 24-30. Poem, 1935.

——, "Whitman and the Problem of Good,"* *The Life of Poetry* (New York: A. A. Wyn, 1949), 73-87. Essay.

STEPHEN VINCENT BENET, "Ode to Walt Whitman,"* *Burning City* (New York: Farrar & Rinehart, 1936), 26-41. Poem, 1935.

WALLACE STEVENS, "Like Decorations in a Nigger Cemetary," part 1,* *The Collected Poems of Wallace Stevens* (New York: Knopf, 1971), 150. Poem, 1936.

GENEVIEVE TAGGARD, "Night Letter to Walt Whitman," *New Frontier*, 1 (June, 1936), 11. Poem.

KATHERINE ANNE PORTER, "1939: The Situation in American Writing," *The Collected Essays and Occasional Writings of Katherine Anne Porter* (New York: Delacorte, 1970), 451-52. Essay, 1939.

DYLAN THOMAS, "The Countryman's Return," *Letters to Vernon Watkins* (New York: New Directions, 1957), 87-90. Poem, 1940.

#NORMAN ROSTEN, "You, Walt Whitman . . .," *Selected Poems* (New York: George Braziller, 1979), 33. Poem, 1940.

#EDWARD DAHLBERG, "Sing O Barren," *Can These Bones Live?* (New York: Harcourt Brace, 1941), 142-50. Essay.

LEON FELIPE, "The Prologue Speaks" [verse prologue to a translation of *Leaves of Grass*], in HWW, 4-5. Poem, 1941.

FLOYD DELL, "To a Poet Once Resident in Washington," *Walt Whitman Review*, 3 (1957), 39. Poem, 1943.

#KARL SHAPIRO, *Essay on Rime* (New York: Reynal & Hitchcock, 1945), 15-16, 29-30, 51, 66. Verse essay, 1944.

PAUL POTTS, "Gettysburg," "People Walking Down the Streets," "To a Dame Who Sneered When She Saw My Sox,"* *Instead of a Sonnet* (London: Editions Poetry London, 1944), 9-10, 12-14, 21. Poems.

#CHARLES ANGOFF "Walt Whitman Contemplates His Biographers," *American Mercury,* 60 (March, 1945), 340, rpt. WHR, 1 (1979), 13. Poem.

LANGSTON HUGHES, "The Ceaseless Rings of Walt Whitman,"* in Hughes, ed., *I Hear the People Singing: Selected Poems of Walt Whitman* (New York: International Publishers, 1946), 7-10. Essay.

——, "Old Walt,"* *Selected Poems of Langston Hughes* (New York: Knopf, 1959), 100. Poem, c. 1950.

#PABLO NERUDA, "Que Despierte el Leñador," *Canto General* (Buenos Aires, Editorial Losada, S.A., 1968), 311-32; first section translated by Robert Bly in Bly, ed., *Neruda and Vallejo: Selected Poems* (Boston: Beacon Press, 1971), 104-11. Poem, 1948.

——, "Ode to Walt Whitman,"* *Nuevas odas elementales* (1956), rpt. HWW, 43-51. Poem.

FLORENCE ROME GARRETT, "To Walt Whitman," *Saturday Review of Literature,* 32 (June 11, 1949), 24. Poem.

KENNETH PATCHEN, "The Orange Bears,"* *The Collected Poems of Kenneth Patchen* (New York: New Directions, 1968), 384. Poem, 1949.

#ALVARO CARDONA-HINE, "Landscape of Antiquity," "Bivoac," reprinted in this volume. Poems, 1949.

EDITH SITWELL, "Whitman and Blake," *Proceedings of the American Academy of Arts and Letters and the National Institute of Arts and Letters,* 2nd series, no. 1 (1951), 52-58. Essay, 1950.

E. B. WHITE, "A Classic Waits for Me," in R. P. Falk, *The Antic Muse* (1955). Parody.

RANDALL JARRELL, "Some Lines from Whitman," *Poetry and the Age* (New York: Vintage, 1953), 101-20. Orig. title, "Walt Whitman: He Had His Nerve," *Kenyon Review,* 14 (Winter, 1952), 63-71. Essay.

#HENRY MILLER, "Letter to Pierre Lesdain," *The Books in My Life* (New York: New Directions, 1952), 221-43. Essay.

PEDRO MIR, "Contracanto a Walt Whitman,"* in Jaime Labastida, ed., *Viaje a la Muchedumbre* (México: Siglo Veintiuno Editores, S.A., 1972), 37-67. Parts translated in HWW, 30-41. Poem, 1952.

ALFREDO CARDONA PENA, "A Reading of Walt Whitman," *Los jardines amantes* (1952), in HWW, 16-17. Poem.

STANLEY BURNSHAW, "Poetry: The Art (In the Form of an Apostrophe to Whitman)," *In the Terrified Radiance* (New York: George Braziller, 1972), 145-49. Poem, 1952.

1955-1980

#ALLEN GINSBERG, "A Supermarket in California,"* *Howl* (San Francisco: City Lights, 1956), 23-4. Poem, 1955.

——, "Ignu," "Death to Van Gogh's Ear," *Kaddish* (San Francisco: City Lights, 1961), 56-65. Poems, 1958.

——, "Love Poem on Theme by Whitman," *Reality Sandwiches* (San Francisco: City Lights, 1963), 41. Poem.

——, "Wichita Vortex Sutra," *Planet News* (San Francisco: City Lights, 1968), 110. Poem.

——, Dedication and "After Words," *The Fall of America* (San Francisco: City Lights, 1972), 190. Prose.

——, "Plutonian Ode," WHR (1979), 38-42, and widely reprinted. Poem.

OCTAVIO PAZ, "Whitman, Poet of America," *The Bow and the Lyre* (Austin: University of Texas, 1973), 271-74. Essay, 1955.

#WILLIAM CARLOS WILLIAMS, "An Essay on *Leaves of Grass*," in Milton Hindus, ed., *Leaves of Grass One Hundred Years After* (Stanford: Stanford University Press, 1955), 22-31.

——, "The American Idiom,"* in Linda Wagner, ed., *Interviews with William Carlos Williams* (New York: New Direction, 1976), 101-2. Essay, 1961.

KENNETH BURKE, "Policy Made Personal: Whitman's Verse and Prose Salient Traits," in Milton Hindus, ed., *Leaves of Grass One Hundred Years Later* (Stanford: Stanford University Press, 1955), 74-108. Essay.

——, "Why Satire, with a Plan for Writing One," *The Michigan Quarterly Review*, 13 (Fall, 1974), 307-37. [Contains two parodies of Whitman on 333-37.] Prose, poems.

RICHARD EBERHART, "Centennial for Whitman,"* *Collected Poems: 1930-1976* (New York: Oxford, 1976), 160-63. Poem, 1955.

——, "Comments,"* WHR (1979), 20. Essay.

EDWIN HONIG, "Walt Whitman,"* *The Moral Circus* (Baltimore: Contemporary Poetry, 1955), 19. [Printed in another form in WWCC.] Poem.

ROSALIE MOORE, "Reunion for Walt Whitman," WWCC, 4. Poem, 1955.

RUSSELL ATKINS, "There She Sits," WWCC, 14-15. Poem, 1955.

NORMAN FRIEDMAN, "Grace is Wild," WWCC, 15. Poem, 1955.

ERNEST KROLL, "A Century of Leaves," WWCC, 17. Poem, 1955.

ALFREDO GIOP DE PALCHI, "Whitmanesque," WWCC, 21. Poem, 1955.

SONIA RAIZISS, "Whitman Today," WWCC, 22. Poem, 1955.

BYRON VAZAKAS, "From Fulton Ferry," WWCC, 32. Poem, 1955.

FRANK O'HARA, "A Whitman's Birthday Broadcast with Static," "Ode: Salute to the French Negro Poets," "Bill's Burnoose," in Donald Allen, ed., *The Collected Poems of Frank O'Hara* (New York: Alfred A. Knopf, 1971), 224, 305, 415-16. Poems, 1955, 1958, 1961.

LOUIS ZUKOFSKY, "A-12," *"A"* (Berkeley: University of California Press, 1978), 228. Poem, c. 1955.

GALWAY KINNELL, "The Avenue Bearing the Initial of Christ into the New World," part 9, *The Avenue Bearing the Initial of Christ into the New World* (Boston: Houghton Mifflin, 1974), 113-14. Poem, c. 1957.

——, "Vapor Trail Reflected in the Frog Ponds," *Body Rags* (Boston: Houghton Mifflin, 1968), 7-8. Poem, 1967.

——, "Whitman's Indicative Words,"* *American Poetry Review* (March/April, 1973). Essay, revised and expanded for this volume.

MARGARET TUARELLO, "Poem for Walt Whitman," *Books Abroad,* 30 (1956), 31. Poem.

ROGER NINCK, "Ode á Walt Whitman," *Les Couteaux du Destin* (Paris: Caractè res, 1956), 58-62. Poem.

JOHN BERRYMAN, " 'Song of Myself': Intention and Substance,"* *The Freedom of the Poet* (New York: Farrar, Straus & Giroux, 1976), 227-41. Essay, 1957.

——, #78, #140, #279, *The Dream Songs* (New York: Farrar, Straus and Giroux, 1969), 93, 157, 301. Poems.

——, "Despair,"* *Love & Fame* (New York: Farrar, Straus and Giroux, 1970), 72. Poem.

#HENRY MILLER, "Walt Whitman,"* *Stand Still Like the Hummingbird* (Norfolk, Conn: New Directions, 1962), 107-10. Essay, 1957.

WRIGHT MORRIS, "Open Road: Walt Whitman," *Territory Ahead* (New York: Harcourt, Brace, 1958), 51-66. Essay.

——, "Whitman," *Earthly Delights, Unearthly Adornments* (New York: Harper & Row, 1978), 25-32. Essay.

JULES ROMAINS, Untitled, WWE, 17-18. Essay, c. 1950s.

DANNIE ABSE, "After the Release of Ezra Pound," *Collected Poems 1948-1976* (Pittsburgh: University of Pittsburgh Press, 1977), 64-65. Poem, 1958.

FRED D. L. SQUIRES, "Rendezvous: With Message to Whitman Comrades Everywhere," privately printed, 1959. Poem.

JAMES WRIGHT, "The Morality of Poetry," *Saint Judas* (Middletown: Wesleyan, 1959), 18-19. Poem.

——, "The Delicacy of Walt Whitman,"* in R. W. B. Lewis, ed., *The Presence of Walt Whitman* (New York: Columbia University Press, 1962), 164-88. Essay.

——, "The Minneapolis Poem," "Inscription for the Tank," *Shall We Gather at the River* (Middletown: Wesleyan, 1968), 12-14, 15-16. Poems.

JONATHAN WILLIAMS, "Fastball,"* "Autopsy,"* *The Empire Finals at Verona* (Highlands, N.C.: Jargon 30, 1959), n.p. Poems.

JACK KEROUAC, 130th Chorus, 168th Chorus,* *Mexico City Blues* (New York: Grove Press, 1959), 130, 168. Poems.

ROBERT LOWELL, "Words for Hart Crane," *Life Studies* (New York: Farrar, Straus and Giroux, 1959), 55. Poem.

———, "Shadow," *Day by Day* (New York: Farrar, Straus and Giroux, 1977), 116-17. Poem.

#KARL SHAPIRO, "The First White Aboriginal," *Start with the Sun*, (Lincoln: University of Nebraska, 1960), 57-70. Essay.

———, "Whitman Today," *Walt Whitman Review*, 6 (June, 1960), 31-32. Essay.

#CHARLES ANGOFF, "I Saw Walt Whitman," *Literary Review*, 4 (Autumn, 1960), 32-33. Poem.

DAN PROPPER, "The Fable of the Final Hour," in Seymour Krim, ed., *The Beats* (New York: Fawcett, 1960), 27-33. Poem.

ROBERT DUNCAN, "The Propositions" (section 4), "A Poem Beginning with a Line by Pindar" (section 2), "Another Animadversion," *Opening of the Field* (New York: New Directions, 1960), 36, 63-4, 84-5. Poems.

———, "The Fire, Passages 13," "Passages 26: The Soldiers," *Bending the Bow* (New York: New Directions, 1968), 40-45, 112-16. Poems.

———, "Changing Perspectives in Reading Walt Whitman," in Edwin Haviland Miller, ed., *The Artistic Legacy of Walt Whitman* (New York: New York University Press, 1970), 73-102. Essay, 1969.

———, "The Adventure of Whitman's Line," delivered at Whitman conference at Rutgers-Camden in Nov., 1978, unpublished. Essay and poem.

CHARLES OLSON, "I, Mencius, Pupil of the Master . . ."* *The Distances* (New York: Grove Press, 1960), 61-63. Poem.

EDWARD DORN, "The Open Road," *The Collected Poems* (Bolinas: Four Seasons, 1975), 17-21. Poem, 1961.

EGBERT S. OLIVER, "Walt," *College English*, 23 (November, 1961), 158. Poem.

DENISE LEVERTOV, "A Common Ground,"* *The Jacob's Ladder* (New York: New Directions, 1961), 1-3. Poem.

#JORGE LUIS BORGES, "The Achievements of Walt Whitman," *Texas Quarterly*, 5 (Spring, 1962), 43-48. Essay/lecture.

———, "Camden 1892,"* "Another Poem of Gifts," "Lines I Might Have Written and Lost around 1922," *Selected Poems 1923-1967*, ed. Norman Thomas DiGiovanni (New York: Delacorte Press, 1972), 174-75, 198-203, 208-09. Poems, 1964-66.

———, "Walt Whitman: Man and Myth," *Critical Inquiry*, 1 (1975), 707-718. Essay/lecture, 1968.

———, "Foreward," HWW, xiii-xvii. Essay, 1968.

———, "Preface," *Hojas de hierba* (Buenos Aires, 1969), Borges's translation of selections from *Leaves of Grass*. Essay.

KENNETH KOCH, "Fresh Air," Part 1, *Thank You and Other Poems* (New York: Grove Press, 1962), 54-55. Poem.

——, "The Art of Poetry," *The Art of Love* (New York: Vintage, 1975), 23-45. Poem.

#LOUIS SIMPSON, "In California," "Walt Whitman at Bear Mountain,"* "Pacific Ideas—A Letter to Walt Whitman,"* "Lines Written Near San Francisco," *At the End of the Open Road* (Middletown: Wesleyan University, 1963), 11, 64-65, 66, 67-70. Poems.

——, "Walt Whitman on Bear Mountain," *A Company of Poets* (Ann Arbor: University of Michigan Press, 1981), 31-34. Essay, 1962.

——, "Port Jefferson," "Sacred Objects," "Doubting," *Adventures of the Letter I* (New York: Harper & Row, 1971), 47, 62-3, 25-6. Poems.

ROBERT H. WOODWARD, "Walt Whitman: The White House by Moonlight," *Walt Whitman Review*, 9 (June, 1963), 42. Poem.

THEODORE ROETHKE, "The Abyss,"* *The Collected Poems of Theodore Roethke* (Garden City: Doubleday & Co., 1966), 219-22. Poem, 1964.

JOHN F. KILEY, "Whitman as Player," *Nassau Review*, 1 (Spring, 1965), 80. Poem.

ART SULLIVAN, "Incident at Sunken Meadow," *Nassau Review*, 1 (Spring, 1965), 99-100. Poem.

#EDWARD DAHLBERG, "Walt Whitman,"* *Cipango's Hinder Door* (Austin: Humanities Research Center, University of Texas, 1965), 45-46. Poem.

PAUL HORGAN, *Songs After Lincoln* (New York: Farrar, Straus and Giroux, 1965). Several poems based on Whitman's Civil War observations.

#NORMAN ROSTEN, "Face on the Daguerreotype," *Selected Poems* (New York: George Braziller, 1979), 141. Poem, 1965.

——, "Brooklyn and Whitman's Ghost," WHR (1979), 32-33. Essay.

GEORGE OPPEN, "A Language of New York," Section 8, *This in Which* (New York: New Directions, 1965), 43. Poem.

DAVID IGNATOW, "Communion," "Walt Whitman in the Civil War Hospitals,"* "Waiting Inside,"* *Poems: 1934-1969* (Middletown: Wesleyan, 1970), 66-7, 131, 262. Poems, c. 1960s.

——, #90, *Tread the Dark* (Boston: Little, Brown, 1978), 86. Poem.

——, "Son to Father"* WHR (1979), 29. Essay.

KENNETH REXROTH, "Classics Revisited XXXV," *Saturday Review*, 49 (Sept. 3, 1966), 43. Essay.

KEN DOBEL, *Walt Whitman and the Kid in the Woodshed* (Torrence, California: Hors Commerce Press, 1966). Poem.

VINCENT CLEMENTE, "I Look for You This Evening, Walt Whitman," *Lyrismos*, 1 (Spring, 1967), 5, and "His Last Days on Mickle Street," *Lyrismos*, 1 (Winter, 1967-68), 14. Poems. [See also the four other poems in the Winter issue, Judson Dicks, Bette Stadler Wright, David Conford, and Dan Pfanner, gathered under "A Whitman Tribute from Paumanok," pp. 14-19.]

HOWARD NEMEROV, "A Modern Poet,"* *The Blue Swallows* (Chicago: University of Chicago Press, 1967), 57. Poem.

RONALD JOHNSON, "Emanations," *The Book of the Green Man* (New York: Norton, 1967), 38. Poem.

——, "Letters to Walt Whitman,"* *Valley of the Many-Colored Grasses* (New York: Norton, 1969), 89-98. Poem.

ANTHONY BURGESS, "The Answerer," *Urgent Copy* (New York: W. W. Norton, 1968), 48-53. Essay.

JOHN UPDIKE, "Midpoint" (Canto IV: The Play of Memory), *Midpoint and Other Poems* (New York: Alfred A. Knopf, 1969), 22-37. Poem, 1968.

——, "Walt Whitman: Ego and Art," *New York Review of Books*, 25 (Feb. 9, 1978), 33-36. Essay.

EDGAR SIMMONS, "A Note to Walt Whitman," *Driving to Biloxi* (Baton Rouge: Louisiana State University Press, 1968), 51. Poem.

DONALD HALL, "The Invisible World," introduction to Hall, ed., *A Choice of Whitman's Verse* (London: Faber and Faber, 1968), 7-20. Essay.

LOU LIPSITZ, "Reading a Poem by Walt Whitman I Discover We Are Surrounded by Contemporaries," *Cold Water* (Middletown: Wesleyan, 1968), 18. Poem.

#MURIEL RUKEYSER, "Gibbs," *The Collected Poems* (New York: McGraw-Hill, 1978), 187-90. Poem, 1968.

——, "After Melville," *Collected Poems*, 516-17. Poem, 1973.

WALTER LOWENFELS, "The Eternal Meanings," AD, 5-7. Essay. 1969.

——, "Walt Whitman's Many Loves," *The Tenderest Lover: The Erotic Poetry of Walt Whitman* (New York: Delacorte, 1970), xvii-xxxiii. Essay, 1969.

ROBERT MEZEY, "Happy Birthday Old Man," AD, 28. Essay, 1969.

CLARENCE MAJOR, "Close to the Ground," AD, 35. Essay, 1969.

IVAN DIVIS, "The Death of Walt," AD, 9. Poem, 1969.

ROBERT M. CHUTE, "Interlude on Avenue B," AD, 29. Poem, 1969.

JAMES SCHEVILL, "A Changing Inventory: For Walt Whitman," AD, 30-31. Poem, 1969.

LUCILLE BANTA, "Walt Whitman," AD, 32-34. Poem, 1969.

JOHN ROBERT COLOMBO, "New Poems for Old Walt," AD, 36. Found poems, 1969.

RICHARD WILBUR, "The Present State of Whitman," *Responses: Prose Pieces 1953-1976* (New York: Harcourt Brace Jovanovich, 1976), 146-51. Essay, 1969.

#PABLO NERUDA, "El XIX," *Fin de Mundo*, translated by Ben Belitt in Neruda, *Five Decades* (New York: Grove Press, 1974), 388-91. Poem, 1969.

——, "We Live in a Whitmanesque Age,"* *The New York Times* (April 14, 1972), 37. Essay.

——, "I Begin by Invoking Walt Whitman,"* *A Call for the Destruction of Nixon and Praise for the Chilean Revolution* (Cambridge: West End Press, 1980), n.p. Poem, late 1960s.

WILLIAM MEREDITH, "Whitman to the Poet," in William White, ed., *Walt Whitman in Our Time* (Detroit: Wayne State University Press, 1970), 9-11. Essay.

GREGORY CORSO, "Elegiac Feelings American," section 2, *Elegiac Feelings American* (New York: New Directions, 1970), 6-8. Poem.

WINSTON WEATHERS, "Seven Considerations of Whitman's Creative Spirit," in Lester F. Zimmerman and Winston T. Weathers, eds., *Papers on Walt Whitman* (Tulsa: University of Tulsa, 1970), 1-5. Cycle of poems.

CLINTON KEELER, "Sir William Osler Meets Whitman at Camden—1886," *Calamus*, 3 (October, 1970), 19. Poem.

JORGE GUILLEN, "My Relationship with Whitman" WWE, 32-33. Essay, 1971.

ROBERT CREELEY, "Introduction,"* *Whitman Selected by Robert Creeley* (Baltimore: Penguin, 1973), 7-20. Essay, 1972.

ADRIENNE RICH, "Poetry, Personality and Wholeness: A Response to Galway Kinnell," *Field*, 7 (Fall, 1972), 17-18. Essay.

BILL KNOTT, "Prosepoem to Hart Crane," in Robert Bly, ed., *Leaping Poetry* (Boston: Beacon Press, 1975), 80. Poem, 1972.

MOSES YANES, "Walt Whitman," *Call to Life: Book I, Windows at Daybreak* (Los Gatos, California: Moses Yanes, 1972), 3-4. Poem.

IRVING LAYTON, "Walt's Reply," *Chicago Review*, 24 (Winter, 1972), 126. Poem.

PATRICK D. HAZARD, "Thoughts Composed After Filming a Sunrise on the Walt Whitman Bridge," *Whitman's Camden Centennial Calendar* (Philadelphia, 1973). Poem, 1972.

ROBERT FLANAGAN, "Whitman's Song,"* *Poetry Northwest*, 13 (Winter, 1972-73), 44. Poem.

ANONYMOUS, "Walt Witman," *Lids of Grass* (Albuquerque: Pants Press, 1972). Parody.

DIANE WAKOSKI, "For Whitman,"* *Dancing on the Grave of a Son of a Bitch* (Los Angeles: Black Sparrow, 1974), 54. Poem, 1973.

#LAWRENCE FERLINGHETTI, "Poem for Old Walt," *Open Eye, Open Heart* (New York: New Directions, 1973), 40. Poem.

——, "Populist Manifesto,"* *Who Are We Now?* (New York: New Directions, 1976), 61-64. Poem, 1975.

——, "At the Public Market," *Northwest Ecolog* (San Francisco: City Lights, 1978), 31. Poem, 1977.

FLORENCE B. FREEDMAN, "Lines After Whitman," *November Journey: Poems for My Friends* (New York: 1973), 40. Poem.

WILLIAM RUECKERT, "Letter to Walt Whitman," *The Iowa Review*, 9 (Winter, 1978), 70-71. Poem, 1974.

A. R. AMMONS, Sections 122-126, *Sphere: The Form of a Motion* (New York: Norton, 1974), 64-67. Poem.

RICHARD HOWARD, "Wildflowers: Camden, 1882," *Two-Part Inventions* (New York: Atheneum, 1974), 12-28. Poem.

ERICA JONG, "Testament (Or, Homage to Walt Whitman)," *Loveroot* (New York: Holt, Rinehart and Winston, 1975), 3-7. Poem, 1974.

ROBERT FORREY, "Walt Whitman in Camden," *Walt Whitman Review*, 20 (June, 1974), 75. Poem.

#WILLIAM HEYEN, "The Traffic,"* "Bus Trip," *Long Island Light* (New York: Vanguard Press, 1979), 32-33, 178-79. Poems, 1974.

STEVE JONAS, "Cante Jondo for Soul Brother Jack Spicer, His Beloved California & Andalusia of Lorca," in Morty Sklar and Jim Mulac, eds., *Editor's Choice* (Iowa City: Spirit That Moves Us Press, 1980), 49-50. Poem, 1974.

ANNE WALDMAN, "Light & Shadow," *Fast Speaking Woman* (San Francisco: City Lights, 1975), 68-75. Poem.

ED SANDERS, "Ten Thousand Statues of Walt Whitman on Roller-Skates Hitch-hike Across America" [poem by Reader C], *Tales of Beatnik Glory* (New York: Stonehill Publishing, 1975), 8. Parody.

RICHARD O'CONNELL, "Whitman's Tomb," *ETC: A Review of General Semantics*, 32 (1975), 276. Poem.

#JOSEPH BRUCHAC, "Canticle,"* *Flow* (Austin: Cold Mountain, 1975), 17. Poem.

ROBERT PETERS, "Love Poem for Walt Whitman," *The Poet as Ice-Skater* (South San Francisco: ManRoot, 1975), 8-11. Poem.

TED BERRIGAN, "Whitman in Black," *So Going Around Cities: New & Selected Poems, 1958-1979* (Berkeley: Blue Wind Press, 1980), 365. Poem, c. 1975.

GUY DAVENPORT, "Whitman," *The Geography of the Imagination* (San Francisco: North Point, 1981), 68-79. Essay, 1976.

THEODORE WEISS, "The Good Grey Poet,"* *Fireweeds* (New York: Macmillan, 1976), 72-3. Poem.

DAVE SMITH, "With Walt Whitman at Fredericksburg,"* *Cumberland Station* (Urbana: University of Illinois Press, 1976), 8-9. Poem.

DEREK WALCOTT, "Over Colorado,"* *Sea Grapes* (London: Jonathan Cape, 1976), 56. Poem.

GARY SNYDER, "An Interview with Gary Snyder," by Paul Geneson, *The Ohio Review*, 18 (Fall, 1977), 94-6.

RICHARD HUGO, "Letter to Oberg from Pony," *31 Letters and 13 Dreams* (New York: W. W. Norton, 1977), 63. Poem.

KURT J. FICKERT, "Walt Whitman in West Hills (Long Island)," *Poet Lore*, 72 (Spring, 1977), 5. Poem.

PHILIP DACEY, "Hopkins to Whitman,"* *Poetry Northwest* 19 (Summer, 1978), 5-7. Poem.

——, "Gerard Manley Hopkins Meets Walt Whitman in Heaven: An Entertainment," MSR (1979). [Dacey's entire series of Hopkins-Whitman poems will be published by Penmaen Press this year.]

CHARLES WRIGHT, "Self-Portrait," *Wright: A Profile (New Poems by Charles Wright)* (Iowa City: Grilled Flowers, 1979), 28. Poem.

MILTON KESSLER, "A Page of Thoughts on Walt Whitman," WHR (1979), 58-9. Essay.

JAMES DICKEY, Essay, MSR (1979).

WILLIAM STAFFORD, "For You, Walt Whitman,"* WHR (1979), 34. Poem.

HOWARD NELSON, "Reading 'Crossing Brooklyn Ferry' on a Summer Morning," *Missouri Review*, 2 (Spring, 1979), 57. Poem.

FAY SLAVIN, "Transplant—Long Island," WHR (1979), 48-49. Poem.

RAYMOND ROSELIEP, "Out for a Summer Walk, I 'Lean and Loafe,' Walt Whitman," WHR (1979), 43-47. Poem.

HENRY PETROSKI, "Try Sheet," MSR (1979). Poem.

1980s

#ALLEN GINSBERG, "Walt Whitman: Composed on the Tongue,"* WMS, discourse.

JUNE JORDAN, "For the Sake of a People's Poetry: Walt Whitman and the Rest of Us,"* *Passion: New Poems, 1977-1980* (Boston: Beacon, 1980), ix-xxvi. Essay.

MICHAEL KINCAID, "Some Intricate Purpose,"* WMS, essay.

#WILLIAM HEYEN, "Essay Beginning and Ending with Poems for Whitman,"* WHR (1979), poems and essay revised for WMS.

#ALVARO CARDONA-HINE, "I Teach Straying from Me—Yet Who Can Stray from Me?"* WMS, essay.

C. W. TRUESDALE, "Whitman Exilado,"* WMS, essay.

MERIDEL LESUEUR, "Jelly Roll,"* WMS, essay.

PATRICIA HAMPL, "The Mayflower Moment: Reading Whitman During the Vietnam War,"* WMS, essay.

#JOSEPH BRUCHAC, "To Love the Earth: Some Thoughts on Walt Whitman,"* WMS, essay.

#LOUIS SIMPSON, "Honoring Whitman,"* WMS, essay.

CALVIN HERNTON, "Crossing Brooklyn Bridge at 4 O'Clock in the Morning, August 4th, 1979," WHR 2 (Fall, 1980), 80. Poem.

ROBERT R. HUDSON, "On a Silverpoint Portrait of Whitman," WHR 2 (Fall, 1980), 81. Poem.

GEORGE GEORGAKIS, "All of Us Conjugal," WHR 2 (Fall, 1980), 79. Poem.

EUGENE MCNAMARA, "Calamus," WHR 2 (Fall, 1980), 82-3. Poem.

PHILIP LEVINE, "I Sing the Body Electric," *Antaeus*, 40/41 (Winter/Spring, 1981), 320-21. Poem.

LARRY LEVIS, "Whitman,"* WMS, poem.

ANSELM HOLLO, "Walt's Waltz,"* WMS, poem.

THOMAS MCGRATH, "Revolutionary Frescoes—the Ascension,"* printed in a shorter version in *Praxis*, 2, #4 (1978), 317. Poem.

JUDITH MOFFETT, "Reaching Around,"* *Kenyon Review*, n.s. 2 (Fall, 1980) 95-99. Poem.

PATRICIA GOEDICKE, "For Walt Whitman,"* *Crossing the River* (Amherst: University of Massachusetts Press, 1980), n.p. Poem.

TOM DISCH, "Manhatta Notes," *Contact II*, 4 (Spring, 1981), 11. Poem.

JOHN TAGLIABUE, "American Complicated With Integrity: Homage to Muriel," *Harper's*, 261 (April, 1981), 39. Poem.

ROBERT BLY, "What Whitman Did Not Give Us,"* WMS, essay.

#LAWRENCE FERLINGHETTI, "Adieu á Charlot (Second Populist Manifesto)," and "Third Populist Manifesto (Modern Poetry is Prose)," *The Populist Manifestos* (San Francisco: Grey Fox, 1981), 9-16, 17-27. Poems.

HOWARD MOSS, "A Candidate for the Future," *The New Yorker* (September 14, 1981), 184-99. Essay.

JOHN GILL, "From the Diary of Peter Doyle," *From the Diary of Peter Doyle and Other Poems* (Ithaca: Alembic Press, 1981). Poem.

#JORGES LUIS BORGES, "Walt Whitman, Poet of Democracy," *Commonweal*, 108 (May 22, 1981), 303-305. Essay.

NICHOLAS CHRISTOPHER, "Walt Whitman at the Reburial of Poe," *New Yorker* (August 25, 1980), 93. Poem.

CID CORMAN, *Identities* (Vineyard Haven, Mass.: Salt-Works Press, 1981). Poem.

Notes on Contributors

RALPH WALDO EMERSON (1803-1882), the principal exponent of American transcendentalism, reportedly smiled when he characterized *Leaves of Grass* to F. B. Sanborn as "a combination of the *Baghavat-Gita* and the New York *Herald*." Though Whitman later denied a crucial influence (and Emerson declined to add to his early praise), in the mid-1850s Walt referred to the author of *Nature*, "Self-Reliance," "The Over-Soul," and "The Poet" as "Master."

HENRY DAVID THOREAU (1817-1862) published *Walden; or, Life in the Woods* in 1854. His individualism, sometimes described as "Yankee cussedness," ranks him with Whitman as one of the most highly praised and the most roundly excoriated of American authors.

MATTHEW ARNOLD (1822-1888) wrote comparatively little poetry after his early thirties, the age at which Whitman began as a poet. Walter Whitman entered the 1850s as a polemicising journalist and emerged as Walt Whitman the poet, while Arnold entered the 1850s as a Byronic poet and emerged as the cultural crusader who wrote *Culture and Anarchy* (1869), *Literature and Dogma* (1873), and a host of influential essays.

ALGERNON CHARLES SWINBURNE (1837-1909) shared with Whitman a passionate love of liberty, fascination with the sea, lifelong bachelorhood, and the attentions of Max Beerbohm's caricaturing pen. The Eton- and Oxford-educated Swinburne and Walt had little else in common. Swinburne wrote plays, novels, criticism, and articles for the *Encyclopaedia Britannica*, but is most recognized for the prosodic pyrotechnics of his poetry.

JOAQUIN MILLER (1837-1913), born Cincinnatus Hiner (or Heine) Miller, took his pen name from Joaquin Murrietta, a Mexican brigand he had defended in a newspaper article. Born in Indiana, he grew up on the West Coast. In the 1870s he went to England and there led a flamboyant life, posing as a representative "man of the west," smoking three cigars at once and biting the ankles of débutantes in Mayfair drawing rooms. His *Pacific Poems* was published in England in 1870.

ERNEST PERCIVAL RHYS (1859-1946) was a poet and free-lance critic and editor in London when in 1904 the publisher J. M. Dent invited him to edit a series of inexpensive editions of world classics. Rhys suggested the title Everyman's Library for the series, 983 volumes of which he saw published during his lifetime.

GERARD MANLEY HOPKINS (1844-1889) was born near London and educated at Highgate School, where he wrote prize poems, and at Balliol College, Oxford. On commencing his novitiate in the Jesuit order in 1868 he renounced poetry, but began writing again before his ordination in 1877. He never published his poetry in his lifetime, and it was not until 1918 that his *Poems,* edited by his friend Robert Bridges, appeared.

EDWIN ARLINGTON ROBINSON (1869-1935) said of his sonnet to Whitman, "I was very young when I wrote it, but I knew all the time I was writing it that I didn't really mean it. . . ." Robinson's *Collected Poems* (1921) won a Pulitzer Prize.

LOUIS SULLIVAN (1856-1924) has been called "the spiritual father of American architecture." Much of his best work was accomplished in Chicago, in partnership with Dankmar Adler, where a young Frank Lloyd Wright spent six years as his apprentice. After the partnership with Adler dissolved in 1895, Sullivan's sometimes difficult temperament cost him many commissions. He turned to the writing of important articles on his philosophy of architecture, but by 1920 was reduced to living in one bedroom and subsisting on donations from friends.

RUBEN DARIO (1867-1916), was born in Nicaragua, but lived in Paris for much of his life, an experience that helped him almost singlehandedly renovate Spanish poetry by beginning the movement known as *modernismo.* While he later lost faith in Whitman as an artist, he once called him "the Yankee pontiff with the white beard."

HAMLIN GARLAND (1860-1940) was established b- *Main-Travelled Roads* (1891) as a powerful writer of realistic tales focusing on the tribulations of the midwestern farm life he knew as a youth. *Crumbling Idols* (1894) contains his essays on local color, social protest, and Whitmanic individualism.

EDMUND GOSSE (1849-1928) was a friend of Henry James, Robert Louis Stevenson, and Swinburne (whose biography he wrote). Librarian to the House of Lords, his *Collected Poems* appeared in 1911.

ROBERT BUCHANAN (1841-1901) was a British poet and novelist. His notorious attack on the Pre-Raphaelite poets, "The Fleshy School of Poetry"

(1871), was only one of many vitriolic writings, many aimed at Swinburne. His *Collected Poems* appeared in 1901.

GEORGE CABOT LODGE (1873-1909) was the son of Henry Cabot Lodge. His books included *The Song of the Wave* (1898), *Poems (1902)*, and *The Soul's Inheritance* (1909). Henry Adams, in his book on Lodge, saw him as the emblem of how America isolates her artists.

EZRA POUND (1885-1973) was a prolific Idaho-born poet, critic, and champion of a rigorous poetics. His *Cantos* have exerted a major influence on modern poetry. He wrote his "Pact" with Walt Whitman (now in the Harriet Monroe Poetry Collection at the University of Chicago) in a bold, business-like, and very firm hand.

FERNANDO PESSOA (1888-1935) was born in Lisbon, lived in South Africa as a young man, then returned to Lisbon where in 1914 he sensed the birth within himself of three distinct individuals who would each come to write a poetry distinctly different from the others. "Heteronyms," he came to call them, and under or in one of those heteronyms—the tall, and emotional Alvaro de Campos—he wrote the "Salutation to Walt Whitman."

EDGAR LEE MASTERS (1868-1950) was born in Kansas and educated as a lawyer. Masters's *Spoon River Anthology* (1915) was a high-water mark of the Chicago Renaissance and he wrote a biographical study of Walt Whitman in 1937.

EMANUEL CARNEVALI was an Italian-born poet who, during the time he lived in New York City, was a close friend of William Carlos Williams. He published one book of poetry, *A Hurried Man* (1923), which Williams described as "a book that is all of a man, a young man, superbly alive. Doomed." Mentally afflicted, he was returned to Italy where all traces of him were lost. Kay Boyle has compiled his autobiography (1967).

WITTER BYNNER (1881-1968), a Harvard graduate, author, and editor, whose lyric poems are noted for their melodious style, also wrote books on Laotzu and D. H. Lawrence. He collaborated on the hoax *Spectra* (1916), a satirical parody of the technique and diction of modern poetry. Under a pseudonym, he described himself as "a patent and avowed follower of Whitman."

D. H. LAWRENCE (1885-1930), one of the great English novelists and poets of the twentieth century, lived during the early twenties on a ranch near Taos, New Mexico. His *Studies in Classical American Literature* (1923) is itself a classic.

CARL SANDBURG (1878-1967) wrote to his sister Mary on June 2, 1904, "I was in Walt Whitman's old home last Sunday, and on Memorial Day threw a rose in his tomb at Camden." Sandburg's career as a lecturer began a few years later with enthusiastically-received lectures on Whitman to all kinds of audiences. *Chicago Poems* (1916) marked the beginning of his major publications. His *Abraham Lincoln: The War Years* (1939; Pulitzer Prize) frequently quotes Whitman's accounts of Lincoln and the war from *Specimen Days*.

HART CRANE's (1899-1932) two books of poetry (*The Bridge* in 1930 and *White Buildings* in 1926) were his only poetry published during his lifetime. Crane sought in his poems to express his despair at, and to create a triumphant vision of transcendence over, a world which, in its intolerance of his homosexuality and financial difficulties, propelled his personal disintegration and eventual suicide by drowning.

T. S. ELIOT (1888-1965), who was born in Saint Louis, Missouri, educated at Harvard and later in France, Germany, and England, and who became a British subject in 1927, is among the foremost Anglo-American poets and critics of the twentieth century. Although he was a proponent of a distinctly un-Whitmanlike aesthetic, the degree to which Eliot may have been influenced by Whitman is a question still debated in some quarters.

SHERWOOD ANDERSON (1876-1941) is best known for his prose, especially *Winesburg, Ohio* (1919), but his book of Whitman-like poems, *Mid-American Chants* (1918), has had a small but enthusiastic following, too; Edward Dahlberg said of them, "I have read these *Chants* for over thirty-five years, and they are like birds treading the spirit until it flutters."

EZEQUIEL MARTINEZ ESTRADA (1895-1965) an Argentinian poet and essayist, looked to Whitman for a social vision more than for an artistic one; near the end of his life he went to Cuba in support of Castro's revolution.

FEDERICO GARCIA LORCA (1898-1936), one of the preeminent twentieth century Spanish poets, wrote his "Ode to Walt Whitman" while in New York City at Columbia University.

EDWIN MARKHAM (1852-1940), born in Oregon, and who lived and wrote for many years in California, protested, in *The Man with the Hoe and Other Poems* (1899) and *Lincoln, and Other Poems* (1901), the oppression and degradation of exploited labor.

STEPHEN VINCENT BENET (1898-1943) was born in Bethlehem, Pennsylvania and graduated from Yale. His epic poems *John Brown's Body* (1928) and

Western Star (1943) won Pulitzer Prizes, in 1929 and 1944, respectively. His best known short story, "The Devil and Daniel Webster," was adapted by him as a folk opera in 1939.

WALLACE STEVENS (1879-1955) was, for many years, an executive of the Hartford Accident and Indemnity Company, and wrote among the most memorable poems of his generation. Many of them are collected in *The Palm at the End of the Mind: Selected Poems and a Play,* edited by Holly Stevens (New York: Knopf, 1971).

PAUL POTTS, a British poet, published *Instead of a Sonnet* in 1944, and said, "To read my verse is to share my failure." He sought "to push into the hard still lines of strong and English verse the ideas of social revolution."

LANGSTON HUGHES (1902-1967), born in Joplin, Missouri, was a leading figure of the Harlem Renaissance of the 1920s. A prolific author and editor of formidable range, Hughes was the most influential Black writer of his generation and played a central role in the development of Black writing in America.

KENNETH PATCHEN (1911-1972) was born in Ohio and wrote an amazing variety of poetry, much of it illustrated with his own expressionist art. His *Collected Poems* appeared in 1967.

MURIEL RUKEYSER (1913-1980) was a poet whose work was energized by social protest. During the last years of her life she was jailed in Washington, flew to Hanoi in support of peace in Vietnam, and travelled to Korea to protest the incarceration of the poet Kim Chi-Ha. "People have been comparing me to Whitman," she once said, "and although I love and adore and am a child of Whitman, both of us come from the Bible. . . . We are talking about the endless quarrel between the establishment and the prophets, and I hope to be forever on the side of the prophets." Her *Collected Poems* appeared in 1979.

PEDRO MIR was born in 1912 in the Dominican Republic, from which he was exiled during the Trujillo regime. His "Countersong to Walt Whitman" was first published in Guatemala.

HENRY MILLER (1891-1980) wrote often of Walt Whitman, even in *Tropic of Cancer*. Born in New York the year before Whitman died, his work is charged by his belief that "more obscene than anything is inertia."

WILLIAM CARLOS WILLIAMS (1883-1963) was born in Rutherford, New Jersey, where he lived, practiced pediatrics, and was host to a panoply of visiting avant-garde artists and writers. His first volume of poetry, *Poems,* (privately printed in 1909), he later referred to as "bad Keats, nothing else—oh well, bad Whitman, too." His mature works include such landmark books as *In the American Grain* (1925) and *Paterson* (5 books, 1946-58).

ALLEN GINSBERG was born in 1926 in Paterson, New Jersey, son of the poet Louis Ginsberg. The publication of his first book, *Howl,* made him famous overnight; since then he has published many collections including *Kaddish, Wichita Vortex Sutra, Planet News,* and *The Fall of America.* Galway Kinnell has said, "I feel that Ginsberg is the only one to understand Whitman and to bring into the poetry of our time a comparable music."

RICHARD EBERHART was born in 1904 in Minnesota and educated at Cambridge and Dartmouth where he taught for many years. His *Collected Poems 1930-1976* and *Ways of Light* (1977) are among his recent collections. He has won the Bollingen Prize, the Pulitzer Prize, and the National Book Award. ·

EDWIN HONIG's recent collections are *Selected Poems: 1955-1976* (Texas Center for Writers, 1979), and *The Foibles and Fables of an Abstract Man* (Copper Beach, 1979). He teaches at Brown University.

PABLO NERUDA (1904-1973), the renowned Chilean poet, had a lifelong affection for the works of Whitman. Recalling his early struggles to be a poet, Neruda said, "I had to be myself, striving to branch out like the very land where I was born. Another poet of this same hemisphere helped me along this road, Walt Whitman, my comrade from Manhattan."

JORGE LUIS BORGES, born in Argentina in 1899, began his literary career as a poet, and although he is more famous for his stories and essays, he has produced a distinguished body of poetry, in which Whitman is often mentioned. He recalls that when he "first ran across Whitman, I felt blinded, and dazzled and overwhelmed by him."

JONATHAN WILLIAMS is founder, executive director, editor, publisher, and designer of highly-acclaimed Jargon Books and is executive director of The Jargon Society, Inc. His hiking activities have covered 1,408 miles of the Appalachian Trail and his poetic activities have encompassed a commensurate range of the territory.

ROBERT FLANAGAN's recent collections are *Once You Learn You Never Forget* (Fiddlehead Poetry Books, 1978) and *Maggot* (a novel), in its eighth printing from Warner Books. He teaches at Ohio Wesleyan University in Delaware, Ohio.

JACK KEROUAC (1922-1969), the most thorough chronicler of the beat generation, began with the conventional novel *The Town and the City* (1950), then embarked on the "one vast book," including *On the Road, The Dharma Bums, The Subterraneans, Visions of Cody, Big Sur,* and *Desolation Angels,* that he came to call "The Duluoz Legend."

JOHN BERRYMAN (1914-1972), who taught at the University of Minnesota, was awarded a Pulitzer Prize in 1965 for *77 Dream Songs.* When his *Homage to Mistress Bradstreet* was published by Farrar, Straus in 1956, Edmund Wilson and Frank Kermode hailed it as the most important work of poetry since *The Waste Land* and *Four Quartets.*

DENISE LEVERTOV was born in 1923 in Ilford, Essex, England and was educated at home. She has published many books of poetry, including *O Taste and See, Relearning the Alphabet,* and *To Stay Alive,* as well as a books of essays on poetry, *The Poet in the World.* Her *Collected Earlier Poems* was published in 1979. Forthcoming in Fall, 1981 is a new book, *Light Up the Cave* (New Directions).

JAMES WRIGHT (1927-1980) was the author of seven books of poetry including the Pulitzer Prize winning *Collected Poems.* His last book, published in 1977, was *To a Blossoming Pear Tree.* In November, 1981 his posthumous book *This Journey* will be published. He lived in New York City after 1966 and taught at Hunter College. He and his wife Anne completed an eight month trip to Europe in 1979 when he won a grant from the Guggenheim Foundation.

DAVID IGNATOW's next volume of poems, *Whisper to the Earth,* will be published during Fall, 1981 by Atlantic Monthly Press. His collection of essays, reviews, and interviews entitled *Open Between Us,* was published in 1980 by The University of Michigan Press.

THEODORE ROETHKE (1908-1963) was born and educated in Michigan and taught at the University of Washington. His *Collected Poems* were published by Doubleday in 1966. *On the Poet and His Craft: Selected Prose* (1965), edited by Ralph J. Mills, Jr., was published by the University of Washington Press. In his notebook in the early 1950s, Roethke made this characteristic entry: "Nietzche and Whitman my fathers: and yet I cannot worship power."

EDWARD DAHLBERG (1900-1977) is often linked by critics with Thoreau because of his passionate and iconoclastic writings. His autobiography, *Because I Was Flesh,* was published in 1964, and *The Edward Dahlberg Reader,* edited by Paul Carroll, in 1967, both by New Directions.

HOWARD NEMEROV's *Collected Poems* were published by the University of Chicago Press in 1977. His *Figures of Thought: Speculations on the Meaning of Poetry and Other Essays* was published by Godine in 1978, and *Sentences* by the University of Chicago Press in 1980. He is presently teaching at Washington University.

RONALD JOHNSON was born in 1935 in Ashland, Kansas and he has published several books of poetry, including *The Book of the Green Man* (1967), *Valley of the Many-Colored Grasses* (1969), and *RADI OS I-IV* (1977). He is at work on a three-book work, *ARK*.

CHARLES OLSON (1910-1970), in his influential essay "Projective Verse," gives the poetic line the very Whitmanic definition "the breathing of the man who writes, at the moment that he writes." His *Maximus Poems* was published in 1960.

ROBERT CREELEY is presently Gray Professor of Poetry and Letters at the State University of New York at Buffalo. He has published numerous collections of prose and poetry, among them *For Love, Pieces,* and *Later* (all poetry), a novel, *The Island,* and a collection of short stories, *The Gold Diggers.* His forthcoming book, *The Collected Poems of Robert Creeley, 1945-1975* will be published during Fall, 1981 by the University of California Press.

LAWRENCE FERLINGHETTI was born in 1919 in Yonkers, New York and later received a Ph.D. from the Sorbonne. He is the founder, editor, and publisher of City Lights Books which has published some of the most significant writings of our time. His recent collections of poetry are: *Landscapes of Living and Dying* (New York: New Directions, 1979) and *Northwest Ecolog* (San Francisco: City Lights Books, 1978). As a poet, Ferlinghetti describes himself as an Unblinking Eye.

NORMAN ROSTEN, who lives in Broooklyn, has written a number of plays produced both on and off Broadway, radio verse plays, and the novels *Under the Boardwalk* (1968) and *Over and Out* (1972). His *Selected Poems* was published by Braziller in 1979.

DEREK WALCOTT, one of the Caribbean's most distinguished writers, was born in the West Indies in 1930. A prolific playwright as well as a poet, his books include *Sea Grapes* (1976), *Selected Poems* (1977), and *The Star-Apple Kingdom* (1980).

PHILIP DACEY's second and third books will appear in 1981; *The Boy Under the Bed* (The Johns Hopkins University Press) and *Gerard Manley Hopkins*

Meets Walt Whitman in Heaven and Other Poems (Penmaen Press). Dacey teaches at Southwest State University in Marshall, Minnesota and lives in Cottonwood, Minnesota.

WILLIAM STAFFORD, born in 1914 in Kansas, has lived for many years in Oregon. He received the National Book Award in 1963 for *Traveling Through the Dark*. *Stories that Could Be True: New and Collected Poems* appeared in 1977.

THEODORE WEISS was born in Pennsylvania in 1916 and teaches at Princeton. His books of poems include *Outlanders* (1960), *The World Before Us: Poems 1950-1970*, and *Views and Spectacles: New Poems and Selected Shorter Ones* (1979), and two forthcoming collections entitled *Recoveries* and *The Man from Porlock*.

DIANE WAKOSKI was born in California in 1937. Her many works include *The George Washington Poems* (1967), *Dancing on the Grave of a Son of a Bitch* (1973), and *The Man Who Shook Hands* (1978). Her ideas of language grew out of Whitman's: "My language is dramatic, oral, and as American as I can make it, with the appropriate plain surfaces and rich vocabulary."

GALWAY KINNELL is returning to the East Coast after two years of teaching at the University of Hawaii. His most recent publications are *Mortal Acts, Mortal Words* (Houghton Mifflin Co.) and *Walking Down the Stairs*— selections from interviews published by The University of Michigan Press. Of "Song of Myself" he has said: "A reader is taken through one person into some greater self; there is a continual passing into the 'death of the self'. . . . The final action of the poem, where Whitman dissolves into the air and into the ground, is for me one of the great moments of self-transcendence in poetry."

LOUIS SIMPSON's collection of writings about poetry and poets, entitled *A Company of Poets*, was published in 1981 (The University of Michigan Press). His most recent collection of poetry is *Caviare at the Funeral* (Franklin Watts, New York). In the past year Mr. Simpson has been visiting professor at the universities of Hawaii and Pittsburgh. He returns to Stony Brook in the Fall, 1981.

DAVE SMITH will become the Director of Creative Writing at the University of Florida this Fall. His five collections of writing to be published in 1981 are: *Dream Flights* (poems, University of Illinois Press), *Homage to Edgar Allan Poe* (poems, Louisiana State University Press), *Onliness* (novel, Louisiana State University Press), *The Pure Clear Word: Essays on the Poetry of James*

Wright (edited by Smith, University of Illinois Press), and *Blue Spruce* (poems, Tamarack Editions).

WILLIAM HEYEN lives in Brockport, New York, with his wife and two children. He has been writing for several years, and will be for several more, a book-length poem in which Whitman is an important presence. Recent books include *Lord Dragonfly: Final Sequences* (1981), *Long Island Light: Poems and a Memoir* (1979), and *The Swastika Poems* (1977), all published by Vanguard Press. He edited a collection of essays by contemporary poets entitled *American Poetry in 1976* (Indianapolis: Bobbs-Merrill, 1976).

JOSEPH BRUCHAC's most recent publications include two chapbooks of poetry, *Translator's Son* from Cross Cultural Communications (1980) and *Ancestry* from Great Raven Press (1981). A book entitled *How to Start and Sustain a Literary Magazine* was published in 1980 by Provision House Press. He is the editor of *The Greenfield Review,* and is currently at work on a collection of poems, stories and translations drawn from Abenaki Indian oral traditions.

ALVARO CARDONA-HINE lives in Saint Paul, Minnesota. His most recent book is *The Half-Eaten Angel* (Nodin Press, Minneapolis). He also composes music, paints, and has translated the poetry of several Spanish writers.

LARRY LEVIS's third collection of poetry, *The Dollmaker's Ghost,* was published in May, 1981 by E. P. Dutton. The book was a winner of the 1981 Open Competition of the National Poetry Series and was selected by Stanley Kunitz. His second collection, *The Afterlife,* was the Lamont Poetry Selection for 1976. His recent work appears in *The New Yorker, Antaeus,* and *Field.*

ANSELM HOLLO presently teaches at Sweet Briar College in Virginia. He is the author of several volumes of poetry including *Sojourner Microcosms: New and Selected Poems, 1959-1977* (Berkeley: Blue Wind, 1978), *Heavy Jars* (West Branch: Toothpaste Press, 1977), and a forthcoming book entitled *Small Hand* (Ann Arbor, 1982).

MICHAEL KINCAID lives in Minneapolis and has published his work in *Great River Review* and the Minneapolis *Tribune.* His collection of poems, *To Walk in the Daylight,* was privately published in 1973. He is at work on a new volume of poetry entitled *Underlight.*

PATRICIA GOEDICKE lives in Mexico with her husband, the writer Leonard Wallace Robinson. This past year she was teaching poetry at Sarah Lawrence College. Her recently published collections of poetry include *Crossing the*

Same River (University of Massachusetts Press, 1980), *The Dog That Was Barking Yesterday* (Lynx House Press, 1980), and *The Trail That Turns On Itself* (Ithaca House Press, 1978).

PATRICIA HAMPL's first book, a collection of poems entitled *Woman Before an Aquarium,* was published by the University of Pittsburgh Press in 1978. Her memoir about growing up in Saint Paul, Minnesota and about her travels to Czechoslovakia, *A Romantic Education,* was awarded a Houghton Mifflin Literary Fellowship and was published early in 1981. She lives in Saint Paul and sometimes teaches at the University of Minnesota. Current projects include a novel, an essay on Czeslaw Milosz and poems.

JUDITH MOFFETT's recent collections include *Keeping Time* (poems), and she is at work on a long prose work entitled *James Merrill: An Introduction to the Poetry* to be published by Columbia University Press.

THOMAS MCGRATH was born in North Dakota and educated at the University of North Dakota, Louisiana State, and New College, Oxford, where he was a Rhodes Scholar. His books include *Longshot O'Leary's Garland of Practical Poesy, A Witness to the Times, Figures from a Double World, New and Selected Poems, The Movie at the End of the World* and *Letter to an Imaginary Friend,* a work of epic proportions and still in progress. A book of short poems about his son Tomasito, *letters to tomasito,* was published in 1977 by Holy Cow! Press and recently reprinted. Copper Canyon Press will soon publish a collection of poems entitled *Waiting for the Angel I & II.*

ROBERT BLY will have a new collection of his poetry published this Fall by Dial Press entitled *The Man in the Black Coat Turns.* He has recently published an anthology of nature poems from the eighteenth century to the present entitled *News of the Universe: Poems of Two-Fold Consciousness* (Sierra Club). He has translated the work of many important European and Spanish poets such as Pablo Neruda, Georg Trakl, Cesar Vallejo, Antonio Machado, Tomas Tranströmer and several others. He is editor and founder of The Fifties Press, followed by The Sixties, The Seventies, and, at last report, The Eighties. He spends most of his time in the woods of northern Minnesota.

C. W. TRUESDALE's most recent collections of poetry are: *Cold Harbors* (Latitudes Press, 1974) and *Doctor Vertigo* (Wyrd Press, 1976). A small collection of short fiction, *Legacy* is due out from Crowfoot Press in 1982. He collaborated with John Minczeski and Bonzo on *Born Again Beef,* a collection of political satires published by the Lost Olympics Press in 1980. He is the founding editor and publisher of New Rivers Press which has begun publishing a distinguished collection of books by Minnesotan writers (Minnesota Voices Project). He is also editing, with D. Clinton and Tom Montag, a collection of writing entitled *Retelling the Americas: A Geopoetics Anthology.*

JUNE JORDAN is currently an Associate Professor of English at the State University of New York at Stony Brook. Her recent publications include *Things I Do in the Dark: Selected Poems, 1954-1977* (Revised Edition, Beacon Press, 1981), *Civil Wars: Selected Essays 1964-1980,* (Beacon Press, 1981), and *Passion: New Poems, 1977-1980* (Beacon Press, 1980).

MERIDEL LESUEUR will have an anthology of her work published this Fall by the Feminist Press entitled *Ripenings: The Prose & Poetry of Meridel LeSueur.* She has also written a "nounless novel" which will be published next year along with two other short novels. She lives in Saint Paul, Minnesota.

The Translators: DIDIER TISDEL JAEN, an Associate Professor of Spanish at the University of California, Davis, edited and translated *Homage to Walt Whitman: A Collection of Poems from the Spanish* (University of Alabama Press, 1969). BETTY JEAN CRAIGE, an Associate Professor of Comparative Literature at The University of Georgia, is the author of *Lorca's Poet in New York: The Fall into Consciousness* (University of Kentucky Press, 1977), and editor and translator of *Selected Poems of Antonio Machado* (Louisiana State University Press, 1978). TERESA ANDERSON lives in San Antonio, Texas; her works include a volume of original poetry *Speaking in Sign* (West End Press, 1979) and the authorized translation of Neruda's *A Call for the Destruction of Nixon And Praise for the Chilean Revolution* (West End Press, 1980). RICHARD HOWARD's own poems include *Two-Part Inventions* (Atheneum, 1974), in which appears "Wild Flowers," a long poem about Oscar Wilde's visit with Whitman. He is the author of *Alone with America: Essays on the Art of Poetry in the United States Since 1950* (Atheneum, 1980), and has translated St.-John Perse, Jules Renard, Andre Gide and others. His translations of Borges were done with CESAR RENNERT.

RANDALL W. SCHOLES, whose striking portrait of Whitman appears on the back cover of this collection, has illustrated numerous books of poetry and is currently working on a series of wood engravings for a Herman Melville short story. He is also Art Director for *Milkweed Chronicle,* a Minneapolis Journal of Poetry and Graphics.

The Editors:

DAN CAMPION is a graduate of the University of Chicago and of the Program for Writers at the University of Illinois at Chicago Circle. He has worked as an editor with *Encyclopaedia Britannica* and the Follett Publishing Company and presently attends the University of Iowa.

ED FOLSOM is an associate professor of English and American Studies at the University of Iowa, where he teaches a lot of courses in which Whitman appears. His articles on American poets have appeared in such journals as *American Literature, Shenandoah,* and *Western American Literature.* Most recently he published a study of Walt Whitman and baseball in *The Iowa Review.* He is at work on a book-length study of Whitman.

JIM PERLMAN was born in Minneapolis and educated at the University of Minnesota, the University of Arizona and at the University of Iowa where he presently attends school. He has helped to edit a number of little magazines including *One, Window Rock, Moons and Lion Tailes,* and *The Iowa Review.* He is the founding editor and publisher of Holy Cow! Press and has published collections of poetry by Thomas McGrath (*letters to tomasito*), candyce clayton (*at the barre*), Natalie Goldberg (*Chicken & In Love*), Dorian Brooks Kottler (*A Pause in the Light*), and two anthologies (*Brother Songs: A Male Anthology of Poetry* edited by Jim Perlman and *Believing Everything: An Anthology of New Writing* edited by Mary Logue and Lawrence Sutin).